Gold Portfolio
1929-1939

Compiled by
R.M. Clarke

ISBN 1 85520 1941

Booklands Books Ltd.
PO Box 146, Cobham, KT11 1LG
Surrey, England

Printed in Hong Kong

CONTENTS

Continued

CONTENTS - continued

BROOKLANDS BOOKS

ACKNOWLEDGEMENTS

The history books will tell us the the initials M.G. stand for Morris Garages. This is true , of course, but to countless enthusiasts the world over they more importantly just bring to mind the most popular sporting cars ever built. The cars are cherished and driven long after rival, and more expensive, models have been forgotten. This enthusiasm for the cars has meant that over the years we at Brooklands Books have published a large number of titles covering the period the cars were produced. The books dealing with the early cars have been out of print for some time, and I felt we should now put together this selection of road tests and articles as a Gold Portfolio, following on from the similar collections recently printed covering the MGA, MGB, MGC and MGB V8. Although you will find some material here on the TA and TB, I will in the future be compiling another Gold Portfolio solely on the T- types, covering all models from the TA to the TF 1500.

Our aim has always been to make available to enthusiasts the articles that were current when their cars were new, in the hope that these will assist them to both restore and enjoy them. The leading publishers of motoring journals have generously allowed reproduction of the articles used in this book, and I would like to extend my thanks to the publishers of *Autocar, Car South Africa, Light Car, Motor, Motor Sport, Practical Motorist and Sports Car World.* I would also like to acknowledge the assistance I have received with cover photographs from members of the M.G.Car Club.

Although the first cars bearing the M.G. badge were little more than re-bodied Morris chassis, by the time the period covered by this book had arrived the marque was already becoming established in its own right. The stately 18/80 models can now be seen as the end of an era. The vintage period produced some very fine cars, but by 1929 the economic climate of the times meant that the number of customers for these large and expensive machines was greatly reduced. If you study the massive construction of an 18/80 chassis and see the attention to detail you can understand why these cars were relatively expensive. Although based on Morris components a large part of the car was exclusively M.G. and even today these cars are impressive to ride in or drive.

In 1929 the marque received a tremendous boost when the Managing Director, Cecil Kimber, decided to produce the Midget based on the Morris Minor Chassis. This small car quickly built up a following, as you will see from articles in this book, and before long the demand outstripped the capacity of the Oxford factory and a move was made to premises in Abingdon. This was soon producing the largest number of sporting cars in the world from one factory.

There is not space here to tell the full story of those exciting years but if you study this book you cannot fail to be impressed with the industry and innovation of the small workforce. Before M.G. entered international competition in the voiturette class there were virtually no British cars competing on the continent. The era of The Bentley Boys was now over and it was fortunate for the prestige of the British motor industry that M.G. were so active in competition and record braking in the 1930s.

Most of this effort in competition was ended in 1935 when Lord Nuffield re-organised his empire and put the M.G. factory under the control of Morris Motors. The model range was then revised completely to use more of the standard components available within the group. The cars produced, The TA, VA and SA were quite different from those previously built, but are very attractive and were sold in quite large numbers. The TA was developed post-war into the TC - one of the most popular imports into the United States. The large SA saloon gained an enthusiastic following as a comfortable long distance touring car and the Tickford bodied version must be one of the most elegant cars ever built.

R.M.Clarke

THE 8-33 h.p. M.G. MIDGET

A Thoroughbred Little Sports Car Emanating From a Factory Where Only Sports Cars are Manufactured.

WITH CLEAN-CUT LINES. —— The near side of the M.G. Midget. Note the close-up wings and the absence of running boards. There are two doors and the squab is adjustable for rake and leg-reach. Spare wheels, hood and tools are carried in the tail.

THE 8-33 h.p. M.G. Midget can be summed up by saying that it is a thoroughbred little sports car —and that implies a great deal. It should not be confused with the type of car which represents the sporting edition of a touring model of a given make, for it is designed and produced by specialists in a factory from which nothing but purely sports cars emanate.

Made at present only as a two-seater and with the bare equipment demanded by sports car enthusiasts, it is modelled on advanced lines. There are, for example, no running boards, fairing—with vertical louvres—hiding the frame members on each side. The wings are of the close-up type, a V screen is employed, Hartford shock absorbers are fitted all round and the space between the dumb-irons at the front is covered in with sheet-metal fairing. The distinctive M.G. radiator and the Dunlop-shod wire wheels complete a tout ensemble which is both striking and pleasing.

When we undertake road tests it is not often that we are able to try out two cars of identically the same make and type during the same period. In the case of the M.G. Midget, however, we were fortunate in this respect, for we drove one Midget from London to Oxford and collected another.

A Dual Test.

The dual test was instructive, for it showed that the two separate chassis had an almost identical performance. Another point worthy of note is that neither of the cars had been specially tuned immediately preceding our run, both, in fact, having just returned from the "London-Edinburgh" with its fairly rough going in a northward direction and its inevitable "blind" back to London after the run.

The performance of each car in our hands clearly showed that there had been no loss of tune, whilst features such as the clutch, brakes, steering, suspension and so on gave no cause for adverse criticism.

As we have already indicated, the M.G. Midget is built from the word "Go" as a sports car. The chassis itself is modelled upon that of the larger M.G. sports, being upswept both front and rear and having reasonably long, flat semi-elliptic springs. The engine is of the four-cylinder overhead-valve-and-camshaft type, 57 mm. by 83 mm. (847 c.c.), tax £8, the cylinder block and practically the whole of the crankcase forming a rigid casting.

Bevels on the two-bearing crankshaft drive a vertical spindle which also forms the armature shaft of the dynamo, the dynamo itself being mounted vertically on an extension of the cylinder-block casting.

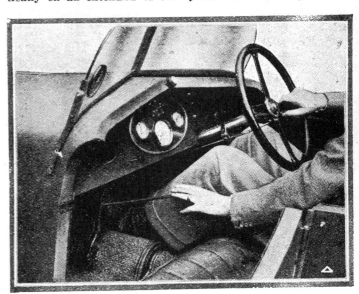

The car provides ample room for two, and the driver's hand falls easily on to the gear lever. The spring-spoke steering wheel makes for comfort.

A metallic universal joint transmits the drive from the upper end of the armature spindle to the half-time gear, thence to the camshaft.

It is claimed that this position for the dynamo tends to obviate backlash and noise in the camshaft driving gear, and we can vouch for the fact that on both the cars we tried the valve gear was commendably silent. The pistons are of aluminium having two rings, and duralumin connecting rods are employed. A special induction pipe and exhaust manifold—both situated on the near side of the engine—are features of the design.

Ignition is by Lucas six-volt coil and battery, the lighting and starting set is of the same make, whilst the carburetter is an S.U. The whole unit is neat, compact and business-like.

With an engine developing some 33 b.h.p. and a car weighing only 10 cwt. 21 lb. moderately high gear ratios can be used with advantage. The ratios of the M.G. Midgets are 4.89, 8.96 and 17 to 1. The respective maximum speeds are first, about 18 m.p.h.; second, just over 40 m.p.h., and top, 63 m.p.h. The gearbox is centrally placed and made as a unit with the engine, the hand brake—mounted on the near side of the gearbox—operating contracting shoes on a drum situated immediately behind the gearbox itself. The four-wheel brakes are, of course, applied by the pedal; in order to give dead smooth brake operation without any suggestion of pedal judder the final connection from the main rods is made by Bowden cable.

Sports Car Equipment.

Although the equipment is not generous in the accepted meaning of the term, it includes everything that is essential—with the possible exception of a screen wiper. There are, for example, a spare wheel, tools, electric horn, spring steering wheel, oil gauge, switchboard, 80 m.p.h. speedometer and a hood of the completely detachable type which provides adequate

Features of the engine are the overhead-valve-and-camshaft gear, the special exhaust and inlet manifolds, and the large size S.U. carburetter.

protection when erected and which is stored in the tail when furled. As a matter of fact, even in a heavy downpour one can keep reasonably dry with the hood furled provided that the car is kept on the move.

The price of this intriguing little vehicle is £175, a sum which obviously does not leave a wide margin for luxuries when a really " hot-stuff " chassis has been created.

We may now turn to our actual road experiences. With so small a car one rather expects the seating position to be slightly cramped. This is not so in the case of the M.G. Midget, which boasts of ample leg and elbow room. The seat squab, incidentally, can be adjusted for both rake and leg reach, thus making it possible for drivers of varying stature to obtain the particular setting which suits them best.

The gear lever is easily reached but, as in most cases where a central lever is used, the hand brake is not so accessible. In view of the fact that it is

Viewed from the front. The fairing over the dumb-irons adds to the sporting appearance of the car.

intended primarily as a parking brake, however, the disadvantage is a small one, and during our test we found it unnecessary to use it except for the purpose named.

The engine starts immediately from cold if the mixture control knob on the dash is momentarily pushed in. There is no hand throttle, the only control on the steering column being the ignition lever.

This view emphasizes the low build of the M.G. Midget and also shows the semi-streamlined tail.

Getting away from rest the sweetness of the clutch is a noticeable feature, and the powerful torque of the engine is reflected in wheel spin even on a dry surface if a semi-racing getaway is attempted.

On second gear the car is extremely lively. If, for

example, one "stands" on the accelerator at about 27 m.p.h. it feels and sounds very much as though a supercharger had come into action.

Keeping the accelerator still hard down, the car rapidly reaches the 40 m.p.h. mark. This does not represent its limit in second gear, but it appears to mark the falling away of the power curve, probably due to valve bounce.

From 40 m.p.h. to 55 m.p.h. in top gear the same lively attributes of acceleration are noticeable; the maximum speed is easily reached, and it is very pleasing to discover that the S.U. carburetter gives a definite increase in power throughout the entire range of throttle control; even the last ¼ in. of travel of the accelerator makes a difference.

At all speeds the car is steady; it holds its direction reasonably well and

snatch at about 10 m.p.h., and top-gear acceleration from this speed is quite good.

For its size the Midget is not so economical as one might expect; for its type, however, the opposite is the case, for when the engine is working at its hardest—the utmost use being made of the gears—the petrol consumption is something over 35 m.p.g., whilst the oil consumption is also very low.

Plans are now well in hand for producing the M.G. Midget on a quantity production basis at the works of the M.G. Car Co., Oxford—one of the many companies controlled by Sir William R. Morris. Bart.

A FACTORY WHICH PRODUCES ONLY SPORTS CARS.

(Oval) A view of the works of the M.G. Car Co., Oxford, and (left) the "giant"—a semi-Diesel of Ruston-Hornsby manufacture—which helps to turn out the "Midgets."

is easily managed. When flat-out it impresses one as being a thoroughly roadworthy vehicle, but a little light on the steering.

Its acceleration is, of course, one of its most pleasing features. Getting smartly off the mark, but without attempting to do anything sensational, 30 m.p.h. can be reached easily in 8 seconds. Braking is reasonably good, and even when the pedal is heavily depressed, say, at 50 m.p.h., the car, despite its low weight, holds the road well and decelerates smoothly. A good feature of the car is its flexibility. After a high-speed turn one can trickle into a busy town and tick along in top gear evenly and without

The M.G. Car Co. is, however, an entirely independent manufacturing concern specializing only in the production of M.G. sports cars, and here, perhaps, we should say that the affinity of the M.G. Midget and the Morris Minor is far less than is popularly believed —many parts of engine and chassis being different.

The company would certainly appear to be on the road to success, and after our experiences with the very sturdy and pleasing M.G. Midget we are not surprised that it is making headway, for the car represents another milestone in the production of high-grade, well-behaved and convincing sports models evolved by British brains and made by British labour.

THE M.G. SIX SPORTS SALOON

A Fascinating Car with a Speed Range of 5 m.p.h. to 78 m.p.h. on Top Gear.

FEW cars created more interest at the last Olympia Show than the M.G. Six Sports, which is in every way a noteworthy production from an engineering and coachwork standpoint. Only a cursory examination of the chassis was necessary to show that the design had been very carefully thought out, while the bodywork was of an exceptionally high order, especially when it is taken into consideration that the complete price of the saloon model, for example, is only £555.

The power unit has a capacity of slightly under 2½ litres, the bore and stroke respectively being 69 mm. and 110 mm., which gives a Treasury rating of 17.7 h.p. The camshaft is carried in four bearings machined all over and balanced statically and dynamically, while the inclined overhead valves are

carburetters with a common float chamber draw the supply through the medium of twin Autopulse pumps from an 11-gallon tank situated between the rear dumb-irons. There is also a tank under the bonnet, that accommodates two gallons, which, in addition to providing a reserve that is available on manipulating a two-way tap, is an excellent additional safeguard in the event of the pump system failing. Likewise provision is also made for carrying a reserve supply of lubricant, this being accommodated in a tank alongside the reserve petrol supply. The pipe leads from the tank into the oil

filler orifice, and thus by turning a tap it is possible to replenish the sump.

The gearbox provides three forward speeds, and is built in unit construction with the engine and clutch. The control is centrally placed and cranked well back, so that there is no necessity for the driver to lean forward when effecting gear changes.

The suspension system comprises semi-elliptic springs fore and aft, and a special feature is the anchoring of the front springs at their rear ends, the shackles being placed forward so as to minimize the effects of spring deflection on braking and steering. Another interesting point is that the springs are inclined upwards so as to improve riding qualities. The latest type of single Hartford shock absorber is fitted all round.

The ignition system is by coil and battery, the distributor being vertically placed high up where it is very accessible and well out of the way from water. Two batteries are fitted, these being carried one on each side of the propeller shaft, where, by tilting the front seats,

operated by an overhead camshaft. The latter is driven by a duplex roller chain which has an automatic tensioning device, and the half-time gear is carried in the head, so that the latter can be removed without upsetting the timing. A full forced system of lubrication is employed.

Special attention has been paid to the fuel-feed system. Two S.U.

(Above) A photograph which shows the lines of the M.G. Six Sports four-door saloon to advantage. (Right) Graph showing the excellent acceleration on top and second gears.

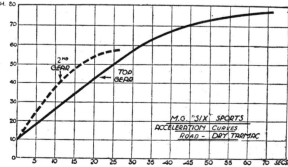

THE M.G. SIX SPORTS SALOON.—Contd.

they are easily accessible through the floorboards. A six-brake system is employed, the pedal operating on all four wheels, and the lever—which operates a separate cross-shaft and rods—operating separate shoes in the rear wheel drums. A single point adjustment of both hand and foot systems is provided.

The excellent specification is set off by the fitting of Rudge-Whitworth racing-type wire wheels with 29-in. by 5.00-in. Dunlop Fort tyres.

The bodywork is a fitting comple-

Showing the neat design of the engine and the two S.U. carburetters.

ment to an excellent chassis, and has undoubtedly been designed by a person who understands the requirements of the owner-driver for a roomy and compact four-seater. The front seats are of the separate armchair type, and the range of adjustment available is approximately 10 ins. Furthermore, the adjustment is so simple that the seats can be slid either backward or forward merely by raising a lever conveniently placed. The seats are also of such a depth as to afford the utmost comfort, while really good support is given to the legs by deep cushions, which are of the pneumatic type.

From a driver's point of view the seating position is ideal, the steering column, which is adjustable, is well raked, the brake lever, which is of the quick-release type, falls naturally to the right hand, and the same can be said of the gear lever, which is in the central position. Furthermore, the visibility all round is exceptionally good, this being achieved by a single-pane windscreen.

The saloon is really of the close-coupled type, and at a glance it does not seem that there is sufficient room to give comfort to the occupants on a long journey. This, however, is far from being the case, for

built-in ladies' and gentlemen's companions, roof light, roof ventilator and blind over the rear window operated from the driver's seat, while on the driver's door is a very neat smoker's companion.

The instrument board is particularly pleasing and all the necessary instruments are artistically grouped thereon. The instruments include revolution counter, speedometer, clock, ammeter, ignition tell-tale, temperature indicator, oil gauge and fuel gauge. These are illuminated at night by two dash lamps.

Another feature which will undoubtedly make a big appeal is an

(Above) The neat instrument panel at each side of which are small lockers. The wheel is of the spring-spoked pattern. (Right) Graph depicting the efficiency of the four-wheel brakes.

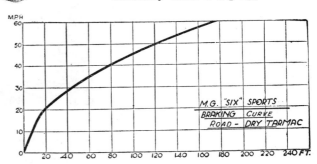

deep wells are sunk on each side of the propeller shaft and in addition the wells are carried underneath the front seats. As a matter of fact, these wells are no less than 10 ins. in depth, and in the car tested two stools 4½ ins. in depth and covered with carpet were fitted; even then, however, the leg-room was ample for a 6 ft. passenger. The rear seat is also equipped with pneumatic upholstery and is divided by an armrest which can be instantaneously removed if so desired.

Leather is used throughout, and the interior furnishing includes blinds to all windows, rope pulls, pockets to the rear doors, armrests,

ingenious built-in luggage container, which has but very little overhang. The back of the container when let down provides a platform on which a full-sized cabin trunk can be placed, while a large and small suitcase can be accommodated inside with the platform not in use. Protection for the luggage is provided by a leather apron, and straps are provided which prevent any possibility of the luggage becoming loose en route. Beneath the luggage container is a very roomy locker for carrying tools. Incidentally, the starting handle is accommodated in special rattle-proof clips underneath the bonnet.

The excellent built-in luggage container.

The M.G. sports does not belie its appearance, and quite a lengthy trial on the road proved that it has a performance of outstanding merit. It is a sports car which is unique in more ways than one. An outstanding feature is that it has a performance expected from the sports vehicle, but on the other hand it behaves in a manner similar to that of any ordinary touring car. Put in another manner, there is no need for one constantly to change gear, for the speed range is from 5 m.p.h. to 78 m.p.h. on top gear. For the person, however, who wants really rapid acceleration the M.G. provides it, and then, of course, it is necessary to change down to second, but because it is nominated as a sports car an ordinary driver need not have any qualms about purchasing it, for the gear change is as simple as that of any ordinary car.

Reference to our acceleration graph will show that without using the gears it is possible to reach the maximum speed from a 10-m.p.h.

start in the very short space of 72 seconds, which must be accredited a particularly fine performance. It can be said that this production is one of the most fascinating it has been our lot to handle, for it does its work with an entire absence of fuss and has a normal touring gait of 60 m.p.h. The engine is absolutely vibrationless throughout the speed range, and there is no roughness even when flat out. In fact, it would be difficult to find a unit which provides a better all-round performance.

Outstanding Features.

With a car capable of such speeds the suspension, steering and brakes must be above criticism. In all three respects the M.G. excels. The steering, which is of the Marles type, is exceptionally light and dead accurate, providing an effortless

all-round compromise. The brakes are not compensated and do not require very heavy pressure. They are also certain and safe in action, while the hand-brake, which is a bad feature on most cars, is particularly good.

Performance on Hills.

Whether on the open road or in congested traffic, the M.G. has an irresistible charm; it is an excellent vehicle for long journeys, while in traffic, owing to a good steering lock and a small overall width, it can be manœuvred with exceptional facility. Ordinary main-road hills are taken in its stride at a mile a minute, and Stokenchurch Hill, between Oxford and High Wycombe, despite the fact that it has some acute bends, did not fetch the car down below 40 m.p.h. on top gear— a very good performance.

"Safety with speed" might well be a slogan for the manufacturers, for this feeling above all is im-

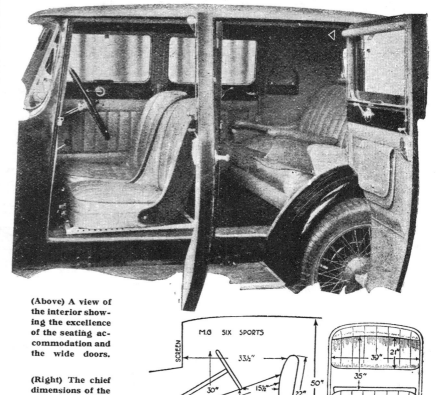

(Above) A view of the interior showing the excellence of the seating accommodation and the wide doors.

(Right) The chief dimensions of the body. The front seats are adjustable over a range of 10 ins.

TYPE : Four-door saloon: price £555.

ENGINE : Six - cylinders ; overhead valves, operated by overhead camshaft ; bore, 69 mm. ; stroke, 110 mm. ; 2,468 c.c.

GEARBOX : Three forward speeds, central control. Ratios : 4.25, 6.58, and 13.2 to 1.

SUSPENSION : Semi-elliptic springs fore and aft, supplemented by single-arm Hartford duplex shock absorbers.

BRAKES : On all four wheels, operated by pedal ; lever, on right-hand side, operates separate set shoes on rear wheels.

MINIMUM SPEED ON TOP GEAR : 5 m.p.h.

MAXIMUM SPEEDS ON GEARS : 1st, 25 m.p.h. ; 2nd, 55 m.p.h. ; top, 78 m.p.h.

FUEL CONSUMPTION : 18-20 m.p.g. (approx.).

TURNING CIRCLE : 43 ft.

DIMENSIONS : Overall length, 13 ft. 2 ins. ; overall height, 5 ft. 6 ins. ; overall width, 5 ft. 1 ins. ; track, 4 ft. ; ground clearance, 8 ins.

WEIGHT : Unladen, 1 ton 5 cwt. 1 qr. ; as tested, 1 ton 9 cwt.

THE M.G. CAR CO.,
Queen Street, Oxford.

control at all speeds. The springing enables corners to be taken at high speeds with safety ; there is not the slightest roll, and although it is slightly better at 30 m.p.h. upwards than it is at lower speeds, it must be regarded as an excellent

pressed upon one after only a short acquaintance with the car.

In conclusion, a very high opinion was formed of this new production which, although a sports model, is a vehicle equally suitable for the average motorist.

The M.G. Midget Sports.

A Fascinating Small Car with an Exceptionally Good Performance.

A side view of the M.G. Midget Sports which shows to advantage the trim lines.

FEW cars in the sports category have aroused more interest than the M.G. Midget, which was first introduced at the last Olympia Show. This exceptionally attractive little vehicle has already more than proved its capabilities in M.C.C. trials, while in the recent J.C.C. High-speed Trial at Brooklands five cars were entered and all secured gold medals. Further, they put up the first, second and third fastest times.

The Midget is designed on very straightforward lines and has a four-cylinder 847 c.c. engine with overhead valves operated by an overhead camshaft. Other features of the design include aluminium pistons, duralumin connecting rods and forced-feed lubrication to the main and big-end bearings and valve gear. The unit is also noteworthy for accessibility in design. Fuel is fed by gravity to the S.U. carburetter and the water circulation is by thermo-siphon, assisted by a fan and a large capacity radiator.

In unit with the engine is a three-forward-speed gearbox and the drive to the spiral bevel back axle is by means of an open propeller shaft. Suspension fore and aft is by long, flat, semi-elliptic springs supplemented by Hartford shock ab-

sorbers. A four-wheel-brake system is, of course, fitted, while the hand brake takes effect on the transmission.

Reference to the illustrations will

TYPE: *Two-seater; price £175.*

ENGINE: *Four-cylinder; overhead crankshaft; 57 mm. bore; 85 mm. stroke; 847 c.c.; tax £8.*

GEARBOX: *Three forward speeds; ratios 4.89, 8.96, and 17 to 1.*

SUSPENSION: *Semi-elliptic springs and Hartford shock absorbers fore and aft.*

BRAKES: *Pedal-operated on all four wheels; hand brake on transmission.*

MINIMUM SPEED ON TOP GEAR: *5 m.p.h.*

MAXIMUM SPEEDS ON GEARS: *1st, 24 m.p.h.; 2nd, 42 m.p.h.; top 65 m.p.h.*

PETROL CONSUMPTION: *40 m.p.g.*

DIMENSIONS: *Overall length, 10 ft.; overall width, 4 ft. 1 in.; wheelbase, 6 ft. 6 ins.; track, 3 ft. 6 ins.*

TURNING CIRCLE: *Left, 36 ft. 3 ins.; right, 39 ft. 2 ins.*

WEIGHT (unladen): *10 cwt. 20 lbs.*

M.G. CAR CO., Queen Street, Oxford.

---

suffice to show the really attractive lines. The car has close-up wings and no running-boards, and is built so low that one can sit in the seat and yet rest one's foot on the ground.

It is equipped with a sloping V windscreen and an entirely detachable hood. The latter, however, can be very easily erected, and, what is more, it provides really good protection from the elements. For those who are keen on entering competitions a good feature is the easy method in which the wings can be detached.

Despite its diminutive size there is plenty of leg room and at least 4 ins. adjustment can be obtained by varying the rake of the squab. The boot of the car has a hinged lid and in the locker is carried the spare wheel and the hood fittings when not in use. This locker is of really ample proportions and enables anyone going on tour to accommodate at least two good-sized suitcases with ease. Pneumatic upholstery is used for the seat cushion and also for the squab, while the floor mat is supplied to match the paintwork. The car is available in two colour schemes, red or light blue fabric to choice, the bonnet valances and wheels being cellulosed to match while the wings are also finished in black cellulose.

During our test nearly 400 miles were covered and no single adjustment had to be made, despite the fact that the car had been in daily

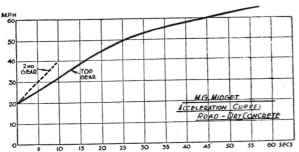

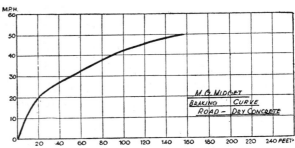

Graphs showing respectively the acceleration on top and second gears and efficiency of the four-wheel brakes.

use for several weeks and had also been on some strenuous trials. The first impressions of the car were gained in traffic, and here it may be said that with its 3 ft. 6 in. track and 6 ft. 6 in. wheelbase it could

The M.G. Midget is an absolute revelation on hills and the Brooklands test hill with its maximum gradient of 1 in 4, was taken as though it did not exist. Starting at 20 m.p.h. on second gear and chang-

there the slightest evidence of roughness. This remark also applies when second gear is being used, the speed on this ratio being 42 m.p.h. Even then there is only the vaguest suspicion of valve bounce and the

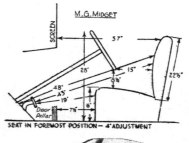

Chief dimensions of the two-seater body.

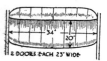

(Above) Showing the distinctive radiator, the close-up wings, V-type windscreen, and the fairing of the dumb-irons. (Right) The doors are wide enough to give unrestricted exit and entry. Note also the gear and brake lever position.

more than hold its own with any type of vehicle. In fact, it was found that owing to its acceleration and general flexibility, journeys taking, for example, half an hour could be done comfortably in twenty minutes with the Midget. Another outstanding thing in traffic was the exceptionally good flexibility on top gear, for it would throttle down to a road speed of 5 m.p.h.

The real charm of this amazing little car, however, is on the open road and driven properly it takes a particularly fast car to pass it. It has a maximum speed of 65 m.p.h., although the makers conservatively only claim 60 m.p.h. and can be driven at this pace with every feeling of safety. Considering its light weight—it is only a fraction over half a ton—it is really astounding how it rides really rough surfaces. Further, it was found that it could be driven against the camber of the road and still feel as steady as a rock.

Ample proof of the exceptional suspension was obtained in a strenuous test at Brooklands. Here this little car covered a flying half-mile against a very strong wind at an average speed of 55.38 m.p.h., while a standing start half-mile, using all the gears, was done at an average of 40 m.p.h.—both particularly fine performances.

ing down to bottom, the climb was made at an average speed of 15.6 m.p.h. Strange to say, however, this performance was bettered by making a standing start on bottom gear. The gearing apparently was just suited to the gradient and when the car went over the top it was doing slightly over 22 m.p.h., while the average speed of the climb was 16.01 m.p.h.

The engine simply revels in being driven flat out and at no speed was

The off-side of the power unit.

engine seems thoroughly happy. On the road we found that by changing down early it took cars in the £1,000 class to hold their own with it on gradients, while all ordinary main road hills could be taken at 45-50 m.p.h. on top.

Despite the fact that the track is only 42 ins., there is not the slightest feeling of insecurity when taking corners at speed, and, furthermore, the steering is finger-light and dead accurate, so that one can place the car exactly where required.

The brakes, of the internal-expanding type and operating on all four wheels by pedal, are quite good and exceptionally safe in operation, and we found that when driving the car on wet surfaces they could be harshly applied without causing the car to deviate from its course.

During the whole of our test, despite the fact that the gears were used more than was really necessary, oil consumption was almost negligible, and the fuel used averaged over 40 m.p.g.

In conclusion we formed the opinion that the M.G. Midget fills a real niche in the sports car world, and is capable of holding its own with any other cars of similar type, whether of British or foreign origin. It is one of the most fascinating little vehicles we have ever driven.

A New M.G. Model for this Season

The 18/80 M.G. Six 2-Seater Sports.

Details of the Mark II.

THE new factory of the M.G. Car Company at Abingdon is now finished, and the first of the Mark II models are on the erecting tracks. The range of models available for the present year is wide, and will appeal to all classes of motor sportsmen.

The Mark I six-cylinder model is unaltered from last year, and embodies an overhead camshaft engine of 2468 c.c., fitted with two S.U. carburettors and coil ignition, and a three speed unit construction gearbox. Drive is taken from a universal joint behind the gearbox through a ball jointed torque tube to the bevel driven back axle. The frame is of heavy section, upswept front and rear, and springing is by four semi elliptic springs assisted by Hartford shock absorbers. Lever and pedal are independently coupled to the four wheel brakes, which are fitted with single point adjustments.

The Mark II retains the good points of the earlier model, but is fitted with a four speed gearbox, embodying a silent third gear, and centre ball bearings for main and layshaft. The frame has been stiffened by a stouter centre cross girder, a front tie rod, and an additional pressing to brace the rear of the chassis. Springs are

wider, and are fitted with Silentbloc shackles. 14in. brake drums are fitted to all wheels

The Mark II, which will be available in the middle of March, costs £550, which the Mark I is available at £445.

Much interest has been caused by the announcement during February of a road racing model. This car, which is called the Mark III, is fitted with an engine of similar capacity to that used in the Mark II, but with a high compression head fitted with two plugs per cylinder and a new camshaft. Dry sump lubrication is a feature, and the crank case sump is separate from the flywheel compartment. An oil tank is carried between the front dumb irons, and is fitted with an oil cleaner.

A large petrol tank holding 25 gallons is used and is provided with a quick filling device. A light four seater body complying with International Regulations is standard, and the price of the complete car is fixed at £895. This model will be raced by private owners during the coming season, and one car has been entered in the Double Twelve.

The M.G. midget is unaltered, but a neat coupé with sliding roof and Triplex glass is now in production at £245.

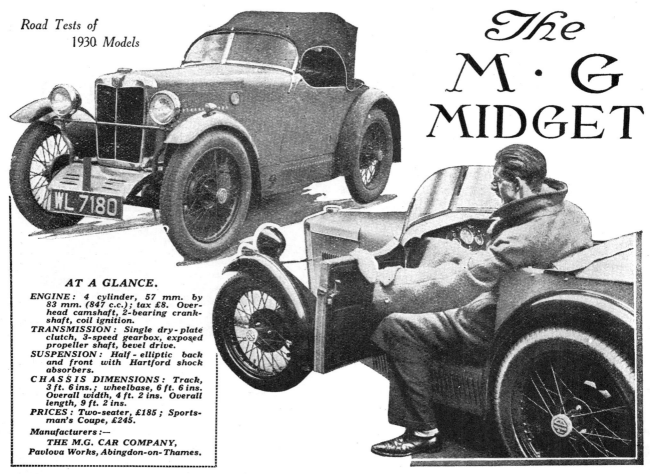

Road Tests of
1930 Models

The M·G MIDGET

AT A GLANCE.

ENGINE: 4 cylinder, 57 mm. by 83 mm. (847 c.c.); tax £8. Overhead camshaft, 2-bearing crankshaft, coil ignition.

TRANSMISSION: Single dry-plate clutch, 3-speed gearbox, exposed propeller shaft, bevel drive.

SUSPENSION: Half-elliptic back and front with Hartford shock absorbers.

CHASSIS DIMENSIONS: Track, 3 ft. 6 ins.; wheelbase, 6 ft. 6 ins. Overall width, 4 ft. 2 ins. Overall length, 9 ft. 2 ins.

PRICES: Two-seater, £185; Sportsman's Coupe, £245.

Manufacturers :—

THE M.G. CAR COMPANY,
Pavlova Works, Abingdon-on-Thames.

A sports car enthusiast, 6 ft. 4 ins. in height and wearing heavy clothes, is able to enter and leave the Midget without contortions.

SOME cars, presumably because their designers are very clever men, are right from the start. This was so in the case of the M.G. Midget which made its debut at the Show before last, and thus is entering upon its second season. The latest model, one of which we have just been able to test, is identical in almost every respect with the original version, the changes which have been made being merely in the nature of cleaning up and adding to the owner's comfort and convenience.

The most noteworthy changes are in the front-brake operating mechanism, which is now schemed so that the Bowden cable pulls in a straight line instead of round a loop. All the brake drums are now of cast aluminium, having deep efficient cooling fins and steel liners, and the hand brake, instead of acting upon the transmission, is linked with the f.w.b. cross-shaft and thus operates on all four wheels.

New Body Features.

As with the chassis, the body has been changed only in minor respects. The most important alteration concerns the door, which is now hinged down its forward instead of its rearward edge. This makes entry and exit no less convenient and is generally agreed to be a more desirable practice. Further small improvements are the use of massive rubber door buffers to prevent any possibility of rattling, a slightly altered method of adjusting the driving seat, which is variable as to the position of the cushion and the rake of the squab, and the fitting of a prop to hold the dickey lid in the open position.

When we called at the new M.G. works at Abingdon to take over a Midget to try it was indeed astonishing to notice the extraordinary activity on the assembly line. At the present time some 60 Midgets a week are being delivered. Everywhere there are rows of axles, springs, steering sets, engines and gearboxes.

Chassis frames are piled in huge stacks, and bodies descend in a steady continuous flow from a floor above.

The assembly is carried out on the most modern lines, elaborate plant having been installed and great pains having been taken to secure speedy output. Even so, we understand, the company is behindhand with deliveries, and will not be able to catch up for some weeks.

The little car handed over to us for test had covered a considerable mileage, and special brackets in front and behind for competition numbers showed that it had seen some service in trials. The work which it had done, however, seemed to have robbed it of none of the "pep" for which it is renowned, and an examination of the chassis showed practically no sign of wear in such important parts as hubs, steering connections, the transmission, and so forth. The electric starter spun the engine perfectly, starting it easily from dead cold and only two or three minutes elapsed before the engine was giving something close to its full power. We felt rather the absence of a hand throttle control which, in our opinion, is always a desirable fitment.

A Concession to B.H.P.

When thoroughly warmed up the engine was found to have a very good tick-over and to need no extra throttle for starting, but when cold the accelerator had to be continually "tickled" to keep the engine alive. Apart from this concession to b.h.p., a pukka sports performance is enjoyed with none of the disadvantages usually associated with it. The clutch frees properly and takes up the drive very sweetly, the gears are easily changed and the engine is almost as flexible as that of the average touring car. Its high

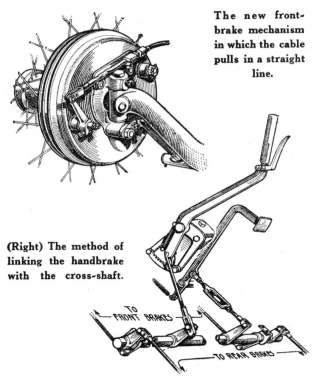

The new front-brake mechanism in which the cable pulls in a straight line.

(Right) The method of linking the handbrake with the cross-shaft.

TO FRONT BRAKES

TO REAR BRAKES

compression, however, makes it necessary for the driver to keep the ignition control on the move in order to get the best results unless a benzole mixture is used or a good non-pinking spirit.

On its gears of (bottom) 17 to 1, (second) 8.96 to 1 and (top) 4.89 to 1, extraordinarily good speeds can be attained. The maximum figures are approximately bottom gear 20 m.p.h., second gear 42 m.p.h. and top gear 62 m.p.h., in each case on a smooth level road. On a favourable downward gradient the car gained and held 68 m.p.h. for nearly half a mile, and at this speed the engine and transmission were perfectly sweet and vibrationless. When the engine was revving really fast on the gears the same could be said of it.

Acceleration Figures.

From a standing start with two occupants the car was capable of reaching 25 m.p.h. in five seconds, 30 m.p.h. in seven seconds and 40 m.p.h. in 12 seconds. During these acceleration tests the change from first to second gear was made at about 18 m.p.h., and it was found at this speed that the change could be made with commendably little pause in neutral.

From a starting speed of 10 m.p.h. the car was able to accelerate to 25 m.p.h. in three seconds, to 30 m.p.h. in six seconds and to 40 m.p.h. in 11 seconds.

With such an engine it is natural that very good average speeds can be maintained. We found that about 52 m.p.h. was a perfectly comfortable speed to maintain indefinitely on good roads, whilst on secondary roads it is easy to keep the speedometer almost continually over the 40 mark.

For high average speeds on the road good brakes are necessary, and these are certainly not lacking on the latest model. We found that the brakes came on in a most convincing manner, and that if heavy pressure were used on the pedal they gave as good results as one could wish. The brake pedal has a good "solid" feel. It rather gave the impression that its travel might, perhaps, be increased with advantage, and the added leverage thus available employed to cut down the pedal pressure.

The suspension and steering were both found to be admirable. An early model which we tried was inclined to wander about the road to some extent when flat out in top gear, but this drawback has now been completely overcome.

When it Rains.

We found that the little two-seater body with its pneumatic upholstery afforded quite a comfortable driving position and that with the hood erected it kept one dry in wet weather. Headroom, however, is perhaps rather too restricted with the hood up—a defect which could be got over by having a slightly taller windscreen.

It remains to add that although we flogged the M.G. Midget in an absolutely ruthless manner no trouble of any kind was experienced, no squeaks or rattles developed and not the slightest falling off in power was noticeable. Whilst the car was in our care it averaged 36 m.p.g. of petrol and used no appreciable quantity of oil. Cheap speed, indeed.

The M.G. MIDGET

An Intriguing Specialized Small Car With a Fine All-round Performance

U NDOUBTEDLY one of the most attractive small sports vehicles available to-day, the M.G. Midget is becoming increasingly popular, combining as it does good performance, excellent appearance and exceptionally cheap transport for two persons. Although primarily a sports

Two views of the M.G. Midget, showing its attractive lines and neat hood.

car, it is just as tractable as the average small car, and consequently does not require any particular skill in handling. It is these attributes that all contribute to the making of a really charming little vehicle.

Despite its diminutive size, there is ample space both as regards width of the seating and legroom, while a 4-in. range of adjustment, together with the provision for altering the rake of the squab, ensures driving comfort. The spare wheel is accommodated in the boot, likewise tools, and the collapsible hood stays and the material that forms the hood itself are stored in the lid of the boot, where they are held in position by two web straps. Incidentally, the hood is particularly easy to erect, and, providing one is not too tall, enables

quite good vision to be obtained. Should it be necessary, as, for example, in competition work, to carry two spare wheels, there is plenty of room in the boot; but, of course, this causes a restriction of luggage space.

TYPE: *Two-seater, price £185.*
ENGINE: *Four-cylinders; o.h. valves operated by o.h. camshaft; bore, 57 mm.; stroke, 83 mm.; 847 c.c.; R.A.C. rating, 8.03 h.p.; tax, £8.*
GEARBOX: *Three forward speeds with central control; Ratios: 4.98, 8.96 and 17 to 1.*
SUSPENSION: *Semi-elliptic springs with Hartford shock absorbers all round.*
BRAKES: *Both foot and hand systems operate on all four wheels.*
MINIMUM SPEED ON TOP GEAR: *5 m.p.h.*
MAXIMUM SPEED ON GEARS: *2nd, 42 m.p.h.; top, 62 m.p.h.*
FUEL CONSUMPTION: *40 m.p.g. (approx.).*
DIMENSIONS: *Wheelbase, 6 ft. 6 ins.; track, 3 ft. 6 ins.; ground clearance, 9 ins.; overall length, 9 ft. 2¼ ins.; width, 4 ft. 2 ins.*
TURNING CIRCLE: *34 ft.*

M.G. CAR CO.,
Pavlova Works, Abingdon-on-Thames, Berks.

A V-type windscreen is fitted, the body sides are high enough to give good protection, and the close-up wings seem quite efficient in the worst of weather. The cowling-in of the front dumbirons also assists materially in preventing mud being flung in all directions. Owing to the low build, running boards or steps are unnecessary, and it is actually possible for one to sit on the seat and rest the feet flat on the ground.

Considering the diminutive engine and its propensities for revving one is not prepared to expect flexibility on top gear to any marked degree. In this, however, one is promptly deceived, and in the thickest of London traffic very little gear changing is really necessary, for the engine can be throttled down to a road speed of 5 m.p.h. without the slightest evidence of snatch. The real enthusiast, however, delights to use the gears, and with but a short acquaintance with the car really quick changes can be executed at high revolutions. The power unit simply revels in high speeds, and, no matter whether it is revved to its utmost capabilities, there is not the slightest sign of roughness. On second gear the car in question did a genuine 42 m.p.h. and 62 m.p.h. on top, while on a slight down grade a speed of 66 m.p.h. was attained.

The car was a perfectly standard product, and, indeed, has been driven very hard by all and sundry, so that this performance is all the more creditable. After covering some 200 miles on the road it was tested, as is our usual practice, at Brooklands. Here are the results obtained:—A flying lap at 53.55 m.p.h.; a flying quarter-mile at 60 m.p.h.; a flying half-mile at 58.06 m.p.h.; and a flying mile at 53.73 m.p.h.

The neat o.h.c. power unit, showing the S.U. carburetter and ribbed exhaust manifold.

The coil mounting, accessible location of the sparking plugs and dynamo drive.

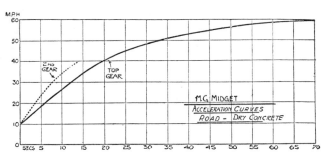

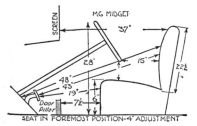

Dimensions of the two-seater body.

The excellent acceleration is plotted on an accompanying graph, and although it will be seen that 70 secs. are taken to reach 60 m.p.h. from a 10 m.p.h. start, it is possible to reach the magic figure in 46 secs. from a 20 m.p.h. beginning.

On the track the M.G. Midget sits down equally as well as on the road. The suspension is a trifle harsh at low speeds, but when "flat out" the road-holding qualities are really amazing for so light a vehicle. In other words, one feels perfectly safe, whether passing another car against the camber, when cornering fast, and at maximum speed. These features naturally give one every confidence and enable high average speeds to be maintained in safety.

On hills this little car is an outstanding performer. For example, on the steepest gradient between Maidenhead and Henley-on-Thames

(Above) Graphs showing respectively the excellent acceleration and the efficiency of the four-wheel braking system.

the speedometer did not drop below 40 m.p.h. on top gear and main-road hills of a little less severity can be negotiated at 50 m.p.h., so it will be seen that it takes hills of the 1-in-6 variety to make a change down to second necessary.

Steering is exceptionally light and accurate; the brakes are smooth in operation and efficient; petrol consumption averages 40 m.p.g. with hard driving, and the oil consumption during our test was so small

that no difference in the quantity of the sump could be detected on the dip rod.

Altogether the M.G. Midget can be safely said to be a very intriguing little car possessed of a superlative performance. Prospective buyers will also be interested to learn that it is being turned out in rapidly increasing numbers in the huge new works which the manufacturers have acquired recently at Abingdon-on-Thames.

The M.G. SIX Mark II.

2,000 Miles on a Fast and Roadworthy British Car

EVEN the most blasé of motorists cannot help liking the latest M.G. Six. It is a car that inspires enthusiasm. It is fast and comfortable and, above all, roadworthy. It can be held at its maximum speed for an apparently indefinite period without ever feeling or sounding overworked; it corners well and has excellent brakes.

A Logical Development.

The "Mark II," as the latest model is called, is the logical development of the well-known "Mark 1" M.G. Six. It has a stiffer frame, giving better road-holding; a wider track, giving steadier cornering; and a beautifully made four-speed gearbox—with a "silent third" speed and lower ratios that give almost equally inaudible service—which gives better acceleration and hill-climbing. The brake gear, too, has been redesigned, so that the car can be brought to a standstill, even from high speeds, more rapidly and more safely than ever.

A mere day on such a car would provide one with little data as to its reliability or wearing qualities. One would appreciate the performance, the ease of handling, the pleasure of it. But one would remain ignorant of the sterling service that it is capable of giving over long periods, its behaviour on wet roads

and dry roads, its easy starting every morning and its general dependability.

For this reason we drove the M.G.

CAR TESTED: *M.G. Six, Mark II, two-seater. Price £625.*

ENGINE: *Six-cylinders, overhead camshaft, 69 mm. bore, 110 mm. stroke, 2,468 c.c.; R.A.C. rating, 17.7 h.p.; tax, £18.*

TRANSMISSION: *Multiplate clutch, four-speed and reverse gearbox (central control), enclosed propeller shaft, spiral-bevel final drive.*

SPEEDS ON GEARS: *Top (4.27 to 1), 78.26 m.p.h. for flying half-mile; laps Brooklands at 72.44 m.p.h.; 3rd (5.58 to 1), 62 m.p.h.; 2nd (8.5 to 1), 40 m.p.h.; 1st gear ratio 14.58 to 1.*

BRAKES: *On all four wheels.*

TURNING CIRCLES: *Right, 40 ft. 2 ins.; left, 43 ft. 11 ins.*

DIMENSIONS: *Wheelbase, 9 ft. 6 ins.; track, 4 ft. 4 ins.; overall length, 13 ft. 2 ins.; width, 5 ft. 3¼ ins.; ground clearance, 8 ins.*

WEIGHT: *In running order, without occupants, 27 cwt. 3 lb.*

THE M.G. CAR COMPANY,
Abingdon-on-Thames.

Six, Mark II, for 2,000 miles before we formed our opinion of it. When it had barely covered its first 500 miles we took it through the

strenuous London-Land's End trial of the Motor Cycling Club. After 1,100 miles we visited Brooklands and the car was timed over the half-mile at 72 m.p.h. Then, when the mileage recorder registered 2,000 miles and the engine and transmission were beginning to be nicely "run in," we again went to Brooklands and covered the same distance at 78.26 m.p.h. So it will be seen that the M.G. improves with hard work.

When taking over the car one is so impressed with the ease of gear-changing and that very silent "third" that one changes gear for the sheer fun of it, snicking into "second" quite unnecessarily to round street corners and dropping into "third" every time one wishes to overtake another vehicle. Moreover, one need have no hesitation in keeping third gear engaged for long periods, particularly when driving in traffic. One thus has almost startling acceleration and correspondingly rapid deceleration to meet every emergency. On the open road this third gear, which allows of well over 60 m.p.h. actual speed, permits of unusually rapid hill-climbing and safe overtaking. Second gear, if the accelerator is fully depressed, gives a maximum of round about 40 m.p.h.

In the course of the London-Land's End trial we used first gear for the **five** observed hills: Grabhurst, Porlock, Lynton, Beggars' Roost and Bluehills Mine, partly because first speed is pretty high (the ratio is 4.27

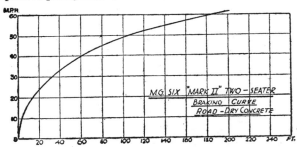

to 1 and the car weighs over 27 cwt. empty) and partly because we had not previously tried the car on the hills and were not taking any chances. On the 1 in 3.2 section of Beggars' Roost, despite a standing start at the foot of the hill, the car proved exceptionally fast, while on Bluehills Mine the M.G. took the acute hair-pin in an easy sweep, although the gradient on the inside of the bend is equally severe.

M.G. SIX "MARK II" TWO-SEATER

SLIDING SEAT PLACED HALF-WAY STEERING COLUMN ADJUSTABLE

On the return journey from Penzance to London we found ourselves, without effort, averaging an extremely satisfactory speed, taking quite sharp bends in absolute safety

(Above) The accessible gear-lever.

(Left) Seating diagram.

even at two-thirds of the top gear maximum and feeling all the time that the car was under perfect control.

The steering is delightful; it is pleasantly light and has a marked self-centring effect. The clutch is one of the smoothest we have ever used, the gear change is smooth and the brakes easily applied.

Acting in large-diameter drums,

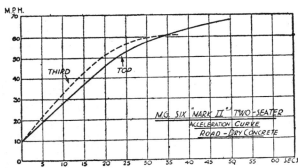

the brakes do not lock the wheels yet provide a praiseworthy degree of retardation. As a result, the car is as safe when pulling up on wet roads as on the rough, dry concrete of Brooklands.

The engine, we found, was prone to "pink" a little when accelerating from low speeds unless the spark was retarded. This was when using ordinary petrol. A motorist who disliked using the very accessible ignition control on the steering wheel could probably overcome this by richening the mixture slightly (very easily done on the S.U. carburetters fitted as standard) or by using benzol mixture.

The M.G., Mark II, is easily handled in traffic, as it will turn in a circle of only just over 40 feet, while its overall length and width are kept within reasonable limits.

High Grade Coachwork.

The bodywork is of the highest grade. The car we tried had a two-seater body of unusually graceful design, with a single-seat dickey. The wings keep the body reasonably clean in bad weather, despite their small wind resistance, and the Leveroll fittings enabled the two bucket seats to be adjusted for legroom. Large door-pockets and dashboard cubby-holes are provided for small articles, while the well-fitting side curtains are stored in a shallow locker behind the front seats. The equipment is quite complete and includes very large Rotax dip-and-switch type headlamps, a double screen wiper, thermometer, revolution counter and all the usual instruments. Both the ignition and gearbox are fitted with thief-proof locks.

The M.G. Six, Mark II, therefore, is a car which we should not hesitate to take anywhere. It has all the charm of a thoroughbred, is very comfortable and, to use the makers' own slogan, it is "faster than most." At the price of £625 it is within reach of all those who appreciate a car that is not only a "good looker" but will give really satisfactory service and really pleasurable driving for tens of thousands of miles.

The "Mark II" has attractive lines.

A "DOUBLE TWELVE" M.G. MIDGET
ON THE ROAD.

WHEN a make of car at its first appearance in a big race, not only carries off the team prize, but is, moreover, the only complete team to finish the course, it is evident that something remarkable has occurred. It is therefore of special interest to be able to give our first-hand impressions of the behaviour under ordinary road conditions of one of the successful cars.

Ready for action. The Midget in " Double Twelve" trim.

The engine, although quite untouched since the race, gave an absolutely effortless cruising speed of 60 m.p.h. on about half throttle, and a good 70 m.p.h. maximum. On one occasion under favourable conditions we reached and held 75 m.p.h., and the road holding was still excellent.

Naturally on such a small engine the gears must be used well if the best performance is to be maintained, but, the running at low speeds was perfectly smooth, and there was absolutely no sign of pinking or roughness when picking up from this speed. This pleasant state of affairs was largely due to the R.O.P. benzole mixture which was used throughout our run, and the next morning the engine started from cold at the first touch of the starter button without even flooding the carburettor. Verb. sap !

Owing to the kindness of Mr. Randall, the entrant and owner of the M.G. Midget team in the Double-Twelve hour race, and of Mr. Kimble of University Motors we were able to take over No. 76, which was the first car of the trio home in the race, and give it a fairly extended test on the road.

One day a party consisting of Mr. Kimble, an assistant, and two members of MOTOR SPORT staff, set out for Waltham Cross to collect the winning cars and bring them up to London. On arrival they were filled up with fuel and oil and forthwith started up. Only one of the cars had had the engine running since being driven down after the race, but all three cars started at once on the starters and we purred merrily off to London. The first part of our run being in dense traffic gave us a chance to appreciate the extreme handiness under such conditions of a small car with real acceleration.

Having left two of the team at University Motors, we set off in No. 76 to find out what effect 24 hours of almost continuous all-out running had had on the behaviour and performance of the 850 c.c. engine.

We had originally intended to do only a short run, but we became so intrigued with the performance of our tiny steed, that we were well down towards the West country almost before we had decided where to go, and the same evening saw over 200 miles more registered on the clock !

The Hartford shock absorbers were, naturally, set for high speed work and made the springing a little hard at low speeds. This is, of course, only what is intended, and once in open country they made the car ride perfectly smoothly and steadily over all sorts of roads.

The K.L.G. 268 plugs, although of the distinctly warm variety functioned well under different conditions, and it was only by allowing the engine to tick over too long that we once contrived to oil up No. 1 cylinder a trifle. This gave an opportunity of proving the accessibility of the unit and a new one was fitted in a matter of seconds.

Naturally, the brakes were ready for slight adjustment after their hard time in the race, but were still adequate. The car as a whole seemed to us a very attractive proposition, which would be economical to run, and after the Double Twelve race, any further comment on its reliability would be superfluous.

TWO MEN AND A MIDGET

An Account of the Part Played in the Belgian "Grand Prix des 24 Heures" by the Smallest Car in the Race.

By F. H. B. SAMUELSON.

SOME little time ago "Casque" said to me that I appeared to specialise in bother of a peculiarly exciting type. Perhaps it was to some extent this penchant for battling against what may sometimes seem unnecessary odds that caused me, while still at Le Mans, where my M.G. Midget had taken part in the Grand Prix d'Endurance, to enter it for the Belgian 24-hour race only twelve days before the Belgian race was due to start.

As is now well known to all those who take an interest in motor racing, my Midget had run extremely well and with the utmost reliability at Le Mans until a fractured oil-pipe put us out of the race. Up till then the performance of the car was such as to convince me that with ordinary luck she was quite capable of going right through any 24-hour race on any road circuit; so immediately after the race was over I made enquiries about the Belgian Grand Prix and eventually entered the car by telegram next day.

Some Hustle !

Time was short, and it was essential that the engine should go back to the M.G. works at Abingdon for overhaul. We therefore took it out of the chassis, which we left at Le Mans, and, putting it in the back of my tried and trusty old French Talbot, bore it back to England.

It was mid-day on Thursday by the time I got the engine to Abingdon, and I had planned to catch the night boat (10 p.m.) back from Newhaven to Dieppe on Friday, so that we might have time to do a little practice on the circuit at Spa, as neither I nor my other driver, F. R. Kindell, had ever seen the course before, nor did we know the roads from Paris to Belgium.

The engine had to be dismantled completely, put up again and tested, and some sort of a cradle made to keep it in place in the back of the Talbot, as I had had to drive with one hand

The author's M.G. Midget in "fighting trim."

and hold it in place with the other most of the way from Le Mans to Abingdon, and it was not improving the upholstery of the much-abused Talbot.

However, all was ready in time, and we got to Newhaven at 9.15 p.m., arriving at Le Mans the next evening. There were just the two of us, and we were short of tools, as in the rush all the tools had been left behind and so had Kindell's luggage! We just had such tools as I usually carry on the Talbot and what we could borrow at the Morris-Léon-Bollée Works at Le Mans. There the English works manager, Mr. Harry Smith, was most kind and helpful to us, putting his whole works at our disposal, helping us with the re-erection and even taking us to his home to real English meals beautifully cooked by his lovely and charming daughter. No wonder we did not finally leave Le Mans until quite late on Monday evening!

We Arrive.

All through France we were haunted by terrific thunderstorms, but we somehow managed to dodge them until we got into Belgium, where they descended upon us from all directions. Finally we arrived at our headquarters at Francorchamps, near Spa, on Wednesday evening completely wet through and very tired. The local Belgians were quite disappointed when they found that we were not going to practise that night.

The Belgian course is a most sporting one and far more difficult and interesting than that at Le Mans. The surface is perfect, the road on the whole narrower, and there are numerous corners and no straight stretches of more than 1½ kilometres in length. It is also decidedly hilly, the difference in level between the highest and lowest points being 490ft. Owing to the scratching of the Bentleys my Midget was the only English car in the race, and, as it was also by far the smallest running, great interest was taken by competitors and spectators alike in its performance.

The race is run in a series of classes according to engine size, and we found ourselves in the 1,100 c.c. class, in which there were eleven other cars, including four Tractas.

How We Fared.

All went well with us for about twenty hours, by which time we were running third in our class, having averaged over 50 m.p.h., including all stops. We were lapping at rather over 55 m.p.h., my best lap working out at 57 m.p.h. Then clutch-slip set in, and as one lap had to be completed in every hour, and three laps during the last hour, no adequate steps could be taken to effect a cure. After using up all the fire extinguishers in the vicinity of our pit we just had to struggle on as best we could to finish 5th in our class and 15th out of twenty-one finishers of all categories, at an average speed of rather over 47 m.p.h. Apart from this clutch-slip the Midget ran marvellously all through, gave no trouble and received a great ovation from the spectators at the finish.

I cannot end this account without a word for my co-driver, Kindell, whose unlimited capacity for hard work and amazing cheerfulness in all conditions were mainly responsible for enabling my Midget to be the first and, so far, only car of its size ever to complete the course in an international twenty-four hours road race.

THE M.G. SIX (MARK I.).

A Closed Car of High Performance.

This four-door saloon on the Mark I. chassis makes an admirable combination.   It sells for £570.

IDEAS on sporting cars have undergone a good deal of change during the past few years.   The days have gone when the owner was content to sacrifice comfort, cleanliness and silence for the sake of speed, and the indifferently-upholstered body with undersized windscreen and scanty wings, which at one time were considered essential in a car which laid claim to high speeds, are no longer in vogue.

The modern sports model, to meet average present day requirements, as well as being capable of fast travel, must also be so equipped as to afford a degree of driving ease comparable with any tourer.   It is this combination of comfort and liveliness which is the outstanding characteristic of the M.G. Six Mark I "Sportsman's Salonette."

The particular model which we had for test had already done many thousands of miles as a service car of the M.G. Company and it was not only just standard, but one which had not been specially tuned or tended for special demonstration purposes.   This was all to the good of our purpose, as we were able to judge what this popular car in perfectly ordinary production form was capable of doing.   On collecting the car from the Pavlova Works at Abingdon, as soon as we got in the driving seat, we found certain little details which call for favourable comment.   The accelerator pedal, for instance, which is placed well away from the other foot controls, is operated against a return spring of just the right tension and works through a conveniently small range of movement, whilst the gear lever of the central change is in a position where it falls readily to hand.   The brake lever is placed on the right-hand side and is of the quick-release racing type.   This is a feature which might well

be included on the most mundane of utility motorcars, for it is a great improvement on the more usual pattern.

From previous experience of low-roofed sports saloons, we were prepared to find the exhaust noise somewhat noticeable, but on the M.G. as soon as the throttle was opened, we found the engine notably unobtrusive. While passing through the country lanes from Abingdon to the main Oxford-London road, it was difficult to realise that our speed had risen to the 50-60 m.p.h. mark, so silky was the running, and on reaching a suitable section of the main road, where we were able to open out, it soon became apparent that it was perfectly easy to "play" the car round the 70 m.p.h. figure without any difficulty at all, and a brief period at full bore brought the speedometer needle round to 75 and finally 80 m.p.h. mark.   When one considers that the M.G. has all the attributes of the well-behaved "town carriage," it must be agreed that this maximum speed, without any fuss or any suggestion of over-driving, is definitely good. There are plenty of motors nowadays, of course, with which one is able to obtain these figures, but it would be difficult to find another which makes less business about it, even if one were to choose a car with an engine of, perhaps, double the capacity.

Another point which genuinely impressed the writer was the braking.   There is nothing so disconcerting in a car than to find on applying the brakes at high speed that its deceleration is violent and uncontrolled. The M.G. brakes which are of perfectly straight forward lay out, make it possible to slow down rapidly from speeds of 70 m.p.h. to a standstill with noteworthy smoothness ;   the steering, which is of the Marles type was well in keeping with the rest of the car.   As for the clutch, this is one of the smoothest that we have ever used.

The springs are long semi-elliptic front and rear with the front ones shackled so that deflections in steering and braking are greatly minimised ; a point which is worthy of note is that all the springs are inclined upwards to the front in such a way that the absorption of road shocks is greatly improved. Hartfords are fitted all round.

The well-arranged facia board on the M.G. Six.

As we have already stated, the model under review was by no means new ; nevertheless, there was a complete absence of any body rattles or drumming. In a good many cars the instrument board is responsible for irritating " dithers " at certain engine speeds and probably one of the reasons of there being no trouble of this sort with the M.G. is that the dash is built up with the chassis and is thus very rigid. It carries the steering column and reserve petrol tank and also a tank for one gallon of engine oil.

The standard equipment includes a Jaegar speedometer and revolution counter, and besides the usual ammeter, clock, oil pressure gauge, petrol gauge and ignition tell-tale, there is also a radiator thermometer.

The engine has a Treasury rating of 17.7 h.p. and a capacity of approximately $2\frac{1}{2}$ litres.

The six cylinders are cast *en bloc* with two separate induction pipes feeding groups of three cylinders. The feed to the two S.U. carburetters is by an Autopulse electric pump. The ignition is by coil and battery (Lucas). The crankshaft is carried on four large bearings and is statically and dynamically balanced, and overhead valves are inclined and operated by an overhead camshaft. Lubrication is by spur gear pump bolted to the outside of the engine. This auxiliary, like other parts of the power unit, is readily accessible. The three speed gear box is built up in one with the engine and the ratios are :—top, $4\frac{1}{4}$-1, second, $6\frac{1}{2}$-1, bottom 13-1. The final drive is by enclosed propeller shaft.

Throughout the M.G. Six, one finds evidence that it has been planned and developed by a designer who is both practical and discriminating, and at the conclusion of our all-too-brief test, we found ourselves in the pleasant and somewhat unusual position of being unable to find anything which we could criticize. And that is all that need be said.

A NEW 80 M.P.H. M.G. SIX

A " Speed Model " with Excellent Acceleration, Braking and Hill-climbing Selling at £525

The M.G. Six (Mark I) speed model.

A NEW M.G. model for 1931 is the Mark I open sports tourer which will be sold with a guarantee of 80 m.p.h. This car is fitted with a very attractive four-seater body of light weight and small wind resistance, with the result that a

---

CAR TESTED: *M.G. Six (Mark I) Speed Model, price £525.*

ENGINE: *Six-cylinder, overhead valves and camshaft; 69 mm. bore, 110 mm. stroke; 2,468 c.c.; R.A.C. rating, 17.7 h.p. Tax £18.*

GEARBOX: *Three speeds and reverse; ratios: 4.25, 6.58 and 13.2 to 1.*

MAXIMUM SPEEDS: *On gears—top, 80.36 m.p.h.; 2nd, 61.22 m.p.h.*

SUSPENSION: *Semi-elliptic springs fore and aft.*

BRAKES: *On all four wheels, operated by Dewandre vacuum servo.*

MINIMUM SPEED: *On top gear, 5 m.p.h.*

DIMENSIONS: *Wheelbase, 9 ft. 6 ins.; track, 4 ft.; ground clearance, 8 ins; overall length, 13 ft.; width, 5 ft.*

TURNING CIRCLES: *Right, 42 ft. 5 ins.; left, 42 ft. 3 ins.*

WEIGHT, *in running order, unoccupied: 22 cwt. 3 qrs. 9 lb.*

THE M.G. CAR CO.,
Pavlova Works, Abingdon-on-Thames.

---

performance above the average is obtained; acceleration is very rapid, gear-changing is much less frequently required and the running costs are appreciably lower than those of the heavier models. So fast is the car on middle gear that one does not miss the four-speed box that is standardized on the more expensive Mark II model.

We recently carried out the first road test of this new M.G. model and found that, owing to the absence of top hamper and the light weight road holding was all that could be desired, and corners could be taken

fast without any sign of rolling. This car, moreover, should be an excellent hill-climber as, from a standing start in first gear, Brooklands test hill was ascended in 12½ seconds —a quite exceptional performance.

In its general specification the new open tourer closely resembles the already well-known Mark I in that it has a six-cylinder overhead camshaft engine of 2,468 c.c. and a three-speed gearbox. The brakes are much improved, however, by the addition of a Dewandre vacuum servo mechanism.

These provide one of the most notable of all improvements to the M.G. Six chassis. A mere touch of the foot brings the powerful brakes

into action, with the result that the car can be brought to rest in an exceptionally short distance. The easy brake operation makes the car quite effortless to drive compared to the earlier models, on which a certain amount of energy had to be expended on braking. The curve which we publish on the next page shows how efficient are these new vacuum brakes.

The springing is very good. Even at 80 m.p.h. on the most bumpy sections of Brooklands track we were perfectly comfortable, while on the road the springing was quite flexible, even at low speeds.

The steering is beautifully light, no reaction from road irregularities

(Right) Showing the neat way in which the hood sticks are stowed away in recesses in the body sides. (Below) Three-quarter rear view, showing method of carrying the spare wheel.

being felt by the driver, while all the controls were easy to operate.

A little more castor action in the steering would, we think, make the car still more pleasant to handle, as there was on the car we tested little or no tendency for the steering to "straighten out" after rounding a bend.

When we tested the car the weather was almost tropical, while a slight wind was blowing across the railway straight at Brooklands. Despite this, a flying half-mile was covered at 80.36 m.p.h. and a complete lap at 78.43 m.p.h. From a standing start to 60 m.p.h., using the gears, occupied 22 4/5 seconds, but to reach 80 m.p.h. the time taken was 94¾ seconds—very little shorter, in fact, than the time taken to accelerate from 10 to 80 m.p.h. on top gear.

The bodywork is well thought out, the hood being particularly neatly arranged to fold flush with the top line of the body, the hood sticks being accommodated in a recess in the body side, which is normally covered by an extension to the hood cover.

The hand brake is situated outside the body, although the gear lever is centrally placed. The scuttle comes very close up to the steering wheel and the windscreen folds

of this type. Even at high speed the car was beautifully quiet, not only mechanically, but also as regards the exhaust. Rudge-Whitworth wire wheels are fitted as standard—a luxury not usually encountered on cars of this price.

The gear change is very easy, the gearbox quiet, and the clutch, which is of the multi-plate type, is smooth.

has been increased by the addition of a de luxe four-door saloon with the now fashionable close-up wings, special interior furnishing, a Pytchley sliding roof, and a new and attractive colour scheme. This will sell at £699.

Modifications to the M.G. Midget sports two-seater consist of the fitting of Triplex glass and other minor improvements. There is also

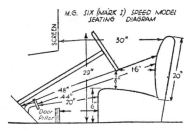

(Right) Seating diagram, giving an indication of the accommodation provided. (Below) Side view, showing the sporting lines of the new model.

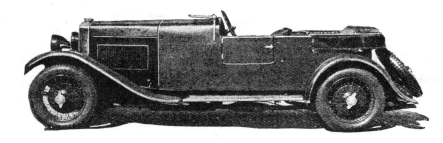

(Left) Acceleration curve, showing the performance obtainable. (Below) Diagram showing pulling-up distances from various speeds.

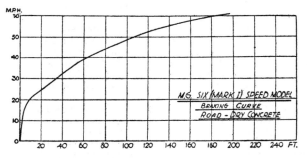

down flat in a forward direction. The body side is cut away to give the driver elbow room, while deep wells are provided for the passengers in the rear compartment. The spare wheel is carried at an angle over the petrol tank between the rear dumbirons, and adds to the sporting appearance of the car. Only two doors are provided, one on the near side giving access to the front compartment, while that on the off side provides entry to the rear seats.

Our test was unfortunately too short to enable us to take the car up any well-known hills, or, in fact, to measure the fuel and oil consumptions, but these we were assured are perfectly reasonable for a car

Selling at £525 complete, this new M.G. should rapidly make itself a name in sporting circles.

In addition to the M.G. Six Mark I speed model, there are several innovations for 1931. For instance, all Mark I models are being fitted with Dewandre servo brakes, and chromium plating and Triplex glass are also being included in the specification. The result is that all existing Mark I models are being priced at £10 more than last year. The sports tourer Mark I is, of course, being retained in addition to the new speed model, and sells at the same price.

The M.G. Six Sports Mark II models remain unaltered in specification and in price, but the range

an additional Midget two-seater available, finished in black with red wheels.

The M.G. Midget sportsman's coupé will have a panelled body and cleaner roof lines, the exterior will be finished in black only, which will, however, be relieved by the standard M.G. upholstery colours.

The complete price list is as follows:—Midget two-seater £185, coupé £245, Mark I chassis £455, two-seater £520, tourer and speed models £525 each, salonette £565, saloon £580. Mark II chassis £550, two-seater £625, tourer £630, salonette £660, saloon £670, saloon de luxe £699. There is also the Mark III, or road-racing model, the price of which has not yet been fixed.

The M.G. MIDGET

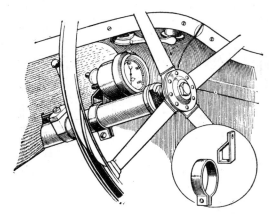

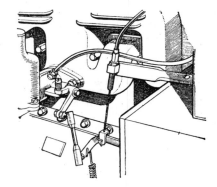

(Left) How the Aric radiator thermometer has been fitted to the steering column and the handy lever for the Bowden hand throttle. (Right) The method of connecting the hand throttle to the existing controls.

A Member of Our Staff Gives His Impressions and Experiences of a Very Popular Sports Car Which is in Everyday Use

WHEN the M.G. Midget was first introduced at the Motor Show of 1928 it marked something new in small sports cars. Previously, of course, there had been sports cars in the £8 tax class, but there had often been something lacking in them; they consisted either of light sports bodies on almost standard chassis and gave performances very little better than the normal product, or they were sports bodies on very much hotted-up standard chassis and gave good performance, but only at the sacrifice of those qualities of flexibility and smoothness which mean so much when one is not merely out for a spot of fun.

Then came the M.G. Midget, and I can well remember the enthusiasm of those who first handled it. To take the wheel was to realize that here was no mock sports car, but a thoroughbred with the convincing feel of the real thing. That was over two years ago. Is it to be wondered at that the Midget is now one of the most attractive and popular of any small sports cars on the road?

Actually, I was one of those who were privileged to handle a Midget in the days when lots of people were talking of them, but few had seen them on the road, much less driven them, and for 18 months afterwards I was "itching" to call one my own. There was, however, a "but" and a rather big one.

For All Purposes.

A journalist on the staff of a journal like *The Light Car and Cyclecar* does not do all his motoring under ideal conditions, for innumerable journeys have to be made, no matter whether it rains. hails, snows or fogs (if there is such a verb), to mention nothing of hackwork, entailing much pottering about in traffic and so on. Much as I had fallen in love with the Midget, I long hesitated before yielding up the many advantages of my 8 h.p. saloon in connection with this work for the many possible drawbacks of an open (very) sports car.

However, I took the plunge at last, and on May 2nd, 1930, duly made the acquaintance of my future car in the delivery depot of The Morris Garages, Ltd., Oxford, who had taken my previous car in part exchange. Perhaps it is one of the greatest tributes I can pay to the Midget when I say that, despite the diversity of uses to which I have put the car, I have never once —even after 200 miles in the pouring rain, followed by a spell of traffic work—regretted the choice.

Versatile Little Car.

Here, in fact, is one of the greatest charms of the Midget. Its capacity for putting up good averages on the open road and its appetite for hills or rough going do not rob it of its docility and general gentlemanly behaviour in traffic; many a six-cylinder car can show up to no better advantage under these varying conditions than this versatile little motor.

I must confess, however, that I am still not in love with the hood. True, it affords good protection, but erecting it is not so simple as putting up a two-seater hood of the non-detachable type, whilst visibility is not all that it might be. The latter drawback has largely been overcome, as will be explained later, but I still prefer to don a large leather coat and dispense entirely with the hood when alone. Of course, no car is yet perfect and this is the only real criticism of the Midget that I have to offer. Moreover, I probably attach more importance to the matter than the average man who buys the two-seater model and who does not so often use the car for purposes for which a sports car was never intended.

Needless to say, I have added a few carefully chosen accessories, whilst various little alterations and additions have been made to suit my own tastes and requirements. Actually, the first gadget to be fitted was a radiator thermometer (made by the Accurate Recording Instrument Co., Ltd., Aric Works, Manor Road, Teddington), of the dial-reading facia-board type. This is an old favourite of mine, which I transferred from my previous car.

Fitting in the case of the Midget presented no difficulty, the bulb being accommodated in the usual manner in the radiator head tank; the dial, however, has been mounted on the steering column just under the wheel to save cutting or disfiguring the already well-filled facia board. The bracket used for this purpose can very easily be made up from strip brass, and is shown in an accompanying illustration.

The need for a screenwiper, whilst not very great with the hood down, was certainly pressing when the hood was up, and accordingly one was purchased. Owing to the arrangement of the Midget screen the normal suction type is awkward to fit, and an electric type has much to recommend it from the point of view of general convenience and ease of fitting.

Those, however, who favour a suction-operated wiper will find a very satisfactory instrument in the special Trico model made for external fitting. This wiper (which is marketed by Trico-Folberth, Ltd., Trico House, Edgware Road, London, N.W.2, and costs 30s.) is the type I am using, and it has the advantage that except in one place rubber tubing is entirely dispensed with, the pipe lines all being of copper tubing, whilst the control is a screw-down valve on the facia board.

On the early Midgets—that is to say, the 1929 and 1930 models—no hand throttle was fitted, and this was found to be something of a drawback when starting up on cold mornings, as it meant that one had to sit in the car and "tickle" the accelerator pedal until the engine was sufficiently warmed up to run at the normal idling speed, or else one had to set the throttle stop in such a way that the engine would tick over when cold, but ran rather fast when warm.

To overcome this point I approached Bowden Wire, Ltd., Victoria Road, Willesden Junction, London, N.W.10, who have provided me with a Bowden-controlled hand throttle which has proved an entire success. Not only is it useful for starting, but, owing to the fact that the lever is fitted on the underside of the scuttle just above the facia board and adjacent to the horn button, it can also be used for driving and is particularly handy for restarting on a hill, as it saves leaning forward to use the hand brake.

Another useful gadget is a Stadium fog lamp (Stadium, Ltd., Stadium House, 75-77, Paul Street, Great Eastern Street, London, E.C.2; price 25s.), which has been mounted on the front dumbiron. I did not, however, have an amber-coloured front, but a clear glass, so that the lamp could be used as a road light, a special oiled silk cover being kept in the door pocket for use when visibility is bad.

Perhaps the most useful of all the additions that have been made to the car is the tonneau cover, which was made by the Plus-One Side Car Co., 20, Alpha Place, London, N.1, at a cost of £1 1s. Not only does this cover keep the cockpit protected from dust or rain when the car is left standing, but it protects the interior from the meddlesome fingers of children.

I have had the cover so arranged that when the car is being driven solo the driver's half can be folded under, the front corner being then anchored on to an additional fastener placed on the underside of the scuttle just above the facia-board on the near side. With the cover in this position the car is much more cosy, whilst if a shower of rain comes on and the hood is not put up any odds and ends on the passenger's seat do not get wet.

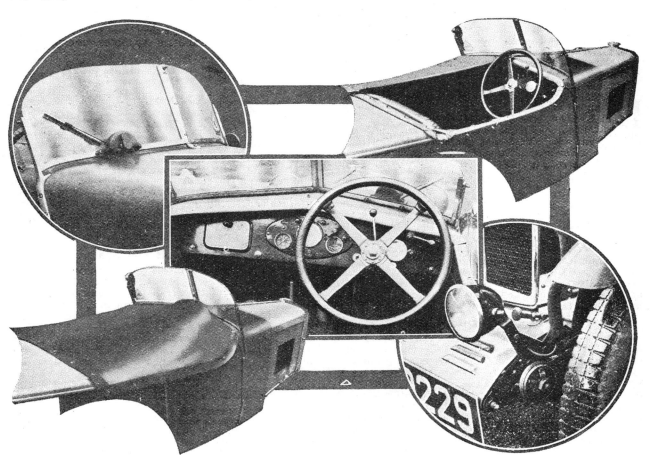

POINTS OF INTEREST. —— A group of detail photographs of the car, showing the external Trico screenwiper, the tonneau cover in its two positions, the Stadium fog and road light and the instrument board; on the last named, the switch for the fog lamp and the valve for the wiper can just be seen to the left and right respectively of the steering-wheel boss.

The M.G. MIDGET

(CONCLUDED)

Impressions and Experiences by a Member of Our Staff

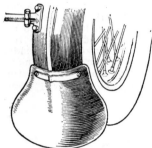

Leather extension flaps for the front wings are easy to make and reduce mud slinging.

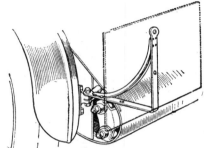

An ordinary shelf bracket bolted to the near - side rear wing stay makes an effective support for a competition number.

LAST week I concluded by mention of the tonneau cover, and this really brings me to the small alterations to my M.G. Midget that have been carried out, for when having the tonneau cover made by the Plus-One Side Car Co. I asked them whether it would be possible to let additional windows into the hood to improve the side visibility; my question was answered in a practical fashion by the fitting of the two neat triangular-shaped windows shown in one of the accompanying photographs. These are of celluloid and the charge made was only 7s. 6d.

Side screens were ordered with the car, but the question arose as to where to carry them safely, and I have overcome the difficulty by making a rough-and-ready American-cloth envelope lined with soft material. There is a flap of this soft material which serves to keep the two screens apart, one screen being inserted and the flap then tucked in over it before the second is stowed away.

Seating Comfort.

So far as comfort is concerned, I have found it a distinct improvement to fit a small ramp or sloping cushion under the front half of each pneumatic cushion. This enables the cushion to be kept very lightly inflated—which is better both from the point of view of comfort and low seating position—but at the same time ensures adequate support for the thighs. Actually, I started experimenting with a pad of newspapers, folded as shown in one of the photographs, to discover the best height for the ramp, but the newspapers have proved so satisfactory that they have remained in position ever since!

Much as I dislike the idea of interfering with the trim lines of the Midget tail, the coming of a holiday, in which luggage for two for a fortnight had to be carried, made increased luggage space necessary, and accordingly I had the spare wheel transferred from inside the boot to the top of the tail. The job was carried out by Tulley Motors, Ltd., Paragon Garage, Hermitage Street, London, W.2, who undertook this work at a cost of 22s. Although the car is certainly neater with the spare wheel inside, the position adopted does not really spoil the lines of the car and has the advantage that one does not have to put a wet wheel amongst the luggage if a puncture occurs on a rainy day, not to mention the great increase in luggage accommodation.

Housing Tools and Spares.

Tools that jump about on the floor of the boot are an annoying source of rattle; therefore, I moved the position of one of the straps previously used to keep the spare wheel in place to a point in the front of the boot, where it now holds the standard toolbag quite firmly, but leaves it readily accessible when required. Items such as the pump, jack, tyre-repair outfit, spares and so on are all tucked away in the separate locker provided in the extreme end of the tail, where they are well out of the way. A quart can of oil and a clip are supplied with the car, and the clip was mounted on the upright frame member of the body just behind the seat on one side.

Partly because I have a weakness for symmetry, and partly because I am one of those cautious persons who like to be doubly sure about everything, I decided to purchase another similar clip for mounting on the other side to carry a spare quart oilcan filled with petrol. This will usually enable a garage to be reached if one is forgetful enough to let the engine peter out when the petrol tap has already been turned on to reserve.

Using the car in all weathers I soon found that there was a tendency for the front wheels to throw up a continuous spray of water, mud and grit on to the front extremities of the rear wings, and this soon began to play havoc with the finish, not to mention the fact that mud in this position is very apt to be wiped off by the driver's or passenger's coat on alighting.

The trouble has been largely reduced by fitting large leather extension flaps to the lower ends of the front wings, the flaps coming to within about an inch of the ground and extending sideways, fan-shaped, distinctly more than the width of the wing. This has not cured the trouble entirely, but it has certainly reduced it to a worthwhile extent. The flaps are fitted in position by means of soft brass strips bent to the shape of the wings.

Most Midget owners are tempted at some time or other to take part in trials, and the question of mounting the competition number at the rear always crops up before the first event. Those who make a regular thing of competition work purchase a rear registration-number plate bracket and fit it to the near side, but this, of course, entails a certain amount of trouble and the man who takes part only in an occasional trial will find that an ordinary right-angle shelf bracket of the type having a cross strut fits nicely on to the rear bolt of the near-side wing bracket, as shown in one of the accompanying sketches. It is then an easy matter to mount a metal or a three-ply board on to the bracket.

The front competition number, of course, presents no great difficulties, as even if no special bracket is fitted it can always be hung on the crossbar.

So far as maintenance work is concerned, there are few tips that the writer can give, as all the normal routine work is dealt with very comprehensively and ably in the makers' instruction book. There are, however, one or two little points which the owner may overlook, or in which he may give himself unnecessary trouble.

Adjusting the rear shock absorbers forms a case in point, quite a number of owners imagining that the only way to do this is to crawl underneath the tail of the car, which is by no means a pleasant business. The job can, however, be done through the hinged flap in the floor of the tail, which is really provided for filling the rear axle.

Similarly, it is possible to apply the grease gun to the nipples on the rear brake cam spindles in the same way, and, although both these operations require a little "wangling" of one's arm to reach the desired point, they are preferable to doing the same jobs when lying on one's back on the floor.

In connection with the brakes wise owners will occasionally remove the drums (not a difficult job) and grease the pivot pins of the shoes, as, although the cam spindles are lubricated, the pivot pins are not. This may be done with advantage at intervals of 10,000 miles or so, when the opportunity may also be taken to inspect the linings.

Incidentally, removing the drums as advised may also enable the driver to prevent grease getting on to the linings, for if the cam spindles are over-lubricated the surplus first creeps down the webs of the lower shoes, whence it finally gets on to the linings. If, however,

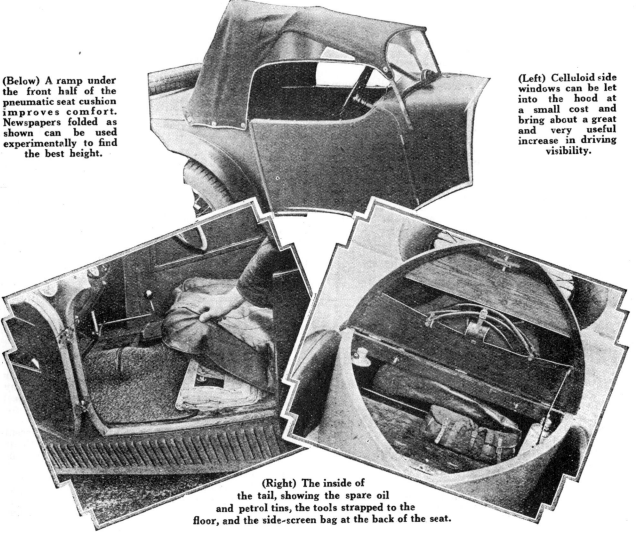

(Below) A ramp under the front half of the pneumatic seat cushion improves comfort. Newspapers folded as shown can be used experimentally to find the best height.

(Left) Celluloid side windows can be let into the hood at a small cost and bring about a great and very useful increase in driving visibility.

(Right) The inside of the tail, showing the spare oil and petrol tins, the tools strapped to the floor, and the side-screen bag at the back of the seat.

the drums are taken off at intervals the owner has a chance to wipe off any surplus grease before it has reached the danger spots.

The earliest models—that is to say, the 1929 and the first batch of the 1930 cars—had rather a small sump, the capacity being only half a gallon. Owners of these cars should take particular care to keep the sump well filled, as, if the level is allowed to drop, there is only a comparatively small quantity of lubricant in circulation, and accordingly it tends to become rather hot.

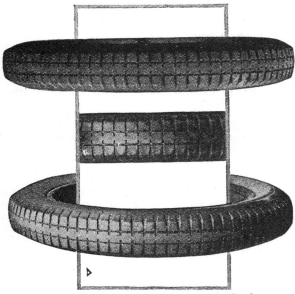

Tyre wear after 10,000 miles' hard work. At the top is the spare, in the centre is one of the front covers and below is one of the rear tyres.

The latest models, of course, have a one-gallon sump of cast aluminium incorporating cooling ribs in the base, and trouble with the oil getting hot never occurs.

The Midget is famous for its excellent road-holding properties, but owners should take care to keep the springs clean and well lubricated, as otherwise a distinct harshness may be noticed at low speeds, especially when travelling without a passenger. This can largely be cured by slacking off the shock absorbers somewhat, but pitching will then be noticeable when the speedometer begins to get upwards of half-way up the scale, and the right combination can be obtained only by keeping the springs themselves supple and adjusting the shock absorbers to suit one's individual needs.

The steering, too, is delightfully easy—it is literally possible to steer the car with one finger—whilst the lock is adequate for almost any hair-pin bends that one can find; the acute turns on Tornapress Hill, in Scotland,

for example, do not call for reversing, although there is certainly little room to spare. The general sense of security is also enhanced by the well-placed spring-spoke steering wheel. Personally, however, I should prefer a slightly higher gear ratio in the steering box, although I quite realize that this would entail a slight sacrifice in lightness; on the other hand, it would make skid correction easier and would save a certain amount of wheel-twiddling when driving in traffic.

Now for a short summary of the car's behaviour over its first 10,000 miles. It has been decarbonized twice—once at the end of the first 2,700 miles, when it was considered thoroughly run in and ready to give of its best, and again when the speedometer registered 6,800. The job will shortly be done again, as I believe in decarbonizing at intervals of not more than 4,000 miles; the engine will run for much longer periods than this, but some of its characteristic smoothness is lost.

Petrol consumption varies considerably, according to the way in which the car is driven. The mixture on my car is set for performance rather than economy, but 40 m.p.g. is attained at normal touring speeds. A long fast run, on the other hand, brings the figure down to nearer 35 m.p.g.

Some 1,500 miles can still be covered on a gallon of oil despite the 10,000 miles of real hard work, including much running with a comparatively cold engine. The tyres, too, are still behaving well and still show plenty of pattern on the tread.

Good General Condition.

So far as general condition is concerned, the car is above reproach, whilst the only repairs are represented by a bill for 30s. for taking up play in the steering and for lining up the cylinder head and dynamo, the latter due to the indifferent workmanship of a garage to whom the last decarbonization was entrusted as I was short of time.

The engine maintains its tune in a surprising manner and does not require the constant valve adjustment, plug cleaning and so forth that one often associates with a sports car. At the moment, for example, it is several weeks since the engine was touched and a number of long fast runs have been undertaken in addition to the usual hack work, but it still does a cheerful 60 m.p.h. in top and well over 40 m.p.h. in second. Moreover, its last long run up to the time of writing consisted of 199.2 miles at an average (carefully checked) of 37.6 m.p.h.

Finally, it is one of the most comfortable small cars I know; if it were not, it would scarcely have been possible for me to have covered 508 miles between 11 p.m. one night and supper-time the next evening, including the ascent of those two notorious Scottish hills—Amulree and Kenmore.

As I said at the outset, it would be difficult to imagine a more versatile little motor coming within the economy car class.   H.

WHY YOU "PARK" YOUR CAR

THE term "parking your car" is so familiar that few owners trouble themselves regarding the origin of the phrase.

After all, it is not so very long ago that few folk spoke of anything other than garaging a vehicle, and I daresay quite a number would suggest that the term "park" may be laid at the door of the films emanating from across the water; but for once this source is entirely innocent of the term.

As a matter of fact, the original word "park" covers a variety of meanings and the standard dictionary definition, according to Nuttall, is in the following terms:—

Park.—A large piece of ground enclosed for public or private recreation; an enclosure around a mansion; AN ARTILLERY ENCAMPMENT; A TRAIN

OF ARTILLERY BELONGING TO AN ARMY; to enclose in a park, etc.

Ignoring the definitions that obviously do not refer to the present use of the term, we hark back to many years ago and find that the term park was freely used in a military sense, referring to a space provided for storing guns, ammunition or military supplies.

From this it would appear obvious that the current use of the word has a very close connection with its original meaning, and is not an Americanism, as some would lead us to imagine.

Although the modern light car can hardly be called artillery, it certainly belongs to an army of satisfied motorists, who trouble little about the origin of the word park, provided they can find a convenient parking ground to leave the car.   G.P.

THE "DOUBLE-TWELVE" M.G. MIDGET

AMONG the models which have been introduced by makers during the past two seasons, few have achieved a greater degree of success than the M.G. Midget; its popularity has been quite out of the ordinary for it is not mass-produced by any means, yet it is rare indeed to travel far on the roads without meeting one.

Appearance counts for a lot, and doubtless the lines of the Midget are responsible, to quite an appreciable extent, for its quick rise to favour. But it is not a sporting machine in looks only, as has been abundantly demonstrated in reliability trials and races.

Probably the most conspicuous performance the Midget has put up so far was in the "Double-Twelve" Race at Brooklands when three of these little vehicles came through that gruelling contest with flying colours.

The cars which were used, as is to be expected, were not absolutely standard. Nevertheless, they were not freaks, and the M.G. concern have now added to their range, the Midget Sports "Double-Twelve" model, which is identical in every respect to those used in the race of that name.

It may be recalled that we have had one of these models placed at our disposal some time ago, and since then we have had the opportunity of giving the "Double-Twelve" Midget a further test. If we were asked what impressed us most about the car we would say its astonishing road-holding qualities at high speeds, and its general "big-car" feeling. Although it weighs only 10 cwt. it "sits" on the road like a heavyweight, and gives the driver a nice sense of control. Without this quality a small, fast motor can be most unpleasant; with it, the new M.G. is distinctly fascinating. In this high degree of control, besides weight distribution, C of G position and springing, the steering plays a vital part. The Midget's steering gear is of the worm-and-wheel type, and the front axle layout gives a caster action, so that straightening out from locking over is almost automatic. A René Thomas wheel is incorporated and the column is set at just the right rake. The brakes are orthodox, the foot control operating on all four wheels and the hand lever is coupled independently. Their action is decisive without being violent. On the particular car we used, the position of the brake lever was not good, being much too far forward and entailing quite a lot of groping. But this matter, together with the accelerator pedal position (which was also rather awkward) has now been rectified. The clutch is of the dry-plate type and although it is fitted with extra strong springs its withdrawal is light and easy.

Turning to the "Double-Twelve" engine, it is found that here the main deviation from the standard unit is in the fitting of a special camshaft, stronger valve springs, a special S.U. carburettor, and special induction and exhaust manifolds. Each engine turned out is very carefully prepared, and before being passed, is freed off and thoroughly run in.

The body fitted has both sides cut away, conforming to International road racing regulations, the general lines being similar to the standard production. There is a special windscreen fitted with Triplex glass, or gauze if necessary, which can be folded flat forward. The upholstery is real leather, whilst the wings and general finish are a pleasing combination of cream and brown.

The model which was loaned us, was the actual car used by Miss Worsley in the "Double-Twelve" and had not been attended to in anyway since that event. The tyres had not been changed, and were the original "five-bar" Palmers, the latest type of cover made by that firm. A Brooklands silencer was fitted which afforded a reasonably silent exhaust under ordinary running conditions, but set up a particularly raucous note on the overrun at high speeds. It was definitely too noisy, and though not unpleasant for the occupants, would certainly sooner or later attract the unwelcome attention of the police. It is only fair to say however, that the makers now recommend and fit a Vortex silencer for road use.

An extra large petrol tank to carry 9 gallons, is fitted in the dash, with quick action filler cap, whilst extra strong road wheels, and a strap to the bonnet, complete the chassis specification. The electrical equipment includes a dynamo specially wound to give an output at high speeds, and the same applies to the coil; the distributor is one made capable of functioning continuously at 6,500 revs, and over.

In addition to the standard speedometer, ammeter, and oil gauge, an oil and water thermometer are fitted, coupled respectively to the sump, and the radiator header tank.

If required an undershield can be fitted, whilst the chassis can also be prepared for long distance racing events by wiring and split pinning all nuts and bolts, and for these two items an additional charge would be made according to requirements.

A MODIFIED MIDGET

ATTRACTIVE JARVIS BODY ON WELL-KNOWN CHASSIS.

WHEN a sports car attains popularity with the swiftness of the M.G. Midget, it is good proof of the soundness of its design, especially when this is backed up by success in competitions. This is certain to lead in its turn to a demand among discriminating owners for a model which will be a little different from the general run in the way of coachwork.

Therefore, although the M.G. Midget was no novelty to us as regards the chassis, we found a great deal to arouse fresh interest in the Jarvis Midget which was in our hands for a few days recently. Some coachwork attracts by its appearance, while some depends on its practical and useful lay-out to capture the owner's fancy. This particular model, however, is one of those rare examples which combine real good looks with a maximum of convenient accommodation.

There are many small sports cars on the road to-day which, while very nice for showing off their owner to advantage on short runs, present considerable difficulties when a long journey is undertaken with any luggage or equipment. Although it must be admitted that there are numbers of sports car owners whose first thought is appearance, and whose journeys rarely extend beyond the main street of their home town, we like to forget them as much as possible, and hope they will decrease rapidly. It is to the normal man, to whom a car means a quick means of getting far afield, that the Jarvis model should appeal. It is, in our opinion, the most practical sports body we have ever tried on a car of this type and size. The actual construction and finish of the body are excellent, as might be expected from a firm who have so long specialised in sporting coachwork, and these may be taken for granted.

The actual lay-out is a miniature of the short 3-4 seater type which is often seen on $1\frac{1}{2}$ litre cars. In this case the rear compartment is intended chiefly for luggage, although it would be useful on occasion to give a lift to an extra passenger for a short journey. A large inspection door in the floor of this compartment gives convenient access to the rear axle for greasing, etc., while a second flap at the rear opens the tool compartment, which is built under the floor level in the form of a dummy petrol tank. This is of ample size, and, as well as a large tool kit, provides room for those many items of spares and equipment which always seem to accumulate. The only criticism of this arrangement is that if the rear compartment is full of luggage, some of this will have to be removed to get at the tools. This is not likely to happen often, however, and the convenience of a really large tool box makes up for it.

The bucket seats are adjustable over a considerable range, and though in the experimental body we tried there was not really sufficient room for anyone over 6 feet, the leg room is being increased in the production model to remedy this. Pneumatic upholstery will also be included in the standard specification.

[Motor Sport Photograph.]

Convenient.   The wide doors on the Jarvis-bodied M.G. Midget.

A neat and really efficient hood is another good point and the lines of the hood are in keeping with the rest of the car. When this is not in use, a combined hood and tonneau cover ensure the contents of the rear compartment, if any, being kept free from dust or damp.

By its behaviour on the road we were able to prove that the weight distribution with this particular body was excellently planned, as the road holding and comfort at speed were really remarkable, and continually gave the impression of a much larger vehicle.

The steering, in common with all Midgets, was very light indeed; in fact, too light for our liking, as we should have preferred rather more caster combined with a somewhat higher gear. At present from full lock to full lock (not a very great angular movement of the front wheels in this case) requires two full revolutions of the wheel. On such a light car a considerably higher gear would still call for no appreciable effort, while when "scrapping" on a winding road it would give a rather quicker and more "live" control. The steering was very pleasant, however, and perfectly steady, while some people may prefer the very low gear.

Although MOTOR SPORT has previously published accounts of the M.G. and its performance, we cannot refrain from again referring to the running of the engine. In addition to its remarkable power for its size, it is one of the smoothest 4-cylinder engines we have ever driven,

and feels almost like a six. With suitable attention to the ignition control it will travel smoothly at a walking pace in top gear, while its maximum was 68 m.p.h., at which speed it was quite free from any signs of over-revving.

On second gear, 40 m.p.h. was reached quickly, and this was the best speed at which to change up if maximum acceleration was required, though considerably more than this could be attained before valve bounce occurred at between 45 and 50 m.p.h. With stronger valve springs this would not occur, but it is evident that its most useful range in second is up to 40 m.p.h. And there is no point in exceeding this in ordinary work, as to do so is simply increasing

[Motor Sport Photograph.]
With hood up or down, the Jarvis-M.G. remains a good looker.

general wear and tear on the engine.

The brakes, operated on all wheels by the pedal, are positive and powerful, and are an improvement on the earlier models of this chassis, making high average speed quite safe. The hand-brake is rather too far forward for convenience, but as this is used chiefly for holding the car when stationary, this small point is of minor consequence.

The job as a whole is well planned and carried out, and is a notable improvement on an already attractive little car. The price with a very full equipment, including side screens, is £225. The makers are Jarvis & Sons, of Victoria Crescent, Wimbledon.

BRITISH CARS IN SOUTH AMERICA

BENEATH the bald statement that nearly a score of British motor manufacturers will be exhibiting at the British Empire Trade Exhibition in Buenos Aires next Spring, there is evidence of an intensive effort to capture a big proportion of the South American car trade.

There are three million inhabitants in Buenos Aires alone, the Argentine Republic has an area of no fewer than 1,500,000 square miles of territory and the annual consumption of cars approaches 100,000. Yet so strong a hold have North American manufacturers obtained in the market that last year only 18 British cars were imported there.

The British motor trade is now making a bold bid to

effect an entry, as is shown by the efforts of some of our leading manufacturers. For this Trade Exhibition is not being considered as an Exhibition alone; certain manufacturers are regarding it as the starting point of a sales' campaign in South America. The Singer Co., for instance, has already appointed a factory representative, Mr. M. H. Flash, who has lived in the Argentine for 21 years and is conversant with all the necessary languages and patois. Accompanied by expert Singer mechanics he will shortly be leaving England with a large fleet of demonstration cars, and on arrival at Buenos Aires he will establish offices, showrooms and service stations. He will then appoint distributors and dealers, and organise a sales campaign throughout the country.

THE M.G. MIDGET· MARK II

Entirely New Montlhery Model with Supercharger, Low Frame and Four-speed Gearbox

A comprehensive view showing the dropped frame, Rudge-Whitworth wheels, four-speed gearbox and 10-gallon fuel tank.

IT is now possible to divulge the fact that the M.G. Midget on which G. E. T. Eyston recently achieved the astonishing speed of 103 m.p.h. was the new M.G. Midget Mark II, otherwise known as the Montlhéry model.

The record-breaking car, together with an example of the standardized chassis which is an improved model of this, were shown to a gathering of racing drivers at the Abingdon works of the M.G. Car Co. on Tuesday last, March 3rd.

A cursory inspection of the chassis reveals that it is extremely low built, the top of the chassis side members being, in fact, only 10⅝ ins. from the ground. A four-speed gearbox is fitted, and a supercharger is carried in front of the radiator between the dumbirons.

A Clever Design.

An examination of the detail work of the chassis reveals an exceptionally clever engineering job.

Perhaps it would be as well, however, to start with a description of the engine, so that the differences between it and the standard job can at once be appreciated.

Outwardly the power unit does not differ materially from that which may be seen in the thousands of Midgets already on the road. There are four cylinders with overhead valves operated by an overhead camshaft, the drive for which is taken through the dynamo, this being mounted vertically in front of the cylinder block. The bore is 57 mm. but the stroke has been reduced to 73 mm., thus bringing the capacity down to 746 c.c. The ordinary Midget, with an engine of 847 c.c. capacity, is not, of course, eligible to run in the 750 c.c. class in races. The alteration in stroke has been

effected by providing a new crankshaft with shorter throws, and very much larger big-end bearings. The rear main bearing has also been increased in size. The crankshaft is, of course, carried in only two bearings, but owing to the effective method of counterbalancing it there is no perceptible vibration when running. Aluminium pistons are fitted, special steel connecting rods being used. Ignition is by coil supplied from a Rotax 6-volt set.

The new exhaust manifold. Note the deeply ribbed sump.

The engine is lubricated on the pressure system throughout by means of a gear-type pump, the oil being carried in a large aluminium sump with cooling fins. The sump contains one gallon, but an auto-

matic device consisting of a large S.U. float chamber is used to replenish the sump from an auxiliary oil tank, which may be of any desired capacity, carried on the dash. Cooling is by a film-type radiator with chromium-plated brass shell, the thermo-siphon system being adopted. It is, however, possible to provide pump cooling and a fan to special order at an extra charge of £15.

Various types of carburetters can be fitted, the mixture being controlled from the dash. An optional fitting is two carburetters for an extra charge of £10 on the unsupercharged model.

The Supercharger.

The supercharger is of Powerplus make and is of the eccentric vane type, working at a pressure of about 8 lb. to 10 lb. An ingenious system of piping has been evolved, whereby a large-bore pipe conveys the mixture at normal speeds from the blower to the induction ports. Running parallel to this, however, is a smaller-bore pipe, and, by a simple arrangement of butterfly valves, at idling speeds the large-bore pipe is shut off and the mixture by-passed through the smaller-bore pipe, so that the velocity of the gas is maintained and "lumpy" running at low speeds is eliminated. Needless to say, this system allows of exceptionally good acceleration. On the model which we inspected, an S.U. carburetter was fitted on the suction side of the blower, which is lubricated by a small pipe from the front end of the overhead-valve cover. Oil is also mixed with the petrol.

An outside exhaust is standardized, a very well made manifold being bolted direct to the block and projecting through the bonnet; this

M.G. MIDGET
MARK II—Contd.

gives a particularly free outlet for the exhaust.

The power unit is supported on two tubular cross-members; one is just behind the radiator and carries the engine at its forward end in a tubular bearing. The other support is beneath the gearbox, which is fitted with a special lug through which passes the tubular frame member. The front engine support carries, in addition, the steering gearbox bracket and radiator, while the lower tube serves as a mounting for the brake pedal.

A dry-plate clutch conveys the drive to an extremely well-made four-speed-and-reverse gearbox. This has a silent third speed and the gate and lever are carried right

The back axle, by the way, is of straightforward design with a straight-toothed-bevel final drive in order to reduce frictional loss, the propeller shaft being fitted with Hardy-Spicer universal joints.

Now we come to the chassis frame. This is dropped considerably, at a point about level with the oil filler on the side of the crankcase, and is then carried straight back and under the rear axle. Between the front and rear dumbirons are massive tubular cross-members which make the frame extremely rigid, yet sufficiently elastic to yield to heavy blows without injury. The springs are flat and underslung both front and rear, and are anchored at their forward extremities and allowed to slide in trunnion blocks at their rear ends, so that there is a maximum of resistance to any transverse movement or side sway.

The steering is quite straightforward, and is of the worm-and-wheel

the lever is depressed. The brakes are of slightly larger diameter than are found on the standard Midget and are applied by enclosed cables.

These are brought through neat slides in the chassis side-members, where grease-gun nipples are fitted, allowing the brake cables to be lubricated under pressure for their entire length. Owing to the use of the flexible connections, the brakes are, of course, unaffected by axle movement, no matter to what extent they are applied.

A 10-gallon petrol tank is mounted on the chassis behind the rear axle and is provided with a large, quick-opening filler cap. It is obvious that larger tanks can be fitted for special purposes, such as long-distance races, without difficulty.

Duplex shock absorbers are supplied as standard, the telecontrol for them from the dash being available as an extra. In addition to the shock absorbers, strip steel hoops secured to the rear of the chassis prevent excessive movement of the latter relative to the axle. An electric fuel pump conveys the petrol from the tank at the rear to the carburetter on the supercharger or cylinder block, according to whether or not a blower is fitted.

Rudge-Whitworth wire wheels of racing design with central "knock-off" locking devices are fitted as standard and are a further example of how no expense has been spared to make this car a really safe and reliable racing model.

Body Built for Speed.

As regards the body, this is similar to that on the record-breaking car and has a streamlined tail, besides an elaborate cowling over the radiator. Needless to say, owing to the design of the chassis frame, the seats are quite exceptionally low, while the height of the steering wheel can be varied according to the requirements of the individual driver. The chassis, by the way, is lubricated throughout by Tecalemit grease gun.

The track of the car remains the same as standard—that is to say, 3 ft. 6 ins.—but the wheelbase is 6 ft. 9 ins., which is 3 ins. longer than standard.

Needless to say, the Montlhéry model M.G. Midget Mark II is a fairly expensive proposition, owing to the amount of special work that has to be carried out on the power unit and other parts. Still, £295, without the supercharger, or £345 with it, are not prohibitive prices.

Incidentally, the four-speed gearbox and supercharger can be supplied, if ordered with the car, on ordinary M.G. Midgets, at an extra charge of £20 and £50 respectively. If fitted subsequently, the prices are £27 10s. and £65 respectively.

This attractive little sports car is made by the M.G. Car Co, Ltd., Pavlova Works, Abingdon-on-Thames.

An unusual view showing the Powerplus blower and its drive, the S.U. carburetter, Andre telecontrol shock absorbers, and the large diameter brake drums.

back, coming approximately in line with the rim of the steering wheel. At the forward end of the casting carrying the gate and operating mechanism is a neat breather, facing forward.

As the smaller unit is designed to run at a higher speed, the back-axle ratio has been lowered to 5.38 to 1. This results in third speed being 7.33 to 1 and second speed 10.7 to 1. An emergency bottom gear of 22 to 1 is provided. It will thus be seen that the three higher ratios are ideal for fast road work, while the lowest should enable the car to climb any gradient that the most thorough-going club secretary could possibly include in a reliability trial. It is conceivable, however, that in certain circumstances it might pay to use the standard rear axle, which has a ratio of 4.89 to 1, and the other gears would be correspondingly higher.

type, with a transverse drag link; a spring spoke steering wheel is fitted.

When we come to examine the brake gear we feel bound to express our admiration for the clever way in which this has been worked out. The whole of the cross-shafts and operating levers is carried within the depth of the side-members; that is to say, within a space of 3 ins., measured vertically. This enables a flat undershield to be secured directly to the under-side of the side-members, while the floorboards can be rested directly upon them.

The foot brake, by means of a special flexible connection, can be adjusted from the instrument board, the hand brake being regulated by an accessible thumb-screw at the base of the lever. The latter, by the way, is of the "fly-off" type, and is only locked in position on the ratchet when the brass cap at the top of

A New Supercharged

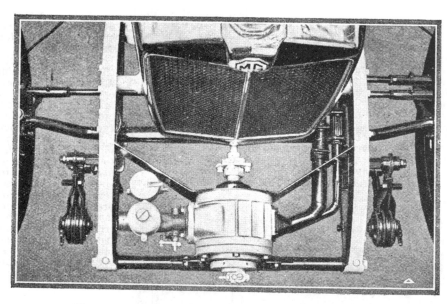

The supercharger viewed from above. Note the main and the
pilot delivery pipes from the blower.

IT is now only just over two years since the M.G. Car Co., Ltd., Pavlova Works, Abingdon-on-Thames, launched the 850 c.c. M.G. Midget. Again the company has caused a stir by announcing this week a new 750 c.c. supercharged model, the chassis of which, although bearing a family resemblance to that of the 850 c.c. job, has been almost entirely re-designed and presents quite a number of interesting points. It will be known as the M.G. Midget Mark II.

The new model has been introduced expressly to meet the needs of the super-sporting enthusiast who wants a car which will be suitable for touring, yet which can at a moment's notice toe the line at Brooklands or elsewhere and take part in even the most gruelling race. With that end in view the whole vehicle has been designed so that it will withstand severe strains and stresses, including that violent "flexing" to which cars of this breed are subjected in road and track events.

The engine has most of the external features of the ordinary M.G. Midget, but the stroke has been shortened by 10 mm., giving dimensions of 57 mm. by 73 mm. (746 c.c.). Moreover, the bore of the cylinders allows for a certain degree of wear which will still keep the capacity well within the 750 c.c. limit.

The pistons are somewhat shorter than standard, and have reinforced crowns, and the compression is, of course, higher than normal. Again, the crankshaft is a stiffer job, the big-ends are larger and there is a more substantial rear main bearing. The connecting rods are of I-section, and the standard overhead valve gear operating mechanism is employed, with the exception that a special cam contour is used. The sump is of cast aluminium, deeply finned to assist cooling; it is fed with oil through a float chamber, the supply being drawn from a tank on the dash.

Engine and gearbox are formed as a unit, the latter having a long cantilevered turret and stubby gear lever which comes nicely to hand. The complete unit is supported at the front by a trunnion and rubber block, the weight being carried by a sturdy cross-member; at the rear a similar cross-member supports the unit beneath the clutch pit. The radiator and the steering box are also carried by the forward cross-member, and the water connections have been altered to suit the arrangement of the Powerplus supercharger.

The supercharger is designed to blow at from 8 lb. to 10 lb. It is carried at its front end by a circular

M.G. MIDGET

gusset secured to a forward cross-member, whilst at the back there is a similar gusset which, however, is swept back so that it can be secured at its ends to the frame members themselves.

The drive is from the nose of the crankshaft via an extension shaft and metallic universal joint. The 1¼-in. S.U. carburetter is mounted on the atmospheric side of the blower, and quite one of the most interesting features of the assembly is the inclusion of a pilot pipe of smaller diameter than the main delivery pipe, the object of which is to overcome flat spots when the engine is turning at moderately low speeds. The change over from the main delivery pipe to the pilot is effected by a butterfly valve working in conjunction with the accelerator pedal.

An ingenious system of lubricating the blower spindle is employed. From the front cylinder head a drain pipe controlled by a tap, which is also connected with the accelerator pedal, connects with the supercharger, thereby supplying hot oil to the instrument and, by means of the tap, cutting off the supply at idling speeds. In addition, oil is mixed with the petrol.

The maximum revs. of the engine are in the neighbourhood of 7,000 per minute. Fuel is supplied to the carburetter from a rear tank holding 10 gallons, the delivery being by air pressure. As an alternative, we

Famous 750 c.c. Montlhery Record Breaker Appears in Standard and Improved Form — With Powerplus Supercharger £345 —Without Blower £295 "All On"

understand, an electric fuel pump can be installed.

Ignition is by Rotax coil, and the very greatest care has been taken in the design and construction of both coil and contact breaker to make them suitable for high speeds. In order to make certain that the added torque can be transmitted satisfactorily, a two-plate clutch is employed, the general design, however, being similar to that of the standard M.G. Midget.

A feature of the four-speed gearbox is the silent third, but to conform with racing practice, the constant mesh wheels are of the straight-cut and not the helical type. This is to eliminate excessive end thrust. The actual gearbox ratios are: top speed direct, third 1.36 to one, second 2 to one and first 4.1 to one; this gives a top gear ratio of just over 5¼ and a bottom gear ratio—which has been purposely incorporated for freak hill-climbing— of approximately 21.5 to one. The final drive is by an open propeller shaft with Hardy Spicer metallic joints at each end, a straight cut bevel and differential.

Rather neat is the arrangement whereby the reverse gear pinion slides right out of engagement when it is not in use. It engages with the normal second gear pinion when required. The speedometer drive is taken from the top of the gearbox so that only a short cable is required.

A very interesting feature of the chassis as a whole is that apart from a slight upsweeping at the front the frame is four-square, the side-members being parallel and the cross-members all straight and of tubular formation. In order to obtain extremely low build the frame members are carried under the rear axle.

The brake gear, moreover, is of the Bowden-operated type and can, therefore, be snugly accommodated along the sides of the frame. By this means a straight undershield ideal for streamlining can be employed, the only excrescence being the sump, which projects through the shield for cooling purposes.

Side view of the chassis, showing all the leading details of the car. The photo should be studied in conjunction with the text.

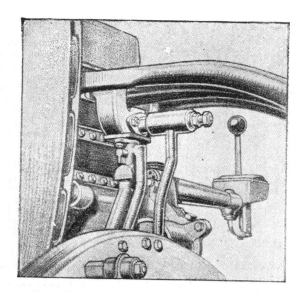

The induction and exhaust arrangements viewed from beneath. The sketch clearly shows the main and pilot delivery pipes from the supercharger, also the exhaust pipe from the blow off valve.

The frame is underslung on long semi-elliptic springs both at the front and at the rear, a special form of split and slotted roller taking the place of the more conventional shackle. These rollers are suitably

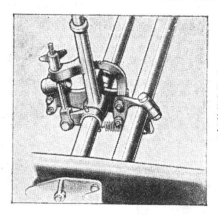

The brake lever moves freely on the cross member but is connected by means of the adjuster itself with a short lever keyed to the shaft.

gaitered so that lubricant can be pumped in and retained. Another very interesting feature of the chassis is the mounting of the rear springs well outside

the frame on extensions of the cross-members. Thus stability is ensured by the springs being as far apart as possible without the frame being unduly wide.

Double Hartford shock absorbers are used all round, the rear shock absorbers, however, being set transversely with one arm bolted rigidly to the frame member; they are of the Telecontrol pattern.

The braking system has been very carefully designed, and a feature which will make a direct appeal is that play can be taken up in the pedal by means of a wheel mounted on the facia board and connected with the brake adjuster by means of a flexible shaft; both lever and pedal apply the four-

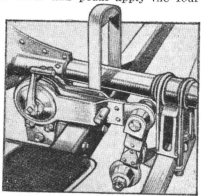

Showing how one arm of each rear shock absorber is fixed to the frame member. The connection for the Telecontrol wire is also visible.

wheel brakes. Adjustment of the hand brake is effected by a turnbuckle above the floorboard. The Bowden brake cables, by the way, are divided at the cable stops and a grease nipple is introduced at these points so that oil can be pumped right through the casings. The brake shoes are fitted as standard with anti-squeak vibration dampers, which consist of small lead weights.

It has not been deemed desirable to alter the design of the steering, which is practically identical with the standard Midget assembly. The car is very nicely set off by the use of Rudge-Whitworth wire wheels of the real racing type.

In addition to the ordinary instruments, the facia board is equipped with a sump thermometer, radiator thermometer and a rev. counter working off the end of the camshaft.

The speed of the car is given as about 85 m.p.h. on top gear and 70 m.p.h. on third. Without supercharger it is listed at £295 and with supercharger £345.

At an early opportunity we hope to present our readers with a test run report of this interesting newcomer.

Near side of engine, showing the triple-branched exhaust pipe and the method of leading the brake cables from the frame at the front.

The special sump and the float chamber, by means of which a constant level of oil is maintained, are features worth examining in this view of the off side of the engine.

The 4-speed "750" M.G. Midget

The new 4-speed gear box employs roller bearings throughout, and engagement of both top and third gears is by means of dog clutches. The brakes themselves are unaltered from those of the standard M.G. Midget, but the operation has been modified so that adjustment can be effected from the dash.

The roadholding and steadiness of the car (always a marked M.G. feature) has been further improved by lowering the chassis frame. This is downswept behind the front axle and passes under the rear axle. The front springs are carried below the axle which has necessitated a new axle beam. The control of the springing is effected by means of the latest type Hartford shock absorber, with control from the dash while running.

The whole car is designed especially for the competition enthusiast and is being introduced in addition to, and not in place of, the standard M.G. Midget. The price of the supercharged car is fixed at £345, while without supercharger it costs £295.

THE enormous popularity of the standard M.G. Midget during last year naturally made enthusiastic owners of the same desirous of somehow competing in 750 c.c. events. It is to this class that such a car morally belongs from its type and size, and small car enthusiasts in general will be glad to learn that the new model will be in this class, and will have many other interesting features which will make it a definite 100% sports car, which should ensure a big demand for the new type.

Not only have all the main points of the standard M.G. been well tried out, but the new car, which has virtually been entirely redesigned, has been intensively developed by experiments in the hands of G. E. T. Eyston, until the final edition has proved capable of over 100 m.p.h. The engine has the same 57 mm. bore as the 850 c.c. but is fitted with a special crankshaft giving a stroke of 73 mm. The shaft is of large diameter and all webs are fully balanced. Steel connecting rods, with the metal poured in direct, and special aluminium alloy pistons are used.

Water circulation is by centrifugal pump mounted between the dumb irons, which location is also chosen for the Powerplus supercharger.

An unusual feature of the induction system is the double inlet pipe. The smaller pipe is used for starting and slow running, the large main pipe being closed. By means of interconnected controls, when the throttle is opened the main pipe is also opened to the main flow of gas. This somewhat unusual arrangement is fitted to ensure easy starting and flexibility which is a most important point in a sports car, as opposed to a purely racing machine.

A useful point for long distance work is the provision of an auxiliary oil supply by means of a tank under the scuttle, which has an automatic feed to the sump by means of a float chamber arranged to keep a constant sump level. The increased power of the engine has been coped with by a redesigned clutch having two discs instead of the single disc used on the old model.

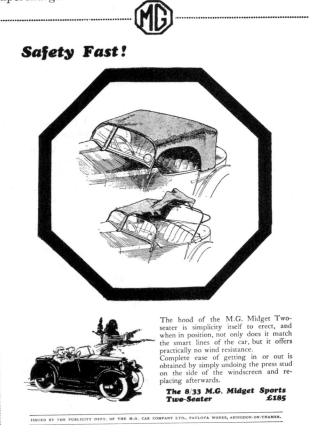

The Midget's First Hundred

What it Feels Like and What it Means to Exceed 100 m.p.h. on a Small Car.

by

G. E. T. EYSTON,

Who Recently Broke 750 c.c. Records at Over 100 m.p.h.

SINCE my return from Montlhéry after breaking the 750 c.c. class record with an M.G. Midget I have been asked many times what it feels like to travel at over a hundred miles an hour on so small a car. To answer such a question would be very easy if I had never driven at this speed before and if I had never before handled a small car at, say, over 60 m.p.h.

Such records as recently obtained at Montlhéry are the result of a gradual increase of speed during the preliminaries, so that when the 100 m.p.h. was eventually timed I had more or less become accustomed to it and was immune from sensations particular to that timed run.

However, the Editor of *The Autocar* has asked me to give my impressions of the record-breaking run, and on marshalling my thoughts for this purpose I find that, after all, I did get a thrill out of it and that there are quite a number of little things which may interest the ordinary motorist.

*   *   *

AFTER a couple of laps of the track to warm up the Midget to its work, I took a quarter-mile run at the "tape" and saw the rev counter creep round to just where I wished it to be—by calculations, about 100 m.p.h. I do not think I had previously touched this speed on a trial run, so I had a real thrill when I entered the

timed stretch at 6,500 r.p.m. I simply put the car at the tape for all I knew, with everything open as wide as ever I could possibly imagine they could be.

Faintly I remember a little knot of people gathered near the timing apparatus standing motionless with strained faces, but looking somewhere in my direction, and, glancing at them as I hurtled along, I hoped to goodness they had remembered that I was really trying for the record. How awful it would be to do all this speeding and find afterwards that they had not been ready!

In any case, there was little time for thoughts of anything but the car; I had to take a glance at all the instruments to see how things were functioning, particularly the oil pressure.

The Midget and I were off the straight and on to the slippery banking before one could say knife. Luckily, I planted the car on the right spot, for as we tore round I had the sensation of being on a pair of gigantic roller skates which wanted to climb higher and higher up the banking.

Although practically unprotected by any screen, I felt no ill-effects of the air pressure, so intent was I to steer what I thought was a straight course. Yet not many years ago doctors said people could not live if they travelled exposed at 60 m.p.h. In the corner of my eye I saw my old friend, Ernest Eldridge, scuttling for a patrol car, and I knew

by this that he, at least, guessed that the real business had begun.

Round into the wind we sailed, and I found it much easier than I expected to hold a true course. Keeping up air pressure in the fuel tank needed continual attention. I had to twist myself to one side to reach the pump handle, but when I got hold of the beastly thing I worked it for dear life; I was almost exhausted before the gauge registered the desired pressure, with the

result that we had struck the far banking again and were half-way round it before I could wriggle myself back to the normal driving position. During that time the car did sundry slides, and I was not feeling altogether happy.

Whenever I turned my head to listen to the engine it seemed to be emitting an unbroken high-pitched squeal from the exhaust, and every time I glanced at the rev. counter I found the needle dancing all over the dial. It was impossible to tell or even to judge the reading. It was not its fault, since it was affected by the tremendous rear-wheel spin due to the wet state of the track.

Back down the straight and over the tapes once more. I had actually completed my first lap, but I wondered whether this had been at 100 m.p.h. or no. If only I could keep up this speed it would be something for one's pains.

More pumping became necessary, and all round the banking I shoved and shoved at the pump handle—slewing about all over the place in consequence—and then we were in the straight again. The machine seemed to like the extra air pressure, so I concentrated on the driving and did the remainder of the lap as decently as I could.

As I crossed the "tape" for the third time I saw 7,000 r.p.m. steady

CONTINUED ON PAGE 43

THE M.G. SIX (Mark I.) SPEED MODEL

A SMOOTH AND SILENT CAR ADMIRABLY SUITED FOR FAST LONG DISTANCE WORK

*Motor Sport
photographs*

THE remarkable recent achievements of the famous M.G. Midget in trials and races, as well as the enormous number of these models on the road, seems to have obscured to some extent the M.G. Six, which is quite as remarkable a car in its own class as its smaller brother. Thanks to University Motors Ltd., of Brick Street, Piccadilly, we recently had the opportunity of seeing for ourselves, not only how the M.G. Six performed on the road, but also, by taking out a much used car with many thousands of miles behind it, how this model stands up to hard driving.

The model tested was the Mark I Speed model, this being the lowest priced range of sixes. The engine is a six-cylinder of 69 mm. x 110 mm. bore and stroke, giving a capacity of 2,468 c.c. A fully balanced 4-bearing crankshaft is fitted, while the inclined overhead valves are operated by an overhead camshaft. Mixture is supplied by two S.U. carburettors. A three speed gear box is fitted in contrast to the 4-speed box on the Mark II chassis, but the remarkable flexibility of the engine and a good choice of gear ratios makes it possible to use the gear box to the best advantage.

The most noticeable characteristic of the car's performance is silence and smoothness. There is no trace of period or drumming at any engine speed, and the behaviour of the car is entirely free from effort or fuss. It is not, of course, a racing car, nor is it intended in any way as such, but rather for fast travel over long distances.

It is an extremely comfortable car to drive for long distances, and we could not help wishing during the test, that we could have the chance of taking this car on a continental tour, where its qualities of comfort and effortless speed on hills or level would show up to great advantage. The acceleration is good for the type of car, the time taken from 10-30 m.p.h. on second gear being 7 secs. When comparing this with other and more fierce "10-30" figures it must be remembered that second gear is fairly high —6.58 to 1, and the maximum speed on this gear is nearly 50 m.p.h. 40 m.p.h. from 10 m.p.h. takes just over 10 secs.

At 60 m.p.h. the car gives the impression of being able to run all day without tiring and only a small throttle opening is required for this speed. The speedometer on this particular car was slightly fast, but the actual maximum on the level we found to be 74 m.p.h.

Good appearance, combined with comfort and utility, are characteristics of all M.G. models. With the Mark I Six these qualities are particularly noticeable.

under none too favourable conditions, and there is no doubt that 80 m.p.h. could be more closely approached on occasion. It must also be noted that the whole test was carried out on a car which as well as being old in service, had received no attention as regards the engine for a considerable period.

It is this feature of being able to give consistent performance over a long period without adjustment or overhaul that is of particular importance to the owner of such a car, who will put in a very big mileage in the year, and has not much spare time to spend on working on the car. With such a quiet engine, great care is required to see that no minor noises occur to spoil the effect, and the silence of the body and chassis were remarkable.

The Marles steering was very light indeed, and made for really effortless control. It is, however, rather low geared and this requires a certain amount of getting used to when driving fast on twisty roads. We should also have preferred a slightly increased self-centring action. The steering is as a whole very much above the average, however, and the car is absolutely steady at speed on all kinds of surface, and gives a great feeling of confidence to the driver. This steadiness is achieved without harshness of springing, and the brakes are smooth and well up to their work. Owing to a slight temporary defect in the servo motor, the pressure required on the brakes was rather higher than normal, but even so was not too high, and when correctly adjusted a light pressure is ample for all needs.

Many points show that much thought has been put into the lay-out of this car. The hand brake for instance, is of the racing type on which the ratchet is only brought into action when required for parking the car, and acts on all wheels. A reserve oil tank, holding a gallon, and connected direct to the sump, is another good point for long distance touring, while a separate 2-gallon petrol tank in the dash, feeding by gravity, ensures reliability in the event of the supply from the 10-gallon rear tank either failing or running out.

The price of the model tested is £525, while a complete range of all M.G. cars to say nothing of other makes, can be inspected at the Showrooms of University Motors Ltd., who are the main London distributors for this make.

THE ARGENTINE AUTUMN GRAND PRIX.

ONLY a month after his victory in the Argentine National Grand Prix, Carlos Zatuszeck has again proved victorious with his Mercédès in a big race in the South American Republic, this time in the Autumn Grand Prix. The race was run on Sunday, 12th April, and competitors had to cover a total distance of 250 miles. The race was unfortunately marred by an accident as two cars collided and ran into the crowd, one person being killed and nine injured. The final result of the race was as follows :—

1. Carlos Zatuszeck (Mercédès), 2h. 54m. 32⅕.
2. Ernesto Blanco (Reo).
3. Florencio Fernandez (Marmon).

The Midget's First Hundred CONTINUED FROM PAGE 41

on the counter and knew, at last, that we were travelling, and even as I did so I saw the lanky Cousins from the M.G. works, all on edge with excitement, rush out the figures "103" in huge lettering on a blackboard. It was most inspiring.

Confound the air pressure ; it had fallen again far too low to sustain the speed for even another lap. Pump, pump, pump—what with everything else I had to look after, it was the absolute limit. Frankly, I felt I could not keep pace with it ; it seemed like bailing a boat with a colander, but still we sped on.

Had Ernest forgotten all about me —or was he looking forward to carrying out some post-mortem on a wrecked engine? We were doing a bit of pioneering in achieving these speeds, and I had a pretty good notion of what the engine and whole car had had to put up with.

I knew Ernest would really love finding out some weakness so that we could improve our performance next time, but underlying this I knew quite well that he must know how I felt about things. I saw Kindall perched on top of the roof of the patrol car, as Jackson and Phillips energetically waved me on from near the timekeepers' box. These men from the M.G. experimental department were obviously confident.

Hard Work.

Goodness knows whether I was still breaking records. I kept shoving at the pump and working with all my strength to keep everything going. When would those fellows think of stopping me? No sign as yet. No sense in going on for the 50 kilometres, as that record has to be made from a standing start. It

seemed to me as if I had covered ten miles at the very least about twice over.

I was glad they were enjoying the fun. I shook my fist at them several times to remind them I was still there, and at last I beheld the vision of Uncle Ernest with the M.G. boys prancing about on the straight, in front of me, waving frantically to "come in."

I throttled down slowly and coasted home.

*   *   *

I got out and sat by the timekeepers' calculating machine whilst the results were "ground out," and as each new record figure became known we had cause to remember February 16th !

Everything had behaved magnificently on the car, as was proved when we subsequently stripped it down.

THE 18-80 h.p. M.G. "SIX" MARK II

An Excellent Sports Car with a Flexible Engine and Refined Performance

THE modern six-cylinder sports car, of which the M.G. "Mark II" is such an excellent example, has effectively dispelled the old impression that in order to provide the necessary speed and acceleration a car of this kind is necessarily made difficult to drive and requires expert handling. Thus, this well-known

on top gear. Each of these road speeds corresponds roughly to an engine speed of 4,000 r.p.m.

Third gear is provided by constant-mesh wheels with helical teeth which are almost inaudible, and is selected by dog clutches. Consequently, the change from top to third and vice versa is absurdly

(Top to bottom) The smart two-seater model tested; the six-cylinder engine, showing the two S.U. carburetters; the dickey seat in which an extra passenger can be carried.

easy and can be carried out faultlessly at 55 m.p.h. if desired. When making such changes at speeds below 30 m.p.h. it is scarcely necessary to double-declutch, as the lever can be pushed straight through. By double-declutching it is quite a simple matter to drop into second speed from top gear or third gear at 35 m.p.h. or so; in short, with just a little skill and practice, the driver obtains complete mastery of the gears.

The getaway from a standstill, which is obtainable by making use of these well-chosen ratios, is nothing short of surprising. One can, for example, reach 60 m.p.h. in a matter of half a minute.

Light Control and Good Road-holding

We have already remarked upon the controllability of the M.G., and this is largely due to the well-thought-out steering gear and suspension system. The former provides light control by means of a large and comfortable wheel with flexible spokes. The suspension system consists of flat semi-elliptic springs thoroughly damped by large André frictional shock-absorbers. The cornering capabilities of the car

M.G. product, with an engine of slightly under 2½ litres capacity, provides acceleration curves which should satisfy the most exacting, yet proves to be almost as flexible and docile in traffic as the woolliest of family saloons.

We tested the M.G. Mark II in two-seater form, covering 400 miles over a great variety of roads and at Brooklands Track. A particular charm of this attractive vehicle is that, sitting close to the wheel and provided with accurate steering and excellent road-holding, the driver really feels part and parcel with his mount. He achieves a degree of

personal control over every action of the car which is extremely pleasurable, and always has the feeling that he knows the exact position of each wheel on the road surface.

At all ordinary cruising speeds the car runs quite quietly with just a low muttering from the exhaust to indicate its potentialities in the way of speed and acceleration. The four-forward speed gearbox is undoubtedly an outstanding feature, the ratios being nicely chosen to give 40 m.p.h. on second, 60 m.p.h. on third and a speed approaching 80 m.p.h., under favourable conditions, are particularly notable, and enable an unusually high average speed to be set up over winding roads. Another good point is that the steering lock provides a turning circle with a diameter well within 40 ft., so making the car easy to handle in traffic.

The brakes inspire confidence in that they give consistent results and stop the car smoothly and squarely. On the other hand, the pedal pressure required to produce emergency retardation is rather high, judged by modern standards.

The long hand-brake lever is conveniently located on the right in such a position as not to obstruct the off-side door. It is fitted with a ratchet of the racing type, which comes into action only when the button at the top of the lever is depressed. Consequently, when slowing down in traffic (or to rest the driver's leg on a long descent), the hand lever can be pulled on to any required extent and, when released, springs freely to the "off" position. There is a great deal to be said in favour of this plan.

Features of the bodywork are an attractive appearance and good workmanship. The two-seater model tested is fitted with comfortable bucket seats with pneumatic upholstery, which are mounted on Leveroll fittings, so that they can readily be adjusted or can, if desired, be lifted out of the body in a few seconds. The driving position is excellent, the steering wheel being well raked and placed close to the sloping single-panel windscreen. The neatly curved tail of the body provides a large space for luggage or, alternatively, a dickey seat in which

A view which shows the neat instrument panel, tandem wiper, spring spoke steering wheel and gear lever. The whole layout is very well planned.

an extra passenger can be accommodated.

The instrument panel carries a number of easily read dials, these being a speedometer, revolution indicator, ammeter, petrol gauge, thermometer, oil gauge and clock. Also on the facia panel are the starter-motor button, a mixture control and two switches, one for the instrument lights and the other for a reversing light at the rear. Above the steering wheel are hand levers for the throttle and spark and just below the wheel an arm projects which carries a switch for the dip-twist headlamps and a horn button.

Care for detail is also exemplified by the excellent arrangement of the windscreen wiper. This is of the tandem type, with two arms, and the makers have sensibly fitted the Lucas electric motor in front of the passenger where, of course, it does not obstruct the driver's view in any way.

As is well known, the six-cylinder engine is fitted with overhead valves operated by an overhead camshaft, and is fed with mixture by two S.U. carburetters. It runs with a high degree of mechanical silence. A lamp is provided secured to the dash under the bonnet which would be very helpful should mechanical trouble be experienced at night. Also fitted to the dash is a Tecalemit oil reservoir for automatic chassis lubrication.

The car tested was supplied to us by University Motors, Ltd., of Brick Street, Piccadilly, W., the well-known London distributors for this famous marque.

TABULATED DATA FOR THE DRIVER

CHASSIS DETAILS.

M.G.: 18-80 Sports two-seater Mark II, six cylinders, 69 mm. by 110 mm. (2,468 c.c.). Tax £18. Overhead valves and camshaft, coil ignition.

Gearbox: Ratios, 4.27, 5.58, 8.5 and 14.58 to 1. Central control, silent third speed. Engine speed, 980 r.p.m. at 20 m.p.h. on "top."

PERFORMANCE.

Speeds on Gears: Top, 74 m.p.h.; 3rd, 60 m.p.h.; 2nd, 40 m.p.h. Minimum speed, top gear, 6 m.p.h.

Petrol Consumption: Driven hard, 19 m.p.g.

Acceleration: Standstill to 65 m.p.h., using 2nd, 3rd and top gears, 36 secs.

DIMENSIONS, Etc.

Wheelbase 9 ft. 6 ins.; track, 4 ft. 4 ins.; overall length, 13 ft.; width, 5 ft. 4 ins.

Turning Circle: 38 ft. 6 ins. diameter.

Weight: As tested, with two up, 30 cwt.

Price: £625.

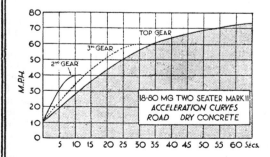

BRAKES.

SPEED m.p.h.	STOP feet.
20	19
30	36
40	80
50	122
60	178

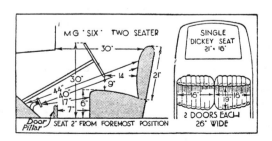

TWENTY-FOUR HOURS *from* LONDON

The Story of a Straight-through Run from London to John o' Groat's in an M.G. Midget

The writer, who is a member of our staff, makes no claim to have established a record, but gives the following account merely as an excellent example of the capabilities of a modern light car

The M.G. Midget outside the John o' Groat's Hotel.

THE idea of making a straight-through run from London to John o' Groat's came when I found myself with an odd week's holiday not booked up, and decided to spend it in Scotland. As I live in London, the obvious thing was to cover the intervening shires 'twixt Thames and Tweed in as short a time as conveniently possible. During a discussion of ways and means, my prospective passenger—a lusty young man who, on numerous previous occasions, has poured his 6 ft. 2 ins. of brawn into the space left in the Midget after I have got in—suggested that the opportunity would be an excellent one for attempting to beat my previous longest straight-away run of 508 miles.

Eventually we decided that, after leaving our respective offices on Friday afternoon, we would forgather at my home and, following a spot of food, would point the Midget radiator northwards and run straight through to Inverness, where, with luck, we proposed to make our headquarters for Saturday night. We should then be right in the heart of the district in which we proposed to spend the week.

The Suggestion Scorned.

Whilst talking things over, my passenger—whom I will call the Tadpole to preserve his anonymity—laughingly said, "Why not go to John o' Groat's and have done with it?" Whereon I laughed a long and scornful laugh and informed him that my name was not either Birkin or Howe.

The long and scornful laugh, together with the reply, would have interested a physchologist, for it was produced for the sole purpose of cloaking the fact that the same thought had occurred to me! However, I was not going to declare John o' Groat's as our destination in case we should not manage it, but I meant to have a good shot at getting there.

At this point, incidentally, it might be as well to emphasize the fact that, although out for personal records, we were essentially on holiday and had no intention whatever of making ourselves thoroughly miserable for the sake of being able to say we had reached Scotland's farthest north in one bite.

At 8.29 p.m. on the appointed Friday the Tadpole lowered his huge bulk into the passenger's seat and I made the best of the space left; followed a little scuffle to get comfortable, and then we sat, watch in hand, waiting for an imaginary starter to drop an imaginary flag punctually at 8.30. Round went the hands of the clock, down came the imaginary flag, and off went the Midget with a full tank, a full sump, and a tail very full of luggage.

Up the North Road.

A fine evening, with a sunset that suggested a fine day to follow, saw us humming merrily up the Royston Road to join that grand highway, the Great North Road, a few miles beyond Huntingdon. Gradually, the shadows lengthened, and on went the headlights, picking out innumerable moths, which ended their all too brief career against the radiator, screen, and headlamps. Seldom have I seen so many.

By this time the traffic had thinned out, and there was little to interrupt the contented growl of the exhaust—a most soothing sound—as the Midget slipped along the great highway at an unhurried 45-50 m.p.h. Only once did I have a momentary qualm as another low sound that did not belong to the exhaust—and was nothing like so musical—suddenly became audible. Visions of faulty ball races and suchlike troubles flashed through my mind, but the alarm was unwarranted; the sound was only the Tadpole crooning soft melodies to himself in sheer contentment.

Precisely at 11.50 p.m. the Midget poked its nose into the yard of an all-night garage at Newark, having come 122.8 miles without—to use the parlance of trials secretaries—the road wheels having ceased to revolve in a forward direction. This, incidentally, smashed record No. 1, as my previous longest distance without a stop of any sort whatever was 111 miles.

In due course a sleepy-eyed attendant appeared, the Midget's tank was filled, and a chamois leather was produced to remove the animal matter which had accumulated on the lamps and screen. As the attendant retired, I suggested that we might make a little more room in the tail by demolishing a few of the sandwiches reposing therein, a suggestion which the Tadpole was nothing loth to follow.

Off Once Again.

Eventually, the top of the tail was shut down—no need to squeeze the luggage now—and off we went after a total stop of 35 minutes.

On up the Great North Road once more, but this time not for long as the bright lights of an all-night garage at Doncaster prompted us to stop for an odd gallon of petrol; nothing like keeping the tank as full as possible when you are not sure how many garages you will find open. For the same reason a petrol stop was again made at Boroughbridge.

Then followed those glorious few miles of dead-straight and flat road which are known as Leeming Lane and Scotch Corner was reached. Taking the left-hand road for Brough, we decided that the effect of the sandwiches had worn off—it was then half-past three—so another halt was called. Food tastes pleasant in the early dawn when you have been driving all night, and in half an hour or so there was yet more space in the Midget's tail!

A quiet smoke, too, seemed indicated, so there we sat, looking somewhat ghostly in the pale half light, silently consuming cigarettes until, by mutual consent, we both had a brief nap. The Tadpole occupied the Midget, whilst I found a comfortable spot on the grass; at least, it seemed comfortable when I dropped off to sleep, but something in the nature of a miniature earthquake must have happened soon afterwards, for a choice line in small mountains was pushing forcibly into one of my off-side ribs when I awoke!

Across the Border.

However, a short nap, even on a mountain top, is very refreshing on an all-night run, and we were soon away, feeling as fresh as the morning which was then breaking. So, on we went over the glorious moorland to Penrith and Carlisle—where more petrol was taken on board—and so to the Scottish border, which was reached by 7.10 a.m. Equally uneventful and equally pleasant was the next 60-odd miles to Lanark, which was reached at 8.50 a.m. In the first 12 hours, that is, by half-past eight, we had, incidentally, put 368 miles behind us, which, so far as I was concerned, was record No. 2 of the trip.

At Lanark we dropped anchor in an hotel and consumed a very welcome breakfast. I believe the Tadpole had thoughts of ordering breakfast for three and eating out of two plates simultaneously, but the rather severe expression on the waitress's face must have made him think better of the idea. Anyway, we both

eventually returned to the Midget feeling fit for anything. This was our only halt at an hotel.

The 36 miles to Stirling, and a few beyond, lie through industrial country, but with the prospect of the exhilarating run over the Grampians on the reconstructed Perth-Inverness road in front of us we made light work of this uninteresting section. The day, moreover, was fine and bright, and we entered Perth shortly before noon in excellent spirits with the best of the trip before us.

Buzzing merrily over the Grampians at our usual cruising speed of about 48 m.p.h., the Tadpole could not restrain himself from singing again, but this time I recognized the noise as soon as it started, and experienced no alarm.

Inverness was passed through at a quarter-past three, and we entered the last lap. The road northwards from this point is very pleasant as it wanders round the Beauly and Cromarty Firths, whilst farther up there is fine coast scenery round Helmsdale. With plenty of time in hand, we called a halt near Bonar Bridge for refreshment and took things leisurely.

Through a Sea Mist.

An hour later we regretted our tardiness, for the road became steadily worse and called for a slower pace, whilst a sea mist suddenly came up, necessitating a further reduction of pace. We began to get anxious; if the roads got worse or the mist thicker, bang would go all our hopes of reaching John o' Groat's within the 24 hours. For a few miles all the Midget's fine road-holding and braking powers were turned to good account.

Then, just as, for the first time, the run was beginning to seem like hard work, the roads smoothed, the mist lifted, and all was plain sailing again.

So it happened that, on a grey, chilly Saturday evening, we drew up in front of the John o' Groat's Hotel, the speedometer showing 715.3 miles and the hands of my watch 8.14 p.m.

*   *   *

Supper and bed both seemed pleasant that night, as is only to be expected, but so comfortable is the Midget for long-distance work and so confident can its owner be of its capacity for unfailing service, that neither physically nor mentally did I feel any strain. Indeed, the next morning I rose without a single ache or trace of stiffness, and the Tadpole had the same tale to tell. We spent the morning leisurely greasing the car—we felt it deserved it—and in the afternoon ran back the 159 miles to Inverness.

And now for a few statistics. The total time from start to finish was 23 hrs. 44 mins., which gives an overall average, including all stops, of 30.13 m.p.h., whilst the total running time was 19 hrs. 29 mins., which gives a running average of 36.7 m.p.h. On coming to top up the sump at John o' Groat's a quart can proved more than adequate, giving an oil consumption in excess of 3,000 m.p.g., and this, despite the fact that the Midget has already some 15,000 miles of hard service to its credit. Petrol consumption worked out at between 35 m.p.g. and 36 m.p.g.

The only point on which I have no statistics concerns the quantity of motoring chocolate consumed by the Tadpole during the run, but perhaps that's just as well!   **H.**

AN ENTIRELY

First Details of a 12 [...]
able of 70 m.p.h. a[...]
Occasional-four Midg[...]
Mod[...]

(Left) The new low-chassis occasional four-seater Midget, which will sell at £210.

THOSE who contend that racing does not improve the breed should study the 1932 programme of the M.G. Car Co., Ltd., Pavlova Works, Abingdon-on-Thames. In it they will find embodied many features which have hitherto been confined to the Montlhéry model, and which, having been proved by the outstanding successes achieved in the racing world by this car, have now been incorporated in some of the other models.

Briefly, the light-car programme of the M.G. concern for the coming season incorporates an entirely new six-cylinder model of 1,271 c.c., a new Midget model with a lower chassis and an occasional four-seater body, and, finally, the ever-popular Midget models exactly the same as for 1931 except for the addition of a new metal-panelled two-seater.

Besides these models, the Montlhéry model in both supercharged and unsupercharged form is being continued without alteration. The prices are £575 and £490 respectively.

The new six-cylinder model, which is known as the Magna, bristles with features of interest, and, as we have already indicated, the influence of racing is to be traced in very many of its features. The engine is really a six-cylinder edition of the well-known M.G. Midget engine, the bore and stroke being the same, namely, 57 mm. and 83 mm., this giving a capacity of 1,271 c.c., and calling for a tax of £12.

As in the case of the Midget, the engine has overhead valves operated by an overhead camshaft through the medium of rocking fingers, the drive to the camshaft being by means of a vertical shaft at the front which also forms the armature shaft of the dynamo.

Forced-feed lubrication by means of a gear-type pump is employed, oil being delivered under pressure to the main bearings, big-ends and overhead valve gear. The sump holds approximately 1½ gallons, and is of a special flat design to allow of adequate ground clearance.

Other features of the power unit are coil ignition, two S.U. carburetters bolted to an induction pipe providing efficient hot spots, a four-bearing crankshaft and a four-bladed fan driven by belt.

The engine is three-point mounted, the front mounting being by means of a bracket bolted to a tubular cross-member of the chassis, and an interesting feature in this connection is that an extension of the bracket is used to carry the radiator which is thus independent of the actual chassis frame.

A four-speed gearbox is employed, the ratios being 4.89, 6.69, 9.78 and 19.55 to 1. It is bolted up in unit with the engine and single-plate clutch, and a very attractive feature of it is the "remote control" gear lever, which is used in place of a lever acting directly on to the box. Actually, the turret on the top of the box is carried backwards

horizontally, and ends in a gate in which is mounted the short, stumpy gear lever beloved of those who like to make full use of a gearbox. The result of the arrangement is an extremely well-placed gear lever, with quite a small travel and a very positive movement—a combination impossible to obtain with a long lever acting direct on the box.

From the back of the gearbox an open propeller shaft carried at each end on Hardy Spicer mechanical universal joints, transmits the drive to a spiral-bevel rear axle and differential of conventional design.

The Racing Influence.

When one turns to an examination of the chassis frame, the influence of racing at once becomes apparent. The chassis is extremely low built, and the floorboards are only 11 ins. from the ground; as a basis for comparison, it may be mentioned that in the normal M.G. Midget—which is quite low—the floorboards are 15½ ins. high. The side members are steeply cambered over the front springs, and there are perfectly flat to the rear and actually pass underneath the back axle. A photograph of this feature appears on page 428.

The rear springs are almost flat, and are carried well outside the frame on stout tubular cross-members, the rear one of which is slotted at each end to accommodate the master leaves which pass through it; this arrangement, of course, is in place of the normal type of spring shackle, and has the advantage that there is less tendency for sideways movement to develop, and so cause the car to "float" when cornering at speed. A similar arrangement is employed in the case of the underslung semi-elliptic front springs, and in both cases moulded rubber covers are used to retain lubricant and keep out dirt. Hartford shock absorbers are fitted at front and rear.

A simple but very businesslike layout is used for the brakes, which are of the usual internal-expanding type, working in large ribbed drums on all four wheels. Operation is by cable, the cables being anchored to small grooved drums on a cross-shaft, rotation of which naturally tends to wind the cables around the drums and so apply the brakes. The extremities of the cables, incidentally, pass through casings and operate on the Bowden principle.

(Left) An interior view of the Magna sliding-roof Foursome, showing the ample room in the back.

NEW M.G. SIX

(Right) The new six-cylinder Magna with a sliding-roof Foursome body, price £289.

The most noteworthy feature of the brake gear is its compactness, the cable drums actually being carried inside the channel-section chassis members, whilst the arm to which the pull rod from the pedal is attached is kept very short so that the brake gear at this point does not protrude above or below the frame members.

The hand brake which is provided with a racing-type ratchet is mounted direct on the cross-shaft, and is adjusted by means of a wing nut, which can, if necessary, be turned whilst actually driving. The main adjustment for the foot brake is also very simple.

Mention of the compactness of the brake gear brings us to another interesting feature of the car, as it enables a shield to be bolted direct to the underside of the chassis members, whilst the floorboards can rest direct on top, so protecting the parts from dust and mud without either reducing the ground clearance or making the seating position any higher. The engine, incidentally, is completely sealed off from the driving compartment, as the space between the clutch housing and the dash is filled in by means of a sheet of stout rubber, whilst there are no slots for the pedals as they are mounted behind the dash. Thus there is practically no possibility of engine fumes reaching the driving compartment.

Accessible Instruments.

The bonnet is carried well back beyond the dash, so that when it is lifted access can be gained to the back of the instrument board. This arrangement is made possible largely owing to the fact that a rear petrol tank is employed; its capacity is 6 gallons.

Pains have obviously been taken to make maintenance as simple as possible, for, in addition to the simple brake adjustments and the rubber covers for the sliding anchorages of the springs, a group system of lubrication is employed.

Other features of the chassis are Rudge-Whitworth racing-type wheels with knock-off hub caps and offset spokes, and a 12-volt electric system. The wheelbase is 7 ft. 10 ins., whilst the track is the same as the normal M.G. Midget, namely, 3 ft. 6 ins.

(Right) The Magna engine. Note the two carburetters and the grouped nipples on the dash support.

The new Magna chassis is available with two styles of bodywork, these being a very attractive sports four-seater selling at £250, and a sliding roof Foursome, which is in the nature of a close-coupled coupé, and sells for £289.

The sports four-seater is of the pannelled type, cellulose finished, and is characterized by its low, graceful yet businesslike lines. A single racing-type flat screen which can be folded forward over the scuttle is provided. The stock colour is ebony black, with a choice of apple green, tudor brown, deep red, cerulean blue or suede grey leather to match. Other external colours are available at an extra charge of £2 10s.

The Foursome is also a most attractive car, a noteworthy feature being that transparent windows are let into the sliding roof in the manner first popularized on the M.G. Midget coupé. The interior is very well fitted up and provides plenty of room, extra width being obtained by recessing the doors to form elbow-rests. The same range of colour scheme is available as in the case of the Magna sports four-seater.

The new low-built Midget chassis does not call for very much description, as practically all the details of the Magna are embodied in it; it is, in fact, a short edition of the Magna with a four-cylinder engine. The only notable differences are that its wheelbase is 7 ft., and that it is provided with a three-speed gearbox which, however, incorporates the remote control provided on the Magna. The four-speed gearbox is available as an extra.

The engine used is the standard Midget type except that it is three-point mounted, and has a special sump to provide extra ground clearance.

A point worth emphasizing is the fact that it is equipped with 12-volt lighting, which is an unusual refinement for an 8 h.p. car, whilst it also has racing-type Rudge-Whitworth wheels. This chassis is available with an occasional four-seater body of the type which has of late become so popular on small cars, and sells for £210.

As we have already mentioned, the normal M.G. Midget range is to be continued without change, but prices have been reduced, the two-seater now selling at £165 and the coupé at £235. In addition, a new two-seater, externally very similar to the fabric two-seater but having a metal-panelled body, is available at £185. Special features of this car are a disappearing hood which remains permanently attached but folds into a recess behind the seat and leather upholstery.

THE £ s. d. of RUNNING
a
SMALL CAR

Actual Results are Always More Useful than Mere Calculations. Here is an M.G. Midget Owner's Carefully Kept Log.

First Year (1930-1931).

Items	£	s.	d.
Tax (quarterly)	8	16	0
Full Insurance	11	5	0
Petrol (223 gallons)	14	17	3
Oil (5 gallons)	1	10	0
Dynamo replacements (2)	2	12	6
Puncture repaired		2	0
Special spotlight bulb *		3	6
Radiator muff *		7	6
Bosch horn tuned		1	6
Lucas MT2 electric wiper *	1	1	0
New half-glass to screen		8	6
Extra dash lamp *		2	0
New S.U. needle		2	6
Flaps on front mudguards *		9	0
Two-way petrol tap (two level) *		9	6
Spotlight glass and rim		5	0
Car washed and polished		4	0
Driving mirror *		4	0
Spare Lucas bulb case *		2	6
(* Extras—not replacements.)			
	42	14	3
Depreciation at 20%	28	7	0
Loss of interest at 5%	7	1	9
	78	3	0

Miles covered	8,468.	
Petrol (consumption)	37.9	m.p.g.
Oil (actually consumed 3 gallons 6 pints)	2,257	m.p.g.
Full cost per mile	2.21d.	
Omitting depreciation, etc...	1.21d.	

WHAT does it cost to run a small car? That is a question which many people ask at this time of year, and, as actual facts always form a more convincing answer than hypothetical calculations, the following, carefully kept records of the running of a popular 8 h.p. car should be both interesting and useful.

The car in question is a 1929 (August) M.G. Midget open two-seater, and was purchased second-hand in 1930 for £141 15s., the list price at that time being £185 for a similar model. The mileage already covered when I purchased it was 8,210.5, and all its previous history was given to me by the original owner, whom I knew well.

Although I knew that the car had been driven pretty hard during its previous ownership, it had received sympathetic treatment and attention and had originally been " run-in " in an intelligent manner, as its previous owner is a really good driver of considerable experience.

Depreciation is always a difficult matter to estimate —until the car is actually sold again—but for purposes of my log I have taken it as 20 per cent. per annum and, in addition, have allowed a further 5 per cent. for loss of interest on capital.

I have not included garage or water rates, as they are, like the poor, always with me, regardless of whether I run a car or not. I am not allocating any of the water rates to my car as I never wash it.

Home Tuning.

Decarbonizing, running adjustments and the few repairs necessary have been done by myself in my own garage, and items such as gear oil for chassis lubrication are not shown, as, having run other vehicles previously, I had a good supply already in my shed.

It will be noticed that the petrol consumption improved vastly during the second twelve months. This was due to fitting a different type of needle in the S.U. carburetter and to spending a great deal of time and patience in getting everything " just right " all through the range. As the car is used every day in and out of town the average consumption seems very creditable, although admittedly long " potters " in the country at low speeds frequently show 52-53 m.p.g.

A number of " unnecessary " items are included in the list, as, during the first year, I fitted numerous extras for my own convenience, and during the second year I fitted a complete set of new covers and tubes prior to going away for a holiday. The original tyres appear to be still good for several thousand miles, but are rather thin—they did 27,500 miles—and I changed them solely as I did not want to be bothered with punctures on holiday.

It will be seen from this that, low as they are, the costs could actually have been reduced quite appreciably by economizing on some of the " extras."

During the two years under review I had two involuntary stops—one during the first year owing to a lead coming off the coil, and one in the second year owing to plunging at speed into a stretch of flooded road in the dark, and soaking the plugs and so forth. Neither delayed me for more than a few minutes.

The information given in the tables is as nearly accurate as it is possible for anything of this nature to be, as an exact log of *every* run is kept, however short it may be. Details of petrol, oil, route and mileage are entered on the spot, together with any work done, so that there is really very little left which may be called "estimated."

To make the story complete one or two details of other points may be given. The highest speed obtained on the level "without any cheating" has been 62 m.p.h. (3,800 r.p.m.)—the mean speed of two runs each way against the watch. Actually the speedometer has been properly checked for accuracy and is now calibrated with r.p.m. as well as m.p.h.

Maximum Speeds.

Normally one can count on a maximum of about 60 m.p.h. in still air on the level, about 55 m.p.h. to 57 m.p.h. if there is any headwind worth mentioning and anything up to about 70 m.p.h. with a good following wind and/or a down grade.

I did on one occasion see what the maximum was in second and bottom. These proved to be 44 m.p.h. (5,000 r.p.m.) in second and 24 m.p.h. (5,100 r.p.m.) in bottom, but in both of these runs valve bounce commenced, as I have the old camshaft and single valve springs. Actually I limit. myself strictly to 4,000 r.p.m. as a maximum on each of these gears, and the acceleration through the gears is quite good enough for all normal purposes. Incidentally, gear changing is vastly improved by the fitting of a McEvoy remote control which drops straight on to the existing box and is infinitely preferable to the normal lever.

Second Year (1931-1932).									
Items						£.	s.	d.	
Tax (quarterly)	..	..	..	..	..	8	16	0	
Full Insurance	..	..	..	..	..	10	2	6	
Petrol (240 gallons) ..	..	..	..	..	..	16	0	0	
Oil (10 gallons)	..	..	..	..	..	3	10	0	
5 new covers and tubes	..	..	..	..	..	11	5	0	
6 volt bulb—parking light ..	..	..	..	..		1	6	
Puncture mended	..	..	..	..	..		2	9	
5 spokes	..	..	..	..	..		1	3	
Brake shoe spring replaced	..	..	..	..		2	3	
Front brake cable assembly	..	..	..	..		11	8	
4 grease nipples	..	..	..	..	..		2	0	
						50	14	11	
Depreciation at 20%	..	..	..	..	..	22	13	7	
Loss of interest at 5%	..	..		..	..	5	13	5	
						79	1	11	
Miles covered	..	-		.	11,090.4				
Petrol (consumption)	..	..	..			46.21 m.p.g.			
Oil (actually consumed 6 gallons 3 pints)	..			1,740 m.p.g.				
Full cost per mile ..	..	..	..	..	..	1.71d.			
Omitting depreciation, etc. ..	..	..	..	..	1.09d.				

In the usual way I never drive for any period on full throttle, but, as my normal runs, apart from town use, are really long ones, I keep at just about 50 m.p.h. whenever the road allows. This is about 3,000 r.p.m., and it can be held all day without distress on a road such as "A1."

As an example—I am not going to be drawn into average speed arguments—the run from N. London to Edinburgh (388.8 miles) was recently accomplished in 11 hours dead from door to door—the actual running time being 10 hours 10 mins., which is an average of slightly over 38 m.p.h. At no time did I exceed 60 m.p.h., and this figure was touched only twice—and, to save the usual letters, at no time during the run was the slightest risk of any description undertaken.

A High Top

Owing to the fact that the top gear is on the high side (4.89 : 1) the "possible" cruising speed is very near the "normal" maximum without straining, as once the engine gets really turning over it keeps its speed with amazingly little throttle. I think that there is no doubt that this accounts for the high average speeds which it is possible to put up on these cars on a long run, and also perhaps accounts for the optimistic ideas of "genuine maximum speed" which are put forward by some owners of similar models!

I am quite prepared to be told that my maximum speed is on the low side for my type of car, but the fact is that it goes a long way in a reasonably short time, and keeps on going.

So far as "buying second-hand" is concerned—it is always said that the acid test of a fair second-hand deal is to sell a car to a friend and still keep your friend. The Midget's previous owner was a friend of mine—we are now even better friends than ever!

THE GIPSY.

HE THOUGHT HER A MUG...

MY cousin Winifred is a woman in a thousand. Not only are her words commendably few, but she is about the quickest diagnoser of a car's minor ailments that I have ever come across. Incidentally, she takes special pride in the tender care she lavishes on her car—particularly the engine and battery.

The other day, in extremely respectable time, Winifred drove from London to a famous resort on the Yorkshire coast, and, finding the chief garages crammed to bursting point, she was forced to store her petted vehicle in a small, dingy and unprepossessing garage in a back street.

Next morning she went round, got into her car, and pressed the starter. Nothing happened—absolutely nothing, not even the protesting groan of a starter hungry for current which a dying accumulator cannot supply. She switched on the dashlight—nothing doing. She thought like lightning for a moment, called one of the hands and commanded him to crank (the car has a mag.—not coil ignition). The lad cranked with a fair show of vigour, but quite without result. Then up strolled the proprietor.

"What have you been doing to this car?" said Winifred—as usual getting her blow in first.

"Nothing, mum," replied the garage man, studying his boots.

"Well, you've stopped it starting, anyway," said Winifred.

The garage man brightened up. "It's an old car, you see," he began, "nearly two years old; nothing will make it start easily except a thorough decarbonizing. P'raps even that won't cure it and then you'd have to have a regrind and new pistons. We could do it by to-morrow for three pounds," he concluded.

Winifred's gaze withered him.

"I give you half an hour to get that engine running," said she, as, like an angry Juno, she strode out into the street. When she returned, the engine was purring gently in its usual docile fashion.

"And," said my cousin Winifred, as she slapped one-and-sixpence on the ledge of the cash window, "next time you disconnect a girl's battery and earth her mag., make sure you've got a real ninny to deal with!

D.H.M.S.

THE SUPERCHARGED M.G. MONTLHERY MIDGET

A REALLY ROADWORTHY 90 M.P.H. 746 c.c. CAR

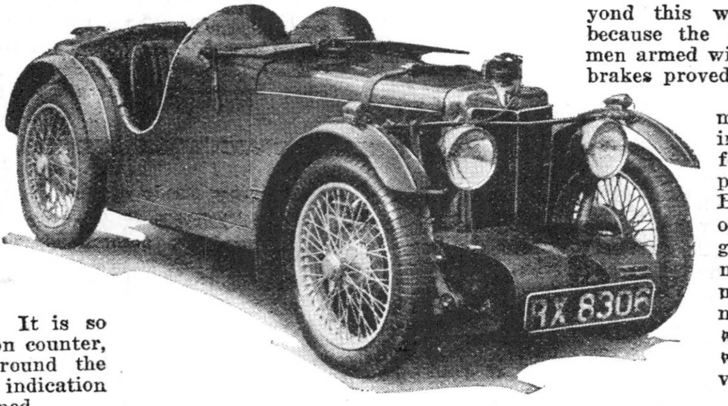

THE Mark II Montlhéry M.G. Midget in supercharged form provides the sports-car enthusiast with the authentic "racing-car" thrill. Its blower makes just the right screaming noise, the exhaust sounds like tearing calico and the whole vehicle smells deliciously of warm castor oil.

One can jump straight into it and tear up to the 90 m.p.h. mark, or very near it, in under a mile. It is so steady that only the revolution counter, with its pointer hovering round the 6,000 r.p.m. mark, gives any indication of the tremendous speed obtained.

What is much more important, from the point of view of the man in the street, is that the car, without modification and with the same R.I. Champion plugs in it, can be taken straight off the track and driven through city traffic and with the engine just ticking over, without oiling-up a single plug, without "overdosing" the cylinders with mixture and without the slightest symptom of overheating.

Indeed, it seems as though its makers do not yet realize what a perfectly delightful and trouble-free vehicle it is for ordinary touring. It is eminently worth while fitting a glass windscreen and a speedometer, and one or two more little comforts (such as anti-dazzle head-lamps) for the high-speed tourist.

It is economical, too. We drove the car good and hard for 400-odd miles and the oil level did not perceptibly get any lower. The rather costly four-tins-of-Benzol-to-one-of-petrol mixture was only consumed at the rate of about 30 m.p.g. As the tank holds 15 gallons the "cruising range" of the car is naturally very considerable.

The engine is silky-smooth up to a very easy 6,000 r.p.m.—beyond that we hadn't the heart to "rev" it—and develops such an amazing amount of power at much lower revs. that one just rushes up quite considerable main-road hills on top gear at 50 m.p.h. or so. Third gear, which is *really* silent, provides astonishing acceleration and except for getting away from a standstill is adequate to meet nearly every demand imposed upon it.

One can run through towns, in gentlemanly style, quite quietly on top gear. On the open road . . . well, one is up in the "seventies" before one has time to realize it!

So far, the supercharged M.G. Midget has covered the fastest "standing half-mile" of any sports car that we have tested, despite the fact that the two occupants of the car scaled 339 lb. between them—over one-fifth of the weight of the complete car (1,500 lb. exactly with 4 gallons of fuel). The quarter-mile was covered, from a standing start, in 19⅘ secs., by which time 65.6 m.p.h. was attained. The half-mile was covered in 33⅕ secs., and the speed reached was 77.6 m.p.h.

The clutch is smooth and light, the gear-change a sheer joy, so easy it is, and the steering feels absolutely safe, inspiring confidence at all speeds. The

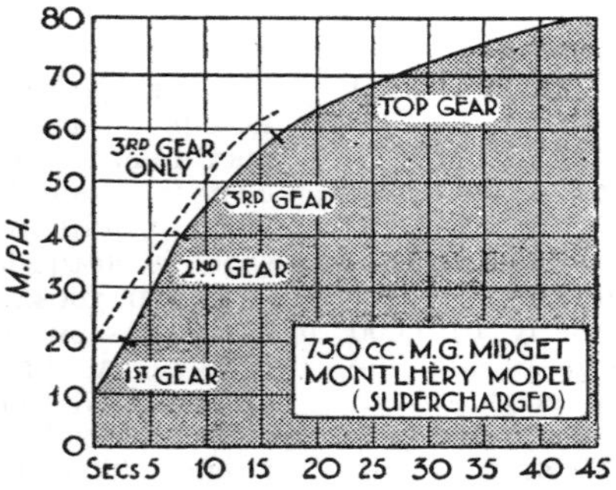

Acceleration curves, using the gearbox.

brakes are not so nice. They are good enough, to be sure, but they lack that "crisp" feeling. The pulling-up distances, using foot and hand brake together (the latter being the more powerful), with the brakes adjusted to the limit, were as follow:—From 20 m.p.h., 15 ft.; 30 m.p.h., 39 ft.; 40 m.p.h., 68 ft.; 50 m.p.h, 105 ft.; 60 m.p.h., 160 ft.; 70 m.p.h., 270 ft. The track was dry.

Normally, one is not expected to exceed 5,500 r.p.m., which is equal to about 20 m.p.h. on first gear (21.5 to 1), 40 m.p.h. on second (10.75 to 1), 59 m.p.h. on third (7.3 to 1), and 81 m.p.h. on top.

The highest speed reached on the track, over the official half-mile, was 88.44 m.p.h. The car was gaining speed all the time and actually covered the last quarter-mile with the rev. counter showing 6,050 r.p.m. = 90 m.p.h. Beyond this we had to stop quickly because the track was covered with men armed with pneumatic drills. The brakes proved adequate.

Our usual run to Sidmouth and back was done in comfort, despite dense fog as far as Staines and pretty opaque going until Basingstoke. The absence of a windscreen (the wire gauze was folded flat) made visors or goggles necessary, but there were no draughts and the car was beautifully cosy and warm. The springing was very good indeed.

We lost time, imperceptibly, on the more winding section of the route because we had not checked the tyre pressures when the manufacturers handed the car over to us, and they were on the low side; enough to cause a trace of wheel dither, particularly when braking, and to make us slow more than we need have done on bends. Subsequently we inflated the tyres to 30 lb. back and 32 lb. front, and the vehicle was transformed. One could throw it lightheartedly round almost any bend. It was incredibly roadworthy, essentially safe, utterly delightful.

Salcombe Hill, near Sidmouth (1 in 5) was climbed at 40 m.p.h. on second gear with the throttle only just open so as not to "over-rev." the engine.

Main Dimensions

The car weighs 13 cwt. 1 qr. 16 lb., the track is 3 ft. 6 ins., and the wheelbase 6 ft. 9 ins. Turning circles 36 ft. 9 ins. (right) and 34 ft. (left). The engine has four cylinders, o.h. camshaft, 57 mm. bore, 73 mm. stroke, 746 c.c. It develops well over 60 b.h.p. at 6,300 r.p.m. Rudge-Whitworth "knock-on" wire wheels are standard. The car costs £575.

Expensive? Well, on the whole, not. The point is that, shorn of wings and lamps, the car is good for anything up to 100 m.p.h. And it feels as though it will hold that speed, or something very near it, indefinitely. What more can one ask for, at any price?

ACCELERATION

From 20 m.p.h. on 3rd gear (7.3 to 1) to		
30 m.p.h.	.. ..	3⅕ secs.
40 m.p.h.	.. ..	6⅗ secs.
50 m.p.h.	.. ..	10 secs.
60 m.p.h.	.. ..	14 secs.
64.26 m.p.h.	.. ..	16⅘ secs.
From 30 m.p.h. on top gear (5.37 to 1) to		
40 m.p.h.	.. ..	6⅗ secs.
50 m.p.h.	.. ..	13⅕ secs.
60 m.p.h.	.. ..	20 secs.
70 m.p.h.	.. ..	26⅘ secs.
80 m.p.h.	.. ..	38 secs.

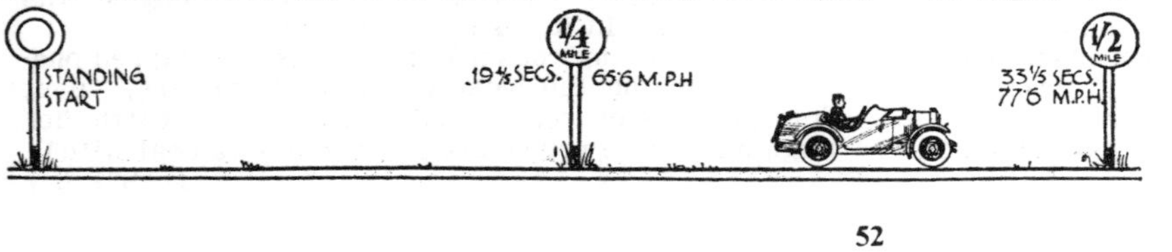

A MAGNA FOLDING-HEAD COUPE

Attractive Body by University Motors

UNIVERSITY MOTORS, LTD., the London distributors of M.G. cars, have supplemented the standard range of coachwork available on the M.G. Magna chassis by the introduction of the very attractive model illustrated on this page. Known as the University folding-head foursome coupé, this body is specially built for University Motors by the Carlton Carriage Co., Ltd., of Willesden.

The main idea in designing the body has been to meet the needs of those who want a good closed car and a good open car but do not want a separate example of each. To fulfil these requirements is not easy, but it has been done with complete success.

Another compromise that has been struck with more than ordinary success, is that between luxury and sportiness. In the matter of comfort, the body is all that could be desired, yet, withal, the sporting appeal that is so essentially a part of the Magna chassis, has been preserved and is present in the sleek lines and low build.

Room for Four.

The body is of the close-coupled type; but it should be emphasized that there is distinctly more room in the back seats than is found in many examples of this style of body on small-car chassis. Admittedly, two grown-ups might be a little cramped at the end of a 200-mile run, but no apology would be needed for offering them the rear seats for a 50-mile trip. For one person, the back should be comfortable for any distance.

These are the points that immediately strike one on examining the body for the first time; the details are no less interesting.

The head is a clever piece of work and it takes a stranger a little while to explore its full possibilities. There are, of course, the fully closed and fully opened positions and it can quickly be changed from one to the other.

If desired, however, the head can be left in the half-erected state, as shown in one of the illustrations on this page —with the windows closed, an excellent arrangement for a cold but fine winter day. Moreover, should there be a shower, it is but the work of a moment to unroll the forward portion of the head and secure it to the screen.

The windows are equally ingenious. Owing to the manner in which the doors are cut away to clear the rear wheel-arches, it is impossible to fit full winding glass panels, so the designers have ingeniously got over the difficulty by a combination of the winding and sliding principles.

Clever Window Arrangement.

The main part of the windows consists of a large panel that drops down into the door in the usual way, but attached to this is a small sliding pane that serves to close the small aperture left. This plan not only gives the convenience of sliding windows for signalling and ventilation, but allows the whole window to disappear when the car is open, as the small panel, when slid forward, drops down into the door with the main one.

At the rear of the body is a large built-in locker that houses the petrol tank and also leaves room for a fairly large suitcase. The rear panel, incidentally, lets down to give access to this and, should there not be enough room in the locker for all the luggage, the panel can be left in the horizontal position and used as a luggage grid.

Another ingenious feature concerns the mudguarding. Most cars without running boards are notorious for the way in which the front wheels sling mud over the body sides, but in this case the trouble has been largely overcome by extending the front wing valances horizontally backwards until they merge with the body just forward of the doors.

How the head can be left in the partly opened position for showery or cold weather.

In the matter of finish, the body is above reproach, whilst all the usual accessories are fitted. A very wide range of either single or dual-tone colour schemes is available.

We were able to take the first example of this model to be produced for a short test run and it fully came up to expectations. It had already covered some four thousand miles, but there were no squeaks or rattles.

The controls are well arranged, and we felt at ease immediately. The rear window, however, proved scarcely large enough for an adequate view when reversing. This point, however, may receive attention on later models.

A Joy to Drive.

The Magna is a sheer joy to drive. Its six cylinders do their job in a smooth and effortless fashion, the brakes give one every confidence to make full use of the extremely snappy performance of the car, the steering is light and positive and the gear change is delightful. The stubby little remote-control lever is just where it should be and the change is quite easy. From top to third is particularly quick and simple, and one can go from one to the other with perfect ease and certainty at 50 m.p.h.

Altogether, a most fascinating car that, considering its many attractions and first-class quality, is not dear at the £335 asked. Further particulars are available from University Motors, Ltd., 4, Brick Street, Park Lane, London.

ON THE M.G. MAGNA CHASSIS.

Two views of the University folding-head foursome coupe which has just been introduced by University Motors, Ltd., for the M.G. Magna chassis. The body possesses many ingenious features and is equally pleasing when open or closed. The price is £335.

TRYING OUT THE M.G. MAGNA

1,200 c.c. SIX WITH ATTRACTIVE FEATURES AND LIVELY PERFORMANCE

Two praiseworthy points of the Magna are revealed in this photograph—the accessibility of the engine and adjacent parts, and the ample door width, features which are lacking in many small cars.

[*Motor Sport photograph*]

ALL of us have at one time or another conjured up visions of the sort of small car we would like to build, if we had the facilities to carry out our ideals. Time and again those ideals have been mentally revised and arranged until they have become increasingly definite.

This car must be fairly small, of course, so that it can nip about in narrow spaces. The chassis must be very low so that it will corner well and be impossible to overturn. It must be light, for this means good acceleration, a most important feature in modern traffic. It also means economy, very essential in these days for most of us, and furthermore, light weight is essential for success in trials.

A really lively engine is taken for granted, and not too small, for we do not want to be constantly tuning or replacing worn parts. Flexibility is another requirement, for at times we feel lazy and do not wish to bother with gears. On the other hand we must have a four-speed gear box with the higher ratios close together for the occasions when we suddenly wish to emulate Chiron or Campari !

The driving position must be carefully arranged, as we shall hope to travel long distances. For the same reason the body must be really comfortable for two people, with pneumatic seats and room for luggage, or occasional extra passengers when necessary. The weather in this country being what it is, we want good weather protection, and as we shall be rather proud of this car of ours it must be very well finished, and have really " snappy " lines.

A very high maximum speed is not essential, as this is usually a very expensive luxury, and about 70 m.p.h. will see the majority of cars left well behind.

All these thoughts have recurred from time to time to any keen motorist, but when we came to take over an M.G. Magna with an Abbey body for test, we realised that here was the car we had really been imagining, only fashioned with more neatness and cunning than the vehicle of our dreams.

This car, which was placed at our disposal by Messrs. Stearns, of 16, Fulham Road, who specialise in sports cars with the Abbey Company's special coachwork, certainly embodies all the points we have enumerated, in addition to many others of which we had never thought.

The chassis frame is upswept over the front axle, and passes under the rear axle, being at a constant level from the engine to the rear.

The six cylinder overhead camshaft engine with twin S.U. carburettors transmits its power through a four-speed box and Hardy-Spicer propeller shaft to the rear axle. There is an emergency bottom gear, very useful for trials work, and three close ratios which suffice for all normal road work including getting off the mark.

Apart from the excellent finish which is apparent to the most casual observer, there are many details of equipment on the body which make a strong appeal to the " all-weather " owner. In addition to the excellent hood arrangement, the screen is provided with twin wipers, and the former is arranged either to open at the bottom, such as for driving in fog with the hood up, or to fold flat on the scuttle like a racing screen when out for some fresh air in decent weather.

The pneumatic seats are fully adjustable, while the rear compartment is excellently arranged for a small car. An eight gallon rear tank is another departure from standard which is extremely useful, and with the good petrol consumption of this motor it would enable a day's run of 250 miles to be covered without filling up, provided that the average speed was not forced too high.

Ease of upkeep of the chassis has been carefully studied, and grouped lubrication points make this important duty easy to carry out.

The first impression on driving the car is of its extreme handiness and excellent acceleration, and these are undoubtedly its chief characteristics. "Pep," and perfect smoothness of engine and transmission throughout the speed range, make it a most fascinating car to drive, and owing to its capacity for leaping past other vehicles at a touch of the throttle, a high average speed is possible even when the way is by no means clear.

The clutch is very smooth, and the gear change positive and rapid, so that no time is lost in running up through the gears. The steering has good self-centering qualities, and once we had adjusted the Hartford shock absorbers to our liking the road holding was very good indeed.

As would be expected from the layout, the car is remarkably steady on corners. We soon came to the conclusion that the speedometer was optimistic, and a careful check of this proved our surmise to be correct. The acceleration figures given show a very high standard of performance for an engine of little over 1,200 c.c., and fully justify the makers' well-known slogan, "Faster than most." Incidentally owners who think their cars show even better figures in standard tune, should remember that ours are fully corrected, and not speedometer readings.

The comfortable maximum speeds on 2nd and 3rd were 35 m.p.h. and 50 m.p.h., while all out in top the car did 66 m.p.h. on the level.

As the car had done little over 500 miles when we tried it for maximum speed, there is no doubt that with a further run-in the speed would be appreciably improved, and the Magna would certainly be a 70 m.p.h. car when thoroughly settled down.

The brakes were a little disappointing, as they were either out of adjustment or required further bedding down, when the stopping distance of 80 ft. which we obtained from 40 m.p.h. should be considerably improved.

[Motor Sport photograph]

A very modern motor car. The M.G. Magna on the road.

Altogether, the latest addition to the M.G. range is a very attractive high performance car, with a special appeal to the man who has to consider reliability and economy, and yet desires a car with individuality.

To anyone who can afford just that amount above standard which the "Abbey" model costs, the extra outlay is certainly well worth while, the price being £298.

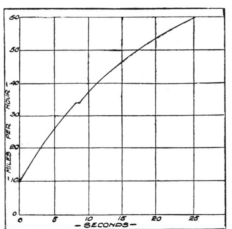

Acceleration graph of the Magna.

NEW TARGA FLORIO COURSE.

OWING to the terrific landslides of the last year, a modified circuit for the 1932 event has been arranged. Once more Vincenzo Florio has given evidence of his amazing energy and devotion to the sport.

Henceforth the course will consist of eight laps, much of it over new roads only just constructed, and the total distance of this classic race will be 600 kilometres. Last year the event had to be run over the old Madonie circuit which runs 146 kilometres to the lap, and the latest course will be of greater interest to spectators, besides still providing the finest test of a racing car it is possible to conceive.

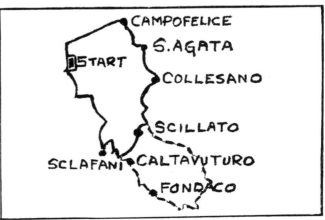

Sketch map showing the new course, with the old marked with dotted line.

POINTS OF VIEW—

G. E. T. EYSTON ON THE MIDGET AT MONTLHÉRY.

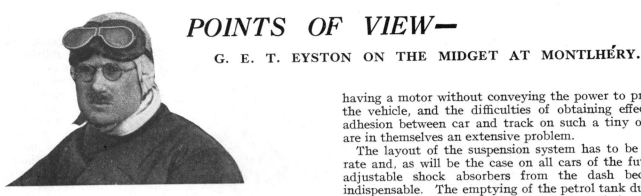

" . . . . . Results are encouraging."

NOW that a 750 c.c. engine has achieved a speed officially timed of nearly 115 m.p.h. it is interesting to look back on the development work which has been carried out during the year 1931.

On December 21st, 1930, the unsupercharged Midget did approximately 87 m.p.h. in records which were taken at Montlhéry up to 100 kilometres. In doing this it broke the existing figures set up by a supercharged model of another make, and therefore this was a good beginning on which to base the effort to attain a much sought after project—namely to be the first to attain over 100 m.p.h. when covering an 'official' distance.

A " Powerplus " supercharger was added and was chosen because of the low horsepower required to drive it, as with a considerable boost this is of extreme importance. It was necessary to insure an engine performance which would give adequate power to pull a higher gear ratio, the maximum revolutions of the engine remaining the same as with atmospheric aspiration.

For particular reasons it was imperative to continue record breaking under wintry conditions, and owing to the intense cold which prevailed, development work was extremely difficult. With the supercharger, however, record speeds were pushed up to 97 m.p.h. for 10 miles at the first attempt.

Certain modifications were then carried out to cope with the low temperature at the carburetter intake and these proved very efficacious.

On February 16th, 1931, the 5 kilometre record was broken at 103 m.p.h. and others at 102 m.p.h., thus the car was the first to achieve the 100 m.p.h. mark and this constituted a milestone in the history of motoring.

The supercharger arrangement in particular has proved its worth in many important competitions during 1931.

1st, 3rd, 7th and 10th in the R.A.C. Tourist Trophy Race, Belfast, being an example, as well as an average of over 92 m.p.h. for 500 miles in the famous B.R.D.C. Race, and the Team prize as well.

Before the racing was over for the season, however, attention was again directed to record breaking, the ambitious plan being to cover over 100 miles in the hour. This may not sound easy on a 750 c.c. engined car, and not so long ago one would have been thought mad to attempt it. It means that the whole car must be 100%. It goes without saying that the engine must run at full bore without losing its tune, and there must be a reserve of power when doing over 100 m.p.h. But it is no good

having a motor without conveying the power to propel the vehicle, and the difficulties of obtaining effective adhesion between car and track on such a tiny outfit are in themselves an extensive problem.

The layout of the suspension system has to be first rate and, as will be the case on all cars of the future, adjustable shock absorbers from the dash become indispensable. The emptying of the petrol tank during the run on such an occasion constitutes a little worry in itself, and this has to be taken care of in the adjustable strength of the suspension.

The class of lubricant used in the engine must be of the highest quality, and additional provision for cooling the oil a *sine qua non*.

It so happened that a model after the style of the Tourist Trophy winner was used for the attempt with the standard sized blower as employed on the road racers. Therefore, the car was in no way a freak. In this way success represented a sheer speed and endurance test for what was virtually a standard production model, and thus its value was increased twofold.

On the 25th of September, 1931, the attack was made.

A gentle start, until things got warmed up to it, meant that after quarter of the distance had been covered the car had to lap Montlhéry track at about 104 m.p.h. continuously.

Actually over 101 miles were covered in the hour and although the driver had an anxious time watching all the instruments and manipulating the controls, the run was accomplished with the greatest regularity.

This only went to prove that development of the 750 c.c. car had reached an advanced stage, sufficient in fact for all practical purposes.

What the ultimate speed of a 750 c.c. engine would be in 1931 was somewhat intriguing, and in order to get some idea of this an M.G. engine was placed in a single seater chassis.

So well had the layout of this been planned that little trouble was experienced in the tuning up, so that it became possible to do over 110 m.p.h. at the first attempt.

Just before Christmas, iu spite of a further cold spell, further records were tackled up to 10 miles, with the result that close on 115 m.p.h. was attained, and this with consistency over 5 kilometres, 5 miles, 10 kilometres and 10 miles.

Whether or no these speeds can be improved remains to be seen.

Anyhow the results so far are extremely encouraging.

MOTOR SPORT ILLUSTRATIONS.

WE have many requests for copies of our drawings by R. A. Nockolds, and in view of this, we can supply copies (artists' proofs) of the reproduction of the illustration which appears on the frontispiece of this month's issue, at 2s. 6d. (signed, 5s.) Application should be made to *The Art Editor*, MOTOR SPORT.

M.G.

Four-cylinder, 57 mm. by 83 mm.
847 c.c. Tax £8.

Six-cylinder, 57 mm. by 71 mm.
1,086 c.c. Tax £12.

Six-cylinder, 57 mm. by 83 mm.
1,271 c.c. Tax £12.

THE M.G. Car Co., Ltd., is a note-worthy concern in that it has always concentrated solely on the production of sports cars, and during the past two years the company has reaped the re-

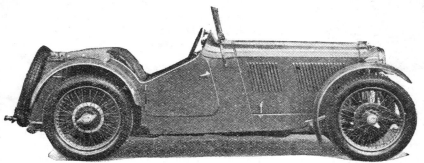

RE-DESIGNED FOR 1933.

The ever popular M.G. Midget appears in much improved form. The J2 two-seater shown here costs £199 10s.

wards of its efforts by a large number of racing successes, not to mention hosts of minor achievements in the trials world.

Last year, for example, Midgets took the five first places in the "Double-Twelve" at Brooklands; first, third and fourth places in the Dublin Grand Prix; and first and third places in the Ulster T.T.; whilst just to round off the season, M.G.s took the team prize in the B.R.D.C. 500 Miles Race.

This year the Midget has had greater difficulties to face, in that its previous successes counted against it when handi-caps were being drawn up, but, in spite of this, a Midget came home first in the recent 500 Miles Race at Brook-lands, whilst these cars took third places in both the 1,000 Miles Race and the Ulster T.T. In record work, too, the make has continued to be prominent, the famous Magic Midget, driven by George Eyston, establishing an international class record at 118.38 m.p.h. At Brook-lands, Horton has lapped the outer cir-cuit at 115.29 m.p.h., whilst Hamilton has lapped the Mountain course at over 69 m.p.h.—both 750 c.c. records.

Five cars and one chassis appear on the M.G. Stand (No. 24), and of these only one is outside the light-car limit. Vieing with each other for the greatest interest are examples of the new Magnette and the new Midget. Actually, the light-car exhibits comprise an M.G. Magnette pillarless four-door saloon with four-speed self-changing gearbox at £445, an M.G. Magnette long chassis priced at £315, one of the new M.G. J2 sports two-seaters costing £199 10s., plus £12 12s. for de luxe equipment, a J2 M.G. Midget saloonette at £255, and an M.G. Magna four-seater at £260.

The new Magnette chassis is fully de-scribed elsewhere in this issue, and its

mechanical features need not, therefore, be dealt with here. The saloon, how-ever, is a particularly interesting model and a description of its main coachwork features cannot be omitted.

Externally, the proportions are very pleasing, the gently curved lines giving the car grace without in any way de-tracting from its fast and businesslike mien. The body is noteworthy in that, although a first glance gives the appear-ance of a two-door job, it proves on

closer examination to be of the four-door pillarless type. Instead of closing on to a central pillar, the doors are posi-tioned at the top and bottom in such a way that there is no loss of rigidity in the body, and exceptional freedom of entry and exit is given.

Another pleasing feature is the slid-ing roof, which, to be in keeping with the pleasing sweep of the body, is slightly curved, and has four large cellu-loid windows let into it so that the interior is light and cheerful, no matter whether the roof is open or closed.

The front screen is of the popular single-pane type hinged at the top, and provided with a single central control, whilst winding windows are fitted in the four doors. All are of Triplex safety glass, whilst a refinement in connection with the rear window is the use of Purdah glass, which makes the fitting of a rear blind unnecessary.

An unusual feature—which, incident-

ally, is the subject of a patent—is the provision for carrying luggage. Nor-mally, the spare wheel is fitted behind the hinged rear panel, but when it is desired to carry a large quantity of luggage the wheel is taken off, when the rear panel can be let down. The wheel is then remounted close to the petrol tank, where it is quite out of the way, and leaves the hinged panel to act as a large platform for the luggage.

Above the petrol tank, the filler of which, incidentally, protrudes through the hinged panel when the latter is closed, is a large locker for tools, whilst just beneath the rear window a distinc-tive direction indicator is provided.

The interior of the car gives an im-pression of great comfort, the uphol-stery and general fittings being very tastefully executed. The front seats are of the separately adjustable bucket type, and are leather upholstered over Hair-lock combined hair and moulded rubber foundations, whilst the back seats have ordinary upholstery and are provided with an armrest on each side.

Well-equipped Facia Board.

The facia board is very tastefully arranged, and in addition to the usual instruments and two enclosed cubby-holes is provided with a rev. counter, water and oil thermometers and two neat lamps, whilst the rest of the equip-ment is on a lavish scale, and includes such items as a dual windscreen wiper and so forth.

So far as the Midget models are con-cerned, the two-seater shown is a par-ticularly businesslike little vehicle with an exceptionally good turn of speed, and should make a pronounced appeal to the open-air sporting enthusiast. The model shown has a duo-tone red panelled body.

The Midget salonette is another very pretty exhibit, with its duo-tone blue cellulose finish and blue leather uphol-stery to match, whilst the other light car on view, the four-seater sports Magna, is another car to delight the eye of the enthusiast for open cars, and is finished in duo-tone green panelled cellulose with green leather upholstery.

Altogether, a stand which must be put down on the list of every sportsman as amongst those not to be missed.

AN ENTIRELY NEW M.G. MODEL.

The M.G. Magnette, which is fully described elsewhere in this issue, shown here in pillarless saloon form. This model has a pre-selector gearbox.

THE AUTOCAR ROAD TESTS

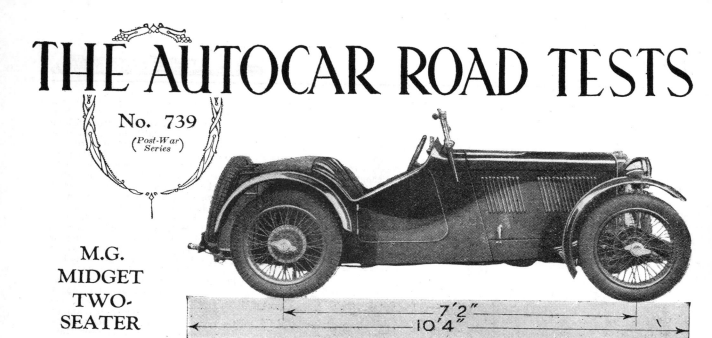

No. 739

(*Post-War Series*)

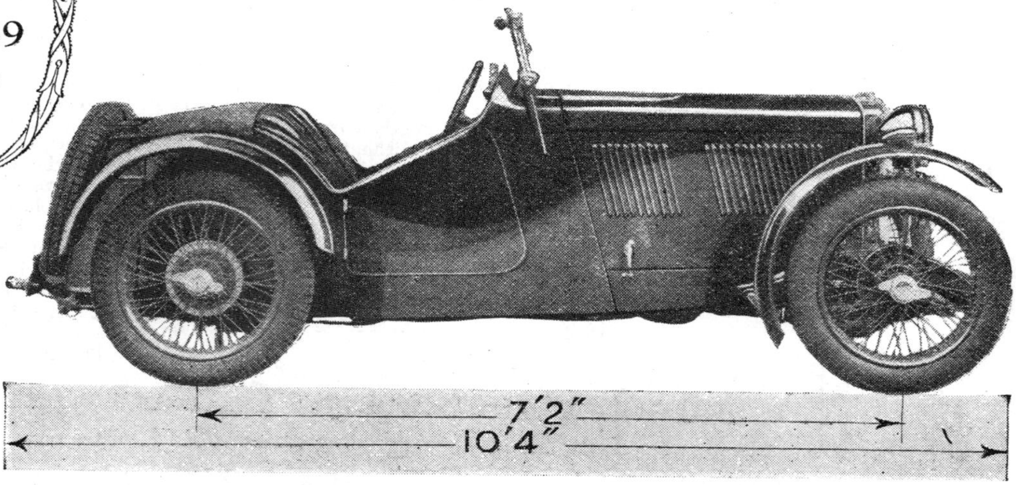

7′ 2″
10′ 4″

M.G. MIDGET TWO-SEATER

THERE is every reason to suppose that the new M.G. Midget will be a great success. The latest car, described in detail elsewhere in this issue, is a direct and logical development from the experience gained by the firm in competition work of all kinds, yet its appeal is not based solely on performance, tremendous though that is for the engine size and the price of the complete car. Comfort has been studied so carefully that it is a remarkably pleasant car to ride in, quite apart from what it is able to do.

It would naturally be expected from the mechanical modifications in this latest car that the performance would be improved as compared with its predecessor, the ordinary Midget. What is not so much expected is that the performance should have gone up to a genuine 80 m.p.h., the car still retaining tractability and flexibility at low speeds. After testing the machine for sheer performance on Brooklands track, and then observing on the road how it behaves in comparison with other much bigger vehicles, there is every reason for the driver to feel amazed at what has been achieved, and to be led into the impression that the engine must be bigger than it actually is.

Apart from speed, not only on top gear but on the indirect gears, the things that matter most about a sports car are the driving position and controls. The new Midget has a driving position which is exactly right, the back rest of the seat being sloped at a natural angle, while the pneumatic cushions for driver and passenger are separate.

The steering wheel comes within easy reach, is bigger than it was formerly, and, of course, is spring-spoked; the short, stiff gear lever is of the remote control type, with a visible gate; the racing type central hand-brake lever is where it should be; in front of the driver is a big, clear dial, consisting of a combined speedometer and rev. counter, the latter applying to top and third gears, and each of the controls works with a minimum pressure of hand or foot.

The charm of the car to the enthusiast, again, is in the ability, in fact the eagerness, of the engine to turn over at extremely high revs., 5,800 r.p.m. being well within its capabilities. This means that though second and first are comparatively low gear ratios, the car gets going very snappily indeed, for it can be run up to 20 m.p.h. on first, 36 on second, and easily to 60 on third, in which connection it may be mentioned that on the cars delivered second gear will be a higher ratio, which should be a considerable improvement.

A highly commendable feature is that the speedometer read slow throughout

M.G. MIDGET TWO-SEATER

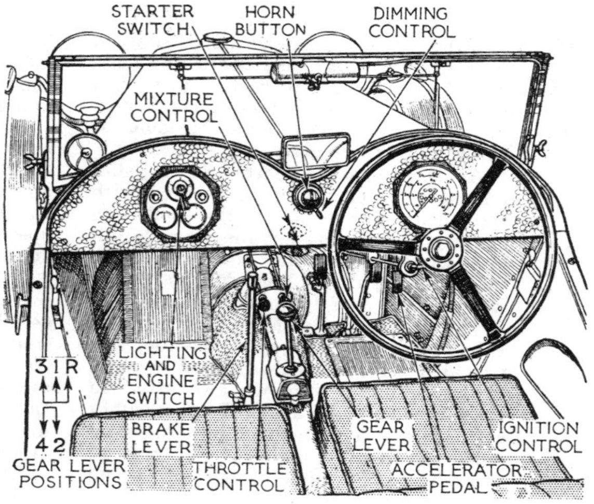

STARTER SWITCH
HORN BUTTON
DIMMING CONTROL
MIXTURE CONTROL
LIGHTING AND ENGINE SWITCH
3 1 R
4 2
GEAR LEVER POSITIONS
BRAKE LEVER
THROTTLE CONTROL
GEAR LEVER
IGNITION CONTROL
ACCELERATOR PEDAL

DATA FOR THE DRIVER

8 h.p., four cylinders, 57 × 83 mm. (847 c.c.).
Tax £8.
Wheelbase 7ft. 2in., track 3ft. 6in.
Overall length 10ft. 4in., width 4ft. 3½in., height 4ft. 4⅝in.
Tyres: 27 × 4.00in. on detachable wire wheels.

Engine—rear axle gear ratios.	Acceleration from steady speed. 10 to 30 m.p.h.	20 to 40 m.p.h.	30 to 50 m.p.h.	Timed speed over ½ mile.
19.24 to 1	—	—	—	
11.50 to 1	5⅘ sec.	—	—	
7.31 to 1	9⅘ sec.	9⅘ sec.	10⅗ sec.	
5.37 to 1	14⅗ sec.	13⅗ sec.	16 sec.	80.35 m.p.h.

Turning circle: 34ft.
Tank capacity 12 gallons, fuel consumption 35 m.p.g. (approx.).
12-volt lighting set cuts in at 12 m.p.h., 7 amps. at 30 m.p.h.
Weight: 11 cwt. 1 qr.
Price, with sports two-seater body, £199 10s.

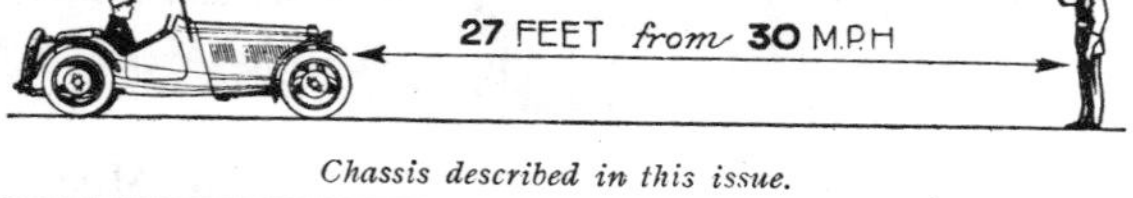

27 FEET from 30 M.P.H

Chassis described in this issue.

M.G. MIDGET TWO-SEATER

the range, and even during the timed test did not go above 78. The maximum speed and acceleration figures were taken with the windscreen folded down flat on the scuttle.

The new Midget swings along beautifully anywhere from 30 to 60 m.p.h., as conditions permit. Yet immediately the driver wishes to increase the performance still more there is the extraordinarily valuable third gear which is not noisy, the change as a whole being delightful, allowing quick upward changes, though with the higher second gear the change from second to third—an important one—will become more rapid.

There is obviously speed in plenty—to a degree, in fact, which means that for the greater part of the time the car will be driven well within itself. What can be called the secondary appeal of the machine is very strong, too, because there is not that fierceness which, while it may be pleasing to the driver, is not, perhaps, regarded in the same way by a passenger.

The occupants sit well down in the car, the cushions and back rest are deep, the doors are wide and make getting in and out easy, and the real abilities of the car are still further disguised because a particularly effective form of silencer makes the exhaust note at ordinary speeds as quiet as that of many normal touring cars.

On the comfort side, again, the car is good at low as well as at high speeds, with the frictional shock

absorbers not too tightly adjusted. The steering is beautifully light and has a little caster action, the brakes are well up to their work, and the clutch takes up the drive smoothly. On top gear with the ignition retarded the engine will pull down to 8 m.p.h., which is an illustration of its flexibility, but is obviously not a thing which the owner of a car of this nature would wish to do.

From a standing start on first gear the Brooklands test hill, with its average gradient of 1 in 5, was climbed at 17 m.p.h., the speed being maintained steadily all the way up the 1 in 4 section. First gear is a low ratio on which there is an immense reserve of power for this kind of work.

Such points as pockets in the doors, a space for small luggage in the tail, and an easily erected hood and side screens for bad weather have not been neglected; it does not follow that an owner who wants high performance does not also require comfort and convenience in one and the same car. The hood is permanently secured, but is stowed out of sight in the tail beneath a neat cover held by quick-action fasteners; the big rear fuel tank is clearly most valuable, giving a range of something like 400 miles without need for replenishment, and there is a reserve supply of three gallons.

At the back the spare wheel is held securely, and the sensible mountings for the wings and head lamps are noteworthy.

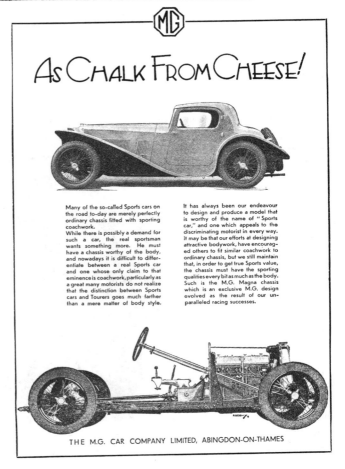

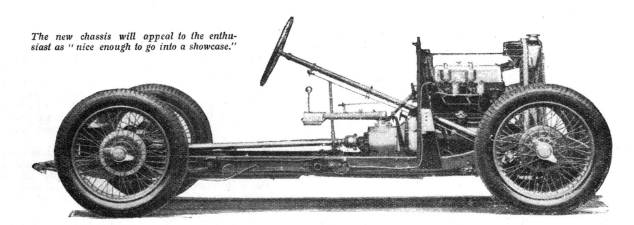

The new chassis will appeal to the enthusiast as " nice enough to go into a showcase."

A NEW M.G. MIDGET

Extremely Interesting 850 c.c. Model, Evolved from the Firm's Racing Experience, which has a Remarkably Fine Performance : Sports Two-Seater Costs £199 10s.

EVERY line of the latest model M.G. Midget shows the influence of the type's previous history in competition, for it is a curious thing but there is always something about a car which has competition behind it that is entirely different from a machine whose success has been gained along a more prosaic path.

The new 850 c.c. Midget, in fact, is a very genuine little sports car, perfectly amenable as far as ordinary touring and everyday use is concerned, but offering the enthusiast all the opportunities he requires if success in trials on the road is his chief ambition. Principally, the engine is altered, because a new type cylinder head has been adopted, with a plain, quite simple type of combustion space, but having two S.U. carburetters on the off side and the exhaust pipe on the other side, an arrangement whereby the ports, which are all separate, become direct and straightforward, allowing the incoming and exhaust gases the best possible chance to enter and depart from the combustion spaces.

Overhead, as before, is a series of valves actuated by an overhead camshaft through rockers, the design of which owes much to racing experience, and the camshaft is driven by gears in front through a shaft around which is incorporated the dynamo, the whole being based on the Montlhéry Midget's design. The change in the head has not affected the position of the plugs, which are on the off side, but are now of the small 14 mm. type, nor that of the ignition distributor, which is driven from the timing gear, but the water passages are bigger and better, there being a special external water manifold running alongside the head, whereby the cooling of the cylinder head is correspondingly improved.

The connecting rods are steel, and the pistons are of aluminium, with three rings. As to lubrication, all the bearings are fed under pressure from the usual geared pump, which sucks lubri-

cant from a ribbed sump holding roughly a gallon of oil, and made of elektron to save weight, being designed to give as much area of metal in contact with the air as possible to maintain the oil at low temperature.

As before, the engine has a large, stiff crankshaft with a plain bearing at the rear end and a special ball race at the front, the crank case itself being of cast-iron and of very sturdy construction.

The gear box now gives four speeds, a most important change, controlled by a lever set on the end of an extension so that the lever is short, stiff, and comes easily to the driver's left hand.

Wisely, the gear box has been given

From the rear the new Midget has a racing car appearance

three close ratios suitable for high speed, but a first speed with the sort of ratio suitable to the stop and restart tests of road trials, or for anything in the nature of a freak hill, a combination which has proved itself invaluable in a car which often has to serve two purposes, being used for speed trials almost as much as it is for ordinary road trials. Very little is lost by having a low-geared first when maximum performance is required, while the very presence of the low gear makes all the difference in the world for road competitions of the usual type. In conformity with modern usage, third speed is relatively silent, and helically cut gears are now standard.

The bell housing, of course, conceals a disc clutch of conventional design, and every part of the transmission bears the modifications suggested by previous competition. Since the rear axle bevel torque is taken by long half-elliptic underslung springs, the open propeller-shaft, which has two universal joints, runs in a narrow tunnel between the driver and passenger, the shaft having at its fore end a splined, sliding joint to allow for the difference of centre of swing between the axle and the propeller-shaft.

As in the earlier cars, the rear axle is of simple design, part of the weight, as well as the drive, being taken through the side shafts, and the brakes expand in ribbed drums on all four wheels, being actuated by cables with separate adjustments. There is a main adjustment, for normal use, reached easily through a trap-door.

To dissipate the heat rapidly the 9in. steel brake drums have aluminium ribs shrunk into position, while nipples are provided so that the brake cables can be greased within their casings. The hand-brake lever—and this is another point taken direct from racing—is so arranged that the pawl does not catch in the ratchet unless the trigger at the top is used, but flies forward immediately it is released.

A New M.G. Midget

Andre friction shock absorbers have been adopted. The frame is practically unaltered, compared with the Montlhéry racing type, having tubular cross-members, and being carried below the side tubes of the rear axle. At the rear there is mounted a large twelve-gallon external racing type fuel tank, for which a large quick-acting filler cap is used, the supply of fuel from this tank to the S.U. carburetters being maintained by an electric pump. A reserve of three gallons is provided.

Behind the tank, again, brackets and a steel strap arrangement carry the spare wheel in approved sports car fashion. In detail, the 17in. steering wheel has spring spokes, the combined specdometer and rev. counter instrument is of considerable size, whilst the windscreen can be folded down horizontally on the scuttle, being fitted with a suction-operated double-blade wiper.

Considerable care has been exercised to ensure not only that the driving position is natural and comfortable, but that the controls are within easy reach of the driver, both the throttle-setting knob and the mixture control for starting being carried on the extension holding the gear lever.

Rudge-Whitworth wire wheels with racing type eared nuts complete the specification—a great improvement from the enthusiast's point of view, as the speed of wheel changing is increased. The whole car is essentially fitting for its intended work; its appearance alone is sufficient attraction for most enthusiasts, appearance being almost as important as performance.

It will be noticed that the hood has been made to disappear entirely under what looks like a tonneau cover, which, in fact, conceals a most convenient compartment in which luggage can be stowed, while the bonnet is extended almost to the screen, and, when open, allows the gear box and pedal mechanism to be more accessible than usual. Also, the grouped lubricators for various chassis bearings can then be attended to with the greatest ease.

The familiar type of steering in which the rod from the drop arm passes athwart the chassis to the tie-rod arm, instead of running parallel with one frame side member in a fore and aft direction, has, of course, been retained.

As far as the steering generally is concerned there is little outward sign of any important modification, yet the steering of the car as a have is vastly improved over that of

the first 850 c.c. M.G. chassis put on the road some years ago.

A twelve-volt lighting set ensures that the head lamps shall give a beam commensurrate with the performance of the car, a six-volt system having been used hitherto, and at the same time gives an efficient reserve for the starting motor under difficult conditions.

In the ordinary way the car with the two-seater body illustrated is

How the frame is underslung at the rear.

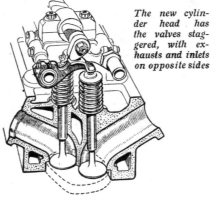

The new cylinder head has the valves staggered, with exhausts and inlets on opposite sides

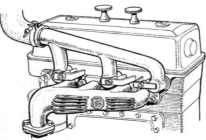

Exhaust and water manifolds.

priced at £199 10s., but for £12 12s. extra further equipment can be obtained in the shape of an electrically operated eight-day clock, an Ashby Brooklands type spring-spoked steering wheel, stone guards for the radiator and lamp glasses, an oil thermometer, the regulation bonnet strap, a racing type fuel tank filler cap with a cam and lever action, an engine thermometer, and the usual combination stop, reverse and tail lamp.

This particular model will be priced as a sports tourer at £220, and as a sports salonette—a very neat little car on modern lines and without running boards —at £255.

In addition, of course, there will be the 750 c.c. car, which will be termed the super-sports Midget, and the supercharged machine to be known as the racing Midget, both having a short-stroke crankshaft fitted to bring them within the competition class capacity limit. In the racing type each valve has three springs, the new type head is, of course used, and there is the special auxiliary oil tank governed by a float-and-needle mechanism which maintains the level of lubricant in the sump while the car is racing.

Superchargers of three different sizes, but all of the eccentric vane type, will be provided, running at three-quarter engine speed, and driven from the front end of the crankshaft, an unusual feature being that the slow running of the engine is assisted because a smaller inlet pipe conducts the gas from the supercharger to the inlet ports, while a larger pipe comes into operation when the throttle is opened. This model also has a Brooklands silencer with a special additional form of baffle making it suitable for ordinary use on the road, while the effective gear ratios usually supplied are 5.37, 7.32, 11.5, and 19.2 to 1, another difference being that the brake drums for this particular car are 12in. in diameter.

A road test of the new Midget appears on pages 251 and 253 in this issue, from which it will be seen, beyond all doubt, that the car has a remarkable performance, especially when the price of the complete machine is remembered, a maximum of 80 m.p.h. being achieved.

With its hood up

80 m.p.h. M.G. MIDGET FOR UNDER £200

A Particularly Interesting Range of Small Cars for 1933. Features Include Underslung Chassis, Two Carburetters, Improved Brakes, 12-volt Lighting and Starting, Rudge-Whitworth Wire Wheels and Better and Roomier Coachwork

A three-quarter rear view of the new 80 m.p.h. Midget two-seater sports showing the petrol tank and spare wheel mounting.

THE new M.G. Midget models were introduced on Thursday of last week at the showrooms of University Motors, Ltd., Stratton House, Piccadilly, London, W.1, who are the London distributors. The outstanding model is an 80 m.p.h. two-seater, Model J2, which sells at £199 10s., the range also including a sports four-seater, Model J1, at £220 and a salonette at £255. The 746 c.c. super-sports two-seater now known as Model J3 and the racing model, J4, are continued. Prices of these may be obtained on application.

The new 80 m.p.h. chassis has a non-supercharged 847 c.c. four-cylinder engine, the bore and stroke being as before—namely, 57 mm. and 83 mm. respectively, which gives an annual tax of £8. The successful M.G. run of racing successes is evident throughout the design. The engine has overhead valves, which are operated through a vertical drive at the forward end by the medium of spiral-bevel gears, and, as before, the dynamo is incorporated in the drive. The extra power has been obtained by the fitting of a new cylinder head, which carries the overhead camshaft and overhead valves as previously. This head is identical in design to that fitted to the famous Montlhéry model. It provides individual exhaust and inlet ports for each cylinder, emerging on opposite sides of the head. Thus, there are four separate exhaust ports on the near side, and the inlet ports are all on the off side. Special care has been given to the design of the ports, so allowing for an easy sweep to give the gases free entry to and escape from the cylinders.

There is a pair of valves for each cylinder, with their stems inclined towards one another, so reducing the distance separating the ends of the stems and allowing shorter and lighter rockers to be employed. The diameter of the inlet valves is also slightly larger than that of the exhaust valves.

With this head a high-compression ratio can be used, and the layout shows the advantages of the new type of small sparking plug, the screwed portion of which measures only 14 mm. compared with the more usual 18 mm. pattern. A special water manifold is also fitted, which has three connections to the water jacket on the near side of the head.

Other features in the design include steel connecting rods, aluminium pistons with three rings, pressure lubrication and a ribbed sump made of Electron. The latter holds approximately one gallon of oil, but owing to its special

(Above) Another view of the 80 m.p.h. two-seater which does over 60 m.p.h. on third gear. Note the cutaway doors. (Left) A close-up of the facia showing the large combined speedometer and revolution counter, and the remote gear control.

shape provides the maximum cooling area to the lubricant, thus allowing a low temperature to be maintained.

The fuel is fed by two S.U. carburetters, which draw their supply by means of an S.U. electric pump from a 12-gallon rear petrol tank, on the top of which is a two-way tap giving a three-gallon reserve supply. The mixture and throttle controls are conveniently placed on the extension carrying the gear lever. Cooling is by thermo-siphon; in the case of the J3 model a fan is also included, and on the special racing model a water pump is fitted in addition.

The exhaust gases are led away from the forward end into a large-capacity expansion chamber mounted amidships, and the exhaust pipe is carried clear of the rear of the car.

All models have four-speed gearboxes of the twin-top type, with helical gears for the constant mesh and third-speed pinions. The gear change is centrally placed, and a neat, short lever is mounted on an extension of the gearbox

so that the driver can change gear without leaning forward in his seat.

On the new model in question the ratios are 5.37, 7.32, 11.5 and 19.2 to 1, with a reverse gear of the same ratio as the first speed. All models, except the special racing type, which has a two-plate dry clutch, have single-plate dry clutches and Hardy Spicer propeller shafts with metal universal joints at each end. The back axle is a straightforward, three-quarter floating pattern.

The chassis is a special underslung design, being built up with tubular cross-members and extremely rigid. The side-members are taken under the rear axle and the front is upswept over the

individual adjustment for all four wheels. Other features of this interesting chassis include a 12-volt Rotax lighting and starting system, Rudge-Whitworth wire wheels with Dunlop 19-in. by 4.00-in. tyres, Marles steering gear adjustable for rake, and a spring-spoked steering wheel.

The attractive new two-seater will accommodate a 6-ft. driver with com-

hood is of the concealed type and behind the squab there is accommodation for quite a good-size suitcase. The tank is mounted at the rear of the back panel, being held in position by sturdy straps, and on the back of the tank a spare wheel is carried and secured in the approved racing style by a triangulated metal band.

The bonnet is taken right up to the scuttle, and so, when it is raised, one can also gain access to the wiring, the brake, clutch and accelerator pedals ; in fact, all controls are rendered very accessible for any adjustment that may be needed.

The scuttle is upswept from the bonnet and is so designed as to form an air-deflecting medium when the single-panel windscreen is folded forward on the bonnet. The windscreen, incidentally, is fitted with a suction wiper, which operates two squeegees. The instrument board is particularly neat. In the centre, only two or three inches away from the rim of the steering wheel, is the horn button and the dimming switch. To the right, in full view of the driver, is a Smith 5-in. combined speedometer and revolution counter,

(Above) The four-seater M.G. Midget and (right) the sliding-roof salonette.

front axle. Thus, the complete car is wonderfully low, and it is possible for a driver of normal stature to touch the ground when seated. The chassis is lubricated by Tecalemit grease gun, the nipples being neatly grouped on the back of the dash wall. Suspension fore and aft is by underslung semi-elliptic springs, which are flat under load, while the springs are mounted in phosphor-bronze slides at their rear extremities in place of shackles. Hartford shock absorbers are fitted front and rear, the latter being mounted in transverse fashion.

The four-wheel brakes can be operated either by pedal or lever and operate in 9-in. drums, which have shrunk-on aluminium cooling ribs. The lever is of the racing type; that is to say, it only locks on when the driver presses the knob at the top of the lever. Quick, single-point adjustments are provided for both foot and hand brake, besides

fort, and also provides plenty of elbow-room for both occupants ; in fact, the excellence of the seating accommodation is one of the outstanding features. The seat cushions have a pneumatic foundation, the squab is sufficiently high to afford ample support for the shoulders, and, owing to the sloping design of the doors, both driver and passenger have unlimited freedom of movement. The

with the figures in white on a black background. To the left, grouped in a neat panel, are the Lucas lighting and starting switch, and the ammeter and oil gauge.

There are no side shields to the wings, for it has been found under test that the type of wing now adopted affords very good protection. An interesting feature, also, is the interposition of rubber discs between the wings and their point of attachment. The headlamps are actually carried on the front wing stays, but, so as to keep the whole ensemble absolutely rigid, these brackets are united by a tubular stay.

On the same chassis the sports four-seater is very roomy and attractive in outline. The instrument board in this case is of different design and provides an enclosed cubby-hole on the near side, while on the off side, so as to make the appearance symmetrical, is a dummy on which is mounted the combined horn push and dimming switch. Here the instruments are grouped centrally.

The salonette is also a particularly attractive car, outstanding features of which are a sliding roof with transparent slats and a rear panel which hinges down to form a means of carrying luggage. Both these models have a six-gallon rear fuel tank.

There is a wide range of colours, and Triplex glass is standardized on all models.

Two views of the four-cylinder o.h.c. engine which is equipped with two S.U. carburetters.

A NEW 80 M.P.H. M.G. MIDGET

PROBABLY the most remarkable progress in automobile practice in recent years has been in the small car field, and to this development a considerable contribution has been made by the M.G. concern. Taking full advantage of the lessons to be learnt from competitions, they have continually entered their cars in races of every description, both at home and abroad, using the data obtained in this way to bring their models to an ever increasing pitch of efficiency.

Now they have surpassed their previous efforts by producing a new M.G. Midget, with an engine capacity of 850 c.c., which, unsupercharged, is capable of a genuine 80 m.p.h.

We recently accepted the kind invitation of the M.G. concern to put the car through its paces for the benefit of our readers, but before going on to an account of our experiences on the road, let us consider the mechanical aspects of this remarkable little machine.

The principal alteration in the engine is the new cylinder head, having the inlet ports on the offside, and the exhaust, with four separate ports, on the nearside. The great advantage of this new design is that the gases have a straight through passage, enabling them to be drawn into and expelled from the combustion chamber with the minimum of delay. Mixture is supplied by two S.U. horizontal carburettors.

The stiff crankshaft, as before, is carried in a ball-race at the front end, and a large white metal bearing at the rear. The connecting rods are steel, and the pistons are made of aluminium, with three rings. The ribbed sump, cunningly shaped to offer the maximum cooling area, is made of Elektron, and holds approximately one gallon of oil. Lubrication is, of course, pressure throughout by a geared pump.

Another improvement lies in the new water manifold, which, in conjunction with bigger water passages, considerably improves the cooling of the head, an important point in an engine capable of a very high speed.

The overhead valves are operated by the usual M.G. overhead cam shaft, driven by a vertical shaft around which is incorporated the dynamo. Although the cylinder head is of different design it has not affected the position of the plugs which, however, are of 14 mm. diameter instead of the usual 18 mm. pattern. Ignition is by a 12 volt Rotax coil and battery system, and the distributor is driven from the timing gear.

A single plate dry clutch is used, and a great improvement has been made in the fitting of a 4-speed gear box, giving the following ratios 1st, 19.2 to 1 ; 2nd, 11.5 to 1 ; 3rd, 7.32 to 1 ; top, 5.37 to 1. Third and top are of the constant mesh twin-top type, while the gear change is by remote control with a short stiff lever situated right beside the driver.

A Hardy-Spicer propellor shaft with metal universal joints takes the drive to the normal three-quarter floating type back axle.

The chassis is a very rigid piece of work, with tubular cross members while the side members pass under the rear axle, but are upswept over the front axle. It is interesting to note that the loading line of the chassis is only 11 inches from the ground, thereby ensuring extraordinarily good road holding qualities. The springs are flat underslung semi-elliptics, swivelling at the front ends, and mounted in phosphor

---

The M.G. Midget Range.

J.1 Model. 4 cyl., 57 x 83 m.m., capacity 847 c.c., 2-seater body, disappearing hood, exterior rear petrol tank. Chassis price £175. Complete car £199 10s.

J.2 Model. Engine as above. Four-seater body. Chassis price as J.1. Complete car £220.

J Model. Engine as above. Salonette body. Chassis price as J.1. Complete car £255.

J.3 Model. 4-cyl., 57 x 75 m.m. Capacity 746 c.c. Suitable for moderate supercharging with Powerplus blower, geared down.

J.4 Model. 4-cyl., 57 x 75 m.m. Capacity 746 c.c. Specially produced for racing and competition and supplied with No. 8 or 9 Powerplus Blower.

On all models the tax is £8, wheelbase 7' 2", track 3' 6".

bronze slides at the rear. Andre shock absorbers are fitted as standard.

The brakes have 9in. drums, with aluminium cooling ribs, and are cable operated. Racing practice

A near side view of the engine.

is again apparent in the unusual hand-brake ratchet, which only works when the button at the top of the lever is depressed. A main, as well as individual, adjustment is provided, while the chafing of cables is eliminated by a special provision of greasing within their casings.

Steering is of the Marles type, and a large rear petrol tank, holding 12 gallons, from which the fuel is delivered by an electric pump, completes the specification.

When we took over the car from the luxurious showrooms of University Motors Ltd., the London Distributors of M.G. cars, we were immediately struck by the genuinely racing appearance of this new Midget. The car is really low, and beautifully proportioned, and possesses that sturdy, workmanlike appearance which can only result from actual participation in racing events. Wire grilles over the headlamps, a folding windscreen, a combined speedometer and rev. counter, two raised fairings above the dash for driver and passenger, racing type Rudge-Whitworth wheels, a really practicable disappearing hood, the exterior rear tank, with a quick-acting filler cap, and a strong spare wheel mounting behind the tank are all details which in the case of the new Midget are not merely ornaments. Incidentally, there is ample room for luggage in the rear compartment, and we noticed the useful feature of the tool kit being strapped securely to the floor.

The driving position makes one feel completely at home, the placing of the steering wheel, gear lever and hand brake being ideal, while our only criticism was that the ignition lever, which is mounted some way down the steering column, might with advantage be placed on the steering wheel boss.

Leaving Town for Brooklands, we were greatly impressed by the liveliness of the wonderful little engine. This, coupled with the small overall size of the car, and light steering, make the new Midget the fastest possible car in traffic.

On the Kingston by pass, with the windscreen folded flat, we settled down to an easy cruising speed of 60 m.p.h., at which speed the car conveyed the feel of working well within its capacity. After a check at a cross-roads, we found the acceleration of the car all that could be desired, the engine displaying an almost uncanny willingness to rev. up to an unlimited maximum. Actually, we reached 5,800 r.p.m. on several occasions, while 60 m.p.h. can be reached with ease on third gear. Second gear we found to be rather low, necessitating a distinct pause on the change up, but we are informed that on production models this ratio will be raised.

Beyond Esher the winding road gave us plenty of opportunities of testing the cornering qualities of the car, and no matter how fast we took the Midget round sharp corners and fast bends, the driver maintained a sense of complete security. On one occasion this procedure provided us with a vital proof of the efficiency of the brakes, for we were suddenly confronted with the spectacle of a

large and heavy lorry slowly passing an equally large farm wagon. Thanks to the powerful M.G. brakes, we need only say that we are alive to tell the tale.

And so to the Track, where we proceeded to put in a few laps at high speed. We were informed by some attendants that there would be a strong headwind blowing against us down the Railway Straight, mitigating our chances of attaining the ultimate maximum of the car over the ½ mile, but in spite of this the little Midget recorded the excellent speed of 75 m.p.h. at which speed the speedometer, guaranteed by the makers to have not more than a 2% error, gave a reading of 74 m.p.h. Continuing under the lee of

This illustration shows the neat combined speedometer and rev. counter and the remote control gear lever.

the Byfleet Banking, the car gained speed, going up to 80 on every lap, a speed which we also attained on the road on our journey back to Town.

Altogether, the new M.G. Midget is a fascinating little car, of infinite possibilities, being genuinely fast but at the same time tractable and quiet in traffic. The comfort provided is that only usually found in cars of much greater overall dimensions, and at the selling price of £199 10s. should prove a complete success.

It is a comforting thought in these critical days to feel that so long as British manufacturers can turn out such cars as this new Midget, we have nothing to fear from competition from the rest of the world.

80 m.p.h. in comfort for under £200 is motoring history indeed!

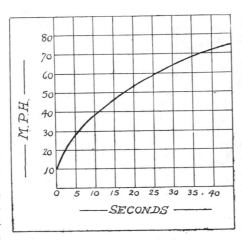

The acceleration curve of the M.G. Midget.

AN ENTIRELY NEW 1,086 c.c. M.G. S

Exclusive Illustrated Description of a Particularly Interesting High-effic
Form. Features Include an Overhead-camshaft Power Unit, Three Car

THE range of highly-efficient and successful sports cars produced by the M.G. Car Co., of Abingdon-on-Thames, has been extended by the introduction of an entirely new 1,086 c.c. six-cylinder chassis which is available in unsupercharged and supercharged form.

There are three types of this new K series to be known as the Magnette. The K1 saloon is priced at £445, and has the Wilson patent self-changing gearbox. The K1 tourer, priced at £385, is also available with this gearbox at £25 extra. The chassis price is £315. Then there is the K2, which has a conventional twin-top gearbox and sells in chassis form at £315, and as a two-seater at £360. K3 is a racing model with the self-changing gearbox as standard. The prices are £595 and £695 in unsupercharged and supercharged form respectively, and the chassis sell at £475 and £575 respectively.

The overhead-camshaft engine of this series is entirely new and was primarily designed for supercharging, consequently there is a very big margin of safety as produced in unsupercharged form. In other words, it is not a "hotted-up" touring car power unit but a racing engine adapted for everyday sporting and touring purposes.

Rated at 12.08 h.p. and carrying an annual tax of £12, the engine, which is three-point mounted, has a capacity of 1,086 c.c., the bore and stroke dimensions being 57 mm. and 71 mm. respectively. It incorporates many of the features that have contributed to the numerous M.G. racing successes. Thus the overhead-valve rocker gear follows on the lines of the racing M.G. Midget, the vertical drive for the overhead camshaft in front of the engine incorporating the dynamo. The cylinder head is also similar to the racing engine and provides for individual exhaust and inlet ports on opposite sides of the block, the port design allowing for an easy sweep to give the gases free entry to and escape from the cylinders. There are two exhaust manifolds, the outlet pipes from which lead into a large-diameter pipe, the spent gases then being led into a Burgess "straight-through" silencer which eliminates back pressure and reduces

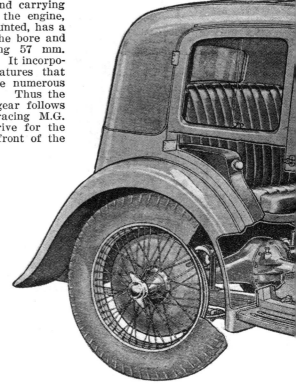

noise to a minimum. The racing model is equipped with an external exhaust system conforming with Brooklands regulations, but if the car is required for normal use a silencing tube is fitted in the expansion chamber.

An interesting feature is the manner in which the valves for each cylinder have their stems inclined towards one another, thereby reducing the distance separating the ends of the stems and allowing lighter and shorter rockers—which have springs between them to prevent rattle—to be used. Double valve springs are fitted. The plugs are located in a practically horizontal position, and have a screwed portion of 14 mm. as against the usual 18 mm. dimension.

A statically and dynamic-

Another view of the four-door saloon body showing the ease of entry and exit provided by the pillarless construction. The car is exceptionally roomy and features include a Purdah glass rear window, sliding windows, telescopic ashtrays in the armrests and recessed interior door handles.

...VITH SELF-CHANGING GEARBOX

...to be Known as the Magnette, and Available also in Supercharged ...Underslung Frame, Large Brake Drums and Very Attractive Bodywork

Cooling is by pump with an R.P. thermostat in the top water pipe, and the film-type radiator has a large header tank. Ignition is supplied by a B.T.H. polar inductor-type magneto, driven by skew gearing enclosed in a box at the forward end of the engine, and the sliding pinion drive 12-volt starter is spigoted into the

end of the crankshaft. The blower, which incorporates reduction gearing, turns at approximately three-quarter engine speed.

As previously mentioned in the introduction, model K1 is fitted with a four-forward-speed pre-selector gearbox, constructed under the well-known Wilson patents. It differs in several respects, however, from the

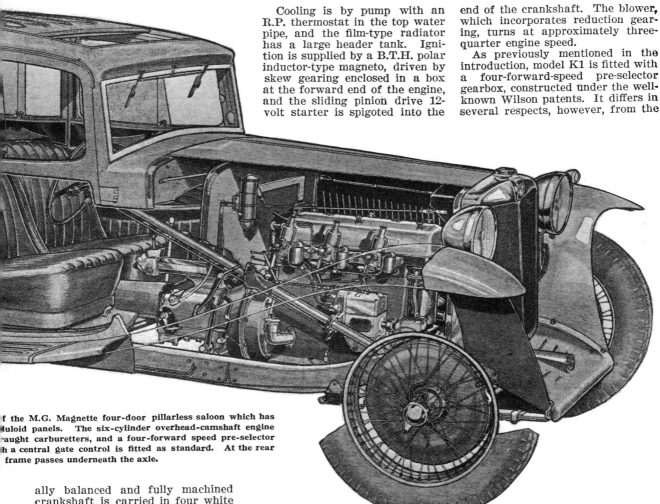

...f the M.G. Magnette four-door pillarless saloon which has ...luloid panels. The six-cylinder overhead-camshaft engine ...aught carburetters, and a four-forward speed pre-selector ...h a central gate control is fitted as standard. At the rear ...frame passes underneath the axle.

ally balanced and fully machined crankshaft is carried in four white metal-lined bearings, the two intermediate ones being of stamped steel white-metalled direct. The H-section connecting rods are specially heat-treated for strength and three-ring aluminium-alloy pistons are used.

It is only natural to find that very careful attention has been paid to lubrication, a forced-feed system being employed throughout. The gear-type pump is enclosed in an external casing low down at the forward end of the sump and a large oil filter is interposed between the pump and the feed to the main bearings. Further to ensure adequate cooling of the lubricant, the large-capacity Elektron sump is copiously ribbed in a longitudinal direction. A large and accessible oil filler is located on the off side and alongside it a dip-rod.

clutch housing on the near side. On the K3 racing model all circuits are wired and fused separately.

On the non-supercharged models three semi-down-draught S.U. carburetters are fitted, fuel being fed to them by an S.U. electric Petrolift. The K1 saloon has an 11-gallon tank with a reserve supply of two gallons, and a 12-gallon tank is fitted on the two-seater. Supercharged models have a single large-bore S.U. carburetter, with a patented twin-induction system; two Petrolifts are standard with a change-over switch, and the fuel lines are duplicated. The supercharger supplied is a Powerplus which is of the eccentric vane type and driven off the front

similar type of box fitted on other makes, for it incorporates an ingenious arrangement of brakes on the epicyclic mechanism, which causes them to operate on a servo principle, giving a strong grip when driving and a weaker grip when the car overruns the engine. Thus the need for an artificial coupling between the engine and gearbox is eliminated. The gear ratios are 5.78, 7.77, 11.56 and 19.7 to 1. A full description of this E.N.V.-produced gearbox appears on page 435.

The control for other models of the self-changing gearbox have been fitted either on top of the steering column or just under the wheel. With the M.G., however, the control consists of a small spring-bladed lever operating in a central notched gate so designed that it is impossible to miss a gear when changing up or down.

On the K2 two-seater and racing model the transmission system is conventional, a two-plate large-diameter clutch and close-ratio four-forward-speed box in unit construction being used. The clutch has been specially designed to prevent wear on the clutch fingers, which have balance weights, so that they are unaffected by centrifugal force. Effective provision has also been made to prevent oil gaining access to the clutch linings. The ratios of this gearbox, which has helical teeth for constant-mesh and third-speed pinions, are 4.78, 6.52, 9.56 and 19.12

to a point which is level with the centre of the side members. It is rigidly braced with tubular cross-members with a tubular steel brace at the rear. The chassis is equipped with a semi-grouped Tecalemit system of lubrication, with the nipples located in convenient positions.

Suspension is by flat semi-elliptic springs fore and aft, these being supplemented in their action by Andre friction-type shock absorbers mounted transversely. The springs

are anchored in a normal manner at the front ends, but at the rear they are carried in phosphor-bronze slides. Check straps are fitted to the rear axle.

Both foot and hand brakes operate on all four wheels, but the systems are entirely independent of each other; operation is in both instances by cable. The heavily ribbed drums, 13 ins. in diameter, are of Elektron with chromium-cast-iron liners. Brake shoes are also Elektron castings, with a back plate of the same material, special provision being made to trap and fling out any water that may gain access to the drums during washing. It is also impossible for grease to find its way on to the linings, a special design of oil thrower being incorporated. The brake shoes have rollers at the cam ends, these being operated by a constant-rate cam.

The steering gear is of the well-known Marles-Weller type, with the column, surmounted by a 17-in. three-arm spring-spoked wheel, adjustable for rake. A divided track rod, for which many advantages are claimed, and the front axle are patented M.G. features.

The chassis is carried on Rudge-Whitworth racing-type wire wheels with splined hubs and knock-off caps. Fort Dunlop tyres are standard, the long chassis being fitted with 4.75-in. by 19-in. covers and the short chassis with 4.40-in. by 19-in. tyres.

to 1. On the K2 racing model the ratios are according to the back-axle ratio selected.

On all models the drive from the gearbox is by a Hardy Spicer open propeller shaft with metal universal joints. With the exception of the racing model, which has a straight bevel final drive, the others have spiral-bevel final drive. A dip-rod enables one readily to ascertain the oil level in the differential.

The frame is of special underslung design, the parallel side members passing under the rear axle and being upswept over the front axle, the dumbirons curving downwards

(Above and right) Showing the ingenious scheme whereby the spare wheel can be alternatively mounted in the event of luggage being carried on the platform formed by the lid of the boot. Note also the neat direction indicator.

(Left) The exhaust side of the engine, showing the two branch outlets, the large oil filter, the dynamo, and storage for the jack and wheel hammer.

The dimension are: length, 12 ft. 6 ins.; width, 4 ft. 10 ins.; wheelbase, 9 ft. (two-seater and racing model, 7 ft. 10 ins.); track, 4 ft.

Perhaps the most interesting model of the K series is the four-door saloon on the K1 chassis, which sells at £445. It is a splendidly proportioned car of really artistic appearance, in which lines, however,

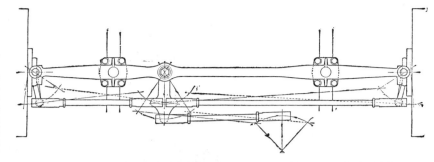

The front axle and divided track rod are patented features of the M.G. Magnette. The design gives very definite positioning of the wheels and is a contributory feature to the exceptional road-holding and cornering.

have not been sacrificed for comfort. The radiator is of the well-known M.G. type, but is set at less slope in comparison to other models of the Magna. The front of the car is neatly encased by a metal fairing and the wings, which have a V-shaped front edge, are nicely swept down into the curved metal-slatted running boards.

A Pillarless Saloon

Externally the body looks as though it is of the two-door type, for only one handle is visible on each side of the car. The body, as a matter of fact, is of the pillarless type and constructed under Dcste patents. The doors are positioned top and bottom and in every way the structure is just as rigid and free from rattle as though pillars were used. Door handles are, of course, fitted on the inside of the rear doors, being recessed within oval-shaped holes. Sliding windows are fitted all round and the rear window, which is of sensible proportions, is glazed with Purdah glass, so making the fitting of a rear blind unnecessary. A sliding roof with four large celluloid inserts is standard, and the roof, like the rear panel, has a very nicely curved line.

An Ingenious Scheme for Carrying Luggage

The back panel is taken right out to the edge of the wings and incorporates a very ingenious scheme for carrying luggage, which is the subject of a patent. Normally, the spare wheel is mounted externally, but when luggage is to be carried the spare wheel is removed, the locker lid is hinged down and the spare wheel is remounted close up against the back of the petrol tank. It is thus completely out of the way and enables the whole space on the lid to be utilized for luggage. The petrol filler orifice projects through the panel, and just above the tank is a capacious locker for carrying tools. Another interesting feature is the incorporation of a direction indicator in the panel just underneath the rear window. This consists of arrows pointing left and right respectively with the letters M.G. in the centre, which are illuminated to form a " stop " light.

Good Equipment and Furnishing

Due to the pillarless construction of the body, it is a particularly easy matter to get into or out of either compartment. The front seats are of the separate adjustable armchair type and have leather upholstery over Hairlock combined hair and moulded rubber founda-

tions. The back seat is in ordinary upholstery, with an armrest on each side, the latter being fitted with telescopic ashtrays at their forward edges. In the rear quarters are combined mirror and ladies' companions, and there is an interior roof light. The woodwork throughout is of walnut, and on the nicely balanced facia board, at each end of which is an enclosed cubby hole, there is a central panel carrying an 80 m.p.h. speedometer, clock, water and oil thermometers, ammeter, two dash lamps, oil gauge, a revolution counter, which is driven off the rear end of the camshaft, and the usual lighting and starting switches, which are controlled by a Yale key.

A combined horn button, dimming switch and direction indicator control is fitted on the steering column, just underneath the wheel, and the normal M.G. controls have been very much improved. This has been effected by completely enclosing within an aluminium tunnel all the control rods operating the mixture, ignition, etc. Thus there are very neat octagonal-headed levers protruding from the tunnel which operate the ignition, mixture and slow-running controls and serve to turn off the petrol, or, alternatively, to switch over to the reserve supply. The gear lever operating the self-changing box, as previously mentioned, is also fitted on this exten-

sion. Two batteries are fitted, these being carried one on each side of the axle and being accessible by raising the rear floorboards.

Other features of a very comprehensive equipment include an electric windscreen wiper which operates two squeegee arms, driving mirror, special brackets for the fitting of bumpers, if so desired, and a handle-operated single-pane screen which works a self-tightening chain and thereby enables one to open the windscreen to its fullest extent.

Open Models

The K2 two-seater model has cutaway doors and is identical in outline to that fitted on the 1,250 c.c. Magna chassis. Features include a flared scuttle, a windscreen that folds down flat, a large external petrol tank and rigid side screens. On this model the speedometer and revolution counter are combined.

The K3 racing model is supplied with a body to comply with international racing conditions and has a variety of extra equipment.

A short run at the wheel of the saloon model served to demonstrate that the performance is outstanding, the speeds obtainable on third and top gears respectively being in excess of 60 m.p.h. and 75 m.p.h. Steering and road-holding are also particularly good.

TWO TRANSMISSION DEVELOPMENTS
A New Singer Gearbox and Self-changing Gearbox Available on the Crossley Ten

ALL Singer models for 1933 are equipped with four-forward-speed gearboxes with silent second and third gears. Another interesting feature in this concern's programme is the introduction of two new models on the Nine Sports chassis, viz., an open four-seater and a coupé. The chassis specification includes a " hot spot " manifold, twin carburetters, remote control gearbox, long steering column, Brooklands spring-steering wheel, radiator stoneguard, Rudge-Whitworth wire wheels with self-locking hubs, Andre shock absorbers, special Brooklands

instruments, revolution counter, and special silencing system.

Both models have long bonnets, while features of the coupé include furniture hide upholstery, sliding roof, safety glass all round, ashtrays, roof light, walnut cappings, and sliding bucket seats with folding backs.

Crossley Motors, Ltd., announce that their 10 h.p. range can be fitted with the Wilson patent four-speed pre-selector self-changing gearbox at an extra charge of £20. This box is of E.N.V. manufacture and is fully described on page 435.

A NEW 1,086 c.c. M.G. MAGNA

Prices Range from £285 to £345

AN entirely new six-cylinder M.G. Magna, to be known as the L type, is announced by the M.G. Car Co., of Abingdon - on - Thames. The engine is rated at 12.08 h.p. and carries an annual tax of £12. The bore and stroke dimensions are 57 mm. and 71 mm. respectively, this being the same as the Magnette. Right throughout the design is noteworthy for the features that have contributed to the long list of M.G. racing successes. It has an exceptionally sturdy four-bearing crankshaft machined all over; the valves are overhead and operated through fingers by an overhead camshaft, the drive for which is situated in front of the engine and has the dynamo interposed.

The cylinder head provides for individual exhaust and inlet ports on opposite sides of the block, the port design permitting an easy sweep to give the gases free entry to and escape from the cylinder. There are two exhaust manifolds, the outlet pipes from which lead into a large diameter pipe, the spent gases being expelled through a Burgess straight-through silencer which provides an effective degree of silence and at the same time eliminates back pressure. Other features of the engine design include three-ring aluminium pistons,

A chassis view of the new M.G. Magna, which is underslung at the rear and upswept in the front. The semi-elliptic springs are also underslung.

The fuel tank is situated externally at the rear, and fuel is fed to the engine by electric pump, which supplies twin S.U. semi - down - draught automatic piston-type carburetters, provided with mixture and slow-running controls placed within easy reach of the driver. The reserve supply is controlled by a two-way tap.

The transmission system comprises a two-plate large-diameter clutch, which, with the gearbox, is in unit with the engine. The gearbox provides four forward speeds and has a remote central control. From the gearbox the drive is by means of a Hardy Spicer propeller shaft with metal universal joints at each end to a three-quarter floating spiral-bevel rear axle.

Other items in the specification include Marles Weller steering gear.

cable-operated four-wheel brakes with 12-in. drums, and Rudge-Whitworth detachable racing-type wire wheels fitted with Dunlop Fort tyres. The track is 3 ft. 6 ins. and the wheelbase is 7 ft. 10 ins.

Altogether, three models are listed—a tourer at £299, a two-seater at £285 and a saloon at £345.

Regarding the tourer, the body width across the outside is 1½ ins. more than on the F type, while the seats are more upright and more comfortable than on the particular model in question. Other features include a 10-gallon fuel tank, an aluminium instrument board and windswept scuttle similar to that fitted to the J2 Midget, and an outline practically identical to the M.G. Magnette K tourer.

The two-seater has a 12-gallon fuel tank and the body is the same as the J2 Midget except for the wing design.

The saloon body is of a new type, providing 4 ins. more room fore and aft in the back seats than on the F model. The front seats are of tubular framework, as on the K model, and there is also a luggage locker at the rear.

Items common to all L models are a combined speedometer and revolution counter, clock, oil thermometer, oil and petrol gauges, dipper switch, two dashlamps and electric screen wiper.

Two views of the new M.G. Magna "L" four-seater.

steel connecting rods, double valve springs and 14 mm. sparking plugs.

The lubrication system is by pressure throughout, and an oil filter is interposed between the gear-type pump and the feed to the main and big-end bearings. The Elektron sump is provided with cooling ribs and has a capacity of 1¾ gallons.

Cooling is by pump, and the water circulation system has an R.P. thermostat located in the top water pipe. Ignition is by coil.

AN "ELEVEN-HUNDRED" MAGNA

Latest Model has New Engine and Important Chassis and Coach-work Modifications

A S announced briefly in *The Autocar* last week, a new version of the popular M.G. Magna has been introduced, and one of its interesting points is that a new six-cylinder engine is used, having a capacity of 1,086 c.c., the bore and stroke being 57 by 71 mm. as compared with the 83 mm. stroke of the former type.

Apart from changes in the coachwork and important modifications to the chassis, there are many features about the latest engine worth detailing. Overhead valves, operated from an overhead camshaft, are retained, the crankshaft, which is machined all over, is exceptionally sturdy, being carried in four bearings, and there is still the arrangement whereby the drive to the camshaft is through a vertical shaft at the front of the engine, the dynamo forming part of this drive. The connecting rods are of steel and the aluminium pistons each carry three rings.

A big ribbed sump, made of the metal elektron, which has a high heat conductivity, carries approximately 1¾ gallons of oil, and between the gear-type oil pump and the feed under pressure to the main and big end bearings is a really big filter, mounted accessibly on the near side of the crank case, where it is easy to withdraw for cleaning.

A pump is used to circulate the cooling water, both inlet and outlet passages between cylinder block and radiator being at the near side of the block. Two S.U. semi-downdraught carburetters are used, the fuel tank being at the back of the car as before, and for the feed to the carburetters there is an electrically operated S.U. Petrolift.

On the near side of the engine the exhaust manifold is formed in two branches shaped so as to afford an easy exit for the gases, the pipes merging in a Burgess straight-through silencer, which is a special type used in the past, and peculiar in not possessing baffles of the ordinary kind, the degree of silencing afforded being high.

Clutch and gear box are, of course, in unit with the engine, the box is a four-speed type with remote-control lever working in a visible gate, and the hand brake lever is of the usual M.G. pattern, the brake remaining on only when the knob on top of the lever is depressed.

Allowing for the differences in dimensions, the new-type chassis, termed the L model, can be described as being on the lines of the J2 Midget, the frame

being carried under the rear axle sleeves, having deep section side-members, and braced by tubular cross-members. The springs are, of course, half-elliptics, being mounted below both front and rear axles. The track remains at 3ft. 6in. and the wheelbase at 7ft. 10in.

Latest M.G. Magna open tourer. The swept wings and running boards will be noticed.

The steering is a Marles-Weller gear, and the column, with a spring-spoked wheel, is adjustable for rake, the wheels being Rudge-Whitworth racing type with 19 by 4.50in. Dunlop Fort tyres. Grouped lubricators under the bonnet are provided for the less accessible bearings on the chassis.

Earlier modifications to the previous Magna included alterations to the cylinder head and larger brake drums, the diameter of the latter being 12in. Coil and distributor ignition is used, and there is a big twelve-volt battery carried aft of the back axle. A switch—combined with the horn button on the instrument board—cuts out the off-side head lamp for dimming purposes, the near-side lamp, which is permanently deflected towards the left-hand side of the road, remaining alight.

Equipment includes a big combined speedometer and rev counter instrument, clock, oil-pressure gauge, oil thermometer, fuel gauge, and separate external lamps lighting up the two main groups of instruments.

In the bodywork considerable changes are evident, the car gaining in appearance from its pleasing length of bonnet, besides which the scuttle is formed into two upswept cowls which are of value in deflecting wind to a certain extent when the screen is lowered. An electric screen-wiper with two blades is fitted.

The swept wings follow the style of those used for the M.G. Magnette, running boards are fitted, and, as to the open tourer, which costs £299, the extreme width of the body has been increased by 1½ inches, whilst the separate bucket seats give a more upright position than formerly. Then there is a two-seater, offered at £285, which has a twelve-gallon fuel tank instead of the ten-gallon type used for the tourer, the body being the same as that of the J2 Midget, with the exception of the new type of wings now used for the Magna.

Then there is the saloon, costing £345, with a nine-gallon tank for which the filler is carried inside the rear luggage compartment, that compartment having a slam-lock with a handle to facilitate access. Important changes in this model are that fore and aft space in the back seat has been increased by four inches, whilst for the front seats, which have spring cushions, a tubular framework is used, which again helps in conserving space. A central chain-operated device (a Cox patent) is used for opening the screen, and convenience of the back passengers is increased by the fitting of side windows in the rear quarters.

M.G. Magna L-type chassis. Front and rear springs are underslung.

MAGNETTE—ISM

Being a Powerful Force Which is Controlled With Delightful Ease in the Pre-selector M.G. Magnette

IN BRIEF.

ENGINE: *Six-cylinder, overhead valves and camshaft, 57 mm. by 71 mm. = 1,086 c.c.; tax £12; B.T.H. Polar inductor magneto; three S.U. carburetters.*

TRANSMISSION: *Pre-selector gearbox; ratios, 5.78, 7.76, 11.56 and 19.65 to 1. Open Hardy-Spicer propeller shaft to spiral bevel rear axle. (Note, also available with a two-plate dry clutch and normal four-speed gearbox; ratios, 4.78, 6.52, 9.56 and 19.12 to 1).*

GENERAL: *Wheelbase, 9 ft.; track, 4 ft; overall length, 12 ft. 6 ins.; overall width, 4 ft. 7 ins.; weight (with 5 gallons of petrol), 21 cwt. approx.*

PRICE: *(as tested) £445.*

PUT even a fairly experienced man into the cockpit of the M.G. Magnette in the middle of Piccadilly, make him drive it to Hammersmith, tell him to stop, and then ask him to let you have his impressions. He will sum them up in the one word "Disappointing."

Give him a demonstration of how an M.G. Magnette must be driven, let him take the wheel again, and then, Hey Presto! Eureka! (or whatever the appropriate phrase is), he will tell you a different story: for the secret of the Magnette—of the magnetism of the Magnette—is to drive it as a pukka sports car, ignoring (for this purpose alone) the fact that it has an ultra-comfortable pillarless saloon body and remembering that, complete with pre-selector gearbox, it is the brother of the type which will uphold the prestige of Britain in the Italian 1,000 Miles' Race.

There is only one way to get the best out of a car like this latest product of the M.G. Car Co., Ltd., and that is to keep the engine running within limits of r.p.m. which represent maximum power output. The efficient six-cylinder unit was not designed to give a walking gait in top gear; it loathes and resents treatment of this kind; nor for the matter of that is it particularly willing at 20 m.p.h. in top.

What it does like is a driver who keeps its crankshaft turning at not less than 2,000 r.p.m.; one who knows what gearbox and accelerator pedal are for and one who is not reluctant to use that knowledge wisely but without reserve.

This gives you 4,000 r.p.m. to play with—for 6,000 is a safe limit—and the tunes you can play (audibly represented by a pleasant sound of tearing calico from the exhaust) are several and varied.

Fifty in third, for example, means only 5,000 odd of those useful revs. If some Impertinent Fellow presses you unduly you can still slide up to 55 in that gear—and still have top in reserve, giving you a margin beyond 70 which is quite sufficient to meet the needs of the average situation of this kind.

Or, to suit other circumstances, you can drop from top to, say, second, the rev. counter jumping from 2,000 to 4,000 and your right foot going down with an unhesitating thrust on to the floorboards. Result, a kick in the back and a leap forward which leaves the Impertinent Fellow wondering; nor is that all. Selecting third you watch the rev. counter sweep round to the five-five mark, push your left foot hard down, ease off the accelerator a spot, pause a moment—then up with the left and down with the right and, with hardly a perceptible break in the forward urge, you are sweeping along in third in a breath-taking, exhilarating rush. . . .

Gears Are Made to USE.

And all so sweetly, so smoothly and with such a small amount of effort. *That* is the way to drive a Magnette: don't let it stagger along, use your gears, use your engine, that's what they are *for* in a thoroughbred.

Figures? Well, here are a few to be going on with and all of them obtained without slipping the epicyclic gearbands and thus stealing a few odd seconds. Rest to 30 m.p.h. (using first and second), 10 secs. Not so bad this, because the engine revs. are mostly the wrong side of the 2,000 mark. Rest to 50 m.p.h., using first, second and third, 28 secs.

Sixty is a very comfortable cruising speed by the way. It is easily reached, and if a hill is so long and steep that the revs. begin to fall, slip the gear lever to third, keep the right foot hard down and give the "clutch" pedal the requisite kick. No sound no jerk—just a sudden, very pleasing degree of acceleration.

How long will a Magnette stand this kind of thing? Well, it can be treated more gently and with only slightly less satisfactory results, but it seems to appreciate being caned—it gives you that impression—and

(Above) The off side of the engine showing the three very businesslike carburetters, also the handy way in which the jack and so on are disposed. (Below) "Pillarless luxury" adequately describes the interior of the body.

buretters whilst on the other side a similar lever operates the advance and retard. On the end of the extension there are the slow-running knob and the petrol-tap knob. All so businesslike and so compact. And note how that cunning

motive is incorporated in this, that and the other. They're proud of the famous Octagon at Abingdon.

The facia board is a book in itself. Rev. counter, speedometer, oil gauge, temperature thermometer, switches—they're all there and all made to be easily seen and to provide useful information or to perform essential service.

They're not satisfied with the Magnette yet; experiments and tests are still going forward. An ordinary mortal, however, finds little to criticize: in fact, he wonders just what the Magnette will be like when they've finished these mysterious rites at the Sign of the Octagon.

(Above) The pre-selector remote control which incorporates other controls as well. (Below) How access is gained to the rear locker.

if this is so it should be capable of standing up to these driving methods as long as you like.

The Magnette has the look of a thoroughbred—low built, semi-streamlined, almost squat, but it also has the look of a very comfortable closed carriage, which it is. Seating four easily, plenty of head and elbow room, luxurious equipment, including a bewildering array of instruments, gadgets and what-nots, it represents really de luxe fast motoring on four wheels (No, sir, never on two, for on corners it sits down because it has been designed to keep all its wheels on the road all the time).

The brakes are good—they have to be and they are —the steering is rock steady and true and the suspension, hard below 20 m.p.h., smooths out wonderfully as the speed rises.

The controls are fascinating. The gear-lever is, of course, the first pre-selector arranged after the manner of a normal gear lever of the remote-control type. It works in a quadrant formed in the gearbox extension and has cunningly arranged lugs so that the lever follows a zig-zag course when moved right across and prevents you making awkward mistakes. On one side of the extension casing there is a smaller lever controlling the mixture strength of the three semi-downdraught car-

Moderate
Priced
M.G.
Midget
Capable
of
90 m.p.h.

The "J.3"
Combines a High
Performance
with Comfortable
Coachwork.

SUPERCHARGING FOR ALL!

THE success of the J.2 M.G. Midget has been an accomplished fact since its introduction, but the merits of the J.3, a supercharged version of the same car, are less widely known, excepting for its fine performance at Montlhéry, where several records, including 1 to 24 hour at 70.61 m.p.h. were put up at the close of 1932. The car we took on test was the actual record-breaker, and we found the combination of speed and tractability almost incredible for a car fitted with an engine of only 750 c.c.

The chassis layout differs little from that of the J.2 described in the September 1932 issue of MOTOR SPORT. The single overhead camshaft engine has inlet and exhaust ports on opposite sides, 14 mm. sparking plugs, and a two-bearing crankshaft. A 6a Powerplus supercharger is driven direct from the front end of the crankshaft, and the S.U. carburettor is supplied from the 11 gallon rear tank, which has a reserve supply, by means of an Autopulse pump. The J.3 crankshaft is heavier than that of the J.2 and has a shorter throw, so as to bring the capacity down to 746 c.c.

The clutch is strengthened, and transmits the drive through a four speed gear-box, with a constant mesh third gear, to the spiral bevel back axle. With the increased power given by the supercharged engine a final ratio of 4.89 has been found suitable, allowing high road speeds without fuss.

The front axle is dropped and the chassis passes under the rear one, with a consequent lowering of the centre of gravity. The springs are flat underslung semi-elliptics sliding in trunnions at their rear ends. Cable-operated brakes are used, and they and the other chassis points are lubricated from nipples grouped under the bonnet.

The car, we were informed, had a maximum speed of about 93 m.p.h., an amazing speed when one considers that two years ago the Mile Record for 750 c.c. cars stood at 94 m.p.h. Changing over from a car of three times the engine capacity and much larger chassis dimensions, we were a little doubtful as to whether this speed would prove agreeable on a small car.

Tyre pressures were checked, the shock-absorbers tightened up hard in front and slightly less so behind and we set off from Abingdon. The pneumatic upholstery damped out any harshness from the tightened suspension, and it was evident that the trial was going to be a success. The steering is unusually light, and so is liable to be overwound by the heavy handed, but once this feature had been recognised, the car was driven with complete confidence. So much so that it was taken down a main-road slope at 90 m.p.h. and proved perfectly controllable, while on corners the short chassis enabled one to get round with the minimum of effort.

The repairs on Brooklands Track prevented a complete circuit being made but starting from the Fork side of the damaged bridge, the car reached 70 m.p.h. by the time it was passing the Vickers Sheds. A strong head wind on the Railway Straight kept the speed down to 80 m.p.h. but once under the shelter of the Byfleet banking it rose steadily to 88 and 90 would undoubtedly have been attained if it had not been necessary to stop before again reaching the bridge.

The acceleration chart reveals an excellent performance which might have been bettered at the top end if the strong wind had not made it difficult to do 80 against it. At the maximum engine revs. of 5,500 the speed in third gear is 7 m.p.h. and there was no sign of period throughout the range. 45 m.p.h. seemed about the safe maximum in second. The brakes were a

Multum in parvo! The "J.3" Midget with an engine capacity of only 750 c.c. can obtain 90 m.p.h.

efficient as the high maximum speed demanded and from 40 m.p.h. the stopping distance was 55-57 feet. They were smooth and progressive in effect.

The J.3 is a very successful example of supercharging properly applied. On its normal fuel—50% Ethyl and 50% Benzol —it runs smoothly down to 500 r.p.m. on top gear, though for a fast get-away a change-down straight into second is a help. The K.L.G. 718 plugs, which are of course of the 14 mm. type, are as happy in traffic as on the open road. The bearings of the blower are lubricated from the sump and the blades get their supply from upper-cylinder oil used in normal quantities in the petrol. Because of this the plugs do not become swamped with oil after an all-night stand in the garage, and the car started instantaneously on all occasions. A possible criticism of the blower-installation is that being fitted on the front end of the crankshaft, a starting handle cannot be fitted, but with a light car like the M.G. a push start should not be difficult.

The blower and the engine were both mechanically silent, but the exhaust note becomes prominent at 3,000 r.p.m., which often seems to happen on a four-cylinder engine. Keeping above or below these revs, the exhaust note in traffic is inoffensive, while in the open country the trumpet note effect fits in well with the exhilarating effect of the car's acceleration.

With a touring car, as distinct from the semi-racing machine, one must have good suspension and comfortable upholstery. Even with the shock-absorbers fully tightened, as they were throughout the test, road shocks were hardly noticed, and the seat was adjustable both for distance from the pedals and for rake. The controls all came easily to hand, and the racing-type brake lever was of great use in traffic.

The gear-change from top to third was a joy, and with the 70 m.p.h. maximum there was no difficulty in getting quickly past any vehicles one normally encounters. All the gears were quiet, and third is a constant-mesh ratio. The gate of the remote-control gear-box is not very definite, as it is possible to catch the lever in the slot leading to reverse gear when changing down to second in a hurry, and one is also liable to put the lever into reverse instead of first gear in a traffic block and to rush rapidly backwards. The enthusiast would overcome this by fitting a gate off one of the larger cars, which is interchangeable with the J. type.

The horn button is fitted to the dash where it can be operated with one finger, and the dipping switch with it. The

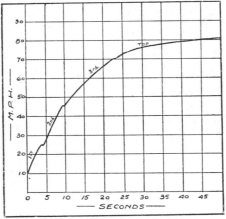

The acceleration chart of the J.3 Midget.

latter simply cuts out one headlight when required. The lamps allow 60 m.p.h. to be maintained with safety.

The J.3 is a car which fits in with one's every mood, and is just as happy humming along at 40 m.p.h. as rushing round corners at full revs. with the inside wheels six inches from the gutter. The good power-weight ratio makes frequent gear-changing unnecessary, and one settles down easily to speeds of 65 to 70 m.p.h., the revs. at the latter speed being just under 4,000. Its maximum with the screen up is about 80 m.p.h.

Heavy rain on the second day of the test prevented the maximum road speed being determined, but it gave a good opportunity of trying the hood. When not in use, this folds down in a locker behind the seat. The sticks are of normal type, pivoted inside the body, and the front part of the fabric clips on to the screen. The latter is rigid and sufficiently high to give a good field of view, but the suction wind-screen wiper did not work when the blower was exerting pressure.

The hood locker is quite spacious, and could hold a pair of useful suitcases, especially if their dimensions were chosen to fill the space available. A removable flap gives access to the back-axle and the transversely placed shock-absorbers. Other manufacturers please copy !

Wet roads in no way affect the car's steadiness and even on tramlines, where the small tyres might have been expected to give trouble, there was no tendency to misbehave. The brakes were also applied fiercely in emergencies without causing any deviation from the desired path.

Considered irrespective of price, this supercharged 750 c.c. car gives real comfort for two people combined with a performance as high as any normal driver could want. Driven with a little consideration, there is no reason why it should not keep its tune over long periods without attention, while the tax, insurance, and running expenses should be small. Costing only £299 10s., the car is quite unique in the value it offers.

Offside view of the engine, showing the single S.U. Carburettor.

Brief Specification.

Engine : 4 *cylinder* 57 *mm. and* 73 *mm. bore and stroke. Capacity* 746 *c.c. R.A.C. rating,* 8.05 *h.p. Single overhead camshaft. Single S.U. carburettor. Coil ignition.*

Gearbox : 4 *speeds and reverse. Constant mesh third. Ratios,* 4.89, 6.65, 10.46, 16.5 *to* 1.

Rear axle : Special bevel. Three quarter floating.

Suspension : Underslung semi-elliptic.

Dimensions : Wheelbase 7ft. 2in. *Track* 3ft. 6in.

Price with open 2 *seater body,* £299 10s. 0d.

OVER HILL AND DALE WITH—

ONE OF THE "J2s"

—And a "Hack" Car at That, But
One Which Still Retained
Plenty of "Pep"

AS a welcome change to a car which is brand new, we were able recently to take over a J2 Midget which had been used—and, we gather, very strenuously used—as a hack car by various members of the staff at Abingdon. As a matter of fact, only the oil, petrol, gearbox and back axle were checked over before the car was driven up from the M.G. works to these offices.

"We want to give you an exact idea of what the performance of an M.G. is like after it has been caned pretty severely for many hundreds of miles," said the M.G. Car Co., Ltd. "You may find that the tune of the engine has lost its edge a little and that there are one or two minor squeaks and rattles. Anyway, there it is . . ."

Far from being downcast at this somewhat lugubrious introduction to the J2, we looked forward with considerable interest to the forthcoming test, and with every confidence turned the radiator of the car in the direction of Tenbury Wells.

We may summarize our general impressions at the outset by saying that the J2 brought joy to our heart and suffered from never an impromptu stop; in fact, it carried on the grand tradition of Abingdon by requiring only petrol and oil whilst it was in our keeping, and during which time it covered another 500-odd miles over hill and dale.

The engine ran very sweetly apart from a slight period which developed between 40 and 50 m.p.h., the clutch was one of the sweetest that has come our way, the brakes were powerful, the steering as light as a feather, and the suspension surprisingly good for so light a car, even allowing for the fact that the shock absorbers were done up tight.

Only one rattle was noticeable, and that quickly attained such alarming proportions that an immediate stop to investigate the cause became necessary. Had hack work been too much for the little car, after all? we asked ourselves as we commenced the inevitable process of elimination. The story, however, lacks a sensational crisis, for it was quickly discovered that the turn buckles holding the removable "floor" of the compartment behind the seats had worked themselves round so that the board had become loose. With the turn buckles readjusted the rattle vanished.

The actual performance of the car merits high praise. We have already emphasized the sweetness of the clutch (although one has to become accustomed to the extremely short travel of the clutch pedal); to this must be added a very quick gear change, and an

The businesslike stern of the J2, showing the tank with quick-filler cap, the spare-wheel mounting and the rear-spring anchorage.

engine, incidentally, responsive to the lightest touch on the accelerator.

Getting off the mark was, therefore, a pleasant business, and by making judicious use of the gear lever it was possible to push the speedometer needle round to the "fifties" and "sixties" in a very short space of time. The maximum speed recorded on the facia-board in third was 55 m.p.h. A higher speed might

IN BRIEF.

ENGINE: *Four-cylinder, o.h.v., 57 mm. × 83 mm. (847 c.c., Tax, £8).*

TRANSMISSION: *Plate-clutch to four-speed centrally controlled gearbox; ratios, 5.37, 7.32, 11.5 and 19.2 to 1. Open propeller shaft.*

GENERAL: *Overall length (approx.), 10 ft. 9 ins.; width, 4 ft. 3 ins.; wheelbase, 7 ft. 2 ins.; track, 3 ft. 6 ins.; weight, 11½ cwt.*

PRICE: *£199 10s.*

THE M.G. CAR CO., Ltd.,
Abingdon-on-Thames - - - Berkshire.

have been possible, but not without signs of distress from the engine. The maximum attainable in top—again by the facia-board reading—was 77 m.p.h. The comfortable maxima in the two ratios named were "forty" and just over "sixty."

Road-holding is one of the most striking features of

the J2—as, indeed, it should be in view of the fact that it is the unsupercharged edition of the model which has been raced so successfully. Corners can be taken fast—even to the point of tyres that complain audibly and a tendency on the part of the tail to slide—without any feeling of insecurity; the ability of the car to hold the road, coupled with the liveliness of the engine and the comparatively high speeds attainable, permit very fast, safe and comfortable averages to be maintained.

An accompanying photograph shows several of the main controls, and, incidentally, reveals how additional access can be obtained when the bonnet is lifted. The short, stubby "remote" gear lever falls nicely to hand, whilst the hand brake—necessary only in an emergency or for parking—works on the true racing principle, i.e., the ratchet does not become effective unless the top thimble is depressed—a return spring ensuring that the lever jumps to the "off" position when the thimble is released.

Horizontal rods carried above the remote gear control arm operate the mixture control and slow-running respectively, whilst the starter button is arranged on the toe-board where it is easily accessible with the left foot.

During rough weather it is unnecessary to raise the hood provided the car is kept on the move, but in this connection a more positive action for the screen wiper is desirable.

One of the most surprising features of the car, in view of the excellence of its performance, was the low petrol consumption. At a modest estimate some 35 miles were covered to every gallon, and it is possible that at slightly lower speeds than those which were maintained during our run, 40 m.p.g. would be possible. A large slice of crèdit for this, and for the general performance of the engine, must be given to the twin semi-down-draught S.U. carburetters.

The general appearance of the car is very pleasing indeed. In the front it bears the unmistakable trade-mark of the Abingdon factory, whilst at the back it boasts a "slab" petrol tank holding some 8 gallons and fitted with a snap-on petrol cap. Adjacent to the petrol cap there is a small tap controlling the main and reserve supply. To round off the appearance, the spare wheel is mounted behind the tank and held in place by steel strips which not only provide a very rigid fixing, but permit of instant and easy access to the spare.

Bearing in mind its price (£199 10s.), the M.G. Midget J2 is excellent value for money, and the model which we tested clearly proved that it is capable of maintaining its tune for long periods even when hard worked.

READILY ACCESSIBLE.

When the bonnet is lifted, not only the engine but the forward part of the cockpit is revealed as well. The photograph shows several interesting points, notably the two semi-down-draught carburetters, the sump filler, chassis lubricating nipples, pedal mountings and so on. The general simplicity of the complete layout will not pass unnoticed.

WIDE RANGE OF SMALL CAPACITY M.G. SPORTS CARS.

THE J SERIES, THE NEW MAGNA AND THE MAGNETTE.

THE experience gleaned by the M.G. Car Company from its successes in the 1932 racing season has been embodied in the designs of all the new models. The new type of cylinder head, with its small plugs, first tried in the 1,000 mile Race at Brooklands, the straight underslung frame with flat springs and the cable-operated brakes are found on all models, and the large petrol tanks and other improvements which have been fitted to the more expensive models are now found throughout the range. Dunlop tyres and Rudge Whitworth wheels are also standard.

The J. Series includes all the four-cylinder cars. The J.2, the popular two seater model, and the J.1, which carries a four-seater body, are fitted with 850 c.c. engines, embodying the new type cylinder head, in which inlet and exhaust ports are on opposite sides, and twin S.U. carburettors. A four-speed gear-box with silent third, and 8 in. brakes with aluminium fins all help to improve performance, and the body and equipment is as complete as could be desired. The two-seater at under £200 has placed sports car motoring within the reach of almost everyone.

The J.3 is a supercharged version of the J.2, and is described fully elsewhere in this issue. By shortening the stroke to 73 mm., the engine is brought within the 750 c.c. limit, and is ideal for fast touring or competition work. It costs £299 10s.

The J.4 and J.5 are the supercharged and unsupercharged cars corresponding to the old Montlhéry type. New features are the head, with opposed ports and 14 mm. plugs, and the oiling system with a large Elektron sump holding one gallon. The oil is forced through a Tecalemit filter on its way to the engine, and the oil level is maintained by a float feed, supplied from a two-gallon dash tank. Like the other J models the valves are operated by an overhead camshaft through fingers, and three springs per valve ensures positive closing. The camshaft is driven by bevel gears from a vertical shaft at the front of the engine and the dynamo is incorporated in this.

Coil ignition is used, and a spare unit is supplied as standard. On the J.5 the mixture is supplied by two semi-downdraught S.U. carburettors, and is pumped from the 12 gallon rear tank by two Petrol-lift pumps. These have independent pipe lines, and the second one is only brought into operation when it is desired to use the reserve two gallons. The supercharged cars are fitted with No. 7 Powerplus blowers mounted between the front dumbirons in the familiar cowling. The blower runs at three-quarter speed, and is protected from any end-thrust from the crankshaft by a sliding coupling. A single carburettor is bolted to the casing, and the mixture passes to the engine through the special dual induction pipe, which maintains gas velocity at low speeds. A water pump is fitted.

The J.4 and 5 can either be fitted with the well-tried M.G. close ratio four speed gear-box, or with a pre-selective box of Wilson type, which costs an extra £25. In the first case a two plate clutch is used, but with the second the drive is taken up by the friction bands. A special feature of the pre-selective box is the servo-action of the bands, which increases the pressure when the engine is driving, preventing any possibility of slip on the lower gears. The gear-lever works in a gate carried on an extension of the gear-box, coming under the left hand, and the mixture and slow running controls are mounted below. The brake-lever is of racing type and the ratchet engages only when the knob is depressed and flies off when next the lever is operated.

The transmission follows the lines of the other models, but straight bevels are used in the back axle.

The flat chassis, upswept in front and passing under the rear axle, is retained unaltered, and gives a floor line only 12 inches from the ground. Additional steel bracing has been embodied at the rear. The flat underslung springs slide in trunnions at their rear ends, and are bound with cord and taped to resist the extra strains of violent cornering and braking.

The brake drums are now 12 inches in diameter, and fitted with cooling fins, and the operating cables, like other chassis points are lubricated from nipples grouped under the bonnet. The brakes are adjusted by means of a hand wheel which is situated alongside the driver.

Cam steering is used and the special M.G. divided track rod contributes to the accuracy of the steering.

The J.4 and J.5, fitted with two-seater racing bodies, normal type gear-box, and Brooklands exhaust system cost respectively £445 and £395.

The M.G. Magna appeared on the market a little over a year ago, and made an immediate name for itself by reason of its good lines, brisk acceleration, and economy of upkeep. Soon there were enquiries as to whether a racing version on the lines of the successful Montlhéry could not be produced. An undertaking of this kind requires much research and experiment, and it was not until last Olympia that the six-cylinder racing car, the Magnette made its debut. Its magnificent performance in the Italian 1,000 Mile Race showed that the period of development had not been in vain.

The engine is of course a six cylinder, with bore and stroke of 57 and 71 mm., giving a capacity of 1,086 c.c. The tax is £12. The cylinder block and top half of the crank case are cast in one, and the cylinder head has 6 inlet and 6 exhaust ports on opposite sides, and 14 mm. plugs. The overhead camshaft operates the valves through fingers, and is driven by the vertical shaft-cum-dynamo arrangement as on the 750 c.c. models. There are two valves per cylinder, and on the racing engines these are fitted with three valve springs.

The aluminium pistons carry three rings, and a special type of steel connecting rod is used. The four bearing balanced crankshaft is machined all over.

An unusual feature is the B.T.H. polar inductor magneto, which by reason of its construction sparks four times per revolution, and therefore has to run at thr̥ quarter engine speed.

Three semi-downdraught S.U. carburettors are fitted to the unsupercharged models, and an electric petrolift pump feeds

the petrol from a 12 gallon rear tank, which has a reserve tap. The K.3 racing model has a 23 gallon rear tank, and two electric pumps, one of which is connected to the

This photograph shows the 13″ brake drums, and the method of mounting the Powerplus blower on the M.G. Magnette.

reserve. Quick-acting filler caps are fitted to each end of the tank.

The supercharged cars are fitted with No. 9 Powerplus superchargers, driven off the front end of the crankshaft, and running at three-quarter engine speed. A single carburettor is used and the blower is lubricated from the engine.

Lubrication is an important matter on a high-speed engine, and the Magnette is fitted with a finned Elektron sump which holds 1¾ gallons. The oil is forced through a pressure filter before reaching the bearings, and on the K.3 a further supply is carried in a dash tank which holds nearly two gallons, and is fed into the sump by an automatic float device.

The Magnette chassis can be obtained either with a manual-type gear-box with constant-mesh third gear, or with a Wilson pre-selective box, which is standard on the saloon and the racing chassis. The gear-lever is mounted on an extension, and grouped with it are the ignition, slow running, mixture and reserve petrol controls.

Transmission follows the usual M.G. lines, with an open propellor shaft with two Hardy Spicer joints and a three-quarter floating back axle. On the K.3 straight bevel gears are used.

The chassis, which is upswept in front and straight from the back of the engine to the rear end, passes under the rear axle. It is braced by tubular cross members, and by a special pressing at the rear. The width is greater than that of the Magna, and this with the track of four feet allows really roomy bodywork to be fitted.

The brakes are unusually powerful, and the drums are 13 inches in diameter.

Attention has been paid to the reduction of unsprung weight, however, and the drums, shoes, and back plates are made of Elektron, with chrome cast iron liners in the drums. Cables from the king pins to the chassis relieve the front springs of the K.3 of any twisting strain. Cam steering is used with a large diameter wheel, and the M.G. divided track rod is a feature of all models.

The increased chassis width and track allows a full-sized four-seater and a most attractive four-door saloon to be accommodated on the nine foot chassis. The sweeping lines of the front wings are most graceful, and not being obstructed by a centre pillar no gymnastics are required to get in and out. The clever luggage container at the back is invisible when not in use. The open car costs £385, while

the saloon, which is fitted as standard with pre-selector gear-box, is priced at £445. The K.2 is a short wheel-base model at the same price as the four-seater.

The K.3 racing model has a short chassis, and follows the lines of the rest of the K. series except for the differences

already noted. It can either be had in chassis form, or fitted with the familiar M.G. two-seater racing body. A very full equipment of instruments is standardised, every electric circuit has its own switch and fuse, and the switches and fuse box are mounted on the dash. In fact no item which has been found desirable in racing practise has been omitted. Fitted with T.T. type two-seater bodies and pre-selective gear-boxes the cars cost £650 supercharged, or £100 less without the blower. A streamlined body is also available.

Through the kindness of Mr. G. F. A. Manby Colegrave, of Squire Motors, Henley, we were able to have a short run in a supercharged K.3. The first impressions were the solid and roadworthy feel of the car, partly due no doubt to the width of the track, and the comfortable driving position. The wheel came naturally into the lap, the upholstery soft and the side of the body padded where one's elbow normally gets rubbed. The wind-deflectors and aero screens made it unnecessary to wear a coat even at high speed.

The engine was not run in, so we had to content ourselves with 4,500 r.p.m. on top gear, which was about 80 m.p.h., and of course at this speed the progress of the car was quite effortless. Limitation of revs. also prevented the full benefit of the pre-selective gear-box from being had, for the willing engine reached the limit in each ratio almost in a flash. One can only say that its use is complete joy. The gate is worthy of mention. The lever now moves along a serrated quadrant with a fairly strong spring to ensure engagement, so that the movement is merely a straight pull, but with sufficient resistance to avoid overshooting a notch.

The grouped controls on the gear-lever extension were convenient, and the engine did not appear to be sensitive to the position of the ignition control.

The brakes were powerful, and the general feel of the car was most promising.

The latest M.G. Magna has beautiful lines, and the four seater illustrated above sells at £299.

Corners were taken without effort and the steering, though still a little stiff, held the car on an accurate course. A full road test which we hope to publish in the near future will undoubtedly answer a good many of the pleas of English drivers for a national sports car.

M.G. MAGNETTE to

Capacity Increased to 1,286 c.

junction with Pre-selector Gearbo

Continental Coupe Added to Ran

The built-in trunk of the new Magna Continental coupe; note the interior-illuminated number plate and direction indicator.

FOR the coming season the models marketed by the M.G. Car Co., Ltd., will, as during 1933, be the Midget, the Magna and the Magnette. From this, however, it must not be imagined that the 1934 programme is merely a repetition of that for 1933, as the various models have all received some attention and important alterations are to be found in certain cases.

Briefly, the "high spots" of the programme are a new and very attractive body on the Magna chassis to be known as the Continental coupé, a new Magnette engine 200 c.c. larger than that fitted last year and an important transmission refinement on this chassis in the form of a single-plate clutch in addition to the self-changing gearbox.

Another small point that is rather out of the ordinary is that all closed M.G. models are now being wired for radio as standard, this feature enabling wireless enthusiasts to fit radios to their cars without either pulling the roof to pieces to insert a concealed aerial or, alternatively, fitting an exposed mass of untidy wires for the same purpose. Actually, the M.G. concern is prepared to supply a Philco radio set as a standard extra at an additional cost of £21 on any of the closed models.

In the matter of prices there is practically no change, the majority of the models, in fact, being maintained at their 1933 figures.

Turning to the various models in detail, one finds that the popular J2 Midget is continued with only two changes of note. One is that the small racing-type wings used last year have been abandoned in favour of long, sweeping,

flared wings and short running boards; the front wings merge gracefully into the running boards, and should prove distinctly more efficient as well as better looking. This change has made the J2 Midget very similar in general design to the equivalent Magna model, for the wings follow the same lines.

The other change is an invisible one,

```
1934 M.G. PRICES.
        Midget.
                                    £    s.
2-seater    ...   ...   ...   ...  199   10
Chassis     ...   ...   ...   ...  160    0
   (De luxe equipment, £17 17s. extra.)
        Magna.
2-seater    ...   ...   ...   ...  285    0
4-seater    ...   ...   ...   ...  299    0
Salonette   ...   ...   ...   ...  345    0
Continental coupé   ...   ...  ...  350    0
Chassis     ...   ...   ...   ...  245    0
   (De luxe equipment, £11 extra.)
        Magnette.
2-seater    ...   ...   ...   ...  390    0
4-seater    ...   ...   ...   ...  399    0
Pillarless 4-door saloon   ...  ...  445    0
Chassis     ...   ...   ...   ...  340    0
   (De luxe equipment, £12 extra.)
```

and consists of the fitting of an additional roller bearing at the front end of the crankshaft; this bearing is situated forward of the bevel drive for the overhead camshaft and gives considerable extra support for the crankshaft, so making for sweeter running. The engine, incidentally, is fitted with Aerolite pistons.

The J2 two-seater is now the only model in the Midget range, the tourer and salonette models having been discontinued. A de luxe edition of the two-seater is available, however, the extra equipment including a D.W.S. four-wheel jacking system; this model costs 17 guineas extra.

The Magna Range.

So far as the Magna range is concerned, the 1,100 c.c. L-type, which was introduced last March, has proved so successful that it is being retained practically without change but with the addition of the Continental coupé already mentioned. It will be remembered, incidentally, that although this chassis has been on the market such a short time, its successes include the winning of The Light Car Club Relay Race and the manufacturers' team prize in the 1,100 c.c. class in the International Alpine Trial.

The new coupé, as its name implies, has a distinctly Continental suggestion about its lines, and is a most pleasing model withal. From the low, squat

(Above) The J2 Midget in 1934 form; the only notable change is the use of flared wings and running boards. (Below) The new Continental coupe, which has been added to the Magna range.

radiator the bonnet sweeps straight back in an unbroken horizontal line to meet the screen, which is almost vertical; the top of the roof continues backwards in a slight curve, the line then dropping sharply to an almost vertical rear panel, the whole being offset by a large trunk on the back of which the spare wheel is mounted. The windows are long and comparatively shallow, and the rear quarters are blind. All these features, added to the graceful wings and pleasing forward sweep of the body line where it meets the scuttle, give the car a most distinctive air.

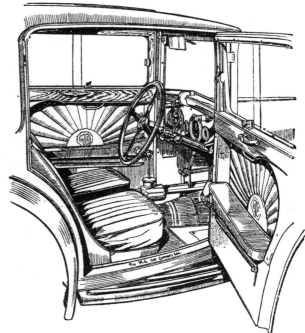

(Right) A sketch of the lavishly equipped interior of the new Magna Continental coupe, which sells for £350.

(Below) The 1934 Magnette two-seater. Externally it is practically unchanged, but has a bigger engine and transmission improvements.

It might be thought from this that the body is one of those in which considerable sacrifices in the matter of convenience and comfort have been made to obtain fascinating lines; this is far from the truth. The body is really comfortable and, owing to the very wide doors, is as easy to enter or leave as one could wish, whilst the low build of the chassis has made it possible to arrange for ample headroom; visibility, too, is good, because, although the rear quarters are blind, the wide doors enable the windows to be carried back to a point well behind the driver's head.

Strictly speaking, the body is a two-seater, but there is a platform behind the front seats which, although intended

primarily for luggage, could, with the aid of a cushion, be utilized quite comfortably for occasional use by two children or one adult.

An examination of the interior fittings and equipment confirms the impression that everything possible has been done for the owner's comfort and convenience. The doors, for example, are deeply recessed and provided with arm rests, so that the occupants have plenty of room as well as somewhere to rest their elbows, whilst below the arm rest in each door is a useful pocket fitted with a Zipp fastener. Also fitted in the doors are neat telescopic cylindrical ashtrays.

Well-placed Controls

The front seats are of the sliding type with a quick release, and the spring-spoke steering wheel and neat remote control gear lever are nicely placed; the hand brake, which has a spring-off racing-type ratchet, is also well within reach.

The front screen is of the usual single-pane type hinged at the top and is controlled by a central winder so that it can easily be opened or closed single-handed. A tandem-type wiper is fitted with the motor on the near side. The facia-board equipment is comprehensive, including a clock, petrol gauge, ammeter, oil-pressure gauge, tell-tale lamp, large combined speedometer and rev. counter, two facia-board lamps, and—unusual but very useful—an oil thermometer.

Other items of equipment include a roof light, large chromium-plated headlamps, with a separate switch to cut out the off-side lamp (the near-side headlamp is permanently deflected) and a special direction indicator at the rear.

The direction indicator forms part of the interior-illuminated number plate built into the rear trunk. This is very well schemed, there being an oval and an arrow arranged on each side of the actual number. The arrows, of course, are backed by red glass and indicate a turn to the left or right, whilst the off-side oval is also backed by red glass and acts as a rear light; the oval on the near side shows amber when the brakes are applied and forms, in effect, a stop-light.

The rear trunk provides room behind the tank for a fair-sized suitcase, the back being hinged to let down and secured by adjustable straps.

The other Magna bodies are almost identical with last year's L-type, and comprise a two-seater, a four-seater and a salonette. De luxe equipment is available on all these models at an extra cost of £11.

So far as the Magnette range is concerned, the cars are almost identical in external appearance with the 1933 models; there are a two-seater, a four-seater and the attractive pillarless four-door saloon.

Mechanically, however, there are two important alterations, the most noteworthy being the new 1,286 c.c.

CONTINUED ON PAGE 86

IN BRIEF.

MIDGET

ENGINE: Four cylinders; o.h. valves and camshaft; 57 mm. by 83 mm.=847 c.c.; tax £8; two-bearing crankshaft.

TRANSMISSION: Single plate clutch; four-speed, "twin-top" gearbox; ratios, 5.37, 7.32, 11.5 and 19.2 to 1; reverse, 19.2 to 1. Open propeller shaft with Hardy Spicer universal joints to spiral bevel rear axle.

DIMENSIONS: Wheelbase, 7 ft. 2 ins.; track, 3 ft. 6 ins.; overall length, 10 ft. 4 ins.; overall width, 4 ft. 4½ ins.

MAGNA

ENGINE: Six cylinders; o.h. valves and camshaft; 57 mm. by 71 mm.=1087 c.c.; tax £12; four-bearing crankshaft.

TRANSMISSION: Two-plate clutch; four-speed "twin-top" gearbox; ratios, 5.375, 7.31, 11.49 and 19.21 to 1; reverse, 19.21 to 1. Open propeller shaft with Hardy Spicer universal joints to spiral bevel rear axle.

DIMENSIONS: Wheelbase, 7 ft. 10 ins.; track, 3 ft. 6 ins.; overall length, (four seater), 12 ft.; overall width, 4 ft. 4 ins.

MAGNETTE

ENGINE: Six cylinders; o.h. valves and camshaft; 57 mm. by 84 mm.=1,286 c.c.; tax £12; four-bearing crankshaft.

TRANSMISSION: Single plate clutch working in conjunction with pre-selector gearbox; ratios, 5.78, 7.76, 11.56, and 19.65 to 1, reverse 25.8 to 1; open propeller shaft with Hardy Spicer universal joints to spiral bevel back axle.

DIMENSIONS: Wheelbase, long chassis, 9 ft.; short chassis, 7 ft. 10 ins.; track, 4 ft.

THE M.G. CAR CO., LTD.,
Abingdon-on-Thames.

M.G. CARS FOR 1934

Slightly Modified J.2 Midget, Continental Coupé Added to Magna Range, Magnette With Greater Engine Capacity, and Pre-selector Gear Box Combined With Plate Clutch

Road Impressions of New Models

Illustrations in Photogravure appear on pages 372 and 373. Road Impressions of the Magna two-seater are given on pages 372 and 373.

VERY little change is being made in the M.G. series of cars for the coming season, for they have been brought to a state of development where extensive modifications are not considered necessary. Prices also are practically unaltered, save for slight variations in the Magnette. The complete range of cars and their prices are as follows:—

M.G. Midget: chassis £160, two-seater £199 10s.

M.G. Magna: chassis £245, open two-seater £285, open four-seater £299, salonette £345, Continental coupé £350.

M.G. Magnette: chassis £340, open two-seater £390, open four-seater £399, open pillarless four-door saloon £445.

It will be noticed that there is a departure in the Midget range, inasmuch as the car is now offered as a two-seater only, other bodies being discontinued. The lines are similar to the previous model, but the appearance has been distinctly improved by fitting a modern type of flared wing, and also the addition of running boards makes sure that the car and its occupants are kept clean in bad weather. In order to preserve and improve the sturdy and sparkling performance which these exceedingly attractive little cars possess on the road —the four-cylinder engine is capable of turning over at pretty well 6,000 r.p.m. —one or two modifications have been introduced, for example, the connecting rods now have fully floating gudgeon pins, and pistons with controlled expansion skirts included, and the compression ratio also has been slightly raised.

Midget Specification

It is interesting to review the specification of the Midget. It has a four-cylinder overhead-valve and camshaft engine, 57 × 83 mm. (84₇ c.c.) tax £8. Twin S.U. semi-downdraught carburetters are fitted, and the fuel from the S.U. petrol pump. The engine is cooled on the thermo-syphon system, and in order to avoid waste of power a Burgess straight-through silencer is used. The

M.G. PRICES FOR 1934.

M.G MIDGET.

	£	s.
Chassis	.. ..	160	0
Two-Seater	.. ..	199	10

M.G. MAGNA.

	£	s.
Chassis	.. ..	245	0
Open Two-Seater	..	285	0
Open Four-Seater	..	299	0
Salonette	.. ..	345	0
Continental Coupé	..	350	0

M.G. MAGNETTE.

	£	s.
Chassis	.. ..	340	0
Open Two-Seater ..		390	0
Open Four-Seater	..	399	0
Pillarless Saloon ..		445	0

M.G. Midget J.2. Two-seater, £199 10s.

3ft. 6in., and the semi-elliptic springs are damped by Hartford shock absorbers. Marles-Weller steering, with a transverse drag link is fitted, and the four wheel brake set is operated through a system of fully enclosed cables provided with proper means of regular lubrication. To handle a Midget on the road is always a pleasure, for the car is fascinating in every way and is not only fast, but has quite a different feel about it from most vehicles. The engine is particularly willing, and also notably smooth for a four-cylinder, and it has a very exhilarating way of going about its work, especially if proper use is made of the gear box.

If a gathering of motor enthusiasts was asked to make a choice out of the M.G. range, the majority would undoubtedly go for the Magna two-seater, for it is a car with just exactly the right balance of bonnet length to body, it sits down to the ground so compactly, and has a distinctly thoroughbred air. That the Magna is capable of doing a great deal more than look well is obvious from the success which it has scored during the recent season—for example, winning the L.C.C. Relay Race, and also the Manufacturers' Team Prize in its group in the International Alpine Trial. Elsewhere in this issue will be found an account of road impressions of one of the current "L" type Magnas.

Magna Revisions

Practically the only alteration to record for 1934 is that larger and more effective head lamps have been fitted. A new type of body, however, is now in production—the Continental coupé. This is a very striking-looking design of two-door four-seater with a large luggage trunk at the back. The interior of the body is most attractively furnished, and there are numerous special points, including elbow rests to the front seats, a sliding roof with windowlets in it, and recessed elbow room. This new body can be finished in black and yellow, in all-black, or various other colours, and is likely to become popular because it is very individual.

Magna Continental coupé.

The M.G. Magna Two-seater

IT is for ever a refreshing experience to change over from the everyday sort of saloon to a piquant and intensely alive little car like the M.G. Magna type "L." The road is no longer a mere highway from place to place, but a path of adventure, as the sea must be adventure to the man who handles a trim sailing craft. There is appeal in the very lines of the Magna, with its long bonnet promising speed, its workmanlike stern view, and long, graceful mudguards. To sense the appeal and try the car is to appreciate in full the very real qualities which are there.

Sitting well down in a deep cockpit, rendered comfortable by pneumatic upholstery, the driver starts the engine, finds a steering wheel tucking itself into his hands, notices the freedom for his arms and elbows, and, looking over the curved scuttle along the distance of the road, drops his left hand instinctively to the little close-up gear lever. A little light footwork, a snick of the gear lever, a flick of the accelerator, and he is away off the mark with the engine note rising.

Smoothness Outstanding

This modern six-cylinder 1,086 c.c. engine in the Magna is a fine design, and it runs with notable smoothness right throughout its range, from a comfortable toddle on top gear right up to nearly 6,000 r.p.m. when all out. Its flexibility and its freedom from vibration or mechanical noise are remarkable, when taken in conjunction with a big power output in relation to size. It responds instantly to the movements of the accelerator pedal, and, as the acceleration figures show, maintains its liveliness right up through the speed range. The car can be depended upon to reach its maximum on the level without hesitation. There is a great fascination in driving the Magna. The steering is

DATA FOR THE DRIVER

12 h.p., six cylinders, 57 × 71 mm. (1,086 c.c.) Tax £12.
Wheelbase 7ft. 10⅛in.; track 3ft. 6in.
Overall length 10ft.; width 4ft. 3½in.; height 4ft. 2in. Hood up.
Tyres: 4.5 × 19 on detachable Rudge-Whitworth wire wheels.
Engine rev. Acceleration from steady gear speed.

ratios.	10 to 30 m.p.h.	20 to 40 m.p.h.	30 to 50 m.p.h.
19.21	6¾	6⅜	—
11.49	6¾	6⅝	17⅛
7.31	14⅛	15⅞	
5.375			

Timed speed over ½ mile, 75 m.p.h.
With screen down 77.59
Acceleration from rest through the gears to 50 m.p.h. 18 sec.; through the gears to 60 m.p.h. 24¾ sec.
15 yards of 1 in 5 gradient from rest 3¾ sec.
Turning circle 32ft. 6in.
Tank capacity 10⅕ gallons; fuel consumption 22-24 m.p.g.
12-volt lighting set.
Weight: 16 cwt.
Price, with two-seater body, £285.

light and quick—at first grasp disconcertingly so—with a strong caster action, but, as soon as it is realised that the wheel is best held with a light grip, the car can be placed neatly, or taken round curves at speed, in an elegant fashion. Although the car is light and lively, the steering has no apparent vices such as incipient wheel tramp, and the radiator and head lamps do not dither about on bad surfaces. Because of the low build and special form of spring anchorages, the car holds the road excellently, and can be driven anywhere with confidence.

One of the features is the four-speed twin-top gear box with remote control. A long extension on the top of the box brings a short gear lever close to the hand, and the gear change is a simple and effective one to handle, whilst the indirect gears are quiet. The ratios are well chosen and the car will reach 40 m.p.h. on second gear, which is pretty useful. The clutch is sweet and light, and is well up to its work. It may be noted that the cockpit of this two-seater does not become uncom-

fortably hot, due no doubt to the metal facings of the dashboard and the rubber sealing around the clutch pit and the steering column, which prevents hot air from blowing through.

Another point which contributes to the general attractiveness of the car is that the large diameter brakes are smooth and progressive, and may be used to pull the car up from high speed without trepidation. Because of the smoothness, they are deceptive in that they pull the car up more quickly than they appear to do, which is always a hall-mark of good brakes. They are armoured-cable operated, but proper provision is made for regular lubrication of the cable sheathing. Except at low speeds, when the shock absorbers can be felt to be doing their work, the comfort of riding is very good, and the stability of the car at any speed of which this model is capable on the track is all that could be desired.

Special Points

There are certain points to attract special attention. The large fuel tank at the rear of the body has a gauge visible on the top, and there is a two-way control which enables some two gallons to be held in reserve. The windscreen is arranged so that it can be folded down flat forwards when needed, and incidentally there is surprisingly little wind when the screen is down, owing to the shape of the dash "humps," and the way that they deflect the wind over the heads of the occupants. It may be mentioned that the maximum speed figure given in the table was an average obtained with the screen down; with it up the maximum was 75 m.p.h.

The speedometer on the car gave a reasonably accurate reading. This instrument is, by the way, a combined speedometer and revolution indicator, for it has separate calibrations showing the engine revolutions equivalent to various road speeds on the different gears. The various controls of the car are well placed and simple to handle; mounted on the tunnel just forward of the gear lever are knobs controlling the jet adjustment and the slow running setting of the twin S.U. carburetters, the ignition advance is automatic, the lights are controlled from the instrument board, and thus the steering wheel is left quite free of encumbrances.

Taken all round, the open two-seater Magna is a most delectable car with the manners, as well as the air, of a thoroughbred.

The Magna L2 two-seater.

HIGH AVERAGE SPEEDS WITH A CAR WHICH HAS THE DEFINITE CHARACTERISTICS OF A RACING ANCESTRY.

On ROAD & TRACK with the "L" Type M.G. MAGNA

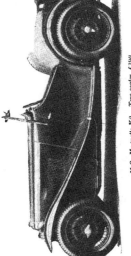

M.G. Magnette K2. Two-seater, £390.

It will be remembered that the Magna specification includes a six-cylinder engine, 57 × 71 mm. (1,087 c.c.), tax £12, with o.h.v. and camshaft, twin S.U. carburetters, external oil filter, separate dynamo and starter, an Elektron sump holding 1¼ gallons of oil, floating connecting rods, and special pistons with controlled expansion skirts, a gear-type oil pump, and pump water circulation.

Magna Details

Transmission is through the two-plate clutch and four-speed gear box, with a remote control gear lever. An open Hardy Spicer propeller-shaft with metal universal joints conveys the drive to a spiral bevel gear, contained in a three-quarter floating design of rear axle. Rudge racing-type wire wheels are fitted and are shod with Dunlop tyres 4.5 × 19in. Jaeger instruments are standardised and include a 5in. diameter speedometer and revolution counter. De luxe equipment is available on all Magna models at an inclusive cost of £11 extra. On the closed cars a No. 5 Philco radio set may also be had at an additional charge of £21, and, incidentally, the salonettes and Continental coupés have, as a part of the standard equipment, an invisible aerial, in case the owner at any time wishes to install a radio set.

It is in the M.G. Magnette that the most notable changes are to be observed. Following the process of development in the course of racing and other experience, a new type of engine has been evolved for the normal models. The design of this follows very closely on the racing engine, with modifications to make it suitable for the needs of the sporting motorist. The new engine has the same horse-power rating and pays the same tax as the old ones, but its dimensions are 57 × 84 mm. (1,286 c.c.). It has, of course, the usual M.G. type of overhead valves and camshaft, but is fitted

with 14 mm. instead of the more usual pattern 18 mm. sparking plugs.

It is equipped with triple S.U. carburetters and has a special coil and automatic distributor designed to meet the high engine speeds which are obtainable. "H" section floating connecting rods are used, the pistons are of the controlled expansion type, and the same features of Elektron sump, pump water circulation, and external oil filter are employed. The water temperature is controlled by an R.P. Thermostat.

There is a particularly interesting change in the transmission of this car. The four-speed pre-selective self-changing gear box is standardised, but between

the gear box and the engine a single-plate Don-Flex clutch has been added. This clutch is so arranged that the first movement of the pedal operates the single-plate clutch, and the further movement is then applied to the busbar of the pre-selector gear striking mechanism. Between the pedal and the two systems is an ingenious balancing arm which ensures that the plate clutch shall always work first.

A Smooth Take-up

On the opposite side of the clutch pit to the pedal is a clever tripping cam which again makes certain that when the gear is in neutral position the plate clutch is held out of engagement, but is automatically released ready, for use when a gear is being engaged. The object of fitting a plate clutch is to give a perfectly smooth and even take-up when starting from rest or when engaging the lower gears. Also, when the engine is running and the gear is in neutral, the gear box is entirely idle and therefore cannot make a noise. The clutch also makes sure that, should too low a gear be engaged inadvertently whilst travelling at a high speed, the plate clutch is able to slip, and this relieves the rest

of the transmission from what might be excessive stress and strain.

A short run on one of the Magnettes fitted with this device showed that a much more smooth and pleasant take-up is the result when starting from rest and gear changing. The Magnette is made in two lengths of wheelbase, the short being 7ft. 10in., and the long 9ft. The frames of both cars are underslung, and the half-elliptic springs have special slides at their rear ends in place of shackles. To ensure rigidity on the long wheelbase models, a cruciform type of cross bracing is fitted in the centre between the side members, in addition to the usual tubular cross-members. The wheel track of the Magnette models is, by the way, 4ft. For the steering a Marles-Weller gear is used, but the car has a special M.G. patented brake of 31 starters. Few cars make such a successful début.

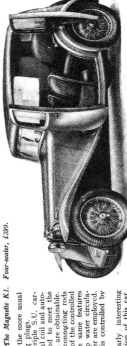

Magnette four-door pillarless saloon.

The Magnette K1. Four-seater, £399.

WE arrived at the M.G. works at Abingdon to collect our mount for the week-end with more than the usual pleasurable anticipations of some real motoring to come. Consider the record of the "L" type Magna this year. A team of three cars was first entered for the Light Car Club's Relay Race at Brooklands, result: a well-earned "first." Then the cars were sent over to the Continent for the Alpine Trial, result: an Alpine Cup for the best team performance up to 1,100 c.c. Finally, the 500 Miles at Brooklands saw a Magna driven by C. E. C. Martin and L. P. Welch come home second out of a field of 31 starters. Few cars make such a successful début.

Through a continual coming and going of M.G.'s of all types, some with only a test "body," others having final adjustments, we eventually arrived at the Delivery Department, where a green 2 seater was waiting for us to put it through its paces. And a very pretty car this "L" type Magna is. The line of the front wings is one of those inspirations which come but seldom in the motoring world, the bonnet and scuttle are exactly the right length, and the squat rear compartment and tank, with the spare wheel just at the right angle, give the car a most workmanlike appearance. But the good looks of the Magna are not merely skin-deep. Those brake-drums, of a generous 12 inch diameter, the underslung chassis at the rear, and the ample Hartford shock absorbers all betoken a car designed from stem to stern for fast work in the hands of a critical owner.

Our immediate destination was the Track. First impressions? Well, effortless cruising at 60 m.p.h., a gluttony for 'revs' on the gears, and light, high-geared steering. A good test of a car is to see how quickly one becomes completely at home with the controls, and the Magna got full marks in this respect. The driver

sits in a nicely upright position, looking *down* on to his front wings, the steering wheel is low, the pedals are correctly spaced and work smoothly in the right arc, and the gear-lever is snugly at his side. The actual gear-change, of course, is simplicity itself.

Brief Specification.

Engine : 6 cyl., 57 x 71 mm., 1,086 c.c., R.A.C. Rating 12 h.p. Tax £12. Single o.h.c. Compression ratio 6.4 to 1. Four-bearing crankshaft. Pump cooling. 2 S.U. carburetters. Single point engine mounting on rubber in front, cross tube through clutch pit at rear. Coil ignition, automatic advance and retard.

Transmission : Double dry-plate clutch, 4 speed normal gear box, silent third, central remote control. Ratios, 1st, 19.21, 2nd, 11.49, 3rd, 7.31, top 5.375 to 1. Road speed at 1,000 r.p.m. on each gear, 1st, 4, 2nd 7, 3rd 11, top 15.5 m.p.h. Hotchkiss drive, Hardy-Spicer propeller shaft, ¾ floating rear axle.

Suspension : ½ elliptic springs, 27 5/16″ front, 37″ rear. Hartford shock absorbers.

Brakes : Cable operated, 2 shoe type, 12″ drums.

Steering : Marles Weller. Adjustable take. Turning circle 37′.

Fuel Supply : 12 gallon rear tank. Electric pump.

Dimensions : R.W. racing wheels. Tyres 4.50 by 19. Wheelbase 7′ 10″ Track 3′ 6″. Ground clearance 6″. Weight of complete 2 seater 15¾ cwt.

Price : 2 seater, as tested, £285 ex works.

At Brooklands we climbed the slope from the Paddock onto the outer circuit, and came to rest on the line marking the beginning of the half-mile Railway Straight. The passenger began to count, *one, two, three* and we were off on our first test, the standing half-mile, which was covered in 38 4/5 seconds. We carried on, the engine as smooth as velvet, and the suspension dealing firmly with the bumps, heaves and depressions which form the surface of Brooklands Track. Off the Members Banking the speedometer registered 79 m.p.h. falling to 77 m.p.h. down the Straight, while our actual speed for the flying half-mile worked out at 75.6 m.p.h.—so that the speedometer is commendably near to accuracy.

The acceleration figures can be seen in the accompanying graph. The willing engine can actually go up to 6,000 r.p.m. on the gears, but taking 5,000 r.p.m. as a more usual maximum, the following speeds are available, 1st 20 m.p.h., 2nd 35 m.p.h. and 3rd 55 m.p.h. The engine of the car we tested was completely smooth throughout its range except for a slight period at 3,700 r.p.m., which was no sooner noticed than it was gone. Using Ethyl there was never a sign of pinking, and the engine was just as tractable as any touring machine.

Finally, to complete our operations at the Track, we tested the brakes from an actual speed of 40 m.p.h., pulling up without a jar in 60 feet. Although no servo mechanism is used, the brakes are extraordinarily easy to operate, and the pedal offers barely more resistance than the clutch pedal. Accuracy of braking is not lost, however, but is reduced to a more delicate process. The hand lever works on the racing principle of the ratchet being engaged at will. In order to release the brake, the lever is just eased back, and then immediately flies forward. For stop and restarts it is ideal.

An Attractive Saloon

Particular interest attaches to the four-door saloon mounted on the Magnette chassis. This body is particularly attractively proportioned, and not only looks well, but allows extreme ease of entry, as it is of the pillarless construction, so that if both doors are open on one side there is nothing in the way of getting in or out. The rear panel of this body can be folded outwards to form a useful luggage carrier, whilst at the same time the spare wheel may be retained in position behind the petrol tank instead of adding to the weight of overhang, as would be the case if the spare wheel were attached to the lid.

Triplex glass is standardised all round on all M.G. models.

The following day we devoted to road work, and the ability of the Magna to average remarkable speeds was very strikingly demonstrated. Making our way from South London to the North West, no fewer than 49 miles were tucked away in the first hour. An average of 40 m.p.h. on ordinary roads requires no attempt at fast driving from the driver, but on one occasion, by making full use of the gear box, brakes and splendid road-holding qualities of the car, we covered 16 miles in 18 minutes, at an average speed of 53 m.p.h.

The road-holding of the M.G. Magna is outstandingly good for its 7' 10" wheelbase. In fact the car encourages the driver to take open bends as fast as possible, just for the pleasure of holding the machine in a slide. The high-geared steering and good weight distribution make the 'L' type Magna one of the most controllable cars on the road to-day.

It was with real regret that we returned our green two seater to the Works. The M.G. Magna 'L' is a car that would inspire affection in the most blasé motorist. One can hardly believe that so much excellence, both in appearance and performance, can be purchased for £285.

Modern art. The Shakespeare Memorial Theatre forms an appropriate setting for the " L " type M.G. Magna.

[*Motor Sport Photographs*]

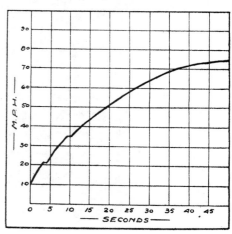

The acceleration chart of the " L " Type Magna.

The New P. Type M.G. Midget. The head lamps are supported on a concealed bar. The direction indicators and the altered body line will be noticed.

NEW M.G. MIDGETS

"P" TYPE WITH THREE BEARING CRANKSHAFT REPLACES THE "J" SERIES.

THE M.G. Car Company announce for March an attractive range of 850 and 750 c.c. models which mark a further advance in the production of small sports cars. Retaining the underslung chassis which proved so successful in the "J" series, the engines, transmission, and brakes have been improved and strengthened, and slight modifications in the coachwork have further improved the line of the "J" type coachwork.

The engine is entirely new. The crankshaft is now carried on three bearings, while the cylinder-head follows the design of the Magnette with a large diameter camshaft carried well above the casting. In this way the size of the water-spaces in the head has been much increased while the cams and camshaft are very substantial. The camshaft is driven by a vertical shaft at the front of the engine combined with the dynamo, with bevel drive top and bottom. The valves are operated by the usual fingers, and 14 m.m. sparking plugs are naturally retained.

The oil filler is situated on the valve cover, covered by a movable plate four inches in diameter which swings aside. All the oil passes through a Tecalemit oil filter in addition to the usual gauze strainer in the sump.

Two semi-downdraft S.U. carburetters are used, fed by an S.U. electric pump, and coil ignition is standard.

The engine is suspended on rubber mountings at three points. A stiff cross-member braces the frame behind the radiator, and the centre part is split horizontally to carry the nose of the crank-case. A bracket from the crank-case carries the radiator, and a stiff plate from the top of it to the cylinder block completes the mounting, so that no flexing of the chassis can effect it.

The gear-box is mounted in unit with the engine. The clutch has been strengthened and the bottom gear-ratio has been lowered for competition-work and emergencies. Third gear is a silent-running ratio with constant-mesh pinions. And open propeller-shaft with Hardy Spicer universal joints is used, and the back axle is now fitted with a four star-wheel differential to stand up to the increased power of the new engine. Luvax hydraulic shock-absorbers are fitted to the back axle,

while the friction-type are used in front.

The chassis follows the lines of the "J" type, upswept in front and underslung at the rear, but has been extended to support the petrol tank and the spare wheel.

Two tubular stays from the chassis carry a dummy Rudge hub which will take either one or two wheels, and the knock-on cap is a great improvement over the metal straps fitted last year.

Twelve-inch brakes are used on the 1934 cars, operated by encased cables. The racing-type hand-brake lever has been retained.

Some alterations have been made in bodywork and equipment. The front wings are stayed by a tube which passes through rubber bushes in the radiator shell, with further bushes where it is fastened to the wings. The bottom stays are also mounted on rubber bushes, so that wing-rattle is positively prevented. The Lucas headlamps have been increased in size and are now chromium-plated. They are carried on the cross-bar. The starting-handle may now be used without removing the dumb-iron fairing.

Direction-indicators are fitted in the scuttle, operated by two push-buttons on the facia-board. The board itself is made of polished wood which is attractive in appearance and avoids the reflection experienced with the aluminium dashes. A large rev-counter is fitted in front of the driver, and carries a scale giving the car's speed on top gear. Trip and season mileages are given through small windows in the plaque in the centre of the facia-board which also carried the horn-button and the dipping switch. The handle of the reserve petrol tap projects alongside the steering wheel. The main electric controls are carried in front of the passenger, with the oil guage.

The windscreen, which is fitted with Triplex toughtened glass, folds flat on the scuttle, and an electric windscreen wiper is standard.

An accessible oil-filler is carried on the cam cover of the new M.G. Midgets. The filter can be seen behind the exhaust pipe.

The squab of the two-seater " P " type cars is supported by notched and slotted plates with bolts and wing-nuts secured in the sides of the body. This does away with the cross-bar behind the seat and affords more easy access to the luggage locker. The main seats adjustment is made by bolts passing through drilled plates.

The four-seater gives more room than last year's J.1 and large foot wells in the back ensure the comfort of the rear passengers.

In a short test of the new two-seater, we were particularly impressed by the smoothness of the engine, which run up to 6,000 r.p.m., although 5,500 is the highest figure recommended, without a trace of period. The clutch was light and smooth, and the new gear-lever gate with a reverse catch is a useful improvement.

It was not possible to attain a high speed in the short time available, but 65 was reached very comfortably on a short stretch of straight road, and close on 60 m.p.h. in third gear. Suspension was good, and the brakes smooth in action and exceptionally powerful when required. The steering seemed to have an increased caster-action, and gave confidence without loosing any of its former lightness.

The " P " type chassis is a worthy successor to the " J " series, and will appeal

[Motor Sport Photographs.
This view shows the new facia board and the spare wheel mounting. The spot-lamp is a useful extra.

even more strongly to the sporting enthusiast and fast motorist. The P2 (two seater) costs £220 and the P1 (four seater) £240. The price of the P4, the supercharged racing car, has not yet been decided.

M.G. MODELS FOR 1934 . . . . CONTINUED FROM PAGE 81

engine which takes the place of the 1,087 c.c. power unit used during the present season. Needless to say, this should result in a greatly improved performance, but the unit itself calls for little description, as the general design is practically identical with that followed in 1933, the main difference lying in the fact that the stroke is now 84 mm. in place of 71 mm.

It is obvious, therefore, that the unit should prove extremely satisfactory in practice, as all its features have been well tried out, both in the hands of private owners and in the racing field, where the Magnette has, of course, met with considerable success.

Features of the engine include an overhead camshaft, twin carburetters, coil ignition with automatic distributor, 14 mm. plugs, large elektron sump, and pump water circulation with temperature control by an R.P. thermostat.

The transmission is noteworthy in that, although the preselector gearbox

is retained and is, in fact, now standardized on all Magnette models, a single-plate clutch of more or less normal type has been interposed between the engine and the gearbox. This is very cleverly arranged so that movement of the clutch pedal serves to operate both the normal clutch and to control the brake bands of the epicyclic gearbox in the normal manner.

Actually, the clutch pedal floats on the withdrawal fork shaft and is connected to it via a floating link which, in turn, is connected to the change-speed mechanism of the preselector box. The clutch is so arranged that the pressure required to disengage the plates is less than that required to operate the epicyclic brake bands, so that, by reason of the floating link, the initial movement of the pedal serves to disengage the clutch; the floating link then comes up against a stop and further movement of the pedal operates the epicyclic gears. The effect is, therefore, that the single-

plate clutch is always disengaged before the epicyclic bands and engaged again after them.

The reason why this design has been adopted is because it has been found in practice that a smoother getaway can be obtained by means of the single-plate clutch and, further, that the risk of serious strains being imposed upon the rear axle by brutal use of the pre-selector box is avoided, because the single-plate clutch gives the slight degree of slip necessary on taking up the drive in these circumstances to prevent any harm being done.

The rest of the chassis follows the same general lines as those adopted in 1933 and employs the well-known M.G. underslung frame. On the long-chassis models, incidentally, a sturdy cross bracing is employed to give rigidity.

To sum up, one may say that the 1934 M.G. programme represents an excellent range of well-tried cars made even better by modifications which have been found in the light of experience to be substantial improvements.

M.G. MIDGET REDESIGNED

Three-bearing Crankshaft Engine—Improved Cylinder Head Design—Strengthened Transmission—New Four-speed Gearbox—More Efficient Brakes—Better Bodywork

The four-seater model, a feature of which is that the rear seat is only one inch higher than the front armchair seats.

DETAILS were announced last week by the M.G. Car Co. of a new M.G. Midget known as the P-type, which supersedes previous models of the J range.

Salient features of the new car are a completely redesigned engine with three-bearing crankshaft, improved design of cylinder head, more robust transmission, a twin-top fourspeed gearbox with a specially low bottom gear for competition work, strengthened back axle with four-pinion differential and 12-in brake drums instead of

stampings of annular H-section, while a thin layer of white metal provides the actual bearing surface. The actual stampings are a light press fit in the crankcase, and the grip of the crankcase, when they are assembled, keeps them in position. The end bearings are of white metal and of very large diameter.

The connecting rods are I-section steel with ribbed caps which further strengthen them. The floating gudgeon pins have Duralumin pads and Aerolite pistons with two rings are used.

The valves are fitted with double springs; the inlets being 1¼ ins. in diameter, whilst those on the exhaust side are 1⅛ ins.

As on the model J, the dynamo is situated at the forward end of the cylinder block, the vertical drive for which forms the motive power between the crankshaft and the overhead camshaft. The distributor drive is also the same, being of the skew variety and driven off the crankshaft direct. An extension of the distributor shaft drives the gear type oil pump,

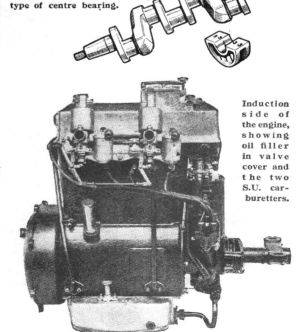

(Right) The new three-bearing crankshaft showing the unusual type of centre bearing.

Induction side of the engine, showing oil filler in valve cover and the two S.U. carburetters.

8-in. The new Midget will be sold as a chassis priced at £175, a two-seater at £220, and a four-seater at £240.

The bore and stroke of the four-cylinder overhead camshaft engine remains the same, namely 57 mm. and 83 mm. respectively, giving a capacity of 847 c.c. As indicated above, three bearings are now used instead of two, the centre one being of a design which has been perfected after long experiment. The bearing is constructed in halves, and takes the form of two steel

The new non-reflecting facia with octagonal-shaped instruments, the one on the right being a combined speedometer and revolution counter. Note also the completely framed screen with the wiper box on the passenger's side.

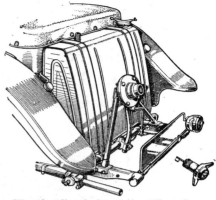

The 12-gallon fuel tank is still at the rear, but a new and very sturdy type of wheel carrier is now fitted.

and there is also provision for a water pump on the other side of the block, it being necessary merely to remove the cover plate and insert the water unit complete with its skew drive. This fitting is provided as an optional extra.

Very careful attention has been paid to the lubrication system. It now incorporates a Tecalemit oil filter which is accessibly fixed on the exhaust side of the engine and filters all the oil on its way to the bearings and valve gear. Another good feature is the provision of a large oil-filling orifice in the valve cover, the lid being so designed that it can be swung aside. Lubricant passes down through the overhead valve gear to the sump, while, so as to protect the pump, the oil suction

centrifugal force, instead of throwing off the lubricant, tends to retain and, in fact, to feed it should any leakage occur from the clutch shaft.

The four forward speed gearbox, as before, is built in unit with the engine and has ratios of 5.375, 7.31, 12.46 and 22.50 to 1. Reverse gear has the same ratio as first. The drive from the gearbox consists of a Hardy Spicer open propeller shaft, the final drive being by spiral bevel with a four-star differential instead of the two-star type previously fitted. The axle casing is also provided with a dip stick, so enabling the level of oil readily to be ascertained.

Springing all round is by semi-elliptic springs, and the detachable wire wheels are shod with 4.00-19

(Above and right) The P-type two-seater Midget in open and closed form.

pipe is enclosed within a cylindrical gauze. The sump of the engine is made of Electron and is copiously ribbed with fins for cooling purposes.

An external petrol tank of large capacity is fitted, and fuel is fed to the engine by means of two semi-downdraught S.U. carburetters. Flexible piping is standardized.

Other improved features include an easily get-at-able dip stick, an improved manifold design and a better method of mounting the radiator. The clutch has been modified, although it is still of the single-plate type. An interesting feature in the design is the provision of a special clutch finger ring faced with Ferobestos. The ring makes contact with the thrust race. which in turn is of such a design that

Dunlop tyres. Hartford shock absorbers are fitted at the front, while at the rear Luvax hydraulic and thermostatically controlled shock absorbers are standard.

The brakes, as previously, are cable operated, although, as already men-

tioned, the drums are now 12-in. diameter and thus are considerably more efficient.

The bodywork has also undergone considerable improvement, and the car now bears an even more attractive appearance than previously. To commence with, an entirely new non-reflecting facia is fitted which carries only three main dials. Directly in front of the driver is a combined rev. counter and speedometer, the latter, incidentally, only giving a true reading in top gear. The dial is also marked with coloured wedges, so indicating the danger zone on the various gears. In the centre is a milo-

meter and two push buttons which operate the Lucas Trafficators, which are situated in the sides of the scuttle. The horn switch and lever for dipping the headlights are at the top of the panel, while on the left-hand side there is the ammeter, oil gauge, coil indicator light, etc. The instruments are also of the non-reflecting type, and in order to make the dials easy to read, convex glasses are fitted.

The equipment is excellent. The screen is of a new and more robust design and fitted with Triplex toughened safety glass. When desired, it can be folded on to the scuttle. Both two-seater and four-seater are fitted with efficient hoods and sidescreens, and on both models the headroom, even when the hood is up, is quite good.

Both the two and four-seaters are available in a number of two-tone colour schemes with leather upholstery to match.

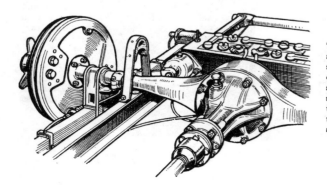

The new P Midget has a straight-side underslung frame of robust design. Brake drums are now of 12-in. instead of 8-in. diameter, there is a dip stick in the differential housing, and the battery is carried at the rear.

1934 RACING CARS
4.—THE M.G. MAGNETTE, K.3.

THE ban on road-racing in Great Britain has prevented the general public from taking the interest in motor-racing which is found in Continental countries, and it is not surprising that since the Sunbeam Motor Company ceased to participate in foreign events, no English racing car capable of taking part in Grand Prix events has been made in a British factory. Happily during the last few years the amazing efficiency of the British 750 c.c. engine has been demonstrated by Austin and by M.G., and with the production by the latter company of the 1,250 c.c. M.G. Magna came a demand for a supercharged version which could be driven in the under 1,100 c.c. events associated with many of the Grand Prix races. The task of the designers was not simplified by the fact that the car must also comply with the international sports car regulations in order to be eligible for the Ulster T.T. race, the only road event held in the British Isles.

In its supercharged form, reduced to 1,100 c.c., the small six-cylinder engine developed surprising power, and at its first public appearance in the 1933 Monte Carlo Rally it was found that the Magnette, as the new car was christened, had been virtually re-designed and was given an engine, chassis and brakes much more substantial than had been the usual practise for 1,100 c.c. cars. In the hand of G. R. W. Wright it won the Mont des Mules Hill Climb in a time only bettered by a Mercédès the previous year.

Development continued, the most notable alteration being the fitting of a Wilson pre-selective gear box. At this time Lord Howe, who had never ceased to hope for a car of British manufacture which he could drive on the Continent, conceived the idea of running a team of Magnettes in the Italian Mille Miglia, after the Targa Florio the most strenuous road race in the world. The cars were completed just in time and were shipped direct from Fowey to Genoa. The cars were soon at Brescia, the starting point of the race, and after a fortnight in which Lord Howe, Sir Henry Birkin and George Eyston, not forgetting their co-drivers Hamilton, Rubin and Lurani got the feeling of their new mounts, the day of the race arrived.

Birkin, whose furious driving was a by-word even on the Continent, was allotted the task of breaking up the opposition Maseratis, and made the terrific average of 87 m.p.h. between Brescia and Bologna. He was forced to retire near Siena with a broken valve, but not before Taruffini on the fastest Maserati had been disposed of. Meanwhile Lord Howe and Eyston forged steadily ahead and after traversing the tortuous Futa and Raticosi Passes came to Rome. The roads north again from Rome were equally arduous, and the drivers' task was made no easier by trouble with ignition and lighting systems. However the little cars were still going splendidly and after regaining Bologna the drivers felt the worst was past. Finally after eighteen hours on the road, the inhabitants of Brescia saw the

The exhaust side of the Magnette eng'ne. The front axle torque cable is seen above the road-spring.

first of the competitors approaching and amid great excitement the cars was made out to be Eyston's Magnette, followed a minute later by the one driven by Lord Howe. In its first appearance in a Continental road-race therefore the Magnette gained first and second places in its class, and also the team prize.

Magnettes were next seen in the International Race at Brooklands, the novelty introduced by the Junior Car Club in which the Double 12 course is used, with varying courses through sandbanks instead of a time handicap. Hall was second, Mrs. Wisdom third and Lord Howe fourth, so the M.G. Company must have been well satisfied with the result.

The combination of acceleration and speed made victory in the Isle of Man Round Town race seem equally certain but all the cars were eliminated by back axle trouble. This was remarkable, considering that they had withstood the stresses of much more arduous Mille Miglia course, but the cause was found to have been the increased power and the constant use of the differential on the right-handed course. As a consequence, later models were fitted with a four-star differential, thus overcoming a fault which only racing could reveal.

Magnettes continued their successes in British events, with a third place for Manby Colegrave in the Empire Trophy, Nuvolari's victory in the R.A.C. Tourist Trophy, and E. R. Hall's win in the 500 Miles Race at 106.53 m.p.h., apart from fine performances at Shelsley and Donington. Abroad Whitney Straight's sensational race in the 1,100 c.c. class of the Coppa Acerbo, in which he beat Barbieri on a Maserati by 1/5 second is especially notable.

The six-cylinder engine has a bore of 57 mm. and a stroke of 71 mm., giving a capacity of 1,086 c.c. The cylinder head carries two vertical overhead valves per cylinder, each with three springs, and they are operated by fingers which pass under a single overhead camshaft.

Each combustion chamber has its own inlet and exhaust port and the 14 mm. plugs are screwed into the off-side of the head. The ribbed induction pipe receives its mixture from the blower at the front end, and has a central explosion valve, while six branch-pipes on the near-side lead into the exhaust manifold.

The cylinder head and the block are both made of high chromium cast iron, and the crankcase is integral with the block. The machined crankshaft is carried in four plain bearings. The alloy pistons have three rings, and steel connecting rods are used with cast-in plain big-ends. The overhead camshaft is driven by a vertical shaft through spiral bevel gears, and the dynamo is integral with the shaft. A water pump is driven by a cross-shaft in front of the engine, and the B.T.H. Polar Inductor magneto, which runs at 2/3 engine speed, is similarly operated on the off-side.

The lubricating oil passes through a Tecalemit filter, and the ribbed elektron sump holds 1½ gallons. The supply is maintained by a float feed from the dash tank which holds a further two gallons. The supercharger is lubricated by a branch pipe from the overhead camshaft.

The standard fuel is 25% Ethyl and 75% benzol.

On last year's models a Powerplus No. 9 supercharger, of the eccentric vane type, was used, carried in front of the radiator and driven by a shaft and reduction gear at 2 3 engine speed. This supercharger will be retained for track races during 1934, but for road work a Marshall 2 vane type will be used, running at engine speed, in order to prevent the oiling of plugs at low speeds.

The compression ratio will be about 5.75 : 1, while the blower pressure will be approximately 12 lbs. No definite horse-power figure is given by the makers, but it is over 100 b.h.p. at 16,300 r.p.m.

A single S.U. carburetter is standard, though two have been used, and it will be fed by an S.U. petrol pump. The fuel tank holds 23 gallons. The induction pipe is without the special slow running hub used on the M.G. Midget, but is fitted with a Kigass spray to assist starting.

No clutch is fitted to the Magnette, as the friction bands in the Wilson pre-selective gear-box also serve to take up the drive. The gears are selected by a short lever mounted on an extension of the gear-box and moving in a serrated quadrant, and other controls such as slow-running adjustment and the ignition lever are also carried there. The gear required is of course engaged by the depression and release of the pedal which replaces the clutch pedal.

With the usual back axle ratio of 4.89 the combined reductions through the gear-box are 4.89, 7.65, 9 78 and 16.6 to 1.

The propellor shaft is of the Hardy Spicer type with all-metal universal joints, while the back axle is of three-quarter floating design with straight-bevel final drive.

The chassis frame is upswept over the front axle and underslung at the rear, and the flat semi-elliptic springs which are bound with cord move in slides at the rear ends. The chassis is braced with

tubular steel members, with a pressing at the rear end and a K shaped strut in the centre of the chassis. Friction shock absorbers are used back and front, four of these, set transversely, being used for the back axle.

The brakes are 13 inches in diameter, with wide drums, but the unsprung weight has been reduced as much as possible by using elektron back plates, shoes and drums with cast iron liners. They are operated by special cased cables. Torque braces from the front axle king-pins to the chassis sides relieve the front springs of the braking torque.

Cam-type steering is used, and a divided track rod has been found to have advantages over the standard lay-out.

During 1933 most of the cars were fitted with a substantial two-seater tour-

A rear view of the body used in 1933. Note the large filler caps on the tank.

ing body with a spare wheel at the back, though Manby-Colegrave and Whitney Straight changed over to streamlined bodies, with a useful improvement in speed. Details of the 1934 bodies have not been settled, but they will probably be light racing bodies similar to the one used by Nuvolari in Ulster, while a short tail may be added. The car with two seater body costs £795.

The chassis weight is approximately 14½ cwt., and with last year's two seater body totalled 17¾ cwt., but with the light body the weight can be reduced to about 15½ cwt. The all-out speed varies of course with the axle-ratio, but an idea can be gained from R. T. Horton's record lap of 115.55 m.p.h. in the British Empire Trophy with the normal road-racing body.

Lord Howe is again taking a team of cars to Italy for the Mille Miglia. He proposes to drive the whole way single-handed, with Thomas, his racing mechanic, as passenger. E. R. Hall will be the second member of the team driving with Mrs. Hall while Penn Hughes and Lurani will be co-drivers on the third car.

Eyston has ordered a team of three cars and will have as his other drivers Penn

PRESENT DAY RACING CARS—*continued*.

Hughes and Wal Handley, the well-known racing motor-cyclist. The Magic Magna, of which more anon, is also being prepared for him, with Denby as spare driver and tuner-in-chief.

Kaye Don has ordered three cars which will be driven by himself, Norman Black, and Jack Field, the Southport driver.

Mere, Yallop, Manby Colegrave and Hall will all be using their last year's cars, while Roy Eccles, Bartlett, C. E. C. Martin, and Ford and Baumer will also have Magnettes for the coming season, and Eccles and Ford have already entered their cars for Le Mans.

Kohlrausch, the well-known German driver, has ordered a Midget and a Magnette and these white-painted English cars will be seen in about 25 events in Germany during the coming season. Fork, another German driver, has also decided to buy a Magnette.

As has already been announced in MOTOR SPORT, Horton is fitting his Magnette with a single-seater body with normal transmission and, with the driver sitting on the right side, an arrangement he used with success on his Midget during 1933. George Eyston is having a special car built with off-set engine and transmission on the lines of the Magic Midget, which will be known as the Magic Magna. R. R. Jackson has also succumbed to the "Monoposto" craze, and is putting a single-seater on his car, which is the original Magnette which won the Mont des Mules Hill Climb. A fourth single seater is

The chassis of the Magic Magna, showing the off-set engine and transmission.

being built by a private individual but is very "hush hush" at present.

The Magnettes have certainly made a excellent showing during the past season, and promise to enliven racing circles at home and abroad during 1934. The next

thing to hope is that Mr. Kimber and his helpers down at Abingdon will turn their attention to something round the three litre mark, with which Great Britain can be adequately represented in the unlimited category.

THE £ s. d. of RUNNING a SMALL CAR

Although his 1929 M.G. Midget has proved strikingly economical, it is not because "The Gipsy" nurses the car. On the left is shown one of his typical holiday loads and, below, how he manages to carry it all; the lid of the tail, it will be observed, is removed for the purpose.

Some Striking Figures by "The Gipsy" Who, Incidentally, Believes in Keeping an Old Friend

SOME readers of *The Light Car* may perhaps remember that about a year ago I gave an account of the running costs of a second-hand 1929 M.G. Midget over a period of two years. The car was bought by me from a friend in 1930 after a mileage of 8,210.8.

I have often seen the recommendation that it is most economical to change cars fairly frequently before depreciation becomes too great, but there must be any number of people—particularly those of a mechanical turn of mind—who, having struck a really trusty and reliable little friend, consider their first purchase price as "money well spent and gone" and keep their car for a number of years.

It may, therefore, be of interest to readers who hold this view if I give some account of the expenses during the fourth year of the Midget's life—the third year of my ownership.

This car, as well as providing my daily transport to and from business, is also by way of being rather a hobby in itself. As a result it probably receives rather more than the usual share of attention so far as the mechanical side is concerned. It also receives a "dry clean" with Karpol occasionally, but I blush to say that it has had a "professional" wash only once in its life! Still, its treatment appears to agree with it as up to the time of writing it had done over 46,000 miles and is going as well as it did the day I bought it.

An accurate log is kept of all runs and any work done, and the petrol and oil consumption are checked up every

RUNNING EXPENSES, 1932-1933.			
	£	s.	d.
Tax (quarterly) ..	8	16	0
Petrol (295 gallons)	20	17	11
Oil (11 gallons)..	2	17	9
Comprehensive insurance	8	16	0
Replacements and repairs (including latest pattern crankshaft and bearings, exhaust valves, rings, and sundry small parts replaced) ..	9	2	9
Extras (including fitting Dunlop Latex upholstery, Burgess silencer, air valve, set of K.L.G. K.1 plugs, tonneau cover, etc.) ..	7	13	0
	58	3	5
Depreciation @ 20% ..	18	2	10
Loss of interest on capital @ 5% ..	4	10	8
Total ..	80	16	11
Distance covered ..	13,534 miles		
Petrol consumption ..	45.88 m.p.g.		
Oil consumption (excluding draining off) ..	1,504 m.p.g.		
Full cost including depreciation ..	1.43d. per mile		
Cost omitting depreciation, etc. ..	1.03d. per mile		

1,000 miles. These at present vary between 45 m.p.g. and 50 m.p.g. for petrol and about 1,100 m.p.g. and 1,800 m.p.g. for oil, according to driving conditions.

In spite of the harrowing tales of excessive cylinder wear which I hear all round, my engine has not yet been rebored and the present oil consumption certainly does not seem to warrant it.

The engine was originally run on "Triple Shell" oil until the advent of "Aero Shell" when a change-over to this grade was made early in 1931. First quality petrol (generally Shell) has been used almost exclusively.

As is natural with a light car with about 40,000 miles to its credit, a certain amount of replacements has been made during the year under review. During this period I have fitted a new set of rings and exhaust valves, a 1932 crankshaft with big ends and rear main bearing and one or two small parts such as roller bearings for the vertical camshaft drive. I also noticed that the rear axle was inclined to "hum" a little, but a new distance piece in the bevel housing cured that.

The actual amount spent on the engine during the year is only just over £7, the remainder being made up of odds and ends and some "extras." Among the latter are two of which I speak very highly. One is a Burgess silencer and the other is Dunlopillo Latex upholstery.

The Burgess silencer, although absolutely "straight through," is really remarkable in its efficiency and has

THE £ s. d. OF A SMALL CAR

Continued

SUMMARY OF RUNNING COSTS, ETC., SINCE NEW.

Year	1929/1930*	1930/1931	1931/1932	1932/1933
Petrol Consumption (m.p.g.)	Approx. 38	37.90	46.21	45.88
Oil Consumption (m.p.g.)	Approx. 2,000	2,257	1,740	1,504
Cost (including depreciation) (pence per mile)	Not known	2.22	1.70	1.43
Cost (less depreciation) (pence per mile)	Not known	1.22	1.08	1.03

*Prior to purchase by the writer.

effectively killed the somewhat harsh exhaust note which was a characteristic of the earlier Midgets.

Having practically worn out some ancient air cushion seats which regularly expired with a dying gasp about every 100 miles, I had some seats made with Dunlop Latex rubber. The difference in all-round comfort was, naturally, marked: these cushions fulfill all the claims made for them. Particularly on long runs of 250 to 300 miles in the day does one appreciate the real comfort they give.

The general performance of the old car does not appear to have fallen off at all as the mileage mounts up.

I generally spend my holidays in the same very hilly part of the country, so that each year I have a good chance of comparing performance. On my last visit to this district, and in spite of having gone there with about 5,000 miles recorded since decarbonizing, the behaviour on my pet roads and hills did not seem to be a bit different from the first visit there.

If the truth be told I expect I am really the sort of customer that Mr. Cecil Kimber—the great White Chief of M.G.'s—would much sooner do without! I am—and always have been—guilty of occasionally using my Midget as a furniture van rather than a sports car! It is really not so much the great weight of luggage which I take as the bulk of it.

I find, on my various excursions into the wilds, that by moving my spare wheel to a temporary and somewhat primitive mounting at the side, I can accommodate quite a considerable amount of "junk." By driving at a reasonable speed and taking things gently round corners and on rough roads I have never been involved in any situations of danger or damage. Although the load looks rather formidable the weight is not really very great and is probably no more than a coupé model with passenger.

Whilst I was away last summer I noticed an article in one of the daily papers on overloading small cars and on the damage that people do to their cars through ignorance. I will perhaps plead guilty to overloading, but I will deny the charge of ignorance! I was perfectly aware of what I intended to do with my car when I bought it, and it is quite an easy thing to point an accusing finger at others when one is backed by a large bank balance and a whole fleet of cars from a Rolls downwards!

Still, in spite of it all, the old 'bus continues its "Jekyll and Hyde" existence—90 per cent. normal open two-seater and 10 per cent. pantechnicon—and so well is it running that I am seriously considering celebrating its next birthday by giving it a four-speed gearbox!

THE GIPSY.

THOSE FLAG SIGNALS

I CANNOT help thinking that the International flag signals used for motor races ought to have a far wider application. For starting purposes the National flag is ideal. By arrangement with one's local station-master one might wave it from a bedroom window as an indication that the last mouthful of egg and bacon had been swallowed and that one was about to sally forth to catch the 8.30, or, better still, it might be televised to the spot where you are waiting for your little bit of trouble and strife as an indication

that she is on her way to the rendezvous (at which you have probably been waiting for an hour-and-a-half).

The yellow flag would be handy in the home. Waved in the face of one's mother-in-law, its message, "Stop instantly!" would be significant. It might be preceded by the dark blue flag waved vigorously by the wife as one returned to the house after a trying day as an indication that the first-named lady has arrived. "Danger

ahead!"—an unmistakable and very useful warning.

Policemen might be equipped with the light blue flag. If, for example, one was being chased by a speed cop, the courteous constable would hold out the flag horizontally, and, obeying its command, one would "keep close to the left to allow another competitor to pass." I have a suspicion, however, that the average unsympathetic bobby would be far more likely to show the black flag ("competitor must stop") and then proceed to do a little scrutineering with a view to disqualification!

As for the green flag (race finished), probably this would be handy at school treats as a signal that the little visitors had gorged to their uttermost, whilst surely no better alternative use could be found for the chequered flag than to hoist it over a disused-car park. Indubitably it would indicate that the cars had "finished the course"!

The new body is scarcely w i d e r than the radiator at any point.

The K3 M.G. Magnette chassis.

appropriate setting of the M.G. dep over at the Brooklands Aerodrome, clos to the track edge, in its stripped guise without wings or electrical gear, as th cars will run in the International Trophy The K3 is, of course, the supercharge 1,100 c.c. six-cylinder design, such a won the Ulster T.T. last year.

One of the principal points of th latest cars is that an entirely differen type of body is now fitted. This is nar rower amidships, in fact, does not exten anywhere much beyond the extrem limits of the radiator sides, looking at th car in front view, though built, naturally to the International code of bod measurements laid down, whilst instea of the cut-off, square-ended tail of las year, with separate fuel tank, there now a streamline shape of tail, of whic the tank is part. The rear view of th latest body looks business-like, withou excrescences or "bits and pieces," an it must be much more efficient in th streamline sense, for "tail drag" fron the suction effect of a square tail is big factor; yet it houses a tank tha holds twenty-seven and a half gallons.

Very Light Body

This body actually is just a ligh aluminium shell, which, they told m you can pick up easily as a unit. is without doors, and has a scuttl "hump" in front of the driver, with small windscreen, for protection.

In the interludes of conversatior whilst we were going over the mai points of the car, I was becoming mor and more intrigued with the idea putting into practice the second part

H E who controls these things summoned me to the presence the other day and, without preamble, as is his way, shot at me the question, "What have you got on?" I knew very well that this had no sartorial significance, and for a split second all manner of possibilities ran through my conscience-stricken head as to what might be about to happen. However, to my ill-concealed relief, the point was that Authority wanted to know what arrangements I had in hand for the immediate future, as I was to see and try, forthwith, a certain product of Abingdon-on-Thames, to wit, an M.G.

There was nothing very unusual in the bare fact itself, but I little realised as I closed the Editorial door behind me quite how entertaining an experience, called work, that this assignment—as I believe they call it in America—was to lead me to. Instructions were that I should acquaint myself with the details of the latest racing Magnette, known as the K3, and, with the co-operation of the M.G. potentates, obtain practical experience of the car in the form in which a number of examples are racing in the International Trophy at Brooklands to-morrow.

So, the details fixed, I hied myself bright and early the next morning to the track, there to meet George Tuck, of M.G.'s, armed with photographs and technical specifications in great detail, and also one of the actual cars, on which preparation in readiness for the race was delayed awhile in order that we might go over the car generally to show me the differences in the 1934 racing

version as compared with last year's model.

Behind that rather bald description, K3 Magnette, a great deal is hidden. Not everyone knows, perhaps, that this is a pukka racing car which anyone with suitable tastes and the necessary cash can purchase, either to compete with—for it

The K3 Magnette in stripped racing form; windscreen, wings, and lamps are supplied for ordinary use.

is designed and built from the very commencement for this purpose—or to use as an ultra high-performance road machine with wings and lamps, at the by no means out-of-reach price of £795. It is, in other words, a production racing car, perhaps hardly paralleled in its availability.

We were considering it, however, on this fine, bright morning, in the entirely

my instructions about actually tryin the car. However, there really are som extremely interesting points on thes machines, the cumulative effect of whic you appreciate when you come to handl the car, but which you can follow, on by one, only by looking round it as stands in front of you, resplendent in it new green paint and seemingly awaitin the human hands that will cause a ful throated crackle of exhaust to issue from that hearty-looking fishtail of official pattern.

What impresses me about the machine in general is that here is a car which, not only as a basic design, but right through all the details appertaining to a machine suitable for racing, is complete, and developed as the result of accumulated practical experience. You can have it with battery, starting motor, and lamps, and then the fuel supply is fed by two of the S.U. electric pumps, one of them constituting a reserve, since only the second pump will feed the last three gallons; but on the car in front of me, as on the others in the race, air pressure maintained by a hand pump in the driving compartment is used to draw the fuel from the tank, there being no battery fitted on these particular cars.

New Type Supercharger

They are using a different type of supercharger from that formerly fitted, the present one being of Roots rotor pattern, and driven, as before, at engine speed from the nose of the crankshaft. An M.G. feature is a big reserve tank for oil in the scuttle, holding three gallons, which automatically replenishes the engine sump as necessary by means of a needle-and-float mechanism resembling that of a carburetter.

A lot has been done in the way of increasing brake efficiency. They use elektron, which has the valuable property of quickly getting rid of heat, besides being light, for the drums, and these are shrunk on to inner drums, of steel, forming the surface on which the fabric of the shoes actually makes contact. The principal change is in the operation of the brakes, in which everything has been aimed at giving a powerful effect from comparatively light pressure on the pedal, and as little loss due to friction anywhere in the system as is practicable.

To this end, for each brake two cam levers are used, one operated by the inner cable and one by the outer casing running from the brake pedal cross-shaft to each drum, thereby greatly increasing the force of application of the shoes for a given foot pressure. Rollers are used as cams to operate the shoes, by which means friction is reduced, and another point is a centralising link designed to bring the shoes truly central and concentric with their drum at the first application of the pedal, thus giving a smooth, even effect, besides ensuring that the linings shall wear down evenly.

Brakes are enormously important, of course, in a car intended for the kind of use which the K3 Magnette will be put to, and it is obvious that the M.G. design people have studied the matter closely. Conveniently in the driving compartment there is a hand wheel which will take up the adjustments of all four brakes to a limited extent while the car is running, though the adjustments for general use are on the inside faces of the drums.

The back axle, I noticed, has two pairs of Hartford Duplex shock absorbers at each side, with their arms parallel with the axle side sleeves, and the front axle has the usual single pair.

Instrument boards always interest me, and the arrangement of the dials on this car is businesslike, in keeping with the character of the machine. Apart from the big rev counter in front of the driver, there are an air pressure gauge—for the fuel supply system when hand-main-

tained pressure feed is used—a super-charger pressure gauge, water thermometer, oil thermometer, the usual oil pressure gauge, and another oil pressure gauge, relating to the supply for the supercharger itself, which is by-passed from the pressure feed to the overhead valve gear.

In addition, these particular cars have only an on-off switch for the magneto, and a control for the Ki-gass fuel spray, which is fitted to facilitate starting. The instrument board is secured to the chassis, and is not part of the body. The ignition advance and retard control is built into the "turret" which houses the pre-selector gear lever, close to the driver's left hand, and the steering wheel is entirely devoid of impedimenta.

It took less time to have these various things impressed upon the memory than it does to record them subsequently, and the great moment for a run on the car

In this overhead view can be seen, in detail, the essentially practical instrument board, and the hand-wheel adjustment for taking up the brakes, whilst a good impression is given of the new streamline tail, which conceals a tank with a capacity of $27\frac{1}{2}$ gallons

had arrived. None of these new-type International Trophy cars had done a very great mileage at the time—this actual machine formed one of the team of cars entered by G. E. T. Eyston—so for my run on the track with it a rev limit of 5,000 r.p.m. was set for the time being. Also, the tank then contained a benzole-petrol mixture, in the proportion of 80 per cent. benzole, and fairly "soft" plugs were fitted, actually K.L.G. 718As, instead of special fuel, as is best for maximum efficiency, and plugs of a type that will withstand high speed.

I had the M.G. mechanic Hounslow as passenger, who will be remembered by many people as mechanic to Nuvolari

Everything about the car as a whole suggests latent power and efficiency.

in the victorious Magnette in last year's T.T. We set off along the aerodrome road, into the paddock, and out on to the track, sedately enough at first, to give the oil time to warm up, and to get the feel of the car to some extent.

Then, when it came to opening it up within the restrictions imposed by the rev limit mentioned, the point that most impressed me about the car was its easy handling at speeds which, except to those who are constantly driving machines of racing type, are high. In the ordinary course of events I get a good deal of experience of testing fairly quick cars on the track, but the Magnette seemed singularly straightforward to deal with, in spite of a quite strong wind that was blowing.

It is interesting that a thousand revs are equivalent to exactly 20 m.p.h. on top gear; so I had been informed, and so a stop-watch reading showed which I took over half a mile at as steady a reading of 4,000 r.p.m. as one can manage in view of the fluctuations in throttle position caused by the bumps. I made the reading to be just over 80 m.p.h., but that was ambling with this machine.

We were not out to "burst" the motor car, naturally, less than normally so in view of the imminence of the race, and it was little use taking acceleration figures through the gears unless the full limits on the indirect ratios could be employed, though readings from rest up to, say, 80, 90 and 100 m.p.h., or from 60 to 100 m.p.h. would be interesting with a car of this type.

A Dead-easy "Touring" 100

What surprised me, however, was that on one run, with the wind, over the half-mile ending past the Vickers sheds, retaining full respect for the rev limit, and without it feeling at all rapid out of the ordinary, I clocked 18 sec., which is 100 m.p.h. dead; and this with the throttle seemingly right back.

The exhaust note is wonderfully satisfactory, and the preselector change entirely suited to the car. It gives, of course, an exceedingly rapid change, and must be marvellous to handle when full revs can be indulged in on the gears—the engine's peak is 6,500 r.p.m., by the way. Secondly, I thought the car comfortable, and not too harsh on the springs at the lower speeds—though much of that depends, naturally, upon the setting of the shock absorbers.

Nothing about the car is for effect alone —every item has its job to do.

M.G. MAGNETTE K3.
Specification.

6 cylinders, 57 × 83 mm., 1,071 c.c. Nominal compression ratio 6.4 to 1 (approx.). Four-bearing crankshaft. Overhead camshaft; triple valve springs. Elektron sump; capacity 2 gallons.

Ignition by polar inductor magneto; 14 mm. sparking plugs. Supercharger pressure 10 to 12 lb. per sq. in.

4-speed pre-selector gear box (Wilson patents). Ratios: 14.7, 8.66, 5.9 and 4.33 to 1, or 16.6, 9.78, 6.65 and 4.89 to 1.

Half-elliptic springs front and rear, underslung, and flat under load; spring leaves taped and bound with cord.

Cam steering gear: patent M.G. divided twin track rod. Threequarter floating rear axle; straight-toothed bevel pinion and crown wheel final drive.

Rudge-Whitworth racing wheels, with 4.75in. Fort Dunlop tyres as standard.

Two-seater body; wings quickly removable.

Standard finish British racing green, with leather upholstery to match; normal M.G. duotone colour schemes available without extra charge. Price £795.

Wheelbase 7ft. 10⅜in.; track 4ft., overall length of two-seater 12ft. 1in. Chassis weight 13½ cwt.

Another remarkable thing is that the car felt as though it could be handled reasonably on the road—I retain vivid recollections of a brief run last year near the works on one of the 1933 Mille Miglia machines. We did not sample that aspect of this car's behaviour—without wings or any semblance of number plates!—and the throttle stop was set too far open to allow throttling down appreciably below 1,000 r.p.m.; but I would certainly take on a main road run joyfully on this type of car, even if not a shopping expedition, though probably something would have to be done about the exhaust note.

Later on, when the tank had been filled with special fuel—in conjunction with Pratts, special fuels have been made up for M.G.s for competition work —and with K.L.G. 689 plugs fitted in place of the others, I had the interesting opportunity of going round with George Eyston in the same car. He called it "pottering round," and he wasn't using anything like the available revs, for similar reasons as applied in the morning, our highest maintained speed being 5,300 r.p.m., which I clocked on the stop-watch as giving 104.65 m.p.h. over the same favourable half-mile as before, and a lap at just under the 100. It was a day when the wind against the car all down the railway straight acted as something approaching a powerful brake.

Riding as passenger in a car travelling at round about the 100 mark on Brooklands is a decidedly different experience from handling the same car oneself. It is not so much that you necessarily expect anything to happen—with Eyston I felt perfectly happy—but especially in a comparatively small car, you are thrown about on the roughest parts of the track, try how you may to brace yourself against the floorboards, and you realise how great a difference it makes having the steering wheel to steady you.

The figures, of course, represent nothing like the ultimate performance possible with the car when entirely run in and free, and with final tuning effected, but they are perhaps interesting as samples of what may be expected.

After that I had to call it a day, resume conventional head gear, climb into a sedate though worthy automobile, and leave the K3 Magnette and that "lair of speed" or "concrete saucer of death," otherwise, except in daily papers, known as Brooklands. And a very good day, too.

LIGHTING BY THE CLOCK
An Automatic Time Switch Operated by a Special Dashboard Timepiece

THE idea of having an automatic switch capable of being set to turn on the side and rear lights at a predetermined moment is not a new one, but for such busy men as doctors, who find it necessary to park their cars for indeterminate periods, a device on these lines would prove a boon.

It is significant that a medical man, Dr. Cyril A. Paulusz, should have developed an automatic switch operated by a dash clock which is normal in every

way save that an "alarm" setting is incorporated. Instead, however, of a bell, the gear is incorporated with a relay consisting of an electro-magnet and an armature connected with a special switch in the lighting system. As soon as the "alarm" operates the armature and the switch, the magnet is electrified, and the armature will remain in the "on" position until the lights are switched off again.

In practice, a small thumb switch on

the dashboard decides whether the system shall be in operation or whether the lighting switch shall operate in the normal manner. With the system in action a thumb screw is used to move the alarm hand, which is turned to the time for lighting up, the main lamp switch turned to "side," and in due course the lights will go on and stay on until the main switch is moved again. The system is patented, and Dr. Paulusz' address is 11, Palmyra Square, Warrington.

The Autocar Road Tests

M.G. MAGNA CONTINENTAL COUPÉ

Very Comfortable, Beautifully Finished Small Quality Car Which Easily Makes High Averages

SOMEHOW it is natural to think of the M.G. as an open car, but there must be a considerable number of owners who require the various advantages of a closed body, and at the same time appreciate the mechanical qualities of a proved sports engine and chassis design such as the M.G. There are many of the closed models, of various types, in use.

For such people there is the Magna Continental coupé, a smart two-seater salonette which was introduced as a new body type at the last Olympia Show, and which is mounted on the 1,100 c.c. six-cylinder chassis. It is a fascinating little car, which handles beautifully and involves practically no sacrifice of usable performance compared with the normal open models, such is the power developed by the very lively overhead camshaft, twin-carburetter engine.

Especially in acceleration through the gears this car is the match of most small sports-type machines one encounters on the road. It gives all the protection of a saloon without the occupants feeling too much shut in, in which matter the M.G. arrangement of transparent panels in the sliding roof has a considerable influence.

It is a deceptive kind of car in the right sense ; for all its power the extremely smooth, quiet engine does not appear to be working at ordinary road speeds. The car floats along happily at 50 to 55 m.p.h. or so without feeling stressed—seems as though it wants to go faster, in fact, besides holding its speed well on gradients, and picking up rapidly after it has been slowed for other traffic.

It is found on a known journey that one has put up an average very nearly as good as that achieved by any type of car one has driven over the same road, yet without effort having to be exerted by the driver or by the car itself. This is an exceedingly valuable attribute and one of the car's principal characteristics.

Whatever may be the conditions of road or traffic, the driver has the most satisfactory feeling that the car will answer exactly. When passing another vehicle at speed, or rounding curves and appreciable corners quite fast, there is still a feeling of certainty and accuracy, yet all the controls are exceptionally light in action. The coupé is as steady to all intents and purposes as an open model, and it rides very well over the wavy type of road which sometimes sets up fore-and-aft pitching in small cars. Friction shock absorbers are used on the M.G.

This Magna exhibits its curious deceptiveness even in the brakes. One discovers that very light pressure on the pedal produces the necessary deceleration for all average requirements, and there is little suggestion of the real decisiveness that the big drums can give until the pedal is pushed hard down for a sudden emergency stop. The figure given in the table, 31 feet from 30 m.p.h., is an average of two tests, and though the braking test had to be made on a wet concrete surface, the car pulled up all square, without grab to either side.

The type of hand brake for long used on M.G.s, in which the lever does not engage with the ratchet unless the knob is depressed, and is freed by a slight backward pull, is exceedingly useful in restarting on a gradient, and the brake holds absolutely firmly.

The other test figures, for speed and acceleration, are increased in value by the fact that conditions at the time were by no means ideal.

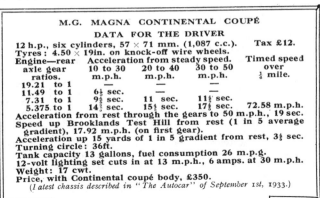

M.G. MAGNA CONTINENTAL COUPÉ			
DATA FOR THE DRIVER			
12 h.p., six cylinders, 57 × 71 mm. (1,087 c.c.).			Tax £12.
Tyres : 4.50 × 19in. on knock-off wire wheels.			
Engine—rear	Acceleration from steady speed.		Timed speed
axle gear	10 to 30	20 to 40	30 to 50	over
ratios.	m.p.h.	m.p.h.	m.p.h.	¼ mile.
19.21 to 1	—	—	—	
11.49 to 1	6¼ sec.	—	—	
7.31 to 1	9½ sec.	11 sec.	11¼ sec.	
5.375 to 1	14¾ sec.	15½ sec.	17½ sec.	72.58 m.p.h.

Acceleration from rest through the gears to 50 m.p.h., 19 sec.
Speed up Brooklands Test Hill from rest (1 in 5 average gradient), 17.92 m.p.h. (on first gear).
Acceleration up 15 yards of 1 in 5 gradient from rest, 3½ sec.
Turning circle: 36ft.
Tank capacity 13 gallons, fuel consumption 26 m.p.g.
12-volt lighting set cuts in at 13 m.p.h., 6 amps. at 30 m.p.h.
Weight: 17 cwt.
Price, with Continental coupé body, £350.
(*Latest chassis described in " The Autocar" of September 1st, 1933.*)

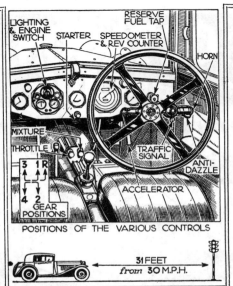

POSITIONS OF THE VARIOUS CONTROLS

A CHEAPER M.G. MAGNETTE

THE "N" TYPE WITH 1250 c.c. ENGINE

LAST year the M.G. range of small sixes included the 1,100 c.c. Magnette with a full four-seater body, and the Magna range with a similar engine in a small chassis. For 1934 the Magna range except for the Continental coupé has been discontinued and in its place is found the "N" Magnette series. A 1,250 c.c. engine is used and the chassis is large enough to give full accommodation for four people.

The engine is of course a six, with dimensions 57 mm. and 83 mm. The new-type cylinder-head with large water spaces and a heavier camshaft is used, and the oil filler is embodied in the cam-case. Twin S.U. carburetters are used, fed by an electric pump. The crankshaft has four bearings and a Tecalemit oil filter is included in the lubrication system. The engine is suspended on rubber at three points.

The clutch is a new single-plate type with laminated centre plate, and the twin-top 4 speed gear box has an improved gate with a reverse stop. The mounting of the mixture and slow-running controls has been improved.

A Hardy-Spicer balanced propeller-shaft with metal universal joints takes the drive to the three-quarter floating rear axle. A four-star differential is now used.

The chassis is upswept in the front and underslung at the rear, and braced with cross tubes of large section. The springs are also underslung, located in silentbloc bushes in front with the rear end sliding in trunnions. Hartford shock-absorbers are fitted in front and hydraulics, thermostatically controlled at the rear. The track is 3' 9" and the wheelbase 7' 10".

A new type of cam-gear steering mechanism is used. The brakes are cable-operated and operate in hardened 12 inch drums. The Rudge wheels are fitted with 18 by 4.75 Dunlop tyres.

Twelve-volt coil ignition is used, and the two six-volt batteries are carried on either side of the propeller shaft. Chromium-plated head and side lights are standard, also a fog lamp, and all main circuits have separate fuses.

A large rev.-counter with a speed scale for top gear is mounted in front of the driver, and other necessary instruments are mounted in a separate panel on the left. In the centre is the mileage indicator with trip and the ignition switch. A reserve petrol tap projects through the dash behind the steering wheel.

The body is mounted on rubber, the sides being carried on a special sub-frame parallel to the chassis members.

The four-seater body is of attractive appearance with graceful swept front wings and upswept scuttle. The doors are cut away to clear the elbows of the front passengers and are noticeably wide considerably facilitating getting into the back and front seats. Traffic indicators are let into the scuttle.

The "N" type M.G. Magnette will be available as an open four-seater, as illustrated, at £335, while a smart two-seater costs £305.

THE P TYPE M.G. MIDGET

THERE can be no dispute that in the smaller sports car classes the British vehicle reigns supreme, and the M.G. Car Company has played a large part in this achievement. In producing the P Type Midget, the successor to the famous " J," another step forward has been made, not so much in all-out speed, for the limit must nearly be reached in that direction, but in good manners and general pleasantness of handling.

An 850 c.c. engine must needs run fast to produce its power, but by using a three-bearing crankshaft the full speed range is utilised on the car under review without a trace of vibration, and by the use of two silencers the exhaust note has been reduced to nothing more than a quiet hum. Consequently the car under review could be kept at between 55 and 60 m.p.h. hours on end without fuss, a most valuable characteristic for those who use their cars for long journeys in addition to the mere week-end breather, where a certain amount of noise and roughness is of minor importance.

The springing, too, reached a high standard of comfort for a small car. Hydraulic shock-absorbers have replaced the friction-type at the rear, with increased comfort at low speeds, while the car can be taken round bends fast enough to make the tyres scream without tending to roll. One setting sufficed for smooth main roads, rough lanes and for all-out running on the track. On main roads corrugated by bus traffic, the Midget pitches rather more than a big car would do, but such behaviour is inevitable with a short wheel-base vehicle.

Lessons doubtless gained from racing experience have been applied to the steering, the ratio has been raised without making it heavy, and altogether it gave confidence up to the highest speeds of which the car is capable. A useful amount of self-centering is provided.

Brief Specification.

Engine : Four cylinders, 57 mm bore, 83 mm. stroke, capacity 847 c.c. Tax £8. Overhead valves, camshaft operated. Coil ignition. Two S.U. carburetters.

Gearbox : Four speeds and reverse. Constant mesh third gear. Ratios 5.37, 7.31, 12.46 and 22.5 to 1.

Dimensions : Wheelbase 7ft. 3½in. Track 3ft. 6in. Weight with two-seater body 14 cwt.

Price with two-seater body £220.

The size of the brake drums has been increased to 12 inches, and the brakes are powerful without any vices. The car can be controlled for any ordinary purpose with the foot-pedal, but in case of emergency stops, the hand-brake lever, which also applies the four brakes, is used. On several occasions the remarkable figure of 48 feet was achieved on dry concrete with only the slightest deviation from the straight. The brake lever is fitted with a racing-type ratchet which only engages when a thimble on the top is pressed and flies off again when the lever is pulled, so there is no possibility of its getting jammed on during the hectic moments of a stop-and-restart test.

The driving position has been as well thought out as the other details, and the spring-spoke steering wheel comes into the lap, the short remote-control gear-lever and the hand brake are readily worked by the left hand, while the pedals are light in operation and set at exactly the right angle. The only criticism one can make is that there is no room for the left foot alongside the clutch pedal, so that it must either rest against it, which is not too good for the clutch race, or be planted high up on the dash. In spite of a long and wide bonnet both wings are clearly seen, and the windscreen affords ample protection for the tallest driver.

As is usual with an unsupercharged engine of small capacity, the power output drops rapidly below 2,500 r.p.m., and to get good acceleration from low speeds it is necessary to drop down to third or even second gear. The change-down to third is a quick one, and as this is a silent ratio and permits a speed of 60 m.p.h. at 5,500 r.p.m., it is particularly useful for fast running on winding roads. Bottom gear is very low, intended primarily for trials use, and second is therefore wider from third than would usually be the case. This wide spacing coupled with apparently a rather heavy

The engine and dashboard are very accessible when the bonnet is lifted. Note the oil-filler on the cam-case.

driven clutch-plate made the second-third change slow, but the timing is not critical, and can be speeded up considerably at the expense of a little noise. On the level the car was usually started on second gear, which gives a maximum speed of 35 m.p.h., while it is interesting to note that at 60 m.p.h. on top the engine is running at 4,000 m.p.h.

Engine speeds such as these appear rather high to the big car enthusiast, but with the smooth-running and silent engine the needle of the rev-counter is the only thing which draws attention to the fact. The chassis layout and road-holding, as has been pointed out, give the driver every confidence, and in fact the P Type Midget is the first small car of its type that suggests itself equally for fast touring and all-out performance. The car runs smoothly down to 15 m.p.h. on top, though as has been stated, for a quick getaway the gears must then be used.

Economy in operation is an important matter nowadays, and it was found that in spite of long spells of flat-out running tests on the track, the petrol consumption worked out at approximately 40 miles to the gallon, and the car ran on benzol mixture or Pratt's Ethyl without any sign of pinking.

On the road, as has been stated, the car can maintain 55 to 60 m.p.h., aided by its good brakes, easy gear-change, and fast cornering. The maximum speed with the screen raised is about 65 m.p.h. On the track we achieved a timed speed of 72 m.p.h. over the half-mile with lowered screen, and top gear is high enough to allow a speed of some 80 m.p.h. down a long slope without over-revving. This relatively high ratio reduces to some extent the acceleration on top, but saves both fuel and engine wear, while a characteristic of the Midget is that once it has reached, say, 65 miles an hour, it hangs on to it well even on an undulating road.

During the past year, J Type Midgets have had numerous successes in reliability trials, and the new car, with its low bottom gear, seemed particularly suited for this job. The car was taken up High Ruse, Shillingridge, Maiden's Grove, and Crowell, all well-known hills in the Chilterns, and climbed them all on half-throttle or less. The surfaces were of course dry after the prolonged spell of fine weather, but under winter conditions, particularly if the car were fitted with competition tyres, the result would have been equally certain.

The track is comparatively narrow, which allows the best path to be chosen even on a narrow lane, and the steering was definite enough to allow the car to be placed exactly where required, and it has a good lock and a useful ground-clearance. The brakes are powerful, as

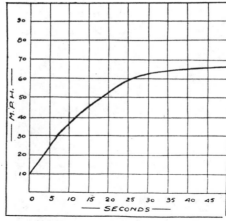

The acceleration chart of the P type M.G. Midget.

[*Motor Sport Photographs*

The front of the latest M.G. Midget has been further improved by concealing the headlamp tie-bar, while the large brake-drums have a more practical appeal.

has already been stated, and by using the hand lever the car can be checked instantly on a downhill grade of 1 in 4 or placed neatly between the lines of a stop-and-restart. The engine and chassis specification were fully described in the March issue of MOTOR SPORT, but a brief summary will be of interest. The four-cylinder engine, which is mounted on rubber at three points, has an overhead camshaft, driven by shaft and bevels at the front end, and the dynamo is carried on this vertical shaft. The valves are operated by fingers, the inlet ports are on one side

of the cylinder block and the exhaust ports on the other side. 14 mm. plugs are used, and automatic advance and retard is provided for the coil ignition.

The two S.U. carburetters are supplied by an electric pump made by the same firm, and the rear tank holds 12 gallons. The cylinder-block and the top half of the crank-case are in one, and the crank-shaft is carried in three plain bearings ; the big ends are also plain.

The clutch has been strengthened, the gear box has a silent third ratio, and a four-star differential is used in the bevel-driven back axle. The chassis is upswept in front and passes under the rear axle, with flat semi-elliptic springs all round. The 12-inch brakes are operated by enclosed cables, and grouped nipples are used for the chassis lubrication.

M.G.s have always been noted for their attractive lines, and the latest bodywork is particularly neat and well appointed. The finish of the cellulose was outstanding and the front view of the car, which has been made more neat by doing away with the outside crossbar, is well set-off by the new chromium-plated lamps.

The engine oil is replenished through a large filler on the cam-case, and the lubricant in circulation is forced through a Tecalemit pressure filter mounted beside the engine.

The long swept wings afford good protection, and all wing-stays are mounted on rubber bushes which can never come loose or rattle. The seats are adjustable and well padded, and the cushions are fitted with Float-on-Air interiors, which are yielding and yet provide support against side-sway. The hood folds neatly into the back of the car, which also provides space for a pair of small suit-cases. The rear of the car is set off by a neat spare wheel carrier supported on tubes from the chassis, and capable of taking two wheels if required.

In refinement of running and pleasing lines the P Type Midget reaches a high standard, and will appeal to an even wider section of the motoring public than its predecessors of similar type. The address of the makers is the M.G. Car Company, Abingdon-on-Thames, who issue an attractive coloured catalogue dealing fully with the salient points of the new car.

THE 1935 P-TYPE M.G. MIDGET

One of the most attractive small sports cars on the road, and capable of over 75 m.p.h.

ON the road the P-type Midget realizes the promise of its sleek and speedy lines. It cruises fast, holding 55-60 m.p.h. with an absence of fuss and engine noise worthy of a car twice the size and price, and its stability is an outstanding feature.

To obtain definite data of the car's performance we took the P-type to Brooklands where, over the quarter-mile, a maximum speed of 76 m.p.h. was obtained; this was checked up on two occasions and the same speed resulted each time, so that it is evident that this excellent performance from the small sports car is not just an occasional happening.

The standing quarter - mile was covered in 23 seconds, which gives an average speed of 39 m.p.h., whilst a speed of 50 m.p.h. was obtained (through the gears) in 17 seconds from a standing start.

Outstanding Stability

One of the characteristics which is most outstanding is the way in which the P-type held the track; even when driven flat out off the banking its road-holding was impressive and gave the driver the utmost feeling of confidence.

We committed much " lappery," the engine revving in the region of 4,500-5,000 r.p.m. the whole time, but there was absolutely no sign of overheating and the power unit was as pleasant at the conclusion of our test as it was when first taken over.

The Test Hill can be described as child's play for the car. On first gear the foot had to be eased off the accele-rator to prevent sending the revs. well over the 6,000 mark; a restart was made with the greatest of ease on the 1-in-4 section.

With a running start of 25 m.p.h., the Test Hill was taken easily in its stride in second gear.

For trials work the new P-type is excellent, and so long as the engine revs. are maintained it should be able comfortably to negotiate practically any gradient included in the average modern event.

The suspension is very good, particularly having regard to the short wheelbase, and in conjunction with the deep and well-upholstered seats, comfort over long and fast runs is an outstanding characteristic. The cornering is, of course, a delight. The car takes its bends as if on rails at much higher speeds than one might expect, and without any particular effort astonishingly good average speeds are put up in the normal way of touring.

One of the most pleasing features is the top-gear performance. On main-road hills the P-type Midget will build up its r.p.m. in top gear until it is moving really fast in the region of 4,000 r.p.m. without suggesting the need for a lower ratio. On the other hand, in third gear (and the change is a real delight) the rev. counter will climb into the neighbourhood of 5,000 r.p.m. and 5,500 r.p.m. without the least worry and with a smooth silkiness that tempts overmuch work with the neat gear lever. In brief, it is an unusually attractive sports model with an outstanding performance.

TABULATED DATA

CHASSIS DETAILS

Engine: Four cylinders; overhead valves; coil ignition; bore, 57 mm.; stroke, 83 mm. (847 c.c.); tax, £8.

Gearbox: Four forward speeds, central control. Ratios, 5.37, 7.31, 12.46 and 22.5 to 1.

PERFORMANCE

Speeds on Gears: Top, 76 m.p.h.; third, 60 m.p.h.; second, 38 m.p.h. Minimum speed on top gear, 7 m.p.h.

Acceleration: Standstill to 50 m.p.h. through the gears, 17 secs.; to 60 m.p.h., 23 secs.

Tapley Performance Figures: Top, 140 lb. per ton; third, 200 lb. per ton; second, 430 lb. per ton. Corresponding gradients climbable at a steady speed are 1 in 16, 1 in 11¼ and 1 in 5¼ respectively.

Braking Efficiency: Measured by Tapley meter, using the pedal only, 75 per cent. from 20 m.p.h.; 80 per cent. from 30 m.p.h.; 80 per cent. from 50 m.p.h. Corresponding stopping distances are 18 ft. from 20 m.p.h., 37 ft. from 30 m.p.h., 67 ft. from 40 m.p.h. and 110 ft. from 50 m.p.h.

Petrol Consumption: 33-35 m.p.g. when driven hard.

DIMENSIONS, Etc.

Leading Measurements: Wheelbase, 7 ft. 3½ ins.; track, 3 ft. 6 ins.; overall length, 10 ft. 11 ins.; width, 4 ft. 4½ ins.

Turning Circles: 34 ft. diameter.

Weight: Unladen, 13 cwt. 2 qrs.

Price: P-type, 2-seater, £222.

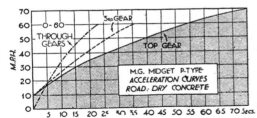

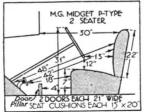

Meet Abingdon's Latest . . .

A New 120 m.p.h. M

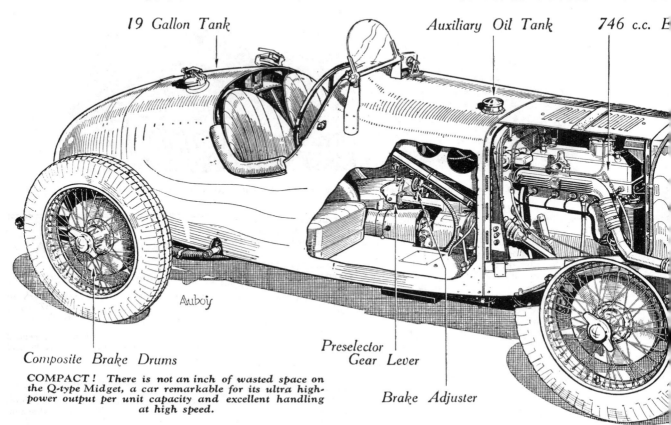

19 Gallon Tank

Auxiliary Oil Tank

746 c.c. E

Composite Brake Drums

Auboy

Preselector Gear Lever

Brake Adjuster

COMPACT! *There is not an inch of wasted space on the Q-type Midget, a car remarkable for its ultra high-power output per unit capacity and excellent handling at high speed.*

NO keen student of racing developments would be likely to dispute that the M.G. Q-type Midget ranks among the most remarkable ultra-high-efficiency small cars to appear in recent years. Its latest achievement (following upon the capturing of the Class H lap records for the Donington circuit) was the lowering last week, at Brooklands, of the world's figures for the standing start mile and kilometre—the former at nearly 80 m.p.h.! (See "Sports Jottings.")

In view of these spectacular successes, special interest attaches to the fact that the "Q" is now to become public property: that is to say, it will be available to ordinary buyers at a price of £550. And though, on the face of it, that may seem a high figure for a car of only 746 c.c., it has to be remembered that each individual vehicle is constructed and tested with the most religious and elaborate care.

The overhead-camshaft four-cylinder engine is similar, fundamentally, to the milder forms of Midget. Separate inlet and exhaust ports are formed on opposite sides of the cylinder head, 14-mm. plugs provide the sparks, and triplicated springs act upon each valve. On the near side a four-branch manifold leads away the exhaust gases, while a second finned manifold, on the off

side, ushers in the mixture as supplied by the Zoller vane-type supercharger. This unit, mounted between the dumb-iron and covered in by a fairing, takes its drive through a reduction gear and a universally jointed spindle; its maximum operating pressure is 25 lb.

The blower itself is lubricated by a separate pump of its own, and draws its charge from a large S.U. carburetter, which, in turn, is fed by S.U fuel pumps communicating with the rear-placed 19-gallon tank.

Constant Level.

To ensure against lubrication irregularities at the high rate of r.p.m. at which the engine runs, the large-capacity Elektron sump is supplemented by an auxiliary one-gallon tank, mounted on the dash. Between the two a float-controlled topping-up device operates. A Tecalemit filter, through which all oil passes *en route* from the pump to the various bearing surfaces, is incorporated in the system.

The motor develops its maximum power—over 100 b.h.p.—at some 7,300 r.p.m.; yet, despite its high rate of turnover, the Q-type Midget is no mere sprinter, as was demonstrated recently in the British Relay Race, when Kenneth Evans turned twenty consecutive Brooklands laps of which the *slowest*

was 102.69 m.p.h. and the fastest 110.68 m.p.h. (On the straight, according to rev. counter readings, 122 m.p.h. was repeatedly exceeded.)

A two-plate clutch of special design serves, as it were, as a shock-absorber in the transmission system, to take the brunt of gear-changes made as changes are made in the heat of a fierce race: no means of operating this clutch is provided, however, for a preselector gearbox, made under Wilson patents, dispenses with the need for it. The final drive ratios may be either 4.5 or 4.875 to 1, at the purchaser's option, while the three gearbox ratios are 1.36, 2.0 and 3.4 to 1. (Reverse, 5.07 to 1.)

The wheelbase provided by the cross-braced and underslung chassis is considerably greater than that of other Midget models. The action of the semi-elliptic underslung springs is controlled by duplex Hartford shock-absorbers at the front and Luvax hydraulics at the rear. To assist air-flow beneath the car, an aluminium undershield, in which are formed air scoops directed upon the gearbox and back axle, is fitted. The torque reaction of the front brakes is resisted by short steel cables made fast to stout steel brackets on the axle and main frame members.

To balance the steering effort apply-

MIDGET—£550

Already-famous Q-type Supercharged Racing Model Goes Into Regular Production: A Replica of Donington 750 c.c. Record Holder, Developing Over 100 b.h.p.

oller Supercharger

;IVENESS *characterizes ecial Zoller supercharger*), designed to deliver the *re at a maximum pres- of 25 lb. to the sq. in. ally the complete blower icealed beneath a neat lumb iron fairing.*

In the course of a visit to the track last week we took the opportunity of covering several laps in one of the Q-type M.G.s. The one in question was, unfortunately, not fully run-in, so that it was thought inadvisable to push it much beyond the 100 m.p.h. mark. At that speed, however, there was ample evidence that the track-worthiness and steering generally are of a most exceptional order: even on some of the bumpiest sections of the concrete both driver and passenger were given an unusually comfortable ride and the car held its course with remarkable certainty.

If further proof were needed of the Midget's breath-taking acceleration (in view of Everitt's new records) there was certainly no lack of it during this conducted tour. It was almost incredible that such thrusting, frantic power should be developed by those four tiny cylinders, each little larger than an inkwell.

This new M.G. undoubtedly has a great future before it on the tracks and road courses of the world.

(Below) A rev. counter, radiator and oil thermometers, an inlet manifold pressure gauge, pressure dials for the main and supercharger oil supplies and an ammeter complete the facia cluster. Note the accessible brake adjuster wheel.

ing to the two front wheels and to reduce whip in the navigating gear, the already-famous M.G. divided track rod system is used.

Built-up drums, specially devised to eliminate distortion, are a feature of the braking system. All four brakes are applied either by pedal or the centrally-located racing-type lever, through the medium of cables working in steel-armoured casings. A conveniently-placed wheel enables brake adjustments to be made from the cockpit.

The broad lines of the vehicle as a whole are clearly seen in the accompanying sketch. The petrol tank, mounted behind the two seats, rests on rubber, being held in position by stranded cables fitting into channels made to conform snugly to their diameters. Wide internal baffles lend rigidity to the tank.

The streamlined tail is, of course, detachable, and conceals the batteries. The weight of the car is approximately 13 cwt., in the semi-stripped state in which it is supplied.

THE M.G. 1935 PROGRAMME

New Saloon with N-type Engine—All Other Models Continued As Before—A Sports Range for Every Purpose— First Road Test of P-type Two-seater

THE NEW KN 1,287 c.c. SALOON

Sporting lines match a sporting performance in this new full-four-seater pillarless saloon. The engine is the popular N-type six-cylinder unit.

"NO Change" is the watchword of the M.G. factory for 1935. So successful has the present range of models proved itself that the cars will be continued for next year absolutely unaltered except for two things—the price of the P-type Midget two-seater (of which a road-test report appears on page 264) will be advanced by £2, to £222, and that a new saloon model will be introduced, to be known as the KN model—embodying the highly successful N-type six-cylinder 1,287 c.c. power unit and a chassis 1 ft. longer and a few inches wider than the existing N-chassis.

The larger chassis has been found better for the accommodation of the pillarless saloon body, in which great pains have been taken to provide real comfort for four people, at the same time retaining the sporting characteristics for which the marque is famous.

Sporting Performance Plus Comfort

The illustration of the KN saloon on this page will indicate the sleek appearance of the car, which has been produced on luxury lines. A sunshine roof combines with a screen, which winds open to an unusual extent, and sliding windows all round to produce adequate ventilation in the worst heat wave. The interior appointments are in the best taste, and are practical withal. Zip-fastener door pockets, recessed armrests, trigger door handles, draught excluders to the pedals, Silent-bloc mounting to the doors and deep, capacious seats fore and aft are items which immediately strike the discriminating owner.

The performance is claimed to match the sporting appearance, and, judging from what is known of the N-type engine, 75 m.p.h. should be within the scope of the KN saloon.

Otherwise the range continues as

before. The P-type Midget and its racing descendant, the Zoller supercharged, preselector-geared 100-odd m.p.h. Q-type chassis, are unaltered. The Magna exists only as a Continental coupé, a sporting two-seater with especially good luggage room, the N-Magnette continues in four body styles, and the supercharged 1,100 c.c. K3 racing-type Magnette is unchanged.

UNCHANGED FOR 1935— THE MAGNA CONTINENTAL COUPE

This smart sports coupe continues as before, featuring luxury motoring for two people, plus ample luggage accommodation.

THE M.G. 1935 RANGE.

Midget (P-type)	
Two-seater	£222
Four-seater	£240
Airline Coupe	£290
Magna (L-type)	
Continental Coupe	£350
Magnette (N-type)	
Two-seater	£305
Four-seater	£335
Airline Coupe	£385
Two-four seater	£350
Magnette (KN-type)	
Pillarless Saloon	£399
Midget (Q-type)	
Racing model	£550
Magnette (K3-type)	
Racing model	£795

Here are a few chassis details of the various models. The P-type has a four-cylinder 847 c.c. engine (bore and stroke 57 mm. by 83 mm.) with overhead camshaft and three-bearing crankshaft. Twin S.U. carburetters, ignition by Rotax 12-volt coil, thermosiphon cooling, a new-design clutch, four-speed "twin-top" gearbox are other items of the specification.

Underslung Chassis

The chassis is underslung at the rear (as in all models) and 12-in. brake drums, Marles Weller steering, Rudge-Whitworth racing type wheels are features of the chassis.

The chassis dimensions are: track 3 ft. 6 ins., wheelbase 7 ft. 3½ ins. The tyres are 19-in. by 4-in. Dunlops.

The L-type Magna has a 1,087 c.c. six-cylinder engine, overhead camshaft, twin carburetters, coil ignition and a general specification similar to the P-model. The wheelbase is 7 ft. 10 ins., track 3 ft. 6 ins. The wheels carry 19-in. by 4.40 Dunlop Fort tyres.

In the case of the N-type chassis the engine is a 1,287 c.c. "Six" with a general layout following that of the other models—overhead camshaft, twin semi-downdraught carburetters and so forth. The steering is rather higher-geared on this chassis, of which the dimensions are 3-ft. 9-in. track and 8-ft. wheelbase. The tyres are 18-in. by 4.75 Dunlops.

All bodies on the N-type chassis are flexibly mounted on special outrigger members, which enable the bodies to withstand normal road shock and chassis movement without protest in the form of squeaks and rattles.

The KN chassis has the same engine as the "N," but the chassis dimensions are 4-ft. track and 9-ft. wheelbase, plus 19-in. by 4.75 Dunlop tyres. On this chassis the brake drums are of 13-in. diameter and the split track rod steering layout is used.

THE P-TYPE M.G. MIDGET

Two-seater Version of Abingdon's Smallest Product Proves Itself Capable of a Genuine 76 m.p.h.   A Car Which Loves High Road Averages, Superbly Braked and with Fine Cornering Qualities

WHY is it, one may have wondered, that in the selection of a small car of high performance a young man's fancy so often turns to the M.G. Midget? What, in short, are the characteristics which have gone to make this vehicle one of England's most popular sports cars?

The bald answers to those questions can be put into a very few words: this car is *really* fast; the act of driving it is a never-failing source of joy; it ridicules attempts to fluster or overdrive it; handled with ordinary intelligence, it is safe at any speed of which it is capable.

Fast Friends Already.

From the M.G. works at Abingdon, Bucks, to the Chiswick end of the Great West Road, London, is a distance of 50¼ miles. When the writer took over the 1935 P-type Midget which forms the subject of this test, he had wind-driven rain for company on the first half of the journey and snow for the latter part. A stranger to the car, he took exactly an hour between the points mentioned. No risks were taken. No scraps were indulged in. The speedometer needle was never urged past the 72 mark. The car was, in fact, driven just as the majority of typical M.G. owners would drive it—quickly, but far from hysterically.

The Midget is not a car which, normally, one often drives flat out. There is little need of its maximum speed in everyday circumstances; but when one's shoe-soles do call a halt on the pedal-board there is remarkably little fear of being overtaken, as the results of against-the-clock speed tests clearly revealed.

As will be seen from the accompanying table, the best timed speed recorded over the measured quarter-mile during test was 76.27 m.p.h. The mean times taken on two-way runs gave a little over 70 m.p.h. On slightly falling gradients a speedometer for whose veracity stern oaths were sworn by the Works went busily up to 82 m.p.h.

On the majority of main-road runs the needle was kept hovering between 60 and 65. The Midget, quite obviously, enjoyed rather than tolerated this urgency. Thanks, doubtless, to its exceptionally rigid crankshaft, supported ungivingly on three ample bearings, the smoothness of power delivery was as marked at frenzied rates of r.p.m. as at a two-thousand-a-minute amble. Absence of vibration is, in fact, outstanding among this engine's varied and subtle charms.

Dancing Figures.

In passing, mention should be made of the combined speedometer and rev. counter, which, for 1935, differs in arrangement from the 1934 instrument. Whereas, formerly, the large figures on the outer circumference of the dial showed top-gear m.p.h., the corresponding figures on the latest type of dial give "r.p.m x 100." Two concentric inner rings show m.p.h. in top and third gears. While having the decided merit of extra informativeness, the modern instrument is, perhaps, the loser in that the top-gear m.p.h. figures, being small and close-clustered, are not so easily read when the road speed approaches furious eighties.

Essentially a vehicle of esoteric qualities, the P-type

M.G. is a car for the man who enjoys driving for driving's own sweet sake; conversely, it is not so much the meat of the press-the-button and leave-the-rest-to-Science class. Third gear is close to top, and the stubby remote-control lever is close to the pilot's hand, for a good reason. That reason is that the engine was designed for a constantly high turnover. If goodwill between car and driver is to be mutual, it is well to make the fullest use of that third gear.

From a standing start, the quarter-mile was covered in 24.4 secs. That figure, although good, hardly does

a curving course at high speed. More particularly is this restfulness appreciated in making the worm-like evolutions demanded by up-town traffic. There are those, on the other hand, whose preference tends towards more direct gearing and the ultra-positive translation of steering motion into road-wheel deflection which it brings. Either way, little fault can be found with a car which may literally be steered with a single finger at upwards of 70 m.p.h.—as this modern Midget can.

The cornering stability and high-speed road-holding qualities of this car have already wrung fervid eulogies from its hardest-bitten Press critics. One can merely echo these earnest avowals of wonder and admiration. With screaming tyre-treads, the Midget can be wrenched round corners at speeds which would mean certain capsize in a machine of less rock-like build. Yet the

```
IN BRIEF

ENGINE: Four-cylinder, overhead valves, 57 mm. by 83 mm. =
    847 c.c.; 1935 tax, £6.
TRANSMISSION: Single dry-plate clutch; four-speed gearbox with
    silent third and remote control; ratios, 5.375, 7.31, 12.46 and
    22.5 to 1; final drive by spiral bevel
GENERAL: Mechanical brakes; semi-elliptic springs front and rear
    with trunnion bearings; 12-gallon rear tank; fold-flat screen.
DIMENSIONS: Wheelbase, 7 ft. 3½ ins.; track, 3 ft. 6 ins.; overall
    length, 10 ft. 11 ins.; overall width, 4 ft. 4½ ins; weight, 13 cwt.
    2 qrs. (unladen); turning circle, 34 ft.
PERFORMANCE: Flying ¼-mile (best speed), 76.27 m.p.h.; mean
    two-way speed, 70.31 m.p.h.; standing ¼-mile, 24.4 secs.; petrol
    consumption, 33-36 m.p.g.
PRICE: £222.

THE M.G. CAR CO., LTD., ABINGDON-ON-THAMES, BUCKS
```

INVITING. Real comfort for two is provided by the Midget. The seat squab and steering rake are both adjustable to individual whims. The placing of the controls and instruments is the subject of favourable comment in this test report.

full justice to the actual powers of pick-up of the engine, and might be appreciably improved upon with a design of clutch requiring shorter pauses between ratios. A degree or so of slickness has, we understand, been sacrificed in the interests of trials-driving owners, who demand, first and foremost, a 100 per cent. slip-proof clutch.

The 12-in. mechanical brakes of the Midget, with their well-ribbed drums, put all of their share of the safety in "Safety Fast." Smooth as silk at no matter what speed they may be crammed on, these brakes have that uncompromising solidity of action which so often is the

suspension is such that there is none of that ease-destroying battery on the spinal column at every bump and pot-hole. It is, indeed, as much to the riding comfort of the car as to any attribute of the engine that its merits as a maker of road averages are due.

The adjustability of the steering column and seat-squab rake make it, moreover, as well-fitting as a tailored suit for any physique, either out- or under-sized. By making judicious use of the available ranges of movement in these components anyone, however irrational of build, may, in a couple of moments, achieve the ideal wheel-in-the-lap driving position.

The Verdict.

All controls and instruments are placed where the eye, hand and foot instinctively seek them. The luggage space behind the seats is ample even for ambitious and far-flung week-ends. The equipment generally is of good standard, from the fold-flat windscreen to the "self-effacing" traffic indicators. The P-type Midget is—as it looks and sounds—a thoroughbred down to the last M.G. octagon. (It *sounds*, when revving briskly, perhaps a little too much of a thoroughbred for an ultra-sensitive ear, but its somewhat hearty exhaust note has that nicely rounded, "dark-brown" quality which seldom leads to tangible unpleasantness.)

It will, in short, be surprising if this vital little motor-car fails to uphold in 1935 the dignity of its status as one of Britain's most popular sports cars.

THE SOURCE of the "seventy-six." Features of note visible in this off-side view of the P-type engine are the large and accessible overhead oil filler and the twin semi-downdraught S.U. carburetters. Note also the spare plug carrier.

saving of a sticky situation. No judder. No trace of squeal.

For a sports car, the M.G. steering—by Marles-Weller—is comparatively low-geared. Naturally, therefore, a bare minimum of effort is sufficient to hold the car on

THE M.G. MAGNETTE "N"

A WELL-FINISHED LIGHT CAR WHICH REVEALS ITS RACING ORIGIN IN HIGH PERFORMANCE, GOOD ROAD HOLDING AND DELIGHTFUL HANDLING.

WHEN one bears in mind the excellence of M.G. sports cars for many years past, it may sound in the nature of hyperbole to say that, in our opinion, the " N " type Magnette is the most delightful car that has emanated to date from the famous Abingdon factory. This is not surprising, for it incorporates in its design, in modified form of course, many of the characteristics which have assisted the K.3 Magnette to gain its laurels in racing and record breaking. In saloon form the " N " is called the "K.N." and a punster could truthfully say that the Magnette is as hot-stuff as its name !

The six-cylinder engine is, in broad outline, an unsupercharged version of that used in the " K.3," with an increased capacity of 1,287 c.c. For those who are unfamiliar with this design, we would add that the crankshaft is carried in four main bearings ; there is a single overhead camshaft, the drive of which incorporates the dynamo ; the inlet and exhaust ports are on opposite sides of the head ; double valve-springs, 14 mm. plugs, and pistons of controlled-expansion type are all used. Unlike the racing " K.3," the " N " has twin S.U. carburettors and a normal type gearbox. The rest of the car follows orthodox M.G. practice, with a strongly braced chassis frame and 12-inch brake drums.

Christmas weather was hardly the most suitable variety for putting a fast car through its paces, but the Magnette is one of those rare cars in which a driver feels completely at home, whatever the conditions. The driving position is extraordinarily well thought out, so that one can sense the slightest movement of the car on a slippery corner. The steering column is actually adjustable for rake, but we found no need to alter it on collecting the car from Abingdon. The pedals are on the small side, but are far enough apart for all but the outsize in shoes. They operate smoothly and are placed at a restful angle—a point in which many cars are badly at fault. The usual M.G. type of remote-control gear lever is

---

Brief Specification.

Engine : 6 cylinders, 57 × 84, 1,287 c.c., 12·08 h.p. Tax £12. Single o.h.c. 4-bearing crankshaft. Twin S.U. carburetters. Rotax battery and coil ignition. 14 mm. plugs. Pump cooling.

Transmission : Heavy-duty type clutch. 4-speed twin-top gearbox, remote control. Ratios 1st 21·5, 2nd 11·9, 3rd 6·98, top 5·125 to 1. Hardy-Spicer prop. shaft with metal universals. ¾ floating back axle, spiral bevel final drive.

Chassis : Underslung at rear. Tubular cross-members, with centre X-shape brace on saloon model.

Suspension : Semi-elliptic springs fore and aft. Friction shock absorbers.

Steering : Cam steering, adjustable-rake. 30 ft. turning circle.

Brakes : Cable operated. 12-inch drums.

Wheels : Rudge Whitworth racing type, knock-off caps, 18 in. rims for 2 and 4-seater, 19 on saloon.

Tyres : 4·75 × 18.

Fuel : 10 gallon rear tznk on 2 and 4-seater ; 11 gallon on saloon. S.U. electric pump. Consumption : 25 m.p.g. approx.

Dimensions : Wheelbase 8ft., track 3ft. 9in.

Price : 2-seater, £305 ; 4-seater, as tested, £335 ; " K.N." Pillarless 4-door saloon, £399.

---

used, in front of which the choke and slow-running controls are easily reached. The racing hand-brake is to our liking, enabling smooth and quick restarts to be made on steep hills.

The dashboard is well panelled and equipped, but we have a slight personal criticism to make of the placing of the dials. The oil gauge and ammeter are two instruments which every driver likes to glance at occasionally on a long run, but both of these are on the extreme left, facing the passenger. Our second minor criticism applies to the combined speedometer and rev. counter, which unfortunately does not indicate the speed of the car when the indirect ratios are being used. On the other hand, revs. are the important thing. Especially useful items of dashboard equipment are the oil thermometer and a reserve fuel tap. A centre panel incorporates mileage and trip indicators, headlight dimming switch, and switches for the direction-signals, dashlamps and fog-lamp.

Encouraged by the general charm and road worthiness of the Magnette, we set off on Boxing Day on a lightning visit to friends at Paignton, South Devon, returning to London the same day. The roads, although wet, were comfortably free from traffic, and as we made our way towards the Great West Road we felt strangely safe on the deserted Chiswick High Road, on normal days a beacon-besprinkled death-trap. We intended the trip to be an easy one, without strain on the driver, passengers (we were three up) or car, and the engine was allowed to find its own restful cruising speed, which proved to be 4,000 r.p.m., or 62 m.p.h. At this gait the Magnette ran with complete effortlessness, giving the impression of consuming the least possible amount of fuel. An approximate checking of the fuel consumption over the whole trip gave a figure of 25 miles per gallon, which is good when bearing the average speed in mind.

The Stockbridge road to Salisbury was taken, and the sight of the magnificent stretches of undulating highway proved too much for our resolutions in regard to steady driving, on more than one occasion. The Magnette quickly reached its maximum of 80 m.p.h., at which speed the road-holding was excellent, and open curves could be taken with a trace of controllable slide. Later on, we found the good handling of the car a great asset on the winding road beyond Salisbury.

In spite of having wet roads to contend with the whole way, we arrived at Paignton at five minutes to one, having left London at ten minutes past eight—197 miles in 4¾ hours, including a stop for petrol and another for personal refreshment—without any hurry, save for a few brief bursts of speed on the Plain. The secret of this ability to cover the ground quickly and safely lies in the Magnette's racing ancestry. Every function of the car has been tested in races at far higher speeds than the " N " model is capable of, and this margin of safety is probably the car's outstanding characteristic. The road-holding at maximum speed, for example, is so good that the driver does not have to wrestle with the steering-wheel in a life-and-death struggle to keep the car on the road. The chassis feels that it could stand another 20 m.p.h. and still be controllable.

As befits a car of high maximum speed, the brakes of the Magnette are extremely powerful and can cope with any situation within reason. Although there is no servo mechanism they are absurdly light in operation, and this may account for the curious absence of braking effect experienced by the driver. The car just pulls up, quickly and smoothly, even when they are applied vigorously. The effect on the passengers is usual in that they tend to pitch forward when dogs or jaywalkers wander off the pavement in their inimitably care-free fashion, but the driver does not notice anything untoward in the behaviour of the car.

A point which impressed us considerably was the silence of the engine. Exhaust note there is a-plenty, of course, but the engine itself is exceptionally quiet up to 4,000 r.p.m. Beyond this point a little of its normal smoothness is lost, and one becomes conscious of the source of one's 65 m.p.h. gait. Higher up the range it becomes smooth once more, and 5,500 r.p.m. is easily and quickly reached on the gears, if required. The rev. counter, by the way, bears a green strip between 5,000 and 5,500 r.p.m., beyond which the dangerous red gives strident warning to over-exuberant drivers.

At five o'clock we bid our friends goodbye, and set off to retrace our tracks to London. In the darkness our speed was rather slower than on the downward journey, speed which was not increased by the untimely, if conscientious indication by an arm of the law that a sidelamp had burnt out. For the illumination provided by the Rotax equipment we have nothing but praise, and a fast cruising speed is made possible. Local fog was dealt with satisfactorily by the special lamp on the dumb irons, and on coming traffic was put at ease by the handily-placed dimming switch.

And so back to London once more, having covered close on 400 miles on as short a day as the English winter can provide. The only one of the party who felt at all weary was the passenger in the back seat, and his troubles were mostly caused by a suppressed desire to be at the wheel himself—a course which the exigencies of insurance did not allow.

By the grace of the M.G. Company we used the Magnette for many more days, and for this we find it difficult to place thanks before reproach—so fond did we become of our willing steed. It was with a grudging heart, indeed, that we motored along the familiar road to Abingdon. A drenching downpour had brought to our notice yet another asset of the Magnette, to wit, a snug hood and all-weather equipment. Here, we reflected, is the ideal small car ; small enough to be economical and handy in traffic, yet possessing roomy coachwork and ample headroom when the hood is erected. At the price of £335 it will meet the requirements of the most fastidious.

Here is the offside of the " N " type M.G. Magnette engine. Prominent features are the typical M.G. dynamo position, and the twin S.U. Carburettors, and the grouped lubrication nipples on the scuttle.

THE "CRESTA" MAGNETTE

Special Two-seater Model in Which Both Light Weight and Comfort Have Been Studied

A SPECIAL model of the M.G. Magnette, to be known as the "Cresta" Magnette, has just been placed on the market by the Cresta Motor Company, Ltd., of Worthing. The coachwork, which is shown in the accompanying photographs, has been carried out by E. Bertelli, Ltd., and the two-seater body is designed with a disappearing hood, an occasional seat, ample luggage accommodation, and a windscreen which, when in the raised position, has flanking screens that can be used as miniature windscreens when the main screen is horizontal. A cover is provided for the rear of the car and for the

passenger's seat when necessary, there is a very large tool box under the bonnet, an Ashby or a Bluemel steering wheel is available, the fuel tank holds 11½ gallons, the seats are adjustable for angle as well as for position, and the detail work of the car is carried out very well indeed, weight being kept down by the use of a special grade of aluminium panel. The finish of the upholstery and paintwork adds very greatly to the attractiveness of the car.

The " Cresta " Magnette has a handsome aluminium-panelled body with many excellent features.

MG

WINS BRITISH EMPIRE TROPHY RACE

CAPT. G. E. T. EYSTON DRIVING HIS SINGLE SEATER M.G. MAGNETTE WON THE B.R.D.C. BRITISH EMPIRE TROPHY RACE AT BROOKLANDS ON SATURDAY, JUNE 23, AT AN AVERAGE SPEED OF 80.01 m.p.h.

M.G. Magnettes also finished —

5th, 6th, 9th and 10th

PROVIDING FIVE OUT OF THE TEN FINISHERS

and won

THE TEAM PRIZE

CAPT. EYSTON'S M.G. MAGNETTE TEAM

(Subject to Official Confirmation)

ISSUED BY THE M.G. CAR COMPANY LTD., ABINGDON-ON-THAMES

(Left) The Magnette at that sporting drivers' Mecca, the Brooklands Paddock. (Below) Showing the gracefully swept tail, recessed spare wheel and deep squab.

Road Tests of 1935 Models

The M.G.

N-Type

MAGNETTE

A Spacious and Tractable Car with Qualities of Lion and Lamb Combined. Quarter Covered at 83 m.p.h.

IN the average philosophy the term " a sports model " used at one time to mean a kind of road-going popgun, the smudge-faced owner of which divided his time about equally between sitting in, and lying under, his vehicle. It is cars like the modern M.G. Magnette—smooth, docile, sweet-mannered, yet fast withal—which have sounded the knell of these old ideas.

The N-type two-seater recently tested would, indeed, exactly typify the new era of sports models, but for its being just a little smoother—and faster—than most.

First, let us consider the car purely from the point of view of high performance. It covered the flying quarter-mile, as the accompanying "In Brief" table shows, at a speed on the right side of 83 m.p.h. Although the conditions prevailing were admittedly on the slightly favourable side, the fact remains that, given a fair run, the M.G. is an absolutely genuine over-80-m.p.h. vehicle. It needs a conscious effort not to drive this car fast.

The time recorded for the standing-start quarter-mile —23⅘ secs.—is one of the best that has ever appeared in *The Light Car* road-test series. Yet that figure does not do full justice to the powers of the engine, for the gear-change calls for a pause if silent engagement is to be made. Particularly is this so in stepping from first to second, of course, for between these two ratios a great gulf is fixed: they are 21.5 to 1 and 11.9 to 1 respectively.

Frankly, this 23⅘ secs. was not "all done by kindness." There *were* noises. A clutch stop would be a boon and a blessing to Magnette owners.

Right through its range of r.p.m., with the exception of a short spell in the 4,000 region, the engine

IN BRIEF

ENGINE : Six-cylinder, o.h. camshaft ; 57 mm. by 84 mm.— 1,287 c.c. Tax, £9.

TRANSMISSION : Single dry-plate clutch, four-speed gearbox with silent third. Ratios, 5.125, 6.98, 11.9 and 21.5 to 1. Reverse, 21.5 to 1. Final drive by Hardy Spicer propeller shaft and spiral bevel.

GENERAL : Mechanical 12-in. brakes, hand on all wheels. Semi-elliptic springs front and rear. Ten-gallon rear tank.

DIMENSIONS : Wheelbase, 8 ft.; track, 3 ft. 9 ins.; overall length, 12 ft. 4 ins.; overall width, 4 ft. 6 ins.; weight, 17½ cwt.; turning circle, 43 ft.

PERFORMANCE : Flying ¼-mile, 83.33 m.p.h.; standing ¼-mile, 23⅘ secs.; petrol consumption, about 26 m.p.g.

PRICE : £305.

THE M.G. CAR CO., LTD.
Pavlova Works,
ABINGDON   -   -   -   BERKS

delivers its power with a fluid smoothness; here, in fact, is perhaps the outstanding characteristic of the car. As for the spell referred to, this does not make itself so much felt as heard, the manifestation being, in fact, one which might easily be thought to come from the gearbox but for the evidence of the revolution counter. It is not sufficiently marked to cause concern once the driver has become at home with it.

Developed, as it is, from racing, this M.G. is decidedly a vehicle which relies upon r.p.m. for its high performance. Although capable of pulling modest loads at low rates of turn-over, it does not find its true element before the needle has reached 4,500 r.p.m. Above that figure its power is thrusting, prodigious. On the level, one can drive in top gear smoothly and without snatch as slowly as 12 m.p.h.

By way of reminder that it is there to be used, the stubby remote-control gear lever all but places itself into the driver's left hand. It could not conceivably be better placed, and, having a short range of motion, it lends itself admirably to well-timed changes.

The exhaust note, as delivered by the Burgess straight-through silencer, is a pleasant oily hum; it would be next to, if not quite, impossible to produce an offensive noise.

The Magnette stands out, even among outstanding contemporaries, for its controllability. Although, admittedly, tastes differ on the question of high-geared steering, it would be impossible to deny that the M.G.'s one-turn-from-lock-to-lock invests it with exceptional cornering qualities. There is, moreover, that absence of "give" and wasted movement which makes all the difference between hair's-breadth accuracy and a scratch on the wing. The steering is, of course, a little heavier than that of the lower-geared Midgets.

In the matter of suspension just the right compromise is achieved. That is to say, with the shock-absorbers set to a nicety all trace of body dance and sway is eliminated without depriving the springs of their primary function—springing. As a feminine passenger put it, after riding fast and far in the Magnette: "Somehow, it doesn't disorganize your spinal column like some sports cars."

The seating accommodation owes much of its comfort and fatigue-resisting propensities to the exceptional depth of the adjustable squab. As one of our pictures shows, this squab extends appreciably above the top line of the body sides, with the result that the shoulders even of a tall man do not overflow into space. The leg room, similarly, is such as to house in comfort the legs of your over-six-footer.

The sweep of the facia-board gives ample visibility for persons of average build, but would, perhaps, necessitate slight neck-stretching on the part of the puny-statured. (There appears to be some little difference between Magnette and Midget in this respect.)

Despite the fact that these two models, differing in weight, share the same braking system, the larger is anything but under-braked, even if it cannot be wrenched to a halt with quite the ferocious suddenness which characterizes the little car. The brakes are equal to the needs of so fast a vehicle and work with a most engaging sweetness.

A studied symmetry is noticeable in the layout of the facia-board, on which are two balanced M.G. octagons, housing, on the one hand, the combined rev. counter and speedometer, and on the other the ammeter, oil-pressure gauge, lighting switch, and ignition tell-tale. The petrol gauge and oil thermometer, likewise octagonally framed, also balance each other, as do the twin lamps. The ability to switch on to the reserve petrol supply from the driving seat is not the least of the Magnette owner's many blessings.

A simple and positive two-point fixing for the peak of the hood to the fold-flat screen deserves mention; the side screens, too, are rigidly made, and, in conjunction with the triangular-shaped and press-studded panels which flank the spacious luggage compartment, make a commendably draught-proof ensemble.

Points with special appeal to the discerning owner are the grouped grease nipples (on the bulkhead supports) which supply the brake cables, the steering column, the rear springs and the brake cross-shaft; the accessible brake adjustment; the large and conveniently placed oil-filling orifice on the rocker box; the twin batteries; the rack for spare plugs; the dip-stick to say "when" to rear-axle replenishments; and many another . . .

The N-type M.G. Magnette, from stem to stem, is a standing testimony to the painstaking brainwork of its designer. It is a thing of which anyone might be proud.

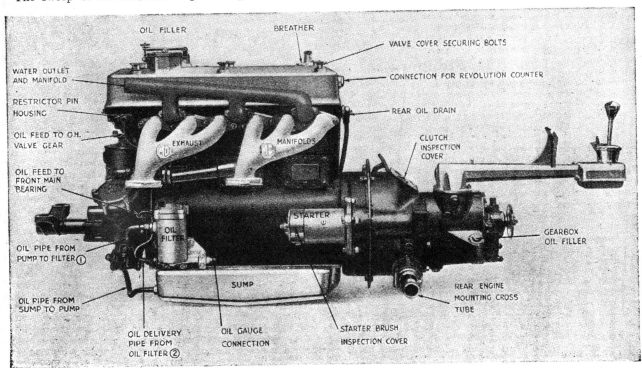

CLOSE UP of the engine gearbox unit of the latest 1,287 c.c. M.G. Magnette.

(Left) A group of experts round one of the new M.G. single-seaters, with the author third from the left (wearing hat). (Below) G. E. T. Eyston, famous M.G. exponent, at the wheel of his International Trophy car

TRY-OUT

An Experience With the New M.G. : The Sports Editor Gives His Opinion and Experiences of the New Supercharged R-type Racing M.G. Midget, Which Has Torsion Bar Independent Suspension

By S. C. H. DAVIS

THE new M.G. chassis, described in *The Autocar* of April 26th, is extraordinarily interesting. Definitely it departs from convention. Any number of nice new experimental components suggest food for thought, but, however interesting a chassis may be, the main, the only, reason for its existence and justification is its performance generally.

It is all very well to have wheels on wishbones, adjustable suspension, and a sort of Menai Bridge spine, but if all that does not mean a car which is easier to handle or, putting it another way, more efficient, however interesting the chassis it is just one more example of what can be called artistic licence without any practical application; not, of course, that one could refer to artistic licence with any effect when so solid a man as Charles is responsible.

The things one hoped for were that the car would ride on relatively loose shock absorbers keeping all four wheels on the ground, which in itself is a revolution because, drivers being drivers, nearly always tighten up the shock absorbers of ordinary cars until the springs cease to act. I have never believed that a car is right which drives most of the time on one rear wheel, steers on one front wheel, and ends by snapping off its shock-absorber brackets. Next, one hoped that it would be possible to accelerate violently without spinning the driving wheels in a highly exciting manner very interesting to the spectator but definitely inefficient as a performance. Finally, if the steering felt real and not as though it controlled the car through one of those much advertised jellies, then the whole thing would be a step in the right direction.

So, when the day came, when the car did arrive at the track, a good deal hinged on the first run, at all events as far as track work is concerned. Well, I can safely say that that first run was very near to what sensational people would call a revelation. One way or another I have driven quite a considerable number of cars, and, as far as the smaller ones are concerned, have been bumped to bits on the track, and rather regarded the process as only natural when a flyweight car is travelling at 100 or more on a surface that is certainly not smooth, while one or two of those small cars at 100 have been harder to keep straight than big ones going at over 120.

Try Out

The predecessor of this particular M.G. was—this is a personal opinion—capable of giving one a very rough ride, partly because it was very fast. Now this new machine is ridiculously comfortable. On the International Trophy course it is bumped about as one comes off the banking into the finishing straight. The wheels left the ground when crossing the worst part of the course, but I do not think there is any car that could ever be built that would stay steady at these two points. Twice during the remainder of the run did the off-side front wheel jump, and all the rest of the way the four wheels sat down solidly on the ground and got on with their work. The result was that one lost a great deal of the impression of speed, which made the approach to the turn off the home banking, when the car is doing 120 or thereabouts, a thing to be judged with some care; but for the rest it was the smoothest run I have ever had in any type of car on that track.

Stable Low or High on the Banking

When you see someone else driving, the body of the car is moving steadily up and down. When you are in the driving seat this is almost unnoticeable, and whether the car goes on to the banking low or high, it appears quite stable. A little enterprise at the turn off the banking resulted in the machine drifting bodily to the left, but the front and back ends went together, which was quite comforting.

The brakes are extraordinarily good, very even, and so powerful that you have to be quite careful not to push hard on the pedal.

"Design" had begun by putting the throttle pedal in the middle of the car, which is always particularly devastating to me, because, in this case, it proves impossible to rev. up the engine when changing down with the Wilson box,

the pedal being well out of reach of one's right heel when braking, and apparently getting lost entirely if one searched for it with the left foot. Oddly enough, it was not over-easy to locate the left "Wilson" pedal either, but the trouble as far as the throttle pedal is concerned can be remedied easily. Changing down without revving the engine is apt, by the way, to create a very nasty mess of the transmission.

The steering was definite, our old friend the jelly having disappeared. It is, I think, a bit too stiff at the moment for the average road circuit, but quite all right for the track. It may be just a question of gear ratio.

The Engine Happy Around 5,500 r.p.m.

The engine, despite its rather exciting boost, feels really good, especially round about 5,500 or 6,000 r.p.m., and though there was not very much chance of trying the acceleration really, I have great hopes that the wheels will not spin overmuch.

All that, I think, means a good deal. It means that a 750 c.c. four-cylinder racing car going really fast can be quite comfortable and can sit on a track which is not over easy to sit on, and that is a very long way indeed towards a decided improvement in cars generally.

As a matter of fact, "Design" got quite thrilled by it and began to take a hand, which is unusual, as designers generally are not to be coaxed into the seats of racing cars; but they tell me that Charles' cornering was really lurid, and I think myself that the moment the car began to slide he began to work out problems on the instrument board with a stump of lead pencil, and consequently the placing of the car might not have been quite accurate. Anyhow, I consider that Charles thoroughly deserves his run.

THE M.G. PROGRAMME

The Price of the "P" Type Midget Substantially Lowered and a New "PB" Type Introduced : The Magnette Modified and Prices Lowered

RUMOUR has been rife concerning the future of the popular M.G. models. It has even been suggested that in future the M.G. range would be but special bodies on existing Morris chassis. Once more, however, rumour is definitely wrong, for the 1936 programme of the M.G. Car Co. Ltd., continues the "P" type Midget and the "N" type Magnette, while an improved version of the Midget, to be known as the "PB" type, is also introduced. Moreover, although the "KN" Magnette saloon is discontinued it will be replaced by a new model, which will make its appearance at Olympia, and which, for the moment, must be dismissed with the comment that it will undoubtedly be of considerable interest.

The "P" type Midget two-seater is continued unchanged as regards chassis and coachwork, but the price has been reduced to £199 10s. in place of £222. The "P" four-seater, however, is discontinued. It will be recalled that the "P" type engine, which replaced the previous "J" type, has a very rigid balanced crankshaft carried in three bearings, light alloy pistons of controlled expansion type, and an improved lubrication system. The bore and stroke are 57 by 83 mm. (847 c.c.), the R.A.C. rating being 8.05 h.p. and the annual tax £6. The transmission of the "P" type was strengthened to cope with the increased power output, and the overall gear ratios are 22.5, 12.46, 7.31, and 5.375 to 1.

Naturally, greatest interest attaches to the latest "PB" type, which is an im-

The new "PB" Midget four-seater.

proved version of the "P" type chassis. This has been produced to give a better acceleration at the lower end of the scale, and the bore has been increased to 60 mm., the stroke remaining the same, and the capacity being 939 c.c., the R.A.C. rating 8.9 h.p., and annual tax £6 15s. Another important difference is that closer gear ratios are pro-

vided, these being 19.24, 11.5, 7.31, and 5.375 to 1.

Apart from these modifications the chassis is the same as that of the "P" type, but the front appearance has been improved by fitting vertical slats to the characteristic M.G. radiator shell, while a new facia board with a neater layout of the instruments is used. The new instrument board has the familiar octagonal mounts for the various dials, and the switch panel is mounted on the extreme left, and is balanced by a large-diameter separate revolution counter on the right in front of the driver. Mounted centrally is the speedometer, and above it the head lamp dipping switch, on each side of which are the push switches for the direction indicators and the switches for fog lamp on the left

" N " Magnette two-seater, has the doors carried on extended hinges and a lower scuttle line.

and dash lamps on the right. The petrol gauge is mounted on the left of these central switches with the oil gauge to the right of them. It is a sign of the times that on the extreme right of the instrument board there is a 30 m.p.h. warning light, which is arranged to light up at 20 m.p.h. and to go out again at 30 m.p.h. The rear tank is also fitted with an improved quick-action filler cap which is hinged to the tank so that it cannot be lost. The price of the "PB" type two-seater is £222, and that of the four-seater £240.

Considerable price reductions have been made in the "N" type Magnette, and the two-seater now costs £280 instead of £305, while the four-seater costs £285 instead of £335. While the chassis is unaltered certain modifications have been made to the coachwork, and the appearance is improved by a slatted stoneguard

The important dimensions of the Magnette may well be recapitulated: the six cylinders have a bore and stroke of 57 by 84 mm. (1,287 c.c.), the R.A.C. rating being 12.08 h.p., and the annual tax £9. The overall gear ratios are 21.5, 11.9, 6.98, and 5.125 to 1, while the wheelbase and track are 8ft. and 3ft. 9in. respectively.

In addition to the open model already outlined, the graceful Airline coupé is

New grouping of the instruments.

It will be recalled that the Airline coupé is a two-door design with a well-curved roof merging into a streamlined rear panel, in which the spare wheel is partly countersunk. The doors carry sliding windows, and the specification includes a sunshine roof.

A short run on the "PB" Midget showed that the increase in engine capacity has had a marked effect on the lower range of acceleration, and has considerably improved also the top gear performance. Moreover, this has been accomplished without in any way impairing the capacity of the engine to attain high rates of revolution, while the closer ratios of the gear box are undoubtedly well suited to the increased

fitted to the radiator shell and by a reduction in the height of the scuttle flares, which has also resulted in giving the driver a better view ahead. The doors are now hinged at the forward edge instead of at the rear, and are carried on substantial chromium-plated hinges which extend on to the sides of the scuttle so that a vertical hinge line is given. The doors do not, therefore, tend to fall to when open.

Apart from these modifications the bodies are similar in appearance to the previous two- and four-seaters, but in the case of the two-seater the luggage space available at the back of the seat has been slightly increased. The seating has also been modified, pneumatic cushions being used, and spring cases for the back squab. A new facia board carries separate speedometer and revolution counter, the instruments and switches being grouped as on the new "PB" type Midget. New and more attractive colour schemes are used, and also serve to improve the appearance.

(Above) The larger-engined "PB" Midget two-seater.

(Below) The "P" Midget Airline coupé.

being retained in the range, and on the "P" type Midget chassis the price will be £267 10s., or £290 on the new "PB" chassis. It is also available on the Magnette "N" type chassis at £355.

engine size. Otherwise, of course, the new model handles in every way like the well-known "P" type, with which it is identical, except for the differences set forth.

CONTINENTAL CHOICE: An M.G. with special radiator and body by Alfred Hanni, of Zurich.

TUNING M.G. CARS

SOME NOTES
by
W. E. WILKINSON
(In an Interview)

Everyone who has anything to do with sports or even touring cars knows that no two cars, apparently identical in every respect, give the same performance. Small variations in valve timing, the casting of the cylinder-head, the fit of the bearings and pistons, all these can affect the ultimate result, though it is almost impossible to detect them until the car is fully run in and tried against the stop-watch. Obviously tuning is of little account unless the chassis is a good one, and this is a point which makes the tuning of M.G. cars particularly worth while. The lay-out of the chassis, brakes and so forth has been determined as a result of racing experience and so there is a margin ample to deal with any extra speed which may be obtained, and it also happens that for a small amount, say £5 to £10, a useful and certain improvement of performance can be expected in every case.

The first car to be considered is obviously the popular " P " type with its three-bearing four-cylinder engine, virtually identical with the unit used on the " Q " and " R " type cars and thus capable of a substantial increase in power without fear of damage.

Before starting work it is advisable that the engine should be run in, so as to be able to detect the improvements in performance which are being made, though of course there is nothing in the tuning which could not be done to a new engine. We usually start with checking the camshaft timing, making sure that the inlet valves open, as they should, 15 degrees before top dead centre. Sometimes the keyway is machined a fraction out of position, and in this case the alteration in timing has to be rectified by making a new key. In the same way the ignition timing must be checked, the correct setting being ⅜-inch before t.d.c. with the ignition fully advanced. If the setting is wrong, and particularly if the owner has been trying a little " private " tuning, the error is nearly always in the direction of too much advance, and an improvement of 2 m.p.h. with smoother running often follows simply through attention to this point.

The next thing to be decided is the compression ratio desired. The standard ratio is 6 to 1 and this can be taken as high as 8.5 to 1 without any major alterations, but in this case the engine will require a mixture of 50 per cent. straight or ethyl petrol and 50 per cent. benzol. Not everyone is prepared to go to the trouble of buying benzol however, so generally we are content with removing ⅛-inch of metal from the head and using a thin gasket. This gives a compression ratio of about 7 to 1 and an increase of speed of 3-5 m.p.h., while the engine still runs smoothly on standard fuels.

The next move is to grind out and polish ports, and to make sure that the openings in the induction pipe, inlet gaskets and cylinder head are smooth and flush. This seems quite a small matter, but in the case of an engine which revs up to 6,500 r.p.m. or more, it may have a substantial effect, and in many cases one may get 2 to 3 m.p.h.

W. E. Wilkinson

Mr. Wilkinson has had a varied experience of sports and racing cars. Some years ago he was head tuner to Captain Eyston and accompanied him and the late Count Compari on their Maseratis in the Double Twelve, the Irish Grand Prix and the T.T. He acted as spare driver to Mr. R. E. Tongue in the 1934 500 miles race, finishing fourth on an M.G. Magnette. He is now racing manager of the Bellevue Garage. ED.

A dynamometer is of the greatest use in checking the effect of small adjustments. This one has just been installed at the Bellevue Garage.

extra as a result of providing a free passage for the incoming mixture. Triple valve springs we also find useful in getting the utmost out of the " P " type engine. The tension is very little greater than that of double springs, but valve bounce is nevertheless avoided since their period is well above any revs. which the engine will reach.

The standard engine components have a sufficient margin of safety to stand the extra power produced by these alterations, but sparking plugs having a higher heat-resistance need to be used, the 14 mm. K.L.G. L.K.I.'s proving satisfactory. With the 7.5 to 1 compression it is also advisable to fit valves of K. steel.

All these attentions cost comparatively little, and a car which previously may have had a maximum of anything between 70 and 78 m.p.h. should now be capable of a genuine 80. If you are an enthusiast with a good supply of ready cash there are other things which add to the car's efficiency, though naturally as this is raised the extra m.p.h. become proportionally difficult to obtain.

One thing which helps in many cases is to have the bearings eased. It is difficult to forecast exactly how much bearings are going to bed down with running in, and occasionally we find them still tight after several thousand miles. A clearance of two-thousandths on main and big-end bearings may actually prolong the life of the engine, since the crankshaft expands just as surely as the pistons or the cylinder block. Another thing necessary to ensure that the engine is giving its best is to make certain that the connecting rods are running parallel with the bores, while those who wish to take part in speed trials may find it worth having the compression raised to 10 to 1 and running on alcohol fuel. Most people with the " P " type car naturally do not contemplate doing anything as drastic as that and for ordinary events such as reliability and speed trials the 7 or the 8.5 compression provides quite enough power.

Nothing has so far been said about the chassis. Very little is required in this direction beyond seeing that the brakes and wheel-bearings are free in all positions, and if high-speed work is contemplated to bind the road springs with insulating tape and then cord, with a final layer of tape to make a neat job. It is assumed of course that spring slides, steering joints and other vital parts are in good condition.

There are still, of course, a great number of the earlier " J " type Midgets in regular use for trials and road work. The same treatment suggested for the " P " type may also be successfully employed on the earlier cars but the two-bearing crankshaft puts a limit to the power which can safely be obtained, and we seldom raise the compression above 7 to 1. This applies even more strongly to the supercharged Montlhéry. As an experiment we had a specially balanced Laystall crankshaft made for one of these cars at a cost of £25 and ran it successfully through an entire season without

116

trouble, and if anyone is thinking of using one of these cars regularly in competitions, I strongly advise obtaining one of these.

Before leaving the Midget it might be well to say something about petrol consumption. The consumption of the standard car is about 30 m.p.g. Raising the compression to 7 to 1 improves the figures slightly, and even on 8.5, where slightly richer needles are required in the carburetters, the increase in fuel consumption is negligible.

The " L " type Magna gave less scope for tuning than most of the later models, as the engine was rather small for the size of the chassis and required to run at high revs. before much power was produced. We have had quite good results with one of these running with an 8.5 to 1 compression, but a more successful way of tackling the problem was found in fitting a small Marshall supercharger blowing at 5 lbs. A larger and more efficient water pump was also found of advantage.

The last type of sports M.G. I deal with is the " N " type Magnette, which is perhaps the most responsive to simple treatment. The engine is dealt with in exactly the same way as that of the " P " type Midget, and the compression may safely be raised to 8.5 to 1. The cars driven by Mr. K. D. and Mr. D. G. Evans have been prepared in his way and we have had excellent results with them, running throughout a season of trials without even dropping the sumps. 75 horse-power is developed at 6,500 r.p.m. Valves, pistons, connecting-rods and other components are all standard, but the clutch springs have been strengthened, and the gear-box pinions originally fitted in the old " J " type Midgets are used, as the standard ratios are rather too low for trials work. Cylinderhead gaskets are dispensed with, the heads being checked on a surface plate and then lapped on to the block.

With trials ratios the all-out speed is 85 m.p.h. though another 5 m.p.h. can be obtained with a higher back-axle. The T.T.-type car which is capable of 95 m.p.h. is identical except for a different camshaft, which gives more overlap, and larger carburetters. The higher speed is obtained, of course, at the cost of power low down.

At the end of the racing season we experimented with a Magnette on which the compression ratio was raised to 9.5 to 1. Alcohol fuel naturally was needed. The car finished first in a Mountain Race and a close third in an outer circuit race, the best lap speed in the latter race being 104.19 m.p.h.

With regard to the racing cars, the supercharged Magnette and " Q " and " R " type Midgets, any modifications we have carried out have been of a minor nature, most of the attention, as usually happens in cars of this type, being given to seeing that every part is free and a good fit. The camshaft on the Magnette

The crankshaft and the centre main bearing of the M.G. Magnette.

which only gives 15 degrees overlap can be changed with advantage for one giving an overlap of 25 to 35 degrees. As regards the chassis considerable weight can be saved by fitting a light body and smaller batteries, while road-holding is improved by removing two leaves from the rear springs.

The wonderful little engines fitted to the " Q " and " R " Midgets are almost identical. They can be revved safely to 7,800 r.p.m. and one we had on the bench the other day gave 116.6 h.p. at 7,500 r.p.m. Beyond rather ticklish jobs such as lightening the rockers and providing special valve cotters, nothing out of the ordinary is needed on them, but we have made some successful experiments with a special cylinder head in which the sparking plugs screw into masked openings. There are no shoulders on the bodies of the special 14 mm. plugs, the copper gaskets being sandwiched in between the bottom of the plugs and the metal of the cylinder head. This method of construction keeps the plugs cool and reduces the size of the opening into the combustion chambers.

Our racing this season concluded with an attempt by Mr. Kenneth Evans on the 750 c.c. Mountain record. Previous attempts we had made showed that though the power developed by the " R " type Midget was quite sufficient to give us the record, the violent braking called for at the corners rendered the brakes almost inoperative after a few laps. This we attributed to the fact that the brake drums were shielded from the air stream and also the fact that the drums and shoes were both made of the same material, so that the heat did not flow away from the linings. Fitting windscoops on the back-plates and fins on the drums completely overcame this trouble, and a few days before the track closed, Mr. Evans took the record at 75.24 m.p.h., a satisfactory finish to a season in which cars tuned at the Bellevue Garage scored 45 awards in racing events and 36 in reliability trials. Racing nowadays is a strenuous business, but for the amateur with a small amount of money to spend, plenty of amusement can still be had from taking part in the smaller speed trials and the Club events at Brooklands, and next season we expect to be busier than ever preparing M.G. and other makes of car for events of this kind.

M.G. Announce a Two-litre

A Handsome and Roomy Four-door Close-coupled Saloon on a 10ft. 3in. Wheelbase Chassis

RUMOUR has had much to say of the M.G. Car Company's eve-of-the-Show surprise. It would be this, and it would be that. It would have this feature and that feature. Now, however, the new model is announced, and is seen to be entirely different from the various forecasts.

Briefly, the M.G. Two-litre is a large, roomy sports saloon of the popular four-door close-coupled type, having essentially modern sweeping lines, with a

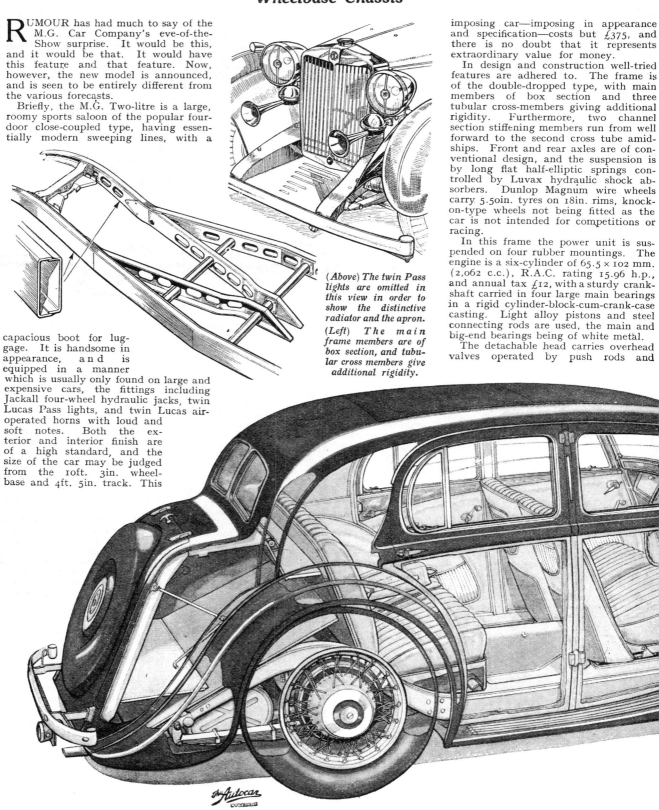

(Above) The twin Pass lights are omitted in this view in order to show the distinctive radiator and the apron.

(Left) The main frame members are of box section, and tubular cross members give additional rigidity.

capacious boot for luggage. It is handsome in appearance, and is equipped in a manner which is usually only found on large and expensive cars, the fittings including Jackall four-wheel hydraulic jacks, twin Lucas Pass lights, and twin Lucas air-operated horns with loud and soft notes. Both the exterior and interior finish are of a high standard, and the size of the car may be judged from the 10ft. 3in. wheelbase and 4ft. 5in. track. This

imposing car—imposing in appearance and specification—costs but £375, and there is no doubt that it represents extraordinary value for money.

In design and construction well-tried features are adhered to. The frame is of the double-dropped type, with main members of box section and three tubular cross-members giving additional rigidity. Furthermore, two channel section stiffening members run from well forward to the second cross tube amidships. Front and rear axles are of conventional design, and the suspension is by long flat half-elliptic springs controlled by Luvax hydraulic shock absorbers. Dunlop Magnum wire wheels carry 5.50in. tyres on 18in. rims, knock-on-type wheels not being fitted as the car is not intended for competitions or racing.

In this frame the power unit is suspended on four rubber mountings. The engine is a six-cylinder of 65.5 × 102 mm. (2,062 c.c.), R.A.C. rating 15.96 h.p., and annual tax £12, with a sturdy crankshaft carried in four large main bearings in a rigid cylinder-block-cum-crank-case casting. Light alloy pistons and steel connecting rods are used, the main and big-end bearings being of white metal.

The detachable head carries overhead valves operated by push rods and

kers from the high-lift camshaft in
crank case. On the off side are twin
ee-branch exhaust manifolds leading
twin silencers, which are carried by
ber-suspended supports to avoid any
aust drumming in the body. The

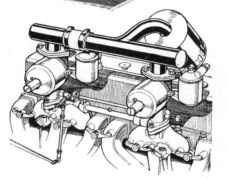

*Possessing good lines and pro-
portions the new M.G. is distinctly imposing and is very
completely equipped.*

nifolds provide hot spots for the in-
tion system, which is fed by two
vndraught S.U. carburetters supplied
twin S.U. fuel pumps from the large
r tank.

Lubrication is forced, and all oil
ses through a Tecalemit filter. The
ge aluminium alloy sump is ribbed for
ling, and the oil filler is accessibly
ced on the valve cover. Cooling is
pump and fan, the system being con-
lled by a thermostat, and the radiator
of the well-known and distinctive
G. design with vertical slats forming
toneguard.

The electrical equipment includes
omatic voltage control of the
amo, and ignition is by coil, with
omatic advance, 14 mm. sparking
gs being used. Twin batteries are

*The induction and exhaust system. Twin
S.U. carburetters of downdraught type take
their air through a large cleaner and silencer.*

tion with the spiral bevel-driven three-
quarter floating rear axle, are 17.82,
10.15, 6.59 and 4.45 to 1. The propeller-shaft has Hardy Spicer needle
roller-type universal joints, which
require no attention.

Lockheed hydraulic brakes with 12in.
diameter drums are operated by the
pedal, while the racing-type brake lever,
which lies horizontally along the tunnel
between the front seats, operates the
rear shoes through cables, and has a very
accessible butterfly nut adjustment.
Steering is by Bishop cam and lever
gear, giving 2¼ turns of the spring-
spoked wheel from lock to lock, the
turning circle being approximately 40ft.

Chassis lubrication is by grouped
nipples on each side of the dash. Large
tools are carried in spring clips on the
dash, and small tools in a box on the off
side beneath the bonnet.

For Four Large Occupants

As regards the body, the occupants
sit well within the wheelbase but have
ample leg room, while the luggage boot
is of unusually large capacity. The front
bucket seats are adjustable, and have
air bags in the spring cases of the
squabs. The rear seat has a wide folding centre arm-rest, and side-rests in
which are mounted ash trays. The
whole scheme of the seating has been
arranged to give ample room and every
comfort to four large occupants, with
room for their luggage in the boot.

The doors are hinged on the centre
pillars, and have winding windows and
"no-draught" ventilating windows also.
Useful pockets are formed in the leather
trimming of the doors, also in the backs
of the front seats. Ash trays are also
fitted in the front doors. The doors are
of good width and give easy access to all
seats.

The interior woodwork is of burr walnut, and cupboards are formed at each
end of the facia board, in the centre of
which the instruments are most attractively grouped. There are from left to
right a combined oil pressure gauge and
ammeter, a 100 m.p.h. speedometer, a
combined rev counter and clock, a combined radiator thermometer and oil-
petrol gauge, with switches and controls
neatly arranged in a row beneath the
instruments. The dials have dull gold

carried at each side of the propeller-
shaft beneath the rear seat.

From the engine power is transmitted
by a cork-faced clutch running in oil to
a four-speed gear box with double helical
gears and synchromesh action for top
and third. The gear ratios, in conjunc-

figures and mounts; and at night are illuminated from behind, a refinement being a rheostat to give a graduated light.

The single-pane screen opens to a wide angle, and has twin wiper blades which lie horizontally out of sight, the motor being in front of the driver but below his line of vision. A Weathershields sliding roof is fitted, as are two visors which when not in use lie beneath the cantrails. Two large rear lights give

Side and centre arm-rests are provided. Note the no-draught ventilation panels.

Easy access is given to the seats and the steering wheel is well raked.

The capacious boot gives ample luggage accommodation.

good visibility for reversing, and are fitted with a blind under the driver's control. Trafficators are mounted in the centre pillars, the switch being in the steering wheel boss, also the loud and soft horn switch. A push-switch on the tunnel changes over from head to Pass lights, and vice versa.

There is much that one could say of the style and finish of the coachwork, but the accompanying illustrations show the graceful modern lines and good proportions. The sweeping wings are well valanced and add to the general appearance, as does the extended bonnet with four ventilator panels in each side. The spare wheel is mounted on the lid of the boot beneath a metal cover.

Altogether the new M.G. Two-litre is bound to attract considerable attention by reason of its striking appearance, its very complete equipment, and its most moderate price.

The neat instrument panel with dull gold dials is set in a burr walnut facia board.

RESEARCH INTO SKIDS AND ROAD WEAR

THE investigations into the causes and cure of skidding form a large part of the first report of the Road Research Board of the Department of Scientific and Industrial Research. It deals with the two years (up to March 31st last) since the Department assumed responsibility for the researches on roads carried out at the Harmondsworth Laboratories, Middlesex.

Sound beginnings have been made with a comprehensive programme of research. As regards skidding, the experiments are to discover the factors favourable to skidding in both vehicle design and road construction. "One obvious method of continuing the research," states the report, "would be to skid full-sized vehicles on a large surface. This method would be too expensive and

somewhat dangerous, but may eventually have to be faced. In the meanwhile, careful consideration has been given to further work with models." A single-wheel trailer has been devised which can be used with circular track road-testing machines, or at the rear of a testing lorry. This apparatus has shown that *wet roads are more slippery in summer than in winter.* Lack of sufficient rain has rather hindered work on some occasions! As a result it may be that artificial wetting of the road will have to take place.

To test the durability of road surfaces —without waiting for deterioration under normal use—experimental stretches are laid down. A speedier method is to use road-wear machines, and one is required that will subject a surface to a normal year's wear in, say, the space of a day.

Some road-wear machines have been developed using circular tracks on which loaded vehicles or wheels travel continuously. A small machine with a 5ft. 6in. track is to be used at Harmondsworth, the "road" itself being revolved under a nearly stationary wheel in this case. A larger machine is being built with a lorry travelling at 45 m.p.h. tethered to a centre post.

Very important is that part of the report dealing with materials for road-making. Work is taking place on the preparation of satisfactory specifications. At present engineers buy materials under trade names, but their composition is not accurately known. British standard specifications exist for tars, but even these are so widely drawn as to allow too much variation.

THE 2-LITRE M.G. IN PRODUCTION

A FAST AND ROOMY SPORTS CAR WHICH IS MODERATELY PRICED AT £375.

The M.G. Two-Litre Saloon

After concentrating for many years on the smaller type of sports cars, the M.G. Company sprang a pleasant surprise just before the Olympia Show by announcing a 2-litre model with a 10 ft. 3 in. chassis, affording space for luxurious and roomy closed coachwork. Certain improvements and modifications have been introduced since then, the principal ones being the increase of engine size to 2,290 c.c., the fitting of a special close-ratio gear-box with central control, and the use of knock-on Rudge wheels. The car is thus eminently suited for sporting use and fast touring, and the open-air enthusiast is now catered for by an open four-seater body by Charlesworth, which is available at the same price as the saloon, and a drop-head coupé made by Salmons of Newport Pagnell. In this latter body the front extension rolls backs and by means of an ingenious winding mechanism the head is then lowered without effort into a recess at the back of the body. The coupé costs £398.

The Abingdon factory has now been completely re-organised, and four assembly lines have been fitted into the space formerly occupied by two. Conveyors for wheels and other heavy parts speed up production, though of course the chassis and bodies still have the same individual attention as in the production of the previous models. The output at present is one car per hour, but when production is in full swing, it will rise as high as 100 cars per week.

Another interesting feature of the factory is the new cellulose spraying plant.

This is in two sections, one of which applies the priming coats and the other a wide choice of finishing colours. Each section has its own oven for drying and hardening the paint, and is capable of handling each week 100 2-litre bodies and a similar number of bodies for the smaller cars.

A short run we had in a 2-litre saloon left us very favourably impressed. The car showed an excellent turn of speed, reaching 70 m.p.h. with very little effort on the winding roads near Abingdon and giving an all-out speed on the open road of approximately 80 m.p.h. The spring-ing was comfortable without any tendency to unsteadiness, and the engine was unnoticed even at speeds around 4,500 r.p.m. The brakes, which are hydraulically operated, proved fully in keeping with the car's speed capabilities.

The seats are roomy and well upholstered and there is plenty of head room. With a sliding roof and ventilating windows there is no excuse for stuffiness on the warmest day. The lines are low and graceful, and a luggage trunk of outstanding size is part of the design. We can safely congratulate Mr. Kimber on his latest venture.

Two-litre M.G.s on the assembly line. Four of these are now installed, making possible an output of 100 cars per week.

The Autocar Road Tests

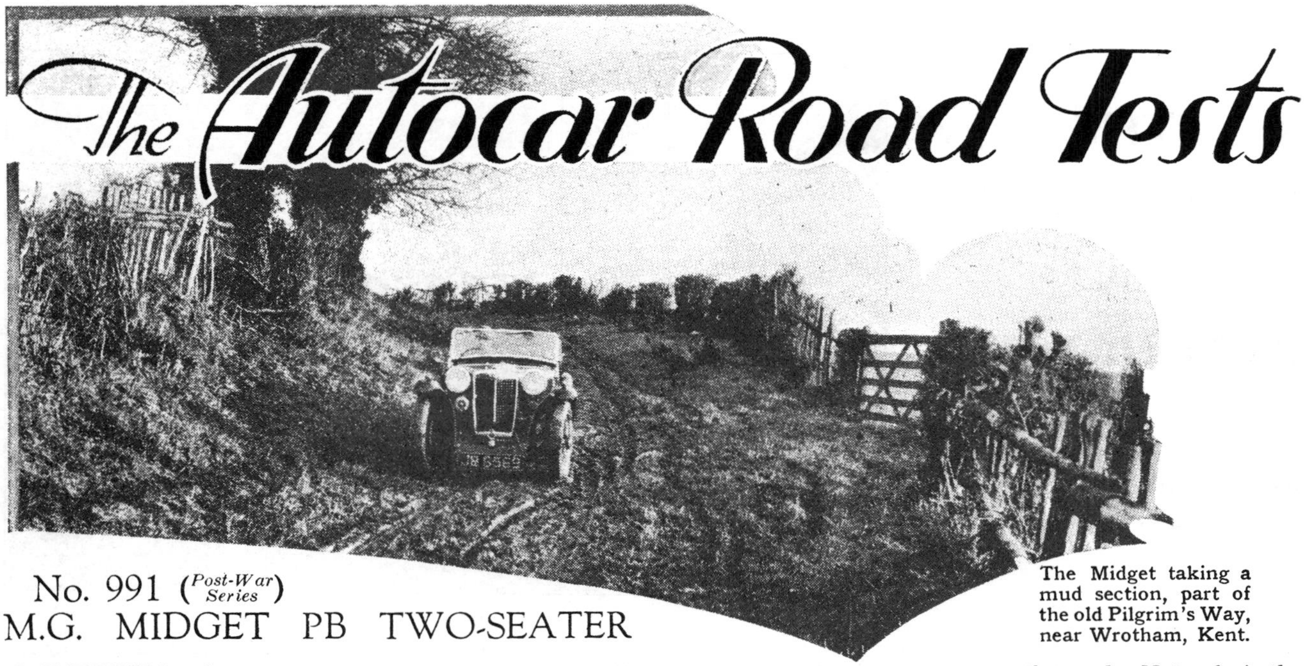

The Midget taking a mud section, part of the old Pilgrim's Way, near Wrotham, Kent.

No. 991 (Post-War Series)

M.G. MIDGET PB TWO-SEATER

A Fascinating Small Sports Car : The Latest Model Shows Marked Improvements in Several Important Points

SOMETIMES the truest expression of opinion upon a car which one has tested in the usual way is to say it is a machine one would like to own oneself. Any such statement is naturally dependent upon the views of the individual expressing it, but, since the M.G. Midget is to be considered as a sports car, appealing to the more enthusiastic type of driver, it is at all events fair comment from someone who tries all manner of cars.

The PB Midget now tested is the model that was introduced just before the last Olympia Show, differing from the earlier P type in having a slightly bigger engine capacity, of 939 c.c. against 847 c.c.—a size retained for what is known now as the PA type. Besides the larger engine there are other points of difference in the PB Midget which contribute towards making it an appreciably improved car.

It would be difficult for anyone free from prejudice and at all capable of being enthused by the performance of a small sports car not to be quickly attracted to this M.G. It does so much for so little. It is almost as fast as can be used reasonably; certainly on either a long or a short journey it covers the ground just about as quickly as any type of car can, and in some circumstances more rapidly than is possible to a bigger, faster but less handy vehicle. Its acceleration is good, and it runs happily at 50, 55 and even 60 m.p.h., for the engine is smooth and will go up to a limit of as much as 5,500 r.p.m. on the indirect gears.

The acceleration shows a distinct gain as a result of the increased engine size—on paper as well as on the road. Not only is the pick-up better from the lower speeds on top and third gears, but in the middle range too, and, if recollections serve, there is a decidedly superior feeling of power in reserve.

Those are points of far more importance than the actual maximum speed. In regard to speed figures, the state of Brooklands at present, undergoing repair as it is, prevented the proper maximum being developed in the available distance. The best that could be managed as a timed speed over a quarter-mile with the windscreen lowered and two up was fractionally below 71 m.p.h.—very definitely that is not the car's limit of speed.

This particular machine was fitted with a speedometer which showed no measurable error at 40, 50, 60 and even 70, and which was slightly *slow* at 30. It is therefore possible to say from the indications the car gave on Brooklands and its subsequent behaviour on the road that the maximum would lie around 75 or 76 m.p.h., given space in which to attain it. That is remarkable for a 9 h.p.-rated car which is flexible, tractable, and thoroughly pleasant for by-way pottering, for instance, and for the slower kind of motoring which often appeals.

Reference has already been made to the high speeds the Midget is capable of keeping up; indeed, about 50 m.p.h. seems a natural speed on open roads. Even without ever driving it faster than that there is a charm about the car it is difficult to express, but which no doubt partly arises from the undeniable efficiency of the small overhead camshaft four-cylinder engine.

DATA FOR THE DRIVER

M.G. MIDGET PB TWO-SEATER

PRICE, with two-seater body, £222. Tax, £6 15s.
RATING : 8.9 h.p., four cylinders, o.h.v., 60 × 83 mm., 939 c.c.
WEIGHT, without passengers, 15 cwt. 2 qr. 16 lb.
TYRE SIZE : 4.00 × 19in. on knock-off wire wheels.
LIGHTING SET : 12-volt ; 9 amps at 30 m.p.h.
TANK CAPACITY : 12 gallons ; fuel consumption, 35 m.p.g. (approx.).
TURNING CIRCLE : (L. and R.) 34ft. GROUND CLEARANCE : 6 in.

ACCELERATION

Overall gear ratios.	From steady m.p.h. of 10 to 30	20 to 40	30 to 50
5.375 to 1	15$\frac{1}{5}$ sec.	16$\frac{3}{5}$ sec.	18$\frac{2}{5}$ sec.
7.31 to 1	10$\frac{3}{5}$ sec.	11 sec.	11$\frac{4}{5}$ sec.
11.50 to 1	6$\frac{3}{5}$ sec.	—	—
19.24 to 1	—	—	—

From rest to 50 m.p.h. through gears, 16$\frac{2}{5}$ sec.

From rest to 60 m.p.h. through gears, 27$\frac{3}{5}$ sec.

25 yards of 1 in 5 gradient from rest, 5$\frac{3}{5}$ sec.

SPEED

	m.p.h.
Mean maximum timed speed over $\frac{1}{4}$ mile	—
Best timed speed over $\frac{1}{4}$ mile ...	—
Speeds attainable on indirect gears—	
1st	22
2nd	37
3rd	55–60
Speed from rest up 1 in 5 Test Hill (on 1st gear)	18.47

Performance figures of acceleration and maximum speed are the means of several runs in opposite directions.

(Latest model described in "The Autocar" of August 30th, 1935.)

This unit has been developed to a fine pitch of performance and generally pleasing behaviour. Not only does it give a remarkable power output for its size, but it has been kept quiet mechanically and smooth for an engine of this description.

A good compromise has now been reached in the matter of the exhaust note; just sufficient remains to indicate that this is a sports and not a perfectly normal touring car, and the peak of the note is reached at about 2,500 r.p.m. No sign of pinking was evident from the engine at any time.

The PB Midget does well in running about slowly in speed-limit areas; indeed, its slow-running capabilities on top gear are extremely good in relation to the performance. Also, it shows a good ability to climb comparatively slowly on top gear on those occasions when it is not desired to rush a gradient or to rev on the gears.

An excellent point is the provision of an amber-tinted warning lamp on the instrument board, which lights up at about 20 m.p.h. and then automatically switches out at 30 to attract the driver's attention. Especially at night this is a prominent warning, and removes any perhaps captious criticism there might be that the "30" range of the centrally mounted speedometer is apt to be obstructed from view by the steering wheel. The separate rev counter now fitted is, however, immediately in front of the driver, and thoroughly visible. Whilst on this same subject of driving in built-up areas, it may be mentioned that, even after adjustment, the view given in the external driving mirror is not all it might be.

It is the handling of the car which gives it much of its appeal. The M.G. is low-built, of course, and it feels in "one piece"; the controls are exact, and very soon the driver is at one with the car. The driving position is right, vision is excellent, both wings being seen from the driving seat, and the big-diameter spring-spoked steering wheel comes in just the right place.

Though most satisfactorily light even when manoeuvring, the steering feels firm as well in a way which is remarkably good for fast work. It is by no means unduly low-geared steering, either, for approximately one and a half turns take the front wheels from full lock on one side to full lock on the other side. There is a delightful sense of having absolute control over the car, and, within reason, the road surface, whether wet or dry, makes practically no difference to the driver's handling of it. It rides so firmly, so safely, takes bends to the proverbial inch, and is able to respond completely to the judgment of an experienced driver.

The brakes do all they should do, too, giving an excellent, regularly achieved emergency test pull-up in less

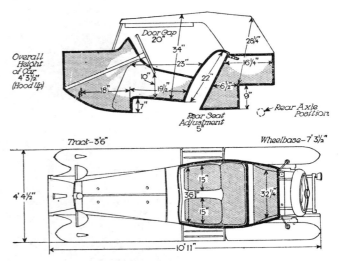

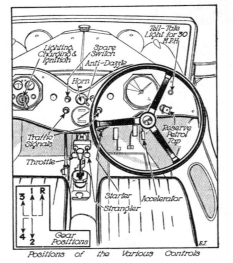

Positions of the Various Controls

29 feet (Dry Surface) from 30 M.P.H

than 30ft. from 30 m.p.h., yet with little actual feeling of brakes having been applied, and without the least pull to either side. The fly-off racing-type hand lever is excellent for holding the car firmly on the steepest gradient.

One of the improvements concerns the gear change. A lighter clutch driving plate is now used, and, in conjunction with appreciably higher first and second gear ratios, the result is a gear change which can be handled really quickly on the upward movements with no more than mild noise from the teeth, or dead silently with a brief, single-clutch pause. Top and third gear ratios remain as before. This is indeed a gear change that handles beautifully as a whole.

The springing is firm to give the stability that has been mentioned, but not really harsh at any time on surfaces which are at all reasonable. There is at times fairly hard movement, this being principally noticeable in towns, but for a car of this description the riding is comfortable and at its best over the middle range of speed.

The hood, which disappears into the body, is raised or lowered and secured really easily. It is not a very natural position for the driver to have his right arm entirely inside the body. There is fair room for small luggage.

The engine has an extremely good oil filler in the top of the valve gear cover; starting is immediate. Grouped "long range" lubricators serve chassis bearings which otherwise would be awkward to reach.

A fascinating, satisfying little car.

The trim appearance of the Midget is not lost when the hood is raised.

THE P.B. TYPE M.G. MIDGET

A SMALL SPORTS CAR WITH A PLEASING PERSONALITY

Good news travels fast. Hearing excellent reports of the new P.B. Midget, which has a 939 c.c. engine, we set off post haste to Abingdon, and demanded one of the new models to try. "Afraid we have no regular press cars available," said Mr. George Tuck, genial advertising manager and welcomer of journalists, "but there's a demonstrator cum works-hack you might like to try. I think you'll like it." And we did.

One's first impression was that the 3 mm. increase in bore, 57 to 60 mm., had made a really substantial difference to the power of the engine at low speeds. Nipping through Abingdon and out into the open country, third gear seemed adequate where second would have been required on the P, and there, was quite a useful performance on top gear. We had been warned that this engine was not quite as smooth as on the production cars, but even so a feeling of power is not unwelcome on a sports car, and the one we tried felt as though it was taking pleasure in pushing the needle to higher speeds.

There are few more pleasant experiences than to be humming along in an open car on a fine day, and the Midget quickly settled down to a steady gait of 55 m.p.h. with inaudible exhaust and a smooth running engine. The seat is raked to give an upright though restful driving position, the steering ratio has been raised so that only a slight movement of the wheel is called for on a thirty degree bend, and a useful castor action centres the steering as the rim is released The steering is positive but remains light, and this ease of control applies equally to the brakes, the clutch and the gear-change.

55 m.p.h. seems only a gentle amble on the Midget in spite of the engine turning over at 4,000 r.p.m., but when a call comes for full speed ahead there is plenty in hand, and the little car gets up to 60 and even 65 quite readily on short stretches of road. Where winding roads are encountered, of course, full use of the gear-box is needed for maximum performance, and the conveniently-placed gear lever and light clutch give one every encouragement. The engine spins up promptly when changing down, a valuable feature when trying to maintain momentum on a trials hill.

Changing up, the shift from first to second has been improved in comparison with that of the "P" type, bottom gear being higher in the case of the new car. Second to third is not so quick, but can be snapped across at the expense of a little noise, while third to top is fastest of all. Third gear is silent; the two lower gears are audible but not unpleasantly so.

With its short wheelbase the car can be thrown round corners and accurately controlled with the high-geared steering. A maximum of nearly 60 m.p.h. is possible in third gear, and if full use is made of this, the car will hold its own with cars of much higher horse-power through being so handy and light to drive.

The brakes are equal to any emergency. In normal use they seem adequate, though not abnormally powerful. With full pedal pressure, however, they pull the car up in the most decisive way, the braking distance working out

BRIEF SPECIFICATION

Engine: Four cylinders. Bore 60 mm., stroke 83 mm., capacity 939 c.c. R.A.C. rating 9 h.p. Single overhead camshaft. Coil ignition. Two S.U. carburetters.

Gearbox: Four speeds and reverse. Constant mesh third gear. Remote control. Ratios 5.75, 7.32, 11.5 and 19.2 to 1

Suspension: Half elliptic springs.

Dimensions: Wheelbase 9ft. 3¼in. Track 3ft. 6in. Weight with open two seater body 14½ cwts.

Price: £222

helping full power to be exerted for braking tests and all four wheels can be locked if required. A racing ratchet, applied by means of a thimble at the top of the lever, is a useful feature.

Comfortable springing is notoriously difficult to arrange on a short-wheelbase car, but the Midget gives no cause for complaint in this respect. With the standard shock absorber setting the car rides comfortably at thirty, and yet contrives to corner steadily when taken round a corner at the limit of tyre adhesion. All out on Brooklands, a light grip with one hand on the steering wheel was all that was required.

Tested over a flying half-mile, the Midget registered exactly 75 m.p.h., a very useful speed for an unblown 9 h.p. car in touring trim. With the screen

valves are actuated by means of fingers and the adjustment is made by rotating the eccentric pivots. 14 mm. sparking plugs are used, with coil ignition. The S.U. carburetters are of semi-down-draught pattern, with an S.U. petrol pump.

The crankshaft is carried in three main bearings, and an accessible pressure

able to pull up outside a shop in a busy street without the manoeuvres which usually attend the parking of the big saloon.

Big men in small motor cars afford a constant source of amusement to the comic papers. On the M.G. the body space on the 7 ft. 3 in. wheelbase has been utilised to the best advantage, and there is plenty of leg-room for a six-foot driver. The seat is not adjustable, but the back squab can be tilted backwards or forwards six or eight inches which gives the same effect. On earlier M.G.s we sometimes had to complain that there was no room for large feet, but on the P.B., the left foot, when not required on the clutch pedal, finds a resting place on the gear-box casing, and there is no fear of applying brake and accelerator at once.

Visibility is good, even with the hood raised, and the car is wide enough for two normal passengers. With the side-curtains in position the driver's elbow is a little restricted, but as the steering is high-geared, this is not a serious point.

The dash equipment comprises a large rev.-counter, speedometer and the usual switches. A knob operating the tap-for the reserve petrol supply of three gallons is mounted under the steering wheel. The petrol consumption works out at 31 m.p.g. and as the tank holds in all twelve gallons, so the car can cover an exceptional distance without refuelling. The headlamps give a good driving light; when meeting oncoming traffic, the off-side one can be extinguished by means of a switch mounted in the middle of the dashboard.

A small amount of space is provided for luggage in the hood well behind the back seat, and with the hood raised a good-sized suitcase can be carried.

The mechanical features of the M.G. are too well-known to require describing in full, but a few points may be recalled. The engine has an overhead camshaft driven from the front end of the crank-shaft through a vertical shaft and bevels. The dynamo forms part of this shaft. The

The chassis is upswept over the front axle and underslung at the rear. Straight half-elliptic springs are used, fixed at the front end and sliding at the rear. The front shock-absorbers are of the friction type, with hydraulics at the rear. The brakes are operated by means of enclosed cables. All inaccessible chassis points are lubricated from two banks of grouped nipples mounted on the scuttle bulkhead.

Mudguards and other chassis parts subject to vibration are mounted on rubber, and the whole car is obviously laid out to make maintenance easy for the private owner. For the P.B. we can safely predict a success even greater than that of its smaller brother.

oil filter is mounted on the near-side of the crankcase. A single dry-plate clutch is used, and the four-speed gear-box, which is mounted in unit with the engine, has constant-mesh third gear. The transmission is orthodox, with an open propeller shaft and a bevel-driven back axle. The

Back and front of the dash are equally accessible on the P.B. Type Midget.

This photograph shows the neat appearance of the new P.B. Type M.G. Midget.

at the excellent figure of 55 ft. from 40 m.p.h. The brake lever, which also operates all four brakes, is useful in

raised, 70 m.p.h. appeared about the maximum. The engine runs quite happily up to 5,500 r.p.m., giving road speeds of 21, 36, 57 and 75 m.p.h. in the four gears. To change up silently it is necessary to pause slightly between each gear, but the lever can be snapped across even at full revs. when maximum acceleration is wanted.

The open road is obviously the place for a sports car, but the 30 m.p.h. limit cannot be ignored. A small yellow dash light connected with the speedometer glows from 20 m.p.h. when the instrument is registering from 20 to 29 m.p.h. and provides a convenient warning day and night. The car runs quite smoothly down to 15 m.p.h. on top gear, and the two finger lightness of the gear-change is appreciated at slower speeds or when accelerating through traffic. Apart from its handiness in slipping through traffic a small car like the M.G. scores heavily in towns because it can be parked so easily in confined spaces and it is gratifying to be

The acceleration chart of the P.B. type M.G. Midget.

SECONDS

Trial Trip

The New Two-litre M.G. Has Its Final Test on a Run to Geneva

THE SCRIBE

EN ROUTE TO GENEVA.

Dinant, Belgium, which has been almost entirely rebuilt since the Great War.

(Above right) The Bayard Rock, which was scaled by the late King Albert.

(Right). The new 2-litre M.G. at Dinant.

others of the present seats, and, what is more, it appears, and feels, much larger than it is. The accommodation for four persons with luggage is roomy: there is actually space for a full-size suitcase between the two front seats, where it forms a convenient arm rest.

If there is anything interesting to see between Antwerp and Malines, we did not see it. Chiesman and I, at least, were too interested in the new car's behaviour. The way the engine pulled suggested a much larger engine than 2,283 c.c.—the capacity has been slightly increased since its premature début at Olympia—in fact, the whole car gives an impression of quality and power found in only a few cars in the 3-litre class.

We stopped in Malines to look at the cathedral: I have since wondered what Mr. Gouvy thought when he found us walking round the car further to admire it instead of gazing up at the great tower of Malines cathedral. Its famous carillon of forty-four bells which has often been broadcast by the B.B.C., brought us back to earth. The guide-books will tell you that on the sides of the cathedral tower there are clock dials 45ft. in diameter, but apparently the past tense should have been used, since the 310ft. tower (about twice as high as Niagara) is still nursing the wounds it sustained in the Great War; it was three times bombarded in the Great War. Malines is a dull old town with a past that has been almost wiped out by the wars of the 17th, 18th and 20th centuries.

A further twenty miles and we were in another Belgian town made famous to us by the Great War—Louvain. Since 1918 it has been almost entirely rebuilt; of the buildings which were worthy of preservation only the fine Hôtel de Ville and a few houses of its period escaped destruction in 1914.

Louvain is a university town and unfortified: the Germans entered it a few days after the war began and the Belgian Army attempted to retake it. There was street fighting and massacre, a large part of the town, including the famous University Library, was burned, and the town was ruthlessly sacked. The library, alongside which we halted, has been rebuilt, through the munificence of an American, I believe. But its precious books can never be replaced. In a little café opposite, where we adjourned for a morning *bock*, we saw a number of students hard at work *with a pack of cards.*

Antwerp, Malines, Louvain! What memories of 1914 the names recalled! A glance at the map showed that as far as Verdun, where we intended to spend the night, our route was over ground which had been swept by the Germans. And everywhere there was evidence of it in the new-looking buildings in each town and village.

IT has lately become the practice of our manufacturers to send any new models they introduce to the Continent for their final tests; some of them, in fact, keep a permanent staff on the Continent for this purpose. This may be regarded as a tribute to easy motoring conditions in this country, for hills several miles long and rising to high altitudes are not to be found north of the English Channel. Neither have we long stretches of bad roads such as are still to be found in certain parts of Belgium, so one may assume that any car which survives several thousands of miles of fast motoring on the Continent has a safety margin for normal conditions considerably in excess of requirements.

The new 2-litre M.G., which attracted so much attention at the last Olympia Show, was tested under such conditions, and to make sure that the new car was quite up to his expectations, the managing director of the M.G. Car Company—Mr. Cecil Kimber—decided to give the car its final trip himself. Mr. F. N. Gouvy, the manager of *Morris Continental Soc. An.*, had business at the Geneva Show, so Geneva became the objective.

There was room for two more passengers; it was much better to have four aboard than to load the car with dead ballast. C. R. B. Chiesman, well known as a keen amateur competition driver, agreed to fill one seat, and the present writer occupied the other. Both of us can report that the comfort of the rear seats is all it should be but very rarely is. I have travelled in the rear seats of many cars, and can say honestly that the comfort of this M.G. has only once been equalled in about three years in my experience,

irrespective of the fact that many of our miles were over the Belgian pavé.

We left London at 8.30 p.m. on Tuesday, March 17th, and at 4.10 p.m. on the following Saturday Chiesman and I were back in England, having journeyed from Antwerp to Geneva in two days, spent one interesting day at the Swiss Show, and returned by air from Zurich, the M.G. being left in Switzerland for a few days to satisfy the demands of prospective buyers who admired its appearance on the M.G. stand in the Show.

When Chiesman and I arrived at Harwich, the good ship *Bruges* had already swallowed the M.G., and Mr. Kimber was in the saloon catching up arrears of correspondence, mainly, I suspect, concerned with his hobbies of yachting and fishing.

In view of the proposed early start next morning, we were comfortably in bed before the ship sailed. Full marks to the clerk of the weather, and the L.N.E.R. steamships, for next morning we agreed that none of us had felt anything to suggest that we had moved from Harwich quay. Full marks also to the stevedores, the R.A.C. representatives, the Customs and the passport officials. Never had any of us entered a foreign country with less formality.

We found the M.G. on the quay, looking very rakish and smart in its shining black paint. We who had not seen it before agreed that it looked much smarter than the one exhibited at Olympia.

We were soon under way with Mr. Gouvy at the wheel. Even in the first few miles on Belgium's notorious pavé

it was evident that the M.G. designers had succeeded in producing a car which combined all a good touring car should be with all the well-known M.G. characteristics. It accelerated like an M.G., it steered like an M.G., and it was taking bends with the same "on a railway track" ease as its predecessors. But this car is much larger than

Namur came next, with its circle of forts which were to hold up, indefinitely, any invader who crossed the Belgian frontier. How bravely they held out, to fall, one by one, before the end of the first month of the war. More street fighting and massacres and burnings: the world had gone mad! The ruins of the forts are still to be seen, and on a 500ft. hill dominating the town there is an ancient citadel, now one of the town's show places, but concerned with wars of more than a hundred years ago. Belgium has always been the cockpit for the squabbles of Europe.

In fact, on the whole of this trip we could not escape the subject of war. In Belgium it was the wars that have gone; in France, preparations for wars to come; in Geneva, discussions of war and its prevention. Soldiering appears to be France's greatest industry. Every French town seems to be a garrison.

The smiling countryside, the sunshine, the singing birds and the smell of freshly turned earth rid our minds for a time of the horrors of war. We were now approaching the Ardennes. A mile or so short of Dinant we stopped for lunch at a roadhouse where the fish for our meal was netted from a stone tank at the rear of the house.

So pleasant was it that we stayed longer than our scheduled time, with the result that, except for a minute or so's halt on the bridge, we could spare no time to look round peaceful Dinant, an almost completely brand-new town after its days of terror in 1914, when more than half of it was destroyed and its women and children screened the enemy from the defenders' guns while a new bridge was thrown over the Meuse to replace the beautiful old stone bridge blown up to hinder the advance. Then on to the Bayard Rock, which towers like an obelisk nearly 200ft. above the road. Apparently it is unclimbable, but the late King Albert scaled it, as a tablet on its side records.

Comfortable Riding at 70-75 m.p.h.

Time was slipping by. Mr. Gouvy spurred on our low black M.G., uphill and down, the speedometer needle between 70 and 75 most of the time, yet the riding was as comfortable as if we had been in a Pullman. It was the first time he had driven the car, and he was obviously enjoying it. Mr. Gouvy is a Belgian-born British subject, well up in the histories of both his native and his adopted countries; his running commentary was most interesting.

Soon we ran into Bouillon, two miles from the French frontier, an ancient little town with a castle dating back to the days of the first Crusade. It was strangely quiet in the town; it seemed that we had it to ourselves, for we saw less than a dozen pedestrians and only one vehicle. It is said to be a holiday centre, but on the day of our visit it was deserted. A cinematograph film of it would have conveyed no more animation than a "still." When one looks up its history one finds that it has not always been so; its record includes mention of such things as torture chambers and dungeons in that silent castle on the hill, and at the Hôtel de la Poste Napoleon III was lodged in 1870, on his way to Germany, a prisoner after the end of the Franco-German war, which was ended with the *débâcle* at Sedan, a few miles farther on.

Mistletoe in France.

Wars! wars!! wars!!!

One could not get away from them. At Dinant we had seen the gap which had been cut at the Bayard Rock in order to facilitate the passage of the army of Louis XIV of France with a train that consisted of 1,600 vehicles requisitioned in the district and loaded with loot. We had seen the memorial to 600 civilians who were shot in the Great War by the Germans, who affirmed that they had been fired on from the houses.

Here in Bouillon tales of more wars. I wondered whether in the last one the Germans passed through without being noticed. A mile or so farther on the Belgian Customs delayed us for a few minutes. At a building very like a toll-house an officer, who had been sitting on a chair outside, sauntered over. In a few minutes we were off again.

The French Customs is a few miles farther on, and here they were more formidable. Great chains were across the road, and officers were dodging in and out of their offices. As at Antwerp and the Belgian frontier only our engine number was taken (why had I not brought more English cigarettes?). The chains were removed, and we were properly in France, but we should have known it even had we, by some mischance, missed the Customs, for the French peasant is not so clean as his neighbours, and outside every front door in the villages there is a manure heap, as in other parts of France. In another three miles we were in Sedan, with a range of hills on our left.

"The Germans were on the hills," said Mr. Gouvy. "The French surrendered, and that ended the war of 1870." More war!

Nature quickly heals the scars of gun fire, and but for the knowledge that there had been war one would pass through without noticing. But at Verdun and in the country around eighteen years has not been long enough for Nature to cover up the past. For many square miles the whole countryside is still a waste, pock-marked by shell holes, and it is still dangerous for anyone to venture on the land that has not been cleared.

Land it is Dangerous to Walk On

Mr. Gouvy, the best of guides, swung off the main road at a point where a signpost directs the traveller to the Fort de Douamont.

"You must see the Trench of Bayonets," he said, "and the fort, and the mausoleum, and the cemetery."

At speed the M.G. took the long, winding climb over a brand-new road, and as the sun dropped towards the misty horizon we halted outside the entrance to *La Tranchée des Baïonnettes,* where several hundred warriors lie in the trench in which they died, their bayonets still sticking out of the ground that caved in on them, and now confined by concrete walls and covered by a roof to form a memorial.

The sun went down large and red as we stood silent and bare-headed, looking at the rusty bayonets over some of which pious pilgrims had thrown their rosaries. Inwardly one raged at the brutality and futility of it all, a rage that increased when, a few minutes later, we halted on the opposite hill outside the mausoleum which crowns a slope where rows of white crosses—which in the gathering dusk looked like fields of tulips in bloom—extend as far as the eye can reach: the graves of over 14,000 Frenchmen who had died defending Verdun.

In the tower of the great granite mausoleum lights appeared to guide aircraft on their way. It was nearly dark, but the door was open. We entered. What light remained was filtered by the amber windows. In the shadows were many great marble caskets containing remains of unknown soldiers. Uncanny? No! In the presence of so much death one felt only reverence—and a resentment against men who make war.

It was dark before we reached the Douamont Fort, which, from the outside, was no more impressive than a disused quarry. It was after visiting hours. We had come a long way. Could we see it? The soldiers in charge left their fireside and conducted us over. I have not the space to describe what we saw and the stories we were told. But imagine a structure like a huge prison, three or four storeys high, built of granite, then buried, with only its entrance and gun turrets left to be camouflaged. Imagine its capture by the Germans; the hand-to-hand fighting inside, for the fort was not fully manned when the war broke out. Then imagine the eight months' fighting before the French recaptured it.

In the streets of ancient Langres.

The Fortunes of War

We were shown the great vault where thousands of hand grenades had been stored by the Germans; we saw enough to visualise what had happened when a French shell got among them, killing, by explosion and gas, hundreds of its garrison. Reoccupied by the French, it held out with the other forts until the end of the war, and, all around, the trenches, dug-outs, wire entanglements, and the débris of war lie about still to be cleared up.

The fort is now a show-piece, as is another fort near by, and has its museum of rusty relics. Only that morning a machine gun had been " dug up " in the neighbourhood and added to the exhibits.

We stayed that night at the Hôtel Belleville, new, like most of the town, and quite comfortable. In spite of all our good intentions, we had covered little more than a third of our journey. The M.G. was none the worse for its run over Belgian pavé; tomorrow it would have to show us its paces if Geneva was to be reached in time for dinner.

*   *   *

" We must step on it," said Kimber next morning as, not over early, we again set off Geneva-wards. " No sightseeing to-day."

But we could not resist a halt, sixty miles on our way, to gaze upon the birthplace of Joan of Arc, in a village, which my notes tell me was Greux, but which, according to history, was Domremy. I am not quite sure, but I think Mr. Gouvy said it was another place altogether. Perhaps, like Ellen Terry, at Coventry, she had two birthplaces, or even three.

However, it is a romantic-looking old house, pleasantly situated behind railings and set back among the trees, at the end of the peaceful village, a link with another war, when the English were in France. We could not get away from wars.

An Ancient Town

We were at Langres for lunch, and spent more time in this old hill-top town than we should have done, considering the number of miles that had still to be covered. It was very pleasant strolling about the narrow streets with their ancient buildings. For once we were in a town without immediate connections with war, although, no doubt, we could have discovered a stirring record had we delved into French history, for it is fortified—the kind of place that would be assailed and defended by men in shining armour.

We were on our way to a city where sits a League of Nations which discusses ways and means for preventing wars. One fervently hopes that their efforts will be crowned with success.

Trial Trip

The New 2-litre M.G. Has Its Final Test on a Run to Geneva.   Part II

By THE SCRIBE

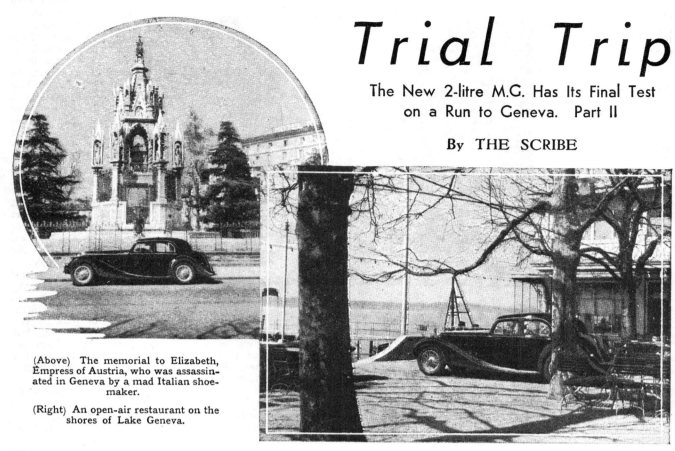

(Above) The memorial to Elizabeth, Empress of Austria, who was assassinated in Geneva by a mad Italian shoemaker.

(Right) An open-air restaurant on the shores of Lake Geneva.

THE trial trip of the new 2-litre M.G. through Belgium *en route* to Geneva (described last week) has been without untoward incident as far as the car was concerned. We have travelled in ease and comfort down that part of the Continent which had seen so much bloodshed in the opening stages of the Great War. From Antwerp we had called at Malines, Louvain, Namur, Dinant, Sedan, and Verdun, all names carrying memories of wars. For lunch on the second day we halted at the ancient town of Langres.

The party consisted of Mr. Cecil Kimber, managing director of the M.G. Car Company, who was giving the new car its final trial himself ; Mr. F. W. Gouvy, the manager of *Morris Continental Soc. An.*, C. R. B. Chiesman, a private owner who competes in the big trials on an M.G., and the writer.

A Source of Information !

Our next objective was Dijon, eighty-three miles away ; we reached it in less than two hours. " We should have lunched here," said Kimber, as we threaded our way through the ancient town. " Dijon is the centre of the Burgundy wine trade. Here is the palace of the former Dukes of Burgundy "—and a lot more, which I afterwards found on the back of the A.A. route booklet.

Onwards to Dole, thirty miles, at a speed that was bringing us back to our schedule, but Geneva was still a hundred miles away. We kept at it. At Poligny we halted for petrol and oil. The Jura Mountains lay immediately ahead ; in fact, the town is at the foot of the first of the passes, the Col de la Savine, which winds through the woods to a height of 3,248ft. The 2-litre took it at speed, the water temperature never above eighty. So far the weather had been so warm and fine that we had forgotten that it was still March. The sight of snow by the sides of the roads and among the trees reminded us that winter was not yet over in the high lands. In places the snow extended over many square miles, and on it we saw the marks of skis.

Followed a glorious run over the mountains, with the air like wine. The sunshine roof was kept open, yet such is the design that we in the back seats did not suffer from draughts.

At La Cure the road forked ; there was a Customs house on each side—the French on the right, the Swiss on the left. On the steps of the Customs house sat a sun-tanned girl in ski-ing regalia, looking very tired. Her companion, too, looked tired, but both appeared to be in the pink of health.

Our route lay to the right, via the Col de la Faucille, from which one drops 4,331ft. into Geneva. But, the Customs officials told us, the Col de la Faucille was still blocked with snow and would not be clear for another six weeks. We must take the left road over the Col de St. Cergues, which means a 4,051ft. descent, in about nine miles, to Nyon, on the shores of Lake Geneva, a few miles north of Geneva.

Descent In The Dark

We descended it by the lights of our head lamps ; through the dusk we could see glorious views over the lake, with a few scattered lights as a foreground at our feet. The brakes were well tested on that descent, for it was not until he had reached the foothills that Mr. Gouvy changed into third to relieve them.

It was quite dark when we ran into the beautiful city of Geneva, with its broad, well-lit, tree-lined promenades alongside the lake. Guide to the last, Mr. Gouvy pointed out the ugly building where the League of Nations first set up in business, then the magnificent home it has just left for the great blocks of offices recently erected on the outskirts of the city. For a moment the M.G. was halted by the memorial to Elizabeth, Empress of Austria, who died there at the hand of a mad Italian. The various great hotels where the would-be peacemakers of the world stay with their suites when the League is in session were inspected in turn.

Then to the Hôtel Cornavin, adjoining the modern railway station, where everything is modern, yet avoiding the bizarre, and where we were booked to stay.

Eventually our faithful M.G. was put away for the night. The log showed she had averaged 19 m.p.g. and that our average speed, without deducting time for our many stops for sightseeing, refreshments, and Customs, had been about 32 m.p.h. We had not set out to break records, but to break anything that would break with hard usage under touring conditions, and in that we had failed.

To Let, one Palace of Peace, in perfect condition : owners moving into something larger.

is "The Thing" to go ; certainly most of the visitors that day were more interested in the jazz band that performed on the balcony.

We dined at a gay little restaurant which reminded one of Vienna ; the food and wine were good and the company *bourgeois* and respectable. Instead of a jazz band which is now considered necessary by so many *restaurateurs,* this place had a quintette of musicians of an older school, and a tenor who sang to us, as distinct from the kind of artiste who merely sings. The

Dazzling sunshine and the much-talked-of but rarely experienced spring weather greeted us next morning. Geneva was looking its best, and that means better than the best of most places. In honour of the automobile exhibition the streets were gay with bunting ; against a sky of brilliant blue Mont Blanc reared its 15,784ft. crest fifty miles away, Europe's highest peak except those in the Caucasus range, where Mount Elbruz goes skywards for 18,526ft.

The New Palace of Peace

On the placid lake the Lausanne steamer was wending its way northwards. Yes, it was very pleasant in Geneva that morning when we fetched the M.G. from the garage to do a little sightseeing before visiting the show.

Mr. Gouvy, still acting as guide, took us to see the Palace of Peace, the new League of Nations headquarters, which strikes one as being a building worthy of its object. But one wonders—while devoutly praying for success—whether the results will be commensurate with its size and magnificence.

A run along the east shore of the lake was very pleasant, and the lakeside restaurant where we lunched in the open air (an open-air lunch in March!) was more pleasant still.

The show was visited in due course, but all of us had seen most of the cars before at Olympia, Paris, or Berlin, so the outstanding impression was of the people. It seemed to us that the Geneva Show is a social function, an annual affair where all the best people go because it

audience was quite enthusiastic. Good food, good wine, good music, good service, what more could one want on a fine night in Geneva?

Later that night we visited the Bavaria Café, the unofficial headquarters of members of the League of Nations' permanent staff, which we found full of intelligent-looking men and women of every nationality, drinking beer and coffee, surrounded by cartoons of men whom the League has made world-famous. It was interesting to hear so many tongues and to note that in many cases these secretaries of secretaries conversed in any language but their own.

Promises of Good Figures

All good things come to an end. To-morrow Chiesman and I would be flying back to England.

The trial trip was over. The 2-litre M.G. had passed with honours. It will shortly be tested by *The Autocar,* when its performance figures will, no doubt, be studied with interest by many readers who have patiently waited to learn more about this car since it was introduced last October. I think we shall find that they will compare favourably with those for cars having much larger engines. The M.G. designers generally manage to extract the most from any given number of cubic centimetres, but the 2-litre on the road does not suggest that this has been done at the expense of smooth running.

Altogether a delightful trip, in delightful company, and in a more than delightful car.

End view of the new Palace of Peace in the suburbs of Geneva.

A Larger M.G. Midget

New Four-cylinder Model with Bigger Engine and Longer Wheelbase Designed Expressly for Sports Enthusiasts and Competition Work

Cut-away doors, a full-width facia, a folding windscreen and disappearing hood are features of the new Series T. Midget: an 80 m.p.h. two-seater priced at £222.

FEW cars have ever enjoyed so big a following amongst sports enthusiasts as has the famous M.G. Midget. Consequently, many keen motorists will be interested in the announcement of a new Midget which is somewhat larger than its prototype both in general dimensions and in cylinder capacity. Known as "Series T," it has been designed throughout for the sportsman, with a particular eye to competition work, and is available only in two-seater form. The maximum speed is about 80 m.p.h. and the price is £222 complete.

Trim Lines; Practical Bodywork

As shown in the photographs and sketches reproduced, the car has trim lines, a very low and sturdy frame (underslung at the back) and comfortable provision for two people. Behind the seats there is quite a large space for luggage and, at the back of the rear panel, a 15-gallon fuel tank and a spare wheel are mounted. The sloping

windscreen can be folded flat and rigid sidescreens are carried in a locker behind the luggage space. The hood drops neatly rearwards into the upper part of the luggage compartment, where it is enclosed by a cover.

In common with the two-litre M.G. model introduced last autumn, the new Midget engine is fitted with push-rod-operated overhead valves. Exhaust and inlet manifolds are located on the off side, the latter being fed from two S.U. semi-down-draught carburetters. The

(Above) The radiator of the new Midget, also showing the "badge bar" which carries a fog lamp and horn.

(Left) The hood folds neatly into the upper part of the luggage compartment and the rake of the seat squab is readily adjustable. Note the large tank and quick-action filler-cap.

LEADING FEATURES

Engine: Four cylinders; push-rod operated overhead valves. 63.5 mm. by 102 mm. (1,292 c.c.). Tax, £7 10s. per annum.

Gearbox: Four forward speeds; remote central control. Overall ratios: 4.875, 6.92, 10.73 and 18.11 to 1. Reverse, 23.26 to 1.

Suspension: By semi-elliptic springs and Luvax hydraulic shock absorbers fore and aft. Dunlop 19-in. by 4.50-in. tyres on centre-lock wire wheels.

Dimensions: Wheelbase, 7 ft. 10 ins.; track, 3 ft. 9 ins.

Price: Two-seater series T model, complete, £222 ex-works.

capacity is 1,292 c.c. and the rating is 10 h.p.

On the near side one finds the oil level dipstick, a large external Tecalemit filter and the distributor for the coil ignition system; 14 mm. sparking plugs are standardized. The ribbed sump is of large capacity and the oil is picked up through a floating suction filter. Engine cooling is assisted by a water pump and a 12-in. fan, temperature being regulated by a thermostat. Fan, pump and dynamo are driven by belt.

The transmission is planned on straightforward lines with a cork-insert, single-plate clutch, running in oil, a four-speed gearbox with remote control, a Hardy Spicer balanced propeller shaft and a spiral-bevel rear axle.

The suspension comprises semi-elliptic springs fore and aft, each of which is pivoted at one end and runs in trunnions at the opposite end as in previous M.G. practice. The low frame, incidentally, is braced by tubular cross-members, and the side

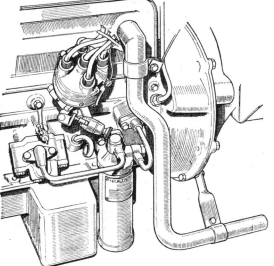

(Above) A view which does justice to the good lines of the new Midget.

(Left) Engine features include an easy timing adjustment, an external oil filter and a crankcase vent pipe.

(Right) Access to the axle, batteries, shock absorbers, etc., is obtained by lifting the floor at the back of the seats.

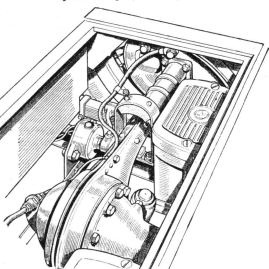

carried by a substantial cross-bar, the central portion of which can be used to carry club badges. The large fuel tank is fitted with a quick-release filler and contains a reserve supply of three gallons. Tool boxes are built into the dash under the bonnet.

A New Two-litre Model

When exhibited at Olympia last year the two-litre six-cylinder M.G. was shown only with sports saloon coachwork. We are now able to illustrate a Tickford foursome drophead coupe which is available on this chassis, the price being moderately fixed at £398.

members are boxed, over a considerable proportion of their length, to increase their torsional rigidity.

Considerable trouble has been taken to ensure a quiet performance. The engine is mounted on rubber, the air intakes of the carburetter are connected to a large silencer and the exhaust traverses a Burgess silencer of the familiar straight-through type.

Centre-lock wire wheels are fitted and carry Dunlop 19-in. by 4.5-in. tyres. The braking system is of the Lockheed hydraulic type with 9-in. drums and Ferodo M.R. linings. The hand-brake lever is centrally mounted and operates the rear shoes through cables. A cam-type steering gear is fitted which is fairly quick in operation and yet gives light control. The rake of the column can be adjusted and a spring-spoked wheel is fitted.

The instruments are laid out clearly and include a 5-in. speedometer and a separate revolution counter of equal size; the latter incorporates a clock. The facia equipment also includes the main lamp switch, map reading lamp, switches for the fog lamp, panel lighting, etc., a control

for the two-way petrol tap and throttle and mixture controls. It carries a warning lamp for use in restricted areas.

The coachwork is very nicely made and its equipment includes Silent Travel door locks; map pockets are provided in both the doors. A wide variety of colour schemes is available without increase of price.

There are many practical features to appeal to the owner-driver. Access to the rear axle, brakes and accumulators, for example, is easily attained by removing the floor of the luggage compartment: a matter of releasing two screws. The horn and fog lamp are

The body is, of course, made by Messrs. Salmons and Sons.

The head is controlled by the familiar Tickford winding mechanism and can be raised or lowered in a few moments. It carries a front extension and consequently can be used either fully closed, half open or fully open.

Two wide doors are fitted, each provided with a frameless window of Triplex glass controlled by a winder.

The front seats are of the bucket type, individually adjustable, and the upholstery is a combination of pneumatic cushions and spring casings covered in leather. This is a very comfortable and practical body.

A Handsome Car : the six-cylinder two-litre M.G. chassis with Tickford coachwork. This foursome drop-head coupe is listed at £398.

A bigger engine, more room for the passengers but the same sporting line, the new T Series M.G. Midget is one of the most attractive of small cars.

A LARGER M.G. MIDGET

THE SERIES T MODEL, PRODUCED ONLY IN TWO-SEATER FORM AND COSTING £222, HAS A BIGGER ENGINE, A ROOMY BODY AND AMPLE LUGGAGE ACCOMMODATION.

Owners of those fast and economical little cars, the J and P type Midgets will possibly heave a sigh of regret at the passing of the little " 850," but the latest small car produced by the M.G. Car Company promises to carry out the same work in an even more satisfying manner. A new and larger power unit has been produced, a four-cylinder with a capacity of 1,292 c.c. and rated at 10 h.p., while the dimensions of the chassis have been increased sufficiently to allow really wide front seats to be fitted, with a spacious luggage compartment behind.

The larger engine should be of great advantage to the trials enthusiast in providing extra power " low down," while at the other end of the scale, the long-distance tourist will appreciate the high top-gear of 4.87 to 1.

A New Push-rod Engine

The engine follows the lead of the 2-litre six-cylinder M.G. recently put on the market, and has vertical overhead valves operated by push-rod, clearance being adjusted by the usual tappet screw and lock-nut. 14 mm. sparking plugs are used, and the coil ignition has automatic advance and retard. The two semi-down-draught carburetters are fitted with a neatly installed air-cleaner, and are supplied from the rear tank by an S.U. electric petrol pump. Oil fumes from the aluminium rocker-cover are piped to the air-cleaner from where they are drawn in to lubricate the inlet-valve stems.

The cylinder-block and the top half of the crank-case are cast as one, and the crank-shaft is supported in three main bearings. The bore and stroke of the cylinders are respectively 63.5 and 102 mm. Alloy pistons are used, with H-section steel connecting rods. The compression ratio is 6.5 to 1. The camshaft is driven by a duplex roller chain.

The lubricating oil is carried in a ribbed aluminium sump which holds 1½ gallons, and the gauge-covered oil intake is pivoted and floats above the level of any impurities which may collect there. A Tecalemit pressure filter is fitted

alongside the crank-case. A large and accessible oil-filler is carried on the valve cover.

The radiator is of the handsome type fitted to the P.B. Midgets and the Magnettes, with chromium-plated top and shoulders and a slatted stone-guard. A three-point rubber belt driven from an extension of the cam-shaft operates a combined fan and water impeller and also the dynamo, which is mounted on the near-side of the engine. A thermostat in the top water joint keeps the engine at its most efficient temperature.

The gear-box is mounted in unit with the engine, and an interesting innovation is a single-plate clutch running in oil and having cork insets. The gear-box employs straight pinions on all gears, the three higher ratios in close relation and bottom an emergency ratio intended for trials work. The overall ratios are 4.875, 6.92, 10.7 and 18.1 to 1. A remote control brings the stiff short gear-lever under the driver's left hand. A balanced propeller-shaft with two Hardy-Spicer joints transmits the power to the semi-floating rear axle.

Underslung Frame and Hydraulic Brakes.

The lay-out of the chassis frame, swept over the front axle and underslung at the rear remains the same as on previous M.G. Midgets, the channels being strengthened around the rear engine mountings by a box section reinforcement of the side-members. The engine is now mounted on rubber at four points. The cross members as hitherto are of tubular section, and the two units of the twelve-volt battery are accommodated on either side of the propeller-shaft.

The chassis dimensions are :—wheelbase 7 ft. 10 in., track 3 ft. 9 in., which are respectively 7 in. and 3 in. larger than those of previous Midgets.

Cable-operated brakes have been abandoned in favour of those of the Lockheed hydraulic pattern. The drums are somewhat smaller than the old pattern, the extra braking area being secured by having wider drums. The shoes are

lined with Ferodo M.R. fabric. The brake-lever, which is centrally mounted and fitted with a racing ratchet, operates the rear brakes through cables.

Flat half-elliptic springs are used at front and back with swivel pins at the front end and trunnions at the rear, and controlled by Luvax shock-absorbers. Cam-steering is fitted, other items of interest being a Burgess straight-through silencer and Rudge wheels.

The petrol tank holds 15 gallons, a feature which will be appreciated by trials drivers, and of this supply three gallons are kept in reserve. A control on the dash-board operates a two-way tap and brings the reserve into use. The throttle and mixture controls have also been moved to the dashboard, and are grouped with the starter button and the switches on the neat instrument panel. The 5-in. rev.-counter is right under the driver's eye and is balanced by a speedometer of similar dimensions on the passenger's side of the facia board.

All-weather Protection

By taking full advantage of the slight increase in track offered by the new model, really commodious front seats, now separate, are available. A further advantage is that the driver's elbow does not overhang the side of the body and the side-curtains can be kept in position without in any way cramping him when rapid movements are required. Four side-curtains instead of the usual two overcome this boxed-in feeling one often experiences in a small car with the hood in position. The well behind the seats is large enough to accommodate four suit-cases, and the hood swings down inside with the sticks below the level of the sides of the body. The cover fits over the back of the body and is secured with three neat straps.

As in appearance as well as in performance the series " T " M.G. Midget yields nothing to its predecessors, and the sweeping wings and the long bonnet remind one of the slightly larger Magnette. Produced in two-seater form at £222, the latest model from the Abingdon factory should be an instant success.

The New 2-litre M G Tourer

A Four-seater Open Car with a Good Performance.   Comfortable Coachwork and Smart Lines are Features

WHEN first displayed to the public at the Motor Show last October, the 2-litre M.G. was available only in the form of a sports saloon. To this model have been added a Tickford drop-head coupé, recently illustrated in *The Motor*, and a Charlesworth open tourer, which is the subject of this

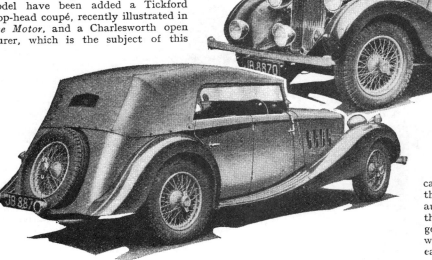

Open and closed : (Above) The new model has a smart appearance and the high sides give good protection. (Left) The hood is neat and is easy to erect or fold.

present description. The tourer is moderately priced at £375 complete, possesses very smart lines, and provides real seating comfort for four people.

The All-weather Equipment

Reference to the illustrations will show how neatly the hood folds away behind the rear-seat squab, so that, when enclosed by a cover, it provides an unbroken line level with the body sides. It is particularly easy to fold or erect and a set of side screens is accessibly carried behind the rear seat.

There are four doors and those at the front are not cut away, so that good protection is afforded to the driver and front passenger when the car is used in open form. The body is unusually wide and, consequently, one can handle the steering wheel without need for the extra elbow-room which a cut-away door provides. The seats are very deep and comfortable and leg-room for the rear passengers is increased by providing wells at each side of the propeller-shaft tunnel.

Performance on the Road

In the course of a road trial extending to about 300 miles we were impressed by the extreme smoothness and quietness of the six-cylinder engine. It will run up to speeds in excess of 4,500 r.p.m. without the slightest fuss or vibration.

The car rides more comfortably than most sports models, and yet holds the road convincingly on a fast bend and steers with lightness and precision. The Lockheed braking system is another

excellent feature, providing plenty of power, with a progressive action. Consequently, the brakes can be freely used on wet roads or at speed. Only a light pedal pressure is required.

Close-ratio Gearbox

The four-speed gearbox, which affords a close-ratio "third," is controlled by a stubby central lever. By exercising a reasonable degree of skill a very quick change, up or down, can be effected. Our only criticism here is that the gears are not very quiet.

A cruising speed of over 60 m.p.h.

can be held at about half-throttle on the level, with the engine scarcely audible. In traffic the smoothness of the clutch, the handy position of the gear lever, and the good range of forward vision are points which make for ease of handling.

Engine Details

The specification includes a two-carburetter engine of 2,288 c.c. capacity, with push-rod-operated overhead valves. It is rated at 17.7 h.p. General equipment is carried out on thorough lines and includes a set of Jackall permanently fitted jacks, centre-lock wire wheels and Dunlop 5.50-in. by 18-in. tyres.

Summed up, this is a very practical car, which is rapidly making an excellent reputation. At the price quoted the open tourer will appeal to the increasing company of fresh-air enthusiasts.

Layout of the facia and controls, showing the short remote-control gear lever and the clearly calibrated dials.

Intermediate M.G. Model

New 1½-litre Four-cylinder Car, Between the Midget and the 2-litre, for Open and Closed Four-seater Bodywork

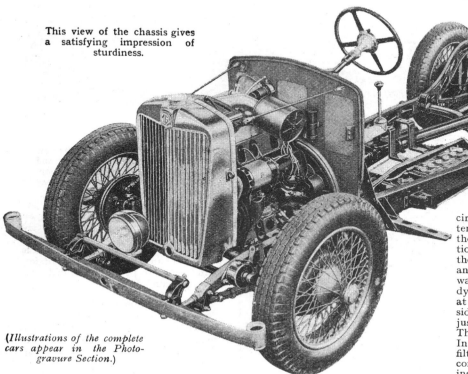

This view of the chassis gives a satisfying impression of sturdiness.

(Illustrations of the complete cars appear in the Photogravure Section.)

AN intermediate M.G. model is now announced, supplementing the 10 h.p. Series T Midget latelv introduced, and replacing the 12 h.p. six-cylinder Magnette. This new model is a 12 h.p. four-cyliuder to be known as the 1½-litre. It is intended to fill the gap in size and price between the Midget, offered only as a two-seater, and the six-cylinder 2-litre M.G., a model which carries roomy saloon, convertible, and open tourer coachwork.

The 1½-litre thus rounds off the range of models and, with a useful wheelbase of 9ft., is to be provided with four-seater bodywork, both an open tourer and a four-door saloon being standardised, at £280 and £325, respectively. The chassis price is £215. Promise of a very good performance in the M.G. manner is given, and, at the same time, this newcomer is aimed at providing quiet, comfortable travel and ample seating accommodation.

In general layout it has a number of items in common with the 2-litre M.G., on a scaled-down version, of course, and certain points of similarity to the latest Midget, though the frame, for instance, is quite different from that of the smaller car. It is not simply and wholly a larger Midget. The four-cylinder engine has push-rod-operated overhead valves, the crankshaft runs in three bearings, there is a ribbed aluminium sump, and mixture is supplied by two semi-downdraught S.U. carburetters, to the intakes of which is attached a large air cleaner

and silencer unit; the pipe connecting this to the carburetters runs transverse to the engine, passing over the valve gear cover. Ignition, of course, is by coil and distributor, the distributor being accessible on the near side, and there is a hand-operated vernier adjustment to enable the timing to be rapidly altered to suit different fuels. The sparking plugs are of the small 14 mm. size, recessed at an angle in the near side of the cylinder block, but readily accessible.

There is thermostatic control of the water temperature, the water when cold, with the thermostat closed, being short-

Steering gear layout, also showing the brake reaction steel-rope link.

circuited through a by-pass system until temperature is gained, when gradually the whole quantity comes into circulation. There is a fan, belt-driven from the crankshaft, in conjunction also with an impeller type of pump to assist the water flow; the same belt drives the dynamo, which is placed fairly high up at the front of the unit on the near side, affording an easy means of adjustment for the tension of the belt. This dynamo is of the ventilated type. In the engine lubrication system is a filter of the renewable element type, conveniently placed for periodical cleaning and eventual renewal.

The bore and stroke of this unit are 69.5 by 102 mm., giving a capacity of 1,546 c.c., the rating being 12 h.p. and the tax £9. A compression ratio of 6.5 to 1 is employed, and maximum engine revs are 4,500 p.m.

In unit with the engine is a single-plate clutch of the cork insert kind, running in oil, together with a four-speed gear box having synchromesh on top and third, and a neat remote-control lever extended back to an excellent position for the left hand. This lever works in an open, visible gate with a positive stop against reverse gear position. Top gear ratio is 5.22 to 1, third is 6.92, second 10.54, and first 18.01 to 1.

Alongside the gear lever, to the right, is the hand-brake lever. This is not of the fly-off type, engaging with its ratchet only when the knob at the top is depressed, but of normal press-down-the-knob-to-release design, though of neat construction, similar in appearance to the previous type of lever.

This ensemble of engine and gear box is mounted flexibly on rubber at four points in the frame—two in front and two at either side of the gear box, a considerable thickness of rubber bonded to the metal being employed. Transmission is by an open propeller-shaft with needle bearing universal joints to a normal pattern of spiral bevel rear axle. At both front and back the suspension is by half-elliptics, and these have the special feature at the shackle ends of side plates which should minimise the

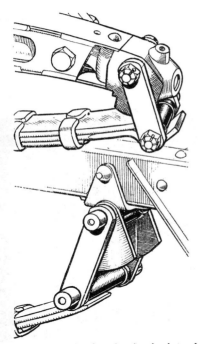

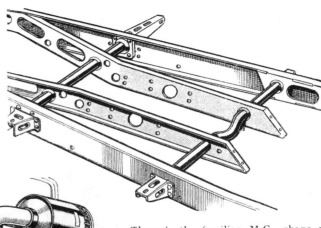

(Left) The spring shackles have special end plates.

(Right) Arrangement of the frame members at the centre of the chassis.

(Below) There are two S.U. carburetters, with air intake silencer and cleaner.

effect of wear in the pins in the later life of the car. A Burman Douglas worm and nut steering gear is employed, the column is well raked, and there is a steering wheel of the spring-spoked kind, with a telescopic quick adjustment.

Both axles have Luvax double-acting shock absorbers of large size; the front axle is nicely laid out and looks sturdy, besides having a special braking torque member. The brake gear is Lockheed hydraulic, with independent control of the rear wheel shoes by cables operated from the hand-brake lever. Dunlop knock-off wire wheels are fitted, and carry 19 by 5.00in. Fort tyres. The chassis wheelbase of this 1½-litre M.G., as already stated, is 9ft., and the track is 4ft. 2in. The frame merits separate mention.

In distinction from the Midget design, the rear members are upswept over the back axle, and from the rear extremity to a point approximately at the centre of the car a latticed box section is given to the side-members. Then, starting from the front of the frame, there is a similar construction, but the extra member which forms the box section layout in front is swept inwards at a point corresponding to about the gear box, the two members in question leaving the side-members and approaching one another at the centre of the frame, where they are welded to cross-members. The tubular cross-members look generous.

There is the familiar M.G. shape of radiator, with its neat name badge and vertical-slatted shell in front of the block, a finishing touch being given by the familiar octagonal cap, which remains in the external position. Carried amidships in the frame is the 12-volt battery. A centrally mounted pass light is provided in front, having a separate switch on the instrument board, and, in common with the layout recently adopted on the 2-litre, separate fuses for the different electrical circuits are provided.

As already indicated, this 1½-litre chassis is destined to take a sports four-seater open body, with a neat hood and complete all-weather equipment, of which a feature is the particularly large area of celluloid material, making for a light interior when this is in use. The saloon is a full four-seater of four-door construction, resembling to some extent a scaled-down version of the most attractive present 2-litre M.G. saloon. A departure for this make is the carrying of the spare wheel in the near-side wing, it being enclosed in a cellulosed metal cover. The body is very well appointed.

This model will be seen at Olympia.

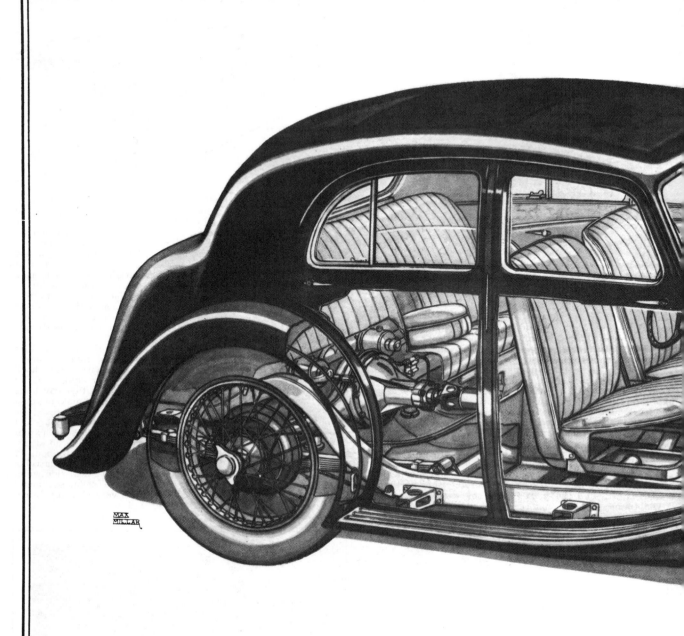

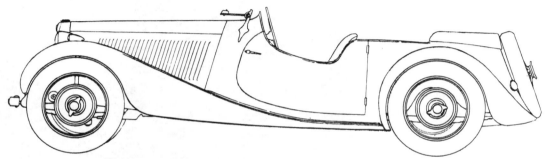

The new 1½-litre chassis will also be obtainable as an
open four-seater.

A NEW M.G.

*Four-Cylinder 1½-litre model on the lines
of the now well-known 2-litre car.*

BRIEF SPECIFICATION

4-Cylinder engine, 69·5 mm. × 102 mm. (1546 c.c.).
Treasury rating 12 h.p. Tax £9. Push-rod operated
over-head valves, Twin S.U. Carburetters, Dunlop " Rudge
Type" hub wheels, 19in. × 5.00 in. Track 4ft. 2in.
Wheelbase 9ft. Overall length 13ft. 6in. Width 5ft. 1¼in.

The
M.G. MIDGET
(T-Series)

As in performance, so in appearance—the T-series M.G. Midget remains every inch an M.G., notwithstanding an all-round increase of dimensions.

THE predominant impression which the T-series M.G. Midget makes upon anyone who has had experience of the superseded PA and PB types is that its designers have done a good and wise thing in increasing the engine size by a substantial margin.

The results of this fattening up— apart from a worthwhile improvement in maximum speed—are what one would expect them to be: more power is available at low revs., the engine never seems to be working so hard as did the smaller units and the "lazy" type of driver who doesn't like gear-changing for the sake of wrist exercise is able to indulge his native indolence.

Our best timed speed over the quarter-mile with two up, viz., 80.36 m.p.h. (see "In Brief" panel), needs no comment. What does remain to be stressed is that on long main-road runs a figure surprisingly near that maximum could be held whenever conditions allowed without the engine appearing to be overworked. An owner of a PA or PB-type Midget who was accustomed to cruise at, say, 60 by speedometer, would probably find himself unconsciously holding the needle at 65 in the "T."

A Quicker Change.

So far as acceleration is concerned, it is immediately obvious that the increased weight is more than counter-balanced by the extra cubic centimetres. On top of that the gear-change with the modern box is decidedly quicker than the old, so that it was not surprising to find the car tested covering the standing quarter-mile in 21⅝ secs.—the best figure by any M.G. which *The Light Car* has recorded.

While some potential owners may feel—and possibly rightly—that they have no need of synchromesh on top and third gears, none will despise the greatly sweetened clutch. Second gear is comparatively high, viz., 10.73 to 1, but on a level road, and even on slight up-grades,

Current Model Outshines its Predecessors in Speed, Acceleration, Comfort, Braking and Ease of Maintenance — Clocks Over 80 m.p.h. for the Flying Quarter-mile

standing starts can be made in second without the necessity for any delicate foot-jugglery.

The remote-control gear lever is placed slightly farther forward relative to the driving seat than is usual on M.G.s, and the range of movement between gear positions is also greater. While none of the four gears is completely silent, noise from this source is not obtrusive.

Reverting to the engine, this unit is uniformly smooth throughout its range of speed and exceptionally flexible withal. The fact that on Cleveland Discol the engine tested positively could not be made to knock by any method known to the heavy footed writer (it had 13,000 miles carbon accumulation), suggests that amateur tuners might find scope in the direction of higher-than-standard compression ratios.

On the score of exhaust noise the T-type Midget compares favourably with its predecessors—the note is rich without being blustery. Despite the presence of a large air silencer-cum-cleaner a certain amount of "power roar" is perceptible when the engine is working hard.

The thermostat now standardized is decidedly an asset, relieving the conscientious driver of perhaps three or four miles tedious warming-up these cold mornings.

Over give-and-take roads this is almost certainly the fastest light car M.G. has ever produced. (Racing models excepted, of course.) It is also the first M.G. light car with hydraulic brakes. To realize the extent to which those two facts are related one must drive the "T," and drive it hard. The Lockheed brakes, with much smaller drums than the old mechanically operated type, are just about as good as modern brakes can be. On the approach to a bend at speed braking can be left until what seems the last split second . . . and then, when the pedal goes down, the driver knows he might have left it even later and still been safe. The racing type hand brake acts through cables on the rear drums only.

The belief that first-class cornering can be achieved only at the expense of a good deal of comfort on bumpy surfaces seems to be losing ground at Abingdon. The springing of the Midget is fairly flexible by usual sports car standards, but the widened track seems to compensate for any adverse effect upon cornering which the new resilience may have had. Unsolicited, two passengers carried during our test passed favourable comment upon the restfulness of the ride.

Getting Comfortable.

With a steering column adjustable for rake, seats which may be slid fore and aft and two sets of squab adjustment—slope and fore and aft position—the Midget owner has no excuse for suffering a driving position other than the ideal one for his height and reach. The span of the seats, which have spring cushions, is adequate for quite bulky occupants, thanks to the widened chassis frame.

The provision of two celluloid weather screens per

side (earlier M.G. two-seaters had one per side, plus a triangular panel of hood material between screen and hood) makes a big improvement in the three-quarter-rear visibility which accurate reversing demands. The wider rear hood window also helps in this connection. On the other hand, it was found that a driver of average height could do with a little more "hat-clearance" when poking his head out for reversing manœuvres. Both wings can be seen from the driving seat, and the windscreen is of the fold-flat type.

The luggage space behind the seats, over which a waterproof cover fits, is spacious enough for all ordinary needs, being 13 ins. deep by 14 ins. wide at the top, increasing to about 20 ins. at the bottom. Elastic-sided door pockets provide accommodation for books, papers and so forth.

As regards the layout of the instruments, for the sake of symmetry the matching speedometer and rev. counter dials are placed at opposite ends of the facia panel, the latter on the right. This means, of course, that the driver must turn "eyes left" to read the speedometer, but it is probable that the majority of sports car owners are more interested in r.p.m. than m.p.h. A warning light—which glares a little disconcertingly into the driver's eye at night, but can be switched off at will—comes on at just above 20 m.p.h. and goes out at 30.

Maintenance Points.

Maintenance work on the Midget is facilitated by the accessibility of the plugs, carburetters, dynamo, distributor and oil filler orifice (in rocker gear cover). The substitution of hydraulic for cable-operated brakes and the provision of Silentbloc oilless bearings at the fore end of each road spring has considerably simplified chassis lubrication, so that the grouped nipples employed on former M.G.s no longer appear. A normal jack is supplied and the tool kit is carried in a box under the bonnet, containing a Sorbo tray recessed for each tool. Improved support for the starting handle is provided by an outrigger bearing, formed in a lug mounted on the plated badge bar which can be seen in the photograph at the top of the preceding page.

IN BRIEF

ENGINE: Four cylinders; overhead valves; 63.5 mm. by 102 mm. stroke = 1,292 c.c.; three-bearing crankshaft; two carburetters. Tax, £7 10s.

TRANSMISSION: Single wet-plate clutch; four-speed gearbox with synchromesh for third and top. Ratios: 4.875, 6.92, 10.73 and 18.11 to 1. Final drive by open propeller shaft and spiral bevel.

GENERAL: Lockheed hydraulic brakes; semi-elliptic springs fore and aft; 9-gallon rear tank.

DIMENSIONS, Etc.: Wheelbase, 7 ft. 10 ins.; track, 3 ft. 9 ins.; overall length, 11 ft. 7½ ins.; overall width, 4 ft. 8 ins.; width across seats, 37 ins.; turning circle, 37 ft.; weight, 15¾ cwt.

PERFORMANCE: Best flying ¼-mile, 80.36 m.p.h.: standing ¼-mile, 21⅜ secs. Petrol consumption, 28 m.p.g. average.

PRICE: £222.

M.G. CAR CO., LTD.,
Pavlova Works, Abingdon-on-Thames.

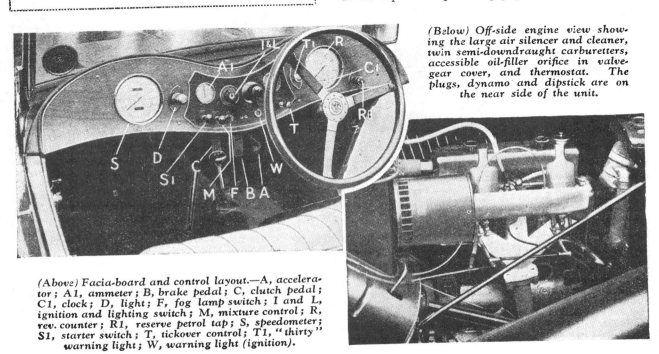

(Below) Off-side engine view showing the large air silencer and cleaner, twin semi-downdraught carburetters, accessible oil-filler orifice in valve-gear cover, and thermostat. The plugs, dynamo and dipstick are on the near side of the unit.

(Above) Facia-board and control layout.—A, accelerator; A1, ammeter; B, brake pedal; C, clutch pedal; C1, clock; D, light; F, fog lamp switch; I and L, ignition and lighting switch; M, mixture control; R, rev. counter; R1, reserve petrol tap; S, speedometer; S1, starter switch; T, tickover control; T1, "thirty" warning light; W, warning light (ignition).

The 1½-litre M.G. Tourer

Attractive model with a wide appeal: brisk performance, good steering and untiring to drive on long journeys

In normal touring trim: these pictures show the very smart lines of the car seen from the front and rear.

The hood folds into a recess behind the rear seat squab and is concealed.

ONE can speak highly in praise of the new 1½-litre M.G.; it is well abreast of the times in general specification and planning; is possessed of particularly attractive bodywork and has a performance which outstrips many other 1½-litre cars. Withal it does it so quietly and smoothly that one can be misled into thinking a six-cylinder power unit (instead of the four-cylinder it is) of a larger capacity than 1½-litres is tucked away beneath the bonnet.

We have completed an extended road test of the 1½-litre tourer—a car of infinite charm and one with a wide appeal, for while it is designed as a normal open tourer, it handles, cruises and rides generally in a way which places it favourably in the eyes of the sports car enthusiast. If one wanted to term it a sports model, then it would have to be classed with the new régime of silent sports motoring which is becoming so popular. It goes to prove that high performance is not necessarily allied with exhaust or mechanical noise.

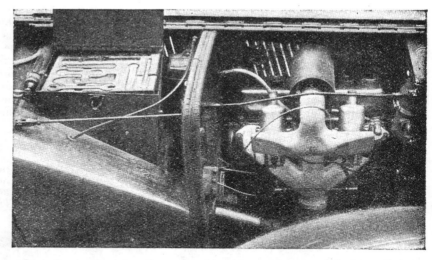

Beneath the bonnet: the two-carburetter, rubber-mounted four-cylinder engine. Observe also the tool storage, the various items fitting snugly into mouldings so that rattle is prevented, yet they are immediately accessible.

77 m.p.h. with Screen Up; Over 80 m.p.h. with Screen Down

Performance in the terms of maximum speed has always been an influential factor where M.G. car owners are concerned, and with the new model there is no disappointment in this direction. At Brooklands figures were obtained with the screen up and folded flush with the scuttle. In the former case, which can be described as normal touring trim, the mean of six timed tests over the flying quarter mile worked out 11.84 secs., representing an average speed of 76.27 m.p.h. The best quarter mile was covered at 77.58 m.p.h.

Subsequent tests made with the screen down showed the car to be capable of over 80 m.p.h., the best timed quarter in these circumstances being 11 secs. dead (equal to 81.82 m.p.h.), the mean of eight tests being 11.2 secs. (80.35 m.p.h.). These are very satisfying figures from a car which weighs some 24 cwt. laden and costs only £280.

Other performance figures included standstill to 60 m.p.h. which occupied 22.6 secs. and standstill to 70 m.p.h., which took 37 secs.

Road holding is fully in keeping with the speed characteristics of the car; shock absorbing is effected by means of a Luvax hydraulic system with a finger-tip control whereby the tension can be varied from the dashboard to suit road and speed conditions. Rock steady riding is obtained at all times, yet there is no harshness. Rough roads can be taken quickly with comfort.

General rigidity is reflected also in the cornering—again demanding the description of very good indeed—so that one has a feeling that the car is really living up to the manufacturer's slogan of "Safety Fast." The M.G. can be "put" just where one wants it, corners hugged as closely as possible and taken at a higher m.p.h. than one might normally indulge.

Rigidity in Chassis Construction

The rear semi-elliptic springs are underslung and the chassis which is of box section throughout is upswept to give adequate clearance for spring deflection and tubular cross-members add reinforcement. A new type of anti-roll spring shackle is employed.

Torque reaction cables between the front axle beam and chassis take care of the braking, being largely responsible for the unusually smooth yet powerful retardation which is always readily obtainable. Repeated tests, using the Tapley meter, enabled us to get figures in the region of 90 per cent. and on one occasion we achieved 95 per cent.; in the main there was practically no deviation from the straight.

Braking Efficiency Maintained

Braking from 50 m.p.h. also gave commendably high figures with the same degree of security. A point calling for comment in this connection is that in spite of repeated brake tests,

the Tapley performance figures showed no tendency to drop appreciably, indicating that the drums and linings were not suffering from overheating.

For long distance cruising this new model is delightful. Passenger comfort has been so well considered that one sits in the car supported adequately on softly sprung cushions with high squabs, and ample weather protection so that long distance motoring becomes a real joy. Once away from town it is possible to settle in to very free and easy untiring cruising speed of 65 m.p.h. with the clock holding higher figures as the occasion demands.

Driving Position

The steering wheel is placed (and it can be adjusted by means of the Bluemel telescopic control) so that one sits "right" and feels right; there is plenty of room for free arm movement in steering, which is light and accurate at speed, and the pedals are at such angles that no ache is created in the leg

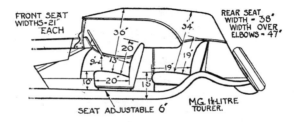

FRONT SEAT WIDTHS - 21" EACH · REAR SEAT WIDTH = 38" · WIDTH OVER ELBOWS = 47" · SEAT ADJUSTABLE 6" · M.G. 1½-LITRE TOURER.

or foot muscles. This combination of effortless cruising and all-round comfort puts high average speed well within the driver's grasp.

The clutch is light and smooth. The gear change embodies synchromesh on second, third and top and the change is simple, when once the timing has been mastered. It is fairly quick, however, and unless the correct synchronization of the cones is struck, the gears engage with a clonk.

Refinement of Finish

There is an air of refinement throughout the entire car. It is beautifully finished, very well upholstered with good quality leather, and thoroughly equipped. The hood folds and drops into a recess behind the rear seats, the whole of the rear compartment and recessed hood being covered by a tonneau cover. The dashboard, in which the various dials with brass coloured surrounds are let into a walnut panel, assumes a rather nautical aspect but one which is pleasing to the eye. Working in conjunction with the speedometer is a Thirtilite giving warning by means of a green light when travelling at about the legal limit. Jackall permanent hydraulic jacks can be fitted.

TheMotor TABULATED DATA—1½-litre M.G. July 6, 1937

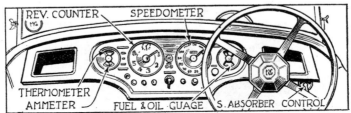

REV. COUNTER · SPEEDOMETER · THERMOMETER · AMMETER · FUEL & OIL GUAGE · S. ABSORBER CONTROL

ENGINE

Four cylinders, o.h.v.; 12-volt coil ignition; 69.5 mm. by 102 mm. (1,548 c.c.); rating, 12 h.p. *Tax:* £9.

MEASUREMENTS

W.b., 9 ft. 0 in.; t., 4 ft. 2 ins.; l., 13 ft. 1½ ins.; w., 5 ft. 1½ ins.; g. clce, 7 ins.; turning circle, 38 ft. left, 42 ft. right.

SPEEDS	m.p.h.
*Maximile mean timed speed ..	74.38
Maximum mean timed speed ..	76.27
Best timed speed (screen down)	81.82
Speed reached on third ..	60
Speed reached on second ..	40

METERED PERFORMANCE†

	Pull lb. per ton	Gradient climbable.
Top (5.22 to 1)..	190	1 in 11.6
Third (7.07 to 1)	250	1 in 8.96
Second (10.18 to 1)	360	1 in 6.2
First (17.64 to 1)	590	1 in 3.8

Petrol Consumption: 25/26 m.p.g., driven hard. Two S.U. carburetters. 12½-gallon rear tank.

Gearbox: Four forward speeds, central control. Synchromesh 2nd, 3rd and top.

M.G. 1½-LITRE. ACCELERATION CURVES ROAD — DRY CONCRETE

SPEED RISING · TOP GEAR · 3RD GEAR

ACCELERATIONS	secs.
10-30 m.p.h., third gear.. ...	9.8
10-30 m.p.h., top gear	13.5
30-50 m.p.h., top gear .. ·..	14.2
0-50 m.p.h., through gears ..	15.8
Standing ¼-mile, through gears ..	22.4

METERED BRAKE TESTS †

	Efficiency. %	Distance. ft.
Pedal only, from 30 m.p.h.	90	33.5
Pedal only, from 50 m.p.h.	80	105
Hand only, from 30 m.p.h.	27	111

(Hydraulic brakes; central hand lever)

Price: £280 (with jacks, £285).

Wheels: Wire, with Dunlop 5 ins. by 19 ins. tyres.

Weight: Unladen, 21¼ cwt.; with two up, as tested, 24 cwt.

*Speed timed over ¼-mile after accelerating for one mile from rest through the gears.
†Pulling power and brake efficiency are recorded by Tapley and Ferodo-Tapley meters respectively.

THE M.G. 1½-LITRE

Acceleration That Can Be Described As 'Terrific': Excellent Road Holding And Commendable Quietness

FOR many years, the M.G. Car Company have used the slogan "Safety Fast". It is, in our opinion, a very good slogan; moreover it gives a true description of the M.G. products. The 1½-litre model that we have recently subjected to a prolonged road test is a good example of the *marque*, despite the fact that it is somewhat more "refined" than its predecessors. By this we mean that it is more docile without being any the less a real sports car with a performance of which any owner could well be proud.

Good Driving Position

Our first impression was that the car was extremely powerful, in addition to being comfortable and silent. It is rare that these three qualities are combined in a car costing less than £300, and we do not believe that they have ever been combined in a manner more likeable than in the M.G. 1½-litre. The seating for both driver and passenger is particularly comfortable and driving visibility is fully satisfactory. Our one criticism in connection with the seating is that the driving seat must be moved backward to permit of reasonable easy exit from the car; this is not difficult because of the simple adjuster provided. We would not suggest modification of the door, because as it is there is convenient entry to the rear seat.

There is a telescopic steering column which, in conjunction with the front seat that can be moved over a wide range, permits of a very comfortable driving position for a driver of any height. The remote-control stub gear lever is also well placed and works splendidly. We found the handbrake lever placed rather too far forward, but it is not difficult to reach by a driver of average height and arm-length provided that he leans forward slightly.

Hand Brake

It is worth noting that the brake-lever ratchet is different from that fitted to other M.G. models; it is released by depressing the spring-loaded end. The more usual arrangement on the M.G. is the provision of a ratchet control that is locked by depressing the lever cap. The system on the car tested will be preferred by drivers who have been accustomed to other makes of car, although M.G. "fans" appear to favour the lever more usually fitted to cars of this make.

Unusual Instrument Panel

The instrument panel is unusual, but not displeasing. It is modelled on the lines of the facia of a motor launch, the instru-

The control for the shock absorbers is set just below the dash, in front of the driver.

ments having enamelled-brass bezels. Instruments include a combined radiator thermometer and ammeter, rev. counter and clock, speedometer and combined oil-pressure gauge, petrol gauge and oil-level gauge. There are seven control knobs arranged in a row, these being, from left to right: mixture control, throttle control, oil-level-gauge switch, ignition and lamp switch, reversing-lamp switch, starter switch and panel-light switch. All of these controls are clearly marked to avoid any confusion.

Other fittings on the facia panel are the ignition warning light, 30-m.p.h. warning light and inspection-lamp sockets. There is a small glove compartment on each side of the facia panel.

Smooth Clutch

On every occasion during our test—and there was a good deal of cold weather—the engine started immediately the switch was pulled out, after setting the mixture control. What is more, the car could be driven away without having to wait for any appreciable time for the engine to warm up. Both when starting from rest and when changing gear, the clutch took up the drive very smoothly indeed. As a test of this we engaged bottom gear, allowed the engine to tick over and then slowly let in the clutch without touching the accelerater. When this test was made on a level road the car moved off very slowly and without jerk. Incidentally, this was good proof of the flexibility of the high-efficiency four-cylinder engine.

Gear-changing proved to be utterly simple, partly because of the clutch but

Rear of a sectioned demonstration chassis. Note the hydraulic shock absorbers which are controlled from the driver's seat.

URER

—could be taken to 62 m.p.h., whilst in top 86 m.p.h. was touched on a few occasions. In favourable conditions on a slight downgrade we actually took the speed up to 90 m.p.h. for a few seconds. This is, of course, exceeding the normal maximum revs., but the engine gave no signs of distress. What is equally important, the car held the road as well as if the speed were no more than 40 m.p.h.; it was in these conditions that "Safety Fast" proved to be no exaggeration, for the brakes were steady and sure.

Whatever the speed of the car, steering was rock steady, sufficiently light for any sports car and sufficiently direct to make high-speed cornering easy. Many drivers who have been accustomed to driving large cars with high-geared steering would be surprised to find how light the steering of this M.G. is, considering the low ratio.

Acceleration Figures

Acceleration, for a comfortable 12 h.p. car, can be described in the one word "terrific". As an example. 50 m.p.h. was reached from a standing start in 13-3/5 secs. using first, second and third gears. Other timed acceleration figures are as follow : 0 to 30 m.p.h., in first and second gears, 7-1/5 secs.; 10 to 30 m.p.h., in second gear, 5-4/5 secs.; 20 to 40 m.p.h., in second, 6-3/5 secs.; 30 to 50 m.p.h., in third gear, 8-4/5 secs.; 30 to 50 m.p.h., in top, 14-1/5 secs. The silence of the engine and transmission in all gears and at all speeds was pleasantly surprising; it was, in fact, more pronounced than is frequently the case with many less "snappy" and slower cars.

The Lockheed hydraulic brakes were well in keeping with the general performance of the car, and gave a stopping distance of 32 ft. 6 in. from 30 m.p.h. Our Ferodo-Tapley meter gave a reading of nearly 93 per-cent. when taking the reading from a steady speed of 30 m.p.h., and of 75 per-cent. from 50 m.p.h. Their action was perfectly smooth, although there was a slight tendency for them to "pull" toward

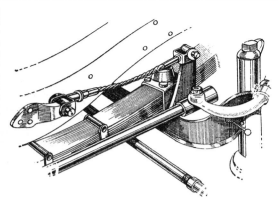

A feature of the 1½-litre model is the fitting of brake torque cables.

the nearside when applied very suddenly at high speeds.

All-Weather Equipment

Our tests were made during a few days when the weather was particularly bad : fog, rain and wind were general. The all-weather equipment had to be used for the whole of the time, with the result that we were, literally, driving a closed car. Draughts were almost entirely absent, but rain did manage to penetrate between the hood and the side screens during a particularly gusty period on an open road. Despite this, we should say that the equipment is as good as any that we have ever found on an "open" sports car.

Due to the wet and slippery nature of the roads it was possible to induce tail-skids when accelerating and when the rear seat was unoccupied, but in no case was the skid of such a nature that correction by the driver was called for; it was necessary only to let the car "have its head" for it to resume its normal straight course.

Engine Flexibility

We have mentioned above that the M.G. was unusually docile for a car with so much "pep". You could slow down to 10 m.p.h. in top gear without any snatch or engine roughness being apparent. At such a speed, steering was so light that it called for no noticeable expenditure of effort to take a right-angle bend. At the other end of the scale, a main-road roundabout could be taken at about 40 m.p.h. without invoking tyre screech.

A feature that was appreciated was the dash-controlled shock-absorber system. While travelling, the small lever working over a quadrant could be set to provide exactly the correct amount of spring damping for the rough surface or driving conditions.

Altogether, we consider that this car is one of the best in its class and one that

Neatly-grouped and easy-to-read instruments. The screen is of the fold-flat type, and the steering wheel is telescopic.

largely due to the use of a good gearbox in which there is synchromesh engagement between top and third, and third and second gears.

Over 80 m.p.h.

It was after reaching the open road that we were able to let the car "have its head", although it had been very pleasing to drive through London traffic on a slightly misty evening. In second gear, in which a start could be made if desired, we were able to reach 43 m.p.h., which speed corresponds with an engine speed slightly above the peak figure of 5,000 r.p.m. In third gear the speedometer—which was sufficiently accurate for all normal purposes

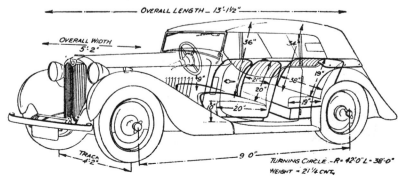

M.G. 1½-LITRE TOURER

could be recommended to any driver who appreciates comfort and at the same time insists upon a performance of a very high standard. The owner-driver is well catered for by the provision of grouped lubrication nipples for the points that are most inaccessible. There is also the "Jackall" jacking system which can be had for £5 extra on the price of £280. The car tested was so fitted and is listed at £285.

Throughout our tests—which naturally included a good deal of hard driving—the petrol consumption averaged 25 m.p.g. It is thus reasonable to expect that a figure

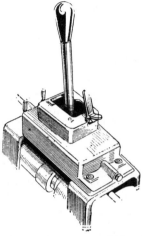

The short remote-control gear lever for the four-speed box.

of 27 or 28 m.p.g. could be obtained during normal touring. Oil consumption was imperceptible, and should average well over 1,500 m.p.g.

Other 1½ litre models are the drop-head coupé and saloon. All three are available in a wide range of colour schemes.

M.G. ... ... STAND 98

Midget Two-seater	... ...	£222
1½-litre Four-seater	...	*£285
1½-litre Saloon	... ...	*£330
1½-litre Sectioned Working Chassis		

*Including Jackall hydraulic jacks.

A VERY successful year in which all models have shown increased popularity is reflected in the M.G. programme for 1938, which is of the no-change order, both in the matter of design and price, the only exception to the latter concerning the models with specialized coachwork where an increase in the cost of the bodies has, of course, had to be passed on to the customer.

In spite of the absence of change, the M.G. stand is of great interest, even to those who are thoroughly familiar with M.G. products, for one of the exhibits is a 1½-litre chassis which is not only ruthlessly cut away to show the design and construction, but somehow or other manages to work despite this drastic treatment.

So far as the complete cars are concerned, the well-known Midget is,

of course, produced in only one form, namely, a sports two-seater, and this is represented on the stand by an example finished in red with red upholstery. Like all M.G. models, it is attractive of line, and coachwork features which will be noted with approval include the neat, efficient and easily erected hood (which disappears into the back when furled), the thin-rimmed side screens, the business-like layout of the facia board, the spring-spoke steering wheel, the well-placed remote-control gear lever and the racing-type handbrake.

The fine performance of these cars on the road is well known (an 80 m.p.h. maximum speed is possible), and the steering, road-holding and braking are well in keeping.

Mechanical features which go to make up these desirable results include a four-cylinder o.h.v. engine of 63.5 mm. bore and 102 mm. stroke (1,292 c.c., tax £7 10s.), a single-plate clutch running in oil, four-speed gearbox with synchromesh for third and top, semi-elliptic springs all round, Lockheed hydraulic brakes and Bishop cam steering.

The 1½-litre model is, in many ways, a bigger edition of the Midget, providing ample room for four with either open, saloon or drop-head

Two very popular sports models —the 1½-litre M.G. tourer (above) and the Midget (below).

coupé coachwork. The coupé, incidentally, is not represented on the maker's own stand, but an example is to be found exhibited in the coachwork section by the manufacturers, Salmons and Sons.

The general engine design is very similar, but the bore is larger, being 69.5 mm., so that the capacity is 1,548 c.c. and the tax £9. Otherwise, such features as twin semi-downdraught carburetters, floating intake oil feed, Tecalemit filter, pump and fan-assisted cooling controlled by

a thermostat, and so on, are similar to the Midget.

The gearbox differs in that the synchromesh is applied to second as well as to the two higher ratios, but otherwise the transmission is similar. Lockheed hydraulic brakes and semi-elliptic springs are other features common to the two cars, but the hydraulic shock absorbers on the 1½-litre are of the type which automatically adjust themselves according to road irregularities and are, moreover, adjustable by means of a driver-operated over-riding control.

How the facia board and controls are arranged on the 1½-litre M.G. Points which will be noted are the large dials for the speedometer and rev. counter, the spring-spoke wheel, the neat remote-control gear lever and the telescopic steering column.

The Performance and Qualities of an M.G. Two-litre Coupé

Story by Laurence Pomeroy, Junr.
Captions by Q. H. Flaccus

THE Greeks had a phrase for it, to wit, that in considering any problem one should start from first principles. On my return from Germany to join *The Motor* I applied this practice to the choice of a motorcar and decided on an M.G. 2-litre with Tickford drop-head coupé body by Salmons for the following reasons.

First, for many years I had had pleasant personal relations with the M.G. company; second, the general layout of the car is in accordance with my needs—moderate size, high cruis-ing speed, a smooth and silent engine, excellent brakes; third, it had a stiff welded steel chassis frame which is vital if one is to obtain satisfaction from a drop-head body. Finally, I considered such a body a paramount necessity in order to enjoy motoring to the full in the ever-changing climate of these not so blessed isles.

There are, I know, those who hold that a saloon with sunshine roof is adequate, but they are condemned beyond controversy by the sheer logic of facts. Every country in the world offers for sale fixed-head saloons and also fully convertible coachwork. England is the only country that fiddles about with movable hatches, and unless we are the only ones in step, we must obviously be wrong.

Choice of Colour

Having made the decision on type, the next matter of importance was choice of colour, and here I think the range is again limited by considerations of logic. It seems obvious that the wings must be black because they are always liable to receive minor scratches and bumps, and touching up by a local

20,000

Fir

garage can obviously be done far more easily if they are this colour than if they are some shade.

An all-black car is, in my opinion, however, completely indefensible. There are so many on the road that familiarity places them beneath contempt, whilst they have the practical disadvantage of needing a first-class wash and polish every day to ensure that any slight merit they may have is not totally sullied. One day I expect what is left of me will ride in a black car, but I shan't know about it.

Of the limited colours for the body matching black wings, cream, I think, is easily the best for it has a resistance to discoloration by dust or mud which is very valuable. The scheme of AMO 604, as it came to be registered, was, therefore, black wings and wheels, cream body, black top and fawn leather upholstery.

Ten Months' Hard Labour

Delivery was taken on July 26, 1937, and in the ensuing 10 months to May 26, 20,146 miles have been covered. This in itself is not remarkable, but two things must be remembered. First, that this car is used in addition to road test cars so that my total mileage during the period was about 30,000; and, second, that the quality of the miles covered in the M.G. has been of first-class order. The car has, in fact, had a hard life in both a physical and moral sense. Physically, because it has been required to do comparatively long runs at consistently high average speeds at any time of the day and on any day of the week; morally, because after a week-end road testing a car costing perhaps £1,500 or even £2,500, with one's critical faculties to be thoroughly sharpened one might expect to be disappointed in the various aspects of a car now marketed at £415. I can quite honestly state that this is not so and that for sheer pleasure in driving I have come across nothing which pleases

READY TO GO. "And as a stag that spies across the vale a wolf's approach, so wilt thou flee."

SUMMER TRIM. "The Southwind lifts at times and straight removes clouds from the sky; nor breed the showers alway."

MILES

me more than the car now reviewed.

What is more, I do not think this is merely a personal idiosyncrasy and, therefore, explicable on the ground of some queer complex due to a mis-

COMFORT
"That is the spot us two to dwell in."

spent youth. Those people who form regular passengers in test cars and also in the M.G. comment quite favourably indeed on the merits of the latter It is, nevertheless, difficult to put into words precisely what they are.

First-class Visibility

However, starting again from absolute beginnings one is pleased when one actually gets into the car and sits at the wheel. The driving position seems just right, the pedals come up through the bottom of the floorboards to connect at the correct angle to the feet and one has extraordinarily good visibility. This is brought about partly because of the relative position of seat to scuttle radiator and wings, both of which are visible; in addition it is due to the large square screen associated with this particular body.

On many saloons the alleged streamlining of the head causes the area of

Triplex to be much restricted and induces one to stoop over the wheel to see out properly. The Salmons body is uncompromisingly square and this, I think, is a great advantage.

Cornering and Stopping

In driving one finds the car remarkably comfortable at normal cruising speeds of between 50 m.p.h. and 70 m.p.h. and although the springing is a little hard on some surfaces at 30 m.p.h., this is a price I think well worth the considerable advantages derived from it. With the low centre of gravity one can hurtle the car round corners without a trace of roll and the brakes thoroughly deserve that most expressive German adjective, "unglaublich," the nearest translation of which is "incredible."

As is generally known, the axle is located by torque stays and this, in conjunction with one of Mr. Lockheed's best systems, enables one to stop the car in remarkably short distances, and at the same time absolutely smoothly.

The body is another point on which the car receives full marks. It is still quite free from rattles, has retained its finish and is reasonably easy to open or close. The latter operation is, of course, particularly important as one may be caught in the rain when doing it. It is, therefore, worth making the point that one can change from the half-open position to fully closed without getting out of the car and under cover except for possibly 15 secs.

Another feature is the width in the front seats. Coupled with the high

roof line one does get an impression of having a first-class railway carriage all to oneself, a feeling that is, so far as I know, the only justification for travelling upon the railways.

Philips Radio Fitted

Since taking over the car certain changes have been made in its specification. The first thing to be done was the installation of a Philips radio, this being the type where the speaker is separate from the set, the latter being mounted underneath the scuttle on the near side and the former on the off side. My ignorance of radio is profound and I cannot claim familiarity with every car set made. With this qualification I can say that the Philips is better than any other I have heard by a considerable margin. It is rather sensitive to interference in towns, but as a musical instrument it is really first class, and this is a point which interests me more than any other.

It has, however, a very good range and on the medium band one can pull in different stations with every few degrees of movement on the scale. At times this can be great fun, as, for instance, when the German-Austrian Anschluss was taking place and one could listen to excited speeches from the appropriate stations. More important to me, however, is the fact that the B.B.C. Symphony Orchestra as relayed from London Regional comes through in a manner which substantially lessens one's regret at not being in the Queen's Hall.

Steering Modifications

The second of the "mods," to use a term now well known in aircraft circles, was fitting the latest type Bishop steering gear in place of the 1937 type. Internal friction has been reduced by using roller bearings and other changes in design, and in consequence the steering has changed from being rather on the heavy side to needing well below the average of controlling effort.

In consequence parking in traffic is far easier than it was before, which is a matter of great importance for a car used in London. In addition, instead of arm movement being required one can now hook the car about at speed with the wrist alone.

A point of particular value when doing long journeys, in conjunction

RACING PEDIGREE. "Horses alike, and cars, the merit prove that was their sires."

with the good seating and suspension, this enables one to arrive at the day's end without the slightest feeling of tiredness, an even more important contribution to this result being the quietness of the car. An unbiased observer would not comment upon this quality as being remarkable at, say, 30 m.p.h. or 40 m.p.h., but would certainly do so at 70 m.p.h., for there is a complete absence of wind noises around the body. These are often of such a magnitude that they render the efforts of engineers to quieten engines completely nugatory, and in this respect the Salmons body is a most refreshing variation from normal present-day practice.

Finally, Lucas Mello-tone horns have been fitted which I like very well indeed and also the Lucas latest FT67 pass light, which is a most effective instrument.

Concerning Performance

Concluding, I find I have said little on performance and my comments on this must, therefore, be condensed. In brief, 20,000 miles have been achieved with no mechanical attention except two tappet adjustments and three brake adjustments. The oil consumption remains as good as new at 1,200 m.p.g., the rear Dunlop tyres are due to be renewed and the front are good for a further 5,000 miles. Two lamp bulbs represent the only toll which has been demanded by Mr. Lucas, and the use of the new light oils of Messrs. Shell and Wakefield have doubtless contributed to the fact that the engine is still in first-class order and is going better than at any period in its history.

The maximum speed is rather over 80 m.p.h. and fuel consumption 16-18 m.p.g., according to average speed. The potentialities of the latter may perhaps be gauged from the fact that one run of 486 miles was covered in a gross time of 14 hrs. 5 mins., including lengthy stops for breakfast, lunch, tea and the taking of a number of photographs.

Mileage without attention would be

VERSATILITY. "Think not if days are gloomy now that will be so ere-long." "The whole canopy of Heaven outspread."

of little merit if the car was now a smoking if perambulating ruin. Such, however, is by no means the case. It is now being thoroughly overhauled at the Works to put it in as good as new condition. The only mechanical work necessary is attention to the clutch, due possibly to my practice of starting in second gear, and to springs and shock absorbers, both of which have had a considerable hammering. The total cost of the work, including touching-up on the body, rechroming certain items, and new tyres, is about £35, to which, of course, must be added £10

OVERALL WIDTH · 5'-6½'
5'-5½'
SEAT ADJUSTABLE · ±5"   TRACK · 4'-5"
10'-3'
16'-5'
M.G. 2 LITRE

spent on routine greasing and oiling during the year.

The total of £45 thus obtained represents a charge of approximately half-penny per mile, so that the overall running cost (as distinct from owning cost) is under twopence per mile.

This, of course, compares very favourably with railway charges and in addition the car can definitely compete with this form of travel in respect of time, and is certainly superior in regard to comfort. At the end of the long journey mentioned previously I went on to a meeting of the Institution of Automobile Engineers and finally did not get to bed until after midnight, but did not feel in the least tired. I am quite sure this would not have been so if I had made the journey in any other form of transport.

It is, therefore, apparent that it is well worth while running a comparatively large car and that such a proceeding is by no means so expensive as might be imagined. Moreover, on the mileage basis that this car has run, the driver spends three hours at the wheel every day of the year, so that comfort and ease of driving become of real importance.

I am pleased to say without hesitation that this is a most excellent car and I have enjoyed every one of my 20,000 first-class miles.

Tickford drop-head foursome coupé on the 2-litre chassis, an attractive and practical style.

M.G. Continuity

Three Main Chassis Types Go On Unaltered : New Open Tourer on the 2-litre Chassis

AS mentioned briefly in *The Autocar* of September 10th, the M.G. Company are continuing their present range of models, in accordance with the policy of introducing new cars when development may make it desirable to do so, not necessarily at fixed annual dates. Thus the 10 h.p. Series T Midget, the 1½-litre four-cylinder—which was new at the time of the last Motor Show—and the 2-litre are carried on without change.

Also, in spite of the increased costs of raw materials, it has been possible to maintain present prices, except in certain cases where specialised coachwork is fitted and where the price is influenced by increased coachwork costs. It is of interest that M.G. sales during the past twelve months have constituted a record, both at home and overseas. The 1½-litre has proved successful since deliveries commenced a few months ago.

On the 2-litre chassis there is a new and very attractive open sports four-seater with coachwork by Charlesworth.

This has cut-away doors and a concealed hood, and is undoubtedly an extremely good-looking car of its type. The price is £399. The other styles of the 2-litre, consisting of the four-door saloon and a folding-head foursome coupé with Tickford body by Salmons, are unchanged.

Thus the complete range and prices are as follows: Midget two-seater, £222. 1½-litre: Chassis £215, four-seater open tourer £280, four-door saloon £325, drop-head foursome £351. 2-litre: Chassis £260, four-seater open tourer £399, four-door saloon £389, drop-head foursome £415. On the 1½-litre permanently attached Jackall hydraulic four-wheel jacks are £5 extra, but are standard equipment on the 2-litre.

It is of interest to recapitulate engine sizes and leading dimensions. The Midget has a four-cylinder engine with push-rod-operated overhead valves, having a bore and stroke of 63.5 by 102 mm. (1,292 c.c.), tax £7 10s. Twin S.U. carburettors are used, there is a four-speed

gear box in unit with the engine, with synchromesh on top and third, half-elliptic springs are employed front and rear, the brakes are of the Lockheed hydraulic type, and knock-off wire wheels are fitted carrying 19 by 4.5in. tyres. The track is 3ft. 9in. and the wheelbase 7ft. 10in., whilst typical overall dimensions for the two-seater are, length, 11ft. 7½in., and width 4ft. 8in.

The 1½-litre has a similar type of engine, with a bore and stroke of 69.5 by 102 mm. (1,546 c.c.), tax £9. The four-door saloon has an overall length of 13ft. 6in., and the width is 1¼in., the chassis track and wheelbase being 4ft. 2in. and 9ft. respectively.

Finally, the 2-litre has a six-cylinder engine of 69 by 102 mm. (2,288 c.c.), tax £13 10s., also with push-rod-operated overhead valves. The wheelbase is 10ft. 3in. and the track 4ft. 5in., whilst overall dimensions of the saloon are, length, 16ft. 2in., and width 5ft. 6½in.

Absent from Earls Court

VISITORS to the Motor Show often wonder why certain makes are not exhibited. A case in point is Jensen Motors, Ltd., whose absence from the Show will no doubt be commented on. The firm state that the reason for the absence is that Jensen Motors, Ltd., have not been building chassis for the requisite length of time to secure registration by the S.M.M.T. as car manufacturers.

This is the new 2-litre open tourer, with a Charlesworth body.

AN M.G. MIDGET IS S

Seven a.m., a fine day and an open two-seater all ready for a 300-mile trip.

SKEGNESS is so bracing. So runs the slogan of the famous East Coast pleasure resort. To test its truthfulness and, at the same time, to try the paces of the Series T M.G. Midget, we set off early one morning with the idea of paying "Skeggy" (as they call it locally) a flying visit. Including an exploration of the coastline beyond, we covered in all over 300 miles in the day—and without fatigue, which would appear to indicate that the bracing qualities of the trip were not confined solely to Skegness.

The Series T Midget is an admirable car for such a journey. It gives you all the kick of the real open sports car. You can push the speedometer needle very easily round to the "70" mark, you can corner accurately at what appear to be almost impossible speeds, and when an emergency arises the brakes stop you in a surprisingly short distance. It is comforting, too, to know that when the tank is full it holds over 10 gallons, so you need not worry about refuelling even on a 300-mile run.

The road to the east coast is interesting and fast. Londoners would probably choose the Barnet By-pass as a beginning, crossing the St. Albans road and joining the Hatfield-Stevenage highway just north of the former town. In Stevenage look out for the "Cromwell Arms" on the right (where they have an excellent cuisine), and almost immediately afterwards fork right, keeping to A1 for Baldock. The left-hand fork will take you to Hitchen along A602.

Now the ground rises, and from the heights between Stevenage and Baldock you will command widespread views on each side. Baldock, by the way, is noted for its fair, and it shares the importance of Letchworth, the "Garden City" that adjoins it. There are reputed to be some almshouses in Baldock dated 1621 founded by John Wynne and designed to last "until the world's end."

Here, too, in Baldock you must watch your step, for at the end of the wide thoroughfare, which marks the beginning of the town, you turn sharp right and then, at traffic lights, sharp left.

Biggleswade is the next stop, but en route you can try the top-gear capabilities of your car, for there are

(Left) The Baldock fork: you take A1. (Above) The first stop (for coffee at such an early hour) is "The White Horse," Eaton Socon. (Bottom, right) Norman Cross: here again you take the right-hand road. (Top, right) The "final check" on the outward journey—"Skeggy's" Clock Tower on the sea front.

two longish hills. (The M.G. romped over them.)

Now you are in Bedfordshire, in the potato and turnip land of which Biggleswade is the centre, within easy reach of the lovely villages of Ickwell and Old Warden; but we must press on.

Still keeping to A1, we come to Eaton Socon, the Eton Slocomb of Dickens's "Nicholas Nickleby," where you will find "The White Horse" at which Mr.

BRACING, TOO!

We Cover 300 Miles in the Day during a Lightning Excursion to Skegness

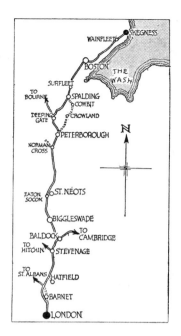

Squeers's coach drew up. Nowadays, however, it has happier associations. Its hostess, Mrs. Langtry, will regale you with stories of many famous opera singers, including Madame Anne Walker, for was she not Anne Walker herself?

Now begins what was once known as the 30-mile slide, but that was many years ago; to-day the road surface is

good and safe, although the road itself cries out for widening. We can soon forget A1, however, for we leave it at Norman Cross, bearing sharp right for Peterborough. Not so many years ago Peterborough was picturesque, but its main street was narrow and awkward to negotiate. To-day there is a wide thoroughfare flanked on one side by a magnificent new town hall. You cross the market-place and then, if you intend to

proceed via the Deepings, turn sharp left at the lights, making for Deeping Gate and Spalding. Alternatively, you can carry straight on at the lights and see some of the real aspect of Fenland by passing through Crowland and over Cowbit Wash.

The writer prefers the road through the Deepings. There are some long, magnificent stretches where a car like the M.G. Midget can show its paces. Be on the lookout for the road to Spalding, however, otherwise you will find yourself progressing towards Bourne and unconsciously looking for the E.R.A. factory instead of the Fun Fair at Skegness.

In Spalding you will find the road well marked to Boston, but here, again, be on the qui vive for a sharp but unobtrusive turn to the left. People who know the road instinctively begin to look for the famous Boston Stump soon after leaving Surfleet. It has recently been restored, but once upon a time this tower, which forms part of "the largest parish church in England," was used as a beacon tower for navigators.

Now we are nearing journey's end. The road winds and twists and there are sharp corners; you will have to make a kind of Z turn in Wainfleet. After that it is all plain sailing and journey's end will indeed have been reached when you pull up outside the clock tower on the famous sea front at Skegness itself.

As a seaside place of amusement, Skegness compares with Brighton and Blackpool, yet it is different from either. The "front" does not run along the edge of the sad sea waves, for the ocean has receded. With characteristic enterprise the land thus uncovered has been reclaimed and designed to add to the undoubted attractions of the place. There are pools and gardens, an open-air swimming bath and a Fun Fair of vast proportions.

Skegness is never desolate, whilst, in the season, it is invaded by thousands of happy holiday makers: and hundreds of them use the camping grounds as their headquarters.

If you take the road out of Skeggy to the north, you will find many places of interest. Not the least is Chapel-St.-Leonards, where the new Vine Hotel will come as an eye-opener if you have not visited the place for some time.

Rain rather spoiled the homeward run in the M.G.; but it served to show that, wet or dry, it is a fast, safe, comfortable and very pleasing motorcar. Allowing for dinner at "The Cromwell Arms," we were back in London by 10 p.m.

New Cars Described —

The 2.6-litre M.G.

High-performance Engine in an Improved Type of Chassis Carrying More Capacious Coachwork

The steering wheel of the new M.G. is offset slightly to give additional room to the right elbow. Below the major instruments can be seen the sub-panel housing those of less importance.

IN last week's issue of *The Autocar* it was announced that a new M.G. model of larger size was to be placed on the market. Full details of this car are now available.

In general conception the new model is akin to the well-tried 2-litre M.G., but the body is of larger capacity, the chassis has a frame of extra strength to match the increased performance, and the engine incorporates special features. In size it is rated at 19.82 h.p. (tax £15) and has six cylinders, 73 by 102 mm. (2,561 c.c.). The cylinder block and the upper part of the crankcase are cast monobloc, while the bottom of the crankcase is closed with an aluminium alloy oil sump, containing two gallons, and ribbed for cooling purposes. Provided with integral balance weights, the crankshaft is large and is mounted in four main bearings. Pistons are of the controlled-expansion type.

Mounted in the detachable high-compression cylinder head are overhead valves placed in line, and these are operated through rockers and push-rods from a side camshaft. Twin semi-down-draught S.U. carburettors feed into a hot-spot type of straight inlet manifold. The intakes of the carburettors have balance-ended pipes coupling them to twin air cleaners and silencers. Below the intake manifold is a six-branch exhaust manifold considerably ribbed for cooling purposes.

At the top of the engine is a neat cast aluminium valve cover on which the oil filler cap is placed conveniently.

One of the most interesting features of this M.G. engine is its lubrication system. Oil is forced round the bearings by a gear pump, but special provision is made for filtering, cooling and rapid warming up from cold. There is a filter on the intake side of this pump which is caused to float a little below the surface of the oil in the sump, so that it is low enough to avoid picking up froth, but high enough to avoid sludge; hence the pump, as it were, automatically selects oil in the best condition.

On the pressure side of the pump the oil has to pass through a 100 per cent. filter before it goes to the bearings, and this filter is easily removable.

Controlled Oil Temperture

Now comes the new and very interesting departure. Before the oil is served under pressure to the bearings it has to pass through a long and closely wound coil of copper pipe which is situated inside a water gallery running from end to end of the base of the cylinder water-jacket. The exterior of this coil is therefore submerged in the water. When the engine is at work, the cool water from the base of the radiator is fed by the water impeller past the coil on its way to the base of the cylinder jacket, and thereby the oil temperature is prevented from rising undesirably high. But when the engine is stone cold and is

In a wide body, broad wells are provided for the rear passengers' feet with toe room below the front seats.

started up, the automatic thermostat control is short-circuiting the radiator (in order that the water in the cylinder jackets shall warm up as rapidly as possible), and this being so, the coil of copper tube of the oil system is warmed up rapidly with the water. Hence the oil flow becomes normal without loss of time.

Ignition, lighting and starting system is 12 volt, and the advance and retard of the ignition are automatically controlled by a suction-operated device. The dynamo is of the ventilated type and has constant voltage control. Wiring circuits have independent fuses.

In unit with the engine is a dry plate,

The spare wheel is carried at the side, leaving the luggage space unimpeded.

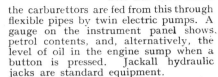

ventilated Borg and Beck clutch, and a four-speed gear box with synchromesh on second, third and top, the ratios being first 17.4, second 10.3, third 6.77, and top 4.78 to 1. The gear box has an improved type of remote control gear change lever, set well back in the centre of the driving compartment and con-

Showing the luggage locker packed and the tool kit, which is housed in a recessed tray in the lid of the locker.

venient to the hand. The hand brake lever is also very conveniently placed on the right of the gear lever. Controls, and an excellent driving position, have always been special features of M.G. cars. The complete engine and gear box unit is rubber mounted on four points, this mounting being flexible, but not so much as to be " floppy."

Transmission to the spiral bevel drive of the three-quarter floating rear axle is through a divided propeller-shaft. That is to say, the first shaft runs to a steady bearing contained in a ring of rubber with a steel housing carried on the frame, while the second-shaft runs from these to the rear axle. This avoids the use of an over-long open propeller-shaft.

Special Frame

In order to keep step with the performance a special design of frame has been introduced. It is of the "double-drop" type, made of manganese steel and electrically welded. Box sections are used throughout. In the centre is a cruciform member of which the forward ends are continued right up to the extreme front cross-member, whereby extra front end rigidity is obtained and a direct support for the four points of the rubber mounting of the engine unit. Another feature of the frame is that the rear springs are outside the side-members, so as to give the widest possible spring base. Half-elliptic springs are used back and front, and are damped with piston type hydraulic shock absorbers. To secure long-wearing qualities and prevent side play, screwed bushes are used on the front springs except for the rear end of the right side, where there is a coil spring loaded

" kick shackle." Silentbloc bushes are employed for the front ends of the rear springs.

For the steering a high-efficiency Bishop cam gear is used, with a medium ratio, a steering column adjustable for length and a spring spoked steering wheel. The wheelbase of the car is 10ft. 3in., the front track 4ft. 5in. and the rear 4ft. 8⅜in. The tyres are Dunlop Fort 5.50 by 18in. on balanced centre-lock wire wheels. Lockheed hydraulic brakes are fitted and have twin master cylinders giving independent balanced operation between front and rear. The brake drums are 14in. in diameter and are machined all over. At the rear of the chasis is a 16-gallon fuel tank, and

This view of the M.G. gives the excellent proportions of the new car. Note the sliding roof and draughtless ventilation.

the carburettors are fed from this through flexible pipes by twin electric pumps. A gauge on the instrument panel shows, petrol contents, and, alternatively, the level of oil in the engine sump when a button is pressed. Jackall hydraulic jacks are standard equipment.

One of the attractions of the driving compartment is to be found in the instrument panel, a new and stylish design arranged so that the large dials of the speedometer and rev counter are high up within easy vision, together with the clock and other dials. Below this panel is a sub-panel with all the minor controls, such as the combined Yale lock-type engine ignition and light switch, and the panel light switch, rheostat, throttle and choke controls. Incidentally, the roof light has a separate switch independent of the main. There is also a light within the luggage boot. The headlight system is arranged so that a foot switch cuts off the head lamps and brings on a pass light mounted in the centre of the front bumper bar, which, by the way, is of the stabiliser type. A rear bumper is fitted.

Characteristic Appearance

In appearance the new 2.6-litre M.G. is characterised by a very long bonnet, with an almost horizontal top line, terminating in a radiator of the famous shape but of slightly larger proportions and V-fronted. The front wings are of an improved style in which the inside valances make a smooth curve with the dome. The style of the coachwork is similar to that of the 2-litre model—in the case of the saloon a four-door four-light design of graceful shape, with a large luggage container built into the rear panel. The whole of this boot is available for luggage, for the spare wheel

is mounted on the left side of the bonnet and scuttle. The lid carries the tool kit countersunk in a partition, and can be used open flat as a platform for extra luggage. This body is broader and more capacious than that of the 2-litre model, and there is additional foot room.

Draughtless ventilation is provided by hinged triangular glass panels in the windows of the doors. A sliding roof is fitted. The windscreen, which has twin wiper blades driven from a silent remote motor, can be opened right up to a horizontal position. There will be three body styles available, saloon £442, four-seater drop-head coupé £468, and an open four-seater £450.

Chassis price is £295.

The "tail-end" of the 2.6-litre M.G. may fairly be described as shapely, the large luggage locker blending well with the car as a whole.

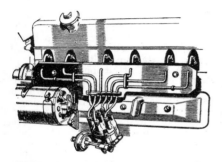

WELL PLANNED. The layout of distributor, leads and plugs of the new 2.6-litre engine. Note the vacuum advance mechanism.

1939 CARS

THE M.G. Car Co., Ltd., are amongst those who do not introduce yearly models and for the year 1939 they are continuing to produce the T-type, 1½-litre and 2.3 litre cars which they have sold in record quantities over the last two years. Additional to these models, however, they are introducing a car of outstanding appeal to all interested in high performance.

This is a 2.6-litre car that has been designed to give a high maximum speed, first-class road holding and, above all, to reach very high standards of reliability and long life. Both engine and chassis have been exhaustibly tested and the following description will show in detail how these ideals have been realized in practice.

The engine is a 2,561 c.c. six-cylinder unit with a bore and stroke of 73 by 102 mm., the R.A.C. rating being 20 h.p. The developed power exceeds 100 b.h.p. and the b.m.e.p. exceeds 135 at 2,600 r.p.m., a figure that is highly creditable to the designers.

Considerable care has been taken in the design of the head, valve timing and the combustion space. A compression ratio of 7.25 to 1 is used in conjunction with alcohol or leaded fuel of 82 octane. There are two inclined S.U. carburetters coupled to dual manifolds having a small balance pipe. Inlet valves with 30.5 mm. throat diameter are used, the exhaust valves being 26 mm., thus having an area of approximately .75 that of the inlets.

This proportion has proved quite adequate at well over 5,000 r.p.m.

Aerolite pistons are employed and the steel connecting rods have thin wall white metal bearings, produced by the Glacier Metal Co. These are also used for the main crankshaft bearings, which have staggered circumferential grooving to prevent wear on the crankshaft.

This latter component is of particular interest, as it is fully counterbalanced. This is the first time that such a design has been used on M.G. production models, although it has been employed with great success on some of their record-breaking cars, notably Major Gardner's.

Lubrication has received special

M.G. 1939 MODELS

T Type

Four cylinders. Bore 63.5, stroke 102, capacity 1,292 c.c.; 10 h.p. (tax £7 10s.). Wheelbase, 7 ft 10 ins.; track, 3 ft. 9 ins.

Two-seater	£222
Drop-head coupé	£269 10

1½-Litre

Four cylinders. Bore 69.5, stroke 102, capacity 1,548 c.c.; 12 h.p. (tax £9). Wheelbase, 9 ft.; track, 4 ft. 2 ins.

Saloon	£325
Drop-head foursome	£351
Tourer	£280

2-Litre

Six cylinders. Bore 69.5, stroke 102, capacity 2,322 c.c.; 17.97 h.p. (tax £13 10s.). Wheelbase, 10 ft. 3 ins.; track, 4 ft. 5 ins.

Saloon	£389
Drop-head foursome	£415
Tourer	£399

2.6-Litre

Six cylinders. Bore 73, stroke 102, capacity 2,561 c.c.; 20 h.p. (tax £15). Wheelbase, 10 ft. 3 ins.; track, 4 ft. 8½ ins.

attention, a large by-pass valve ensuring constant oil pressure under all conditions. As a further contribution towards a stability of lubrication, an oil cooler is fitted, this being fully described, together with an illustration, in "Topical Technics" on another page.

The water cooling also deserves mention, for the whole of the flow is passed from the pump down the side of the block (over the oil cooler) and thence into the back of the cylinder head. It is forced, therefore, through the head under pressure into the radiator, a feature materially assisting cooling of valve and plug seats.

This power unit has been taken up to speeds approaching 6,000 r.p.m. on tests, and on endurance trials, which stress an ordinary engine to the limit in 100 hours, it has run for over 300 hours without showing any signs of distress. It is coupled by a Borg and Beck clutch to a four-speed gearbox with synchronized ratios on top, third and second, actual reductions being 4.8

ATTRACTIVE. The Tickford drop-head coupe on the T-type chassis makes a strong appeal in respect of performance, looks and price, this being £269 10s.

ange includes
New 2.6-Litre

FAST TOURING. "A 2.6-litre car designed to give high maximum speed, first-class road holding and to reach very high standards of reliability and long life."

on top, 6.78 on third, 10.3 on second and 17.43 on first.

The chassis has a relatively long wheelbase (10 ft. 3 ins.) and it has been decided to divide the propeller shaft in the interests of smooth running at high speeds. From a single universal joint immediately behind the gearbox a short and stiff shaft runs to a needle roller joint, rubber mounted part of the way down the chassis frame. Behind this is another short shaft running between two Hardy Spicer joints and connecting to the rear axle.

The rear track is 4 ft. 8½ ins. and this, in conjunction with the wide spring mounting, has made the car exceptionally stable on corners. The brake drums are 14 ins. in diameter and are applied by Lockheed hydraulic operation with a tandem master cylinder. Moreover, the proportions of the wheel cylinders at the front and back end of the car are such as to give a higher proportion of braking to the former than the latter. Ferodo linings are employed.

The chassis frame of this car has been laid out to give great stiffness, particularly at the front end, where the A-form cross bracing is continued right up to the front dumbirons. Luvax piston-type double-acting shock absorbers are fitted and the front springing includes the use of a kick shackle on the off side.

Silentblocs are used for the front of the rear springs and screw-type shackles at the back. The latter have a vastly greater area than the orthodox type and virtual immunity from wear.

General Aspects

Turning now from the technical to the general aspects of the car, a feature which will immediately be apparent is the use of a V-type radiator. A long bonnet gives a fine sweep to the general lines.

The passenger space is separated from the engine-room by the customary M.G. double bulkhead, the pedals coming up through the floor of the body and the steering column being rubber-sealed where it passes through into the engine space. Incidentally, the steering box is mounted very far forward on the frame to give an exceptional rake to the column. Two types of body are available, a four-door saloon and a Tickford drophead coupé.

As compared with the 2-litre car, the major differences are a considerable increase in width and consequently in elbow-room, a modification of the rear

INTERESTING. The power unit of the new model which has the following features: 100 b.h.p., fully counter-balanced crankshaft, oil-cooling, synchro-mesh gearbox, dual inclined S.U. carburetters and carefully proportioned manifolds.

POPULAR. The 1½-litre saloon has sold in large quantities during the past year. It costs £325 and is unchanged for 1939.

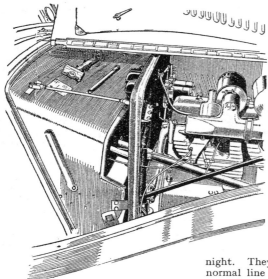

BULKHEADS. Double bulkheads are used on the 2.6-litre, as on other models, to prevent heat, noise and fumes entering the body from the engine compartment.

floor wells, improved tool accommodation in the rear luggage lid and an entirely new instrument panel. This, in common with all other models, has Jaeger instruments and a great deal of experiment has been carried out on giving the best possible visibility at night. They are close to the driver's normal line of vision and their high mounting makes it possible to have large cubby holes.

Turning now to the other cars, these need but a brief description for they are now thoroughly established on the market and are familiar to all keen motorists.

The 2-litre is rated at 18 h.p., has a six-cylinder engine in a chassis of the same wheelbase as the 2.6-litre, but somewhat narrower in track. It has generally similar bodywork with a shorter bonnet and lower radiator, and is priced at £389 for the saloon model, £415 for the Salmons Tickford drophead model, and £399 for the tourer by Charlesworth.

Perhaps the most prominent quality of this car and one which has endeared it to many owners is its exceptional smoothness of running.

Four-cylinder Models

The 1½-litre has a four-cylinder engine of 1,575 c.c., rated at 12 h.p., and is sold with the same three types of body as the 2-litre, prices, however, being £325 for the saloon, £351 for the drophead coupé and £280 for the tourer. This car has a feature not used on the others, to wit, driver-controlled Luvax shock absorbers, and has proved exceptionally popular since it was introduced in 1936.

Finally there is the T-type, which has an international reputation now as a trials and sports car. Hitherto this has only been available with an open two-seater body, priced at £222. It is now, however, supplemented by a particularly smart Tickford drop-

WELL-TRIED. The drophead foursome on the 2-litre chassis remains unchanged for the coming season. The price is £415.

FAMOUS. The T-type open two-seater, priced at £222. This car has won a great reputation for itself in Reliability Trials. With an 80 m.p.h. top speed and 30 m.p.g., it is deservedly popular with the sporting motorist.

head coupé body, which is priced at £269 10s.

Despite its small dimensions this body has all the features associated with the larger Tickford types, including being able to have the top in the half folded or de ville position. It has rather fuller equipment than the normal T-type, extras being: separate bucket seats, Bluemel extensible wheel, Trafficators and remote wiper motor.

All the cars have certain common features of equipment, including, of course, Lucas electrical gear, Lockheed brakes, Bishop steering box, Triplex glass and Dunlop tyres. Smith's Jackall equipment is available on the 1½-litre at an extra price of £5 and is standard equipment on the 2-litre and 2.6-litre cars. An interesting detail refinement on the latter model is the use of fully balanced wheels.

It will be seen that the M.G. company have a range of cars that must make a very strong appeal to the discriminating motorist, whatever type or size of car he needs. Reinforcing the attractiveness of the car's mechanical specification and lines is a wide range of standard colour schemes, these being blue, red, green, duo-green, maroon, black, also grey and metallic grey.

THE M.G. MIDGET DROP-HEAD COUPE

THREE VIEWS OF THE MIDGET COUPE.
(Above, right) The head folded down for dry weather. (Above) With the head half open the M.G. looks like a miniature coupe de ville. (Right) Ready for the worst possible weather conditions. This model costs £269 10s.

By The Blower

THIS is not an ordinary road-test report and anyone who expects the sort of statistics that such articles provide had better stop reading here and now. All I have to offer on these pages are some random remarks about M.G. Midgets in general and the recently introduced drop-head coupé in particular.

I may as well begin by confessing to being something of an M.G. fan—which is not to say that my allegiance is 100 per cent. M.G. and that I won't have anything to do with any vehicle that hasn't a few octagons about the place.

What I do believe is that anyone whose taste in motorcars lies roughly parallel with that part of an M.G. catalogue that deals solely with facts and figures will find Abingdon no bad place to start looking for a new car; and I can speak with some authority in this connection since my acquaintance with the marque includes practically every type of M.G. in the light-car class that the company has ever produced, starting with the original M-type (grand little motorcars in their day) right up to the present T-type (an example of which I have just sold, preparatory to taking delivery of another of the same ilk—which fact saves me the trouble of saying what I think of it). In all, I must have covered well over 70,000 miles in M.G.s.

To confine the subject to the present Midgets, the T-type is not everybody's car. For one thing, it costs a little more than the general run of 10 h.p. models and that is a point these days; equally, for the extra cost you get "that little extra something"—and you do not pay dearly for it. Then there is the matter of accommodation. If you require only two seats and some space for luggage, fine! But if you want your 10 h.p. to pull four seats you will have to look elsewhere.

Just the same applies to a saloon top, although this is where the coupé comes in. Up to the present you had to be an open-car enthusiast to like a T-type. Now, admittedly, you still cannot have a saloon body, but you *can* enjoy closed-car comforts for two—with the option of open-air motoring at will.

If you like the ordinary two-seater T-type you will certainly like the coupé. The latter is naturally a little heavier (1¾ cwt.), but as that figure is just about the equivalent of carrying an extra passenger and a couple of suitcases on the two-seater, the difference in getaway is very slight.

As for cruising speed, the coupé will push the miles behind it just as efficiently as the two-seater and if you are one of those who like to see the milestones go by at minute intervals on a main road, there's no reason why they shouldn't; even higher speeds will not worry the engine, right up to the maximum, which, under good conditions, is nearer 80 m.p.h. than 75.

The Gearbox.

The gearbox is exactly as on the two-seater model with nicely chosen ratios. Second is sufficiently low (in conjunction with a clutch that is at once sweet, but never lacking in grip when fully home) for a comfortable start on the level, but will swing the speedometer needle as far round as the law allows in built-up areas; whereupon one can snick the lever straight into top and amble along in a perfectly legal manner.

Third gear has one of those ratios that is used very extensively in town when the driver wants to have sufficient revs. up his sleeve for acceleration without,

(Below) Near-side view of the 1,292 c.c. push-rod o.h.v. four-cylinder engine. The dash-pots of the twin S.U. carburetters are visible above the valve cover. Note the moulded rubber tool tray.

(Above) The facia panel of the Midget drop-head. Cleanliness of the occupants is assured by the well-protected gear lever and hand brake. The steering wheel, unlike the open Midget, is of the telescopic type.

however, keeping the engine turning over unnecessarily fast; in the country, it is ideal for rapid climbs of main-road hills and for overtaking. The fact that the car will reach the mile-a-minute mark before the engine reaches peak revs. in this gear gives an idea both of its scope and of the wide overlap in the gear performances. The actual ratios are 4.875, 6.44, 9.95 and 16.84 to 1.

It remains to add that bottom and second are very quiet, that third is almost inaudible and that the change (with synchromesh applied to third and top) makes the conveniently placed remote-control lever a delight to handle.

The hand brake, too, is a most convenient control. It has a spring-off racing-type ratchet and, in contrast to the corresponding control on many modern cars, is really powerful—no doubt the result of M.G.'s wide experience of competition work.

Road-holding.

On the score of road holding and cornering, there's really nothing in it between the two cars; both allow you to do things that would be frankly dangerous on some cars without in any way feeling that you have been a naughty boy—as, indeed, you haven't. Brakes go to match—the combination of Lockheeds and a chassis that does not twist into funny shapes under their well-known efficiency; need one say more?

So having reassured any who have their doubts as to whether this new body has "spoilt" the T-type, we can get down to considering the town carriage aspect; and, in spite of what the coupé does on cross-country runs, it certainly has great attractions as a refined motor carriage.

The photographs on these pages give an excellent idea of the lines of the car with the top in any of the three positions at the disposal of the owner. All have their special attractions: fully closed for bad weather or occasions when one desires saloon comfort and convenience; fully open when the idea of *real* motoring seems attractive; half-way for days when one is in an open-car mood and the weather is obliging only at intervals.

As an open car, the coupé is inferior to the two-seater only in so far as the windscreen frame is a little thicker and the occupants do not enjoy the advantages of cut-away doors. Against the latter must be set the added protection and better vision of glass windows compared with celluloid side screens, together with the extra convenience of having that protection instantly available on the mere twiddling of a winder.

In closed car form, the coupé is, quite naturally, incomparably superior to the two-seater with the hood erected—a very snug little machine in which the miles are reeled off with surprisingly little effort and no discomfort whatever the weather.

Two questions always asked about bodies of this type are (a) is the head difficult to raise lower and (b) can you see out of the car when you are in it? The answers are "No" and "Yes" respectively, but a little amplification will do no harm. The entire open-to-closed operation occupies just a little more time than furling the hood of the two-seater, but not so long as coping with quite a number of open-car hoods.

As for visibility, both side lamps and wing tips are well in sight from the driving seat, the screen pillars form little more obstruction than the combination of pillar and side-screen frame on the open model and an external mirror gives a good view to the rear. The back window is not deep, but as it is much nearer to the driver than in most coupés, the view astern is much better than is usual with this type of body.

Interior refinements not found on the two-seater include a telescopic steering column, direction indicators, an ashtray, separate adjustable bucket seats, a roof light and an under-scuttle mounting for the dual screen wiper. But there is no need to go deeply into matters of that kind; as I said at the beginning, this is not intended to be an ordinary road test report—simply a few random remarks inspired by a few days at the wheel of one of the new coupés.

I enjoyed those few days and, although I am at the moment waiting for my new two-seater to emerge from the assembly line, I will freely admit that if ever a car came near to converting me from my present 100 per cent. open-car enthusiasm, the latest M.G. Midget drop-head coupé is that car. For those whose enthusiasm for open-air motoring is not quite 100 per cent. . . . well, need I say more?

A view of the 1½-litre M.G. saloon not often seen by other road users.

A 1½-LITRE M.G. CAN TAKE IT!

A Memorable Run from London to Scotland in a Modern Sports Saloon

AVERAGE speeds, like fishing stories, are apt to lead to heated arguments and much spilling of ink. Yet I am prepared to leave myself open to a perfect fusillade of brickbats (or bouquets) by recording faithfully a certain run to Scotland in an altogether delightful 1½-litre M.G. saloon in February of this year.

I believe that one or two people have achieved extraordinary average speeds between London and Glasgow, and I know of one man who actually accomplished the 400 miles in under 6¾ hours under the auspices of a certain national daily newspaper. This was just before the "30" limit came in, and his car was such that its entry for the T.T. or Le Mans would have raised no comment.

The 1½-litre M.G. lays no especial claim to remarkable high speeds. When pushed it will do a genuine 85 m.p.h. or a dependable 80 m.p.h. where circumstances allow. People often say "Where can you do 85 m.p.h. for long?" I reply: "Scores and scores of places." In fact, I know quite a few stretches of road where, given a 120 m.p.h. vehicle, it is possible to let it out to 120 m.p.h.

Many cars—but not very many light cars—are considerably faster than the 1½-litre M.G., yet I would rather set out on a 400-mile journey in this car than in so-and-so's supercharged "Roadburner" two-seater. In the past I have often attempted very high average speeds with genuine T.T. replicas and hyper-sports thingumybobs. For 200 miles or so I could average fantastic speeds, but afterwards aching wrists, a sore back and a general feeling of having been tramped on, slowed me down considerably.

For sheer consistent and comfortable high-speed motoring the 1½-litre M.G. is one of the best of all the light cars

I have ever driven. At the end of 400 miles I was as fresh as when I started out. The same applied to the car, except for the paintwork, which had vanished under a covering of mud.

If you are interested in average speeds, the M.G.'s time should make interesting reading. My wife took the times, and our actual *running* time from East Finchley to Hamilton was 7 hrs. 47 mins. The distance is about 390 miles, so work that out, you maths. experts! This was achieved by cruising as fast as possible—often the rev.-counter needle was about $\frac{1}{16}$ in. from the "red" mark and, on one occasion, it was well over it—without driving recklessly. This is, of course, contrary to all the best recommended ways of driving a fine motor-car, yet I must admit to a certain curiosity regarding maximum speeds. This M.G. unit had the knack of revving up to its peak (4,800 r.p.m.) without any effort at all, and no funny noises from the vicinity of the valves were apparent either.

The steady hum from the well-tuned o.h.v. unit was a delight. The M.G. Company's motto "Safety Fast" can be understood when you are behind the wheel and have your foot near the pedal of the powerful Lockheed hydraulic brakes. Racing experience has gone into the M.G.'s chassis. The car has the same "feel" as some Abingdon road-racing productions I have tried. Strangely enough, the makers have achieved a real sports-car suspension without any annoying bucketing at low speeds.

For hours on end I sat and never experienced any jolts. Never a shock was transmitted to my wrists, and my wife was as comfortable as she would be in an armchair. As we started out about 4 a.m. we had nearly 3½ hours of complete darkness. Speed at night is apt to be deceptive, and often I didn't realize I was

The M.G. looks, and is, every inch a thoroughbred.

travelling as fast as I was. For instance, at a point between Baldock and Biggleswade I received a mild shock when I saw 85 m.p.h. on the speedometer. Truly well-focused head lamps can make a world of difference. Miles and miles were rattled off without effort. It was odd to see so many farm workers about before 6 a.m. Most of the cottages en route had their lamps lit—no doubt the man of the house was having his breakfast.

This is not a test-run report, nor is it a descriptive tour, but merely a eulogy on the merits of one of our best "quality" light cars. Scrapping on the road is frowned upon by authorities, yet, given a fast car, how many people can resist trying to beat the other fellow? When one's vehicle can corner at very high speeds, it is logical to presume that the driver will endeavour to put as much distance between his car and the one he has just passed.

I kept as close to his rear as possible, and in coming out of one corner managed to pass him. I could see that he was a trifle annoyed, and I anticipated that he would whizz past when we got on to the straight. Fortunately for me there was a stream of traffic coming down from Scotch Corner, and I reached the landmark (where a new hotel is now being built) before he did.

He kept right behind the M.G. until we started to cross the Pennines, and it was there that the M.G.'s cornering abilities came into prominence. He receded farther and farther away in my mirror, until I could just see him like a speck about half a mile back. Eventually, I lost sight of him altogether and felt like patting the fleet little saloon on the radiator. If it had been "autobahn-ening" it would have been another story.

Most of the way the roads were wet, but this didn't make the slightest difference to the M.G.; in fact, it

(Right) The beautifully finished M.G. 1½-litre power-unit. Two S.U. carburetters are used and the induction manifold is plated.

(Below) Seating provides almost arm-chair comfort, and the upholstery is carried out in real leather.

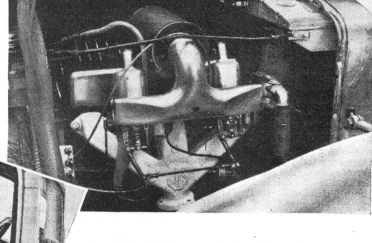

made a lot of difference to the driver, for wet roads mean freedom from ice.

Some people may accuse me of being too enthusiastic about this car, but who can blame me for it? After all, I caned it mercilessly, I wrenched it round corners, I indulged in fierce acceleration, I drove it in the craziest possible way; yet the M.G. engine was still as lively after the return journey from Scotland as it was at the beginning.

Before concluding, I should like to say a word about one or two things. First, the gear-change is as near fool-proof as possible and, secondly, the equipment borders on the lavish. The polished gold finish of the instruments and the smooth walnut finish of the facia panel would delight the most critical craftsman. Upholstery is beautifully carried out in real leather. This particular car was finished in an attractive shade of red, which went very well with the pale grey coach-work. Even after such hectic running the petrol consumption worked out at about 22 m.p.g., which, for driver and passenger, is still considerably cheaper (including meals) than the corresponding railway fare.

With reasonable care (and less hectic driving than mine, perhaps) this well-built 1½-litre M.G. saloon at £325 will ensure many years of trouble-free and pleasurable running, besides giving the owner the obvious pride of having a car that looks and is a thoroughbred.

GEE-GEE.

This cornering business is quite amusing. On the open road between Boroughbridge and Catterick the M.G. was tailing a large American car with "Super-charged" written in large letters on the bonnet (I read this afterwards). The maximum speed of this car was roughly between 95-100 m.p.h., and I knew if I did pass, it could immediately repass me. However, I could see that the car was rather a handful for the driver on corners. His tell-tale stoplights went "on" remarkably soon.

Major A. T. G. Gardner Tells Readers of "The Light Car" His Own Story of Breaking 1,100 c.c. and 1½-litre Records at Over 200 m.p.h.

THE TIMES AND SPEEDS.

Distance.		Times.	Mean.	Speed.	Speed.
WEDNESDAY, MAY 31. 1,100 c.c.					
1 kilom.	...	10.84 secs. 11.14 secs.	10.99 secs.	327.570 k.p.h.	203.5 m.p.h.
1 mile	...	17.36 secs. 18.07 secs.	17.72 secs.	326.254 k.p.h.	203.2 m.p.h.
5 kiloms.	...	55.44 secs. 57.79 secs.	56.62 secs.	317.909 k.p.h.	197.5 m.p.h.
FRIDAY, JUNE 2. 1,500 c.c.					
1 kilom.	...	10.84 secs. 11.05 secs.	10.95 secs.	328.767 k.p.h.	204.2 m.p.h.
1 mile	...	17.46 secs. 17.85 secs.	17.66 secs.	328.065 k.p.h.	203.8 m.p.h.
5 kiloms.	...	55.10 secs. 56.39 secs.	55.75 secs.	322.869 k.p.h.	200.6 m.p.h.

(Subject to Official Confirmation.)

MY aim after last November's records was to get 200 m.p.h. in the 1,100 c.c. class, and then, if the car stood the speed, to go as fast as possible with the engine bored out to bring it into the 1,500 c.c. class.

I realized the technical difficulties of increasing the engine size, but hoped that I should get 200 m.p.h. My main idea was to beat Lockhart's 1,500 c.c. Miller record, which had stood for 12 years, at 164 m.p.h. I also wanted to be the first man to travel at over 200 m.p.h. with a light car. The results far exceeded my expectations, because all but one of my six records were taken at over the 200 m.p.h. mark.

I decided to run for the five-kilometre records because the O.N.S. can operate six timing tapes at Dessau; this meant that I could attack the kilometre, the mile and the five kilometres with one outward run and one return run. All the cables and timing points are permanently on the autobahn; the timing was in the hands of Herr Schäfer, Germany's No. 1 timekeeper.

On my very first run I knew that 200 m.p.h. was in the bag. The engine felt just perfect and the weather was good except for a diagonal cross-wind. On all runs this wind naturally made the car a bit unsteady and must have cost us about 5 m.p.h. The steering and general handling were perfect, and I did not have an anxious moment; in fact, I was able to keep an eye on the rev. counter and knew fairly accurately before the times were published what speeds had been reached.

I changed up from second to third at 90 m.p.h. and into top at 140 m.p.h. At 7,000 r.p.m. I was getting 206.5 m.p.h. on top gear.

I do not think the Dessau stretch is faster than Frankfurt, but the double-width track, 94 ft. across, definitely does give one a comfortable feeling in case the car should be deflected from its course by the wind.

After we had taken the 1,100 c.c. records Reg Jackson and Sid Enever, of the M.G. factory, Mr. Kesterton, of S.U., and Mr. Shorrock, of Centric, set to work to bore out the cylinders of the engine to give a capacity of 1,106 c.c. For technical reasons it was desirable not to increase the bore dimension more than was strictly necessary to get over 1,100 c.c. [An interesting point and one that needs stressing.—ED.]

When the engine was reassembled the car went straight out and did its 200 m.p.h. without any preliminary running-in. It was a fine engineering achievement. The Germans were greatly impressed.

The only real bother, which cropped up when the engine was being reassembled, was that a camshaft bearing carrier was found to be cracked. A most effective repair was made, due to the good offices of the technical director of the Junkers engine factory. The

LIGHT CAR

by *G.E.T. Gardner*

Junkers works are at Dessau, and they offered the use of their workshops for anything that wanted doing.

The only other bother we had with the car was that, on the first run on Friday (1,500 c.c.), I applied the brakes too hard at the end of the five-kilometre stretch. On this car there are no front-wheel brakes. Heavy use of the back brakes caused one nearside shoe to distort and Jackson decided that it would have to be removed. So I made the return run with brakes operating on the offside rear wheel only.

I must thank Herr Dienemann, of the O.N.S., for perfect organization, the mobile police of Dessau and Leipzig, the leader and members of the Dessau N.S.K.K., and the Dessau police, all of whom were most welcoming and helpful.

My thanks are also due to the Burgomaster of Dessau,

Major Gardner waits for the cockpit cowling to be fastened down before starting one of his runs.

(Above) This three-quarter rear view gives a good idea of the beautiful streamlining

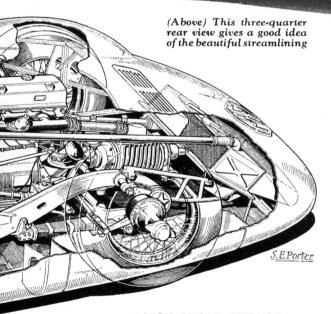

S.E.Porter

MECHANICAL DETAILS.

This special drawing by a staff artist shows all the salient details of the famous M.G. Note how the six-cylinder engine, gearbox and propeller shaft are arranged at an angle to allow the driver to sit between the shaft and the chassis frame.

who provided us with much-appreciated refreshments on the course. The Germans were most charming hosts.

Whilst I had contemplated attacking five-mile, 10-kilometre and 10-mile records in both classes, I felt the car had done marvellously and did not proceed with this plan. The wind would have been very troublesome for the longer records and the course is not straight for the necessary distance.

I did actually try a standing-start run for data purposes, but the car was equipped, of course, for flying-start attempts.

My new screen gave much-improved visibility and the equipment of the car was excellent. I was very impressed with the condition of the tyres, which were cool after the runs and showed no signs of wear at all.

I still feel confident the car has not reached its limit. I found that certain fairings could be altered to give a slight reduction in height and thus reduce windage. Also, I think I was a bit over-geared. I actually ran on an axle ratio of 3.09 to 1.

What next? I am already being asked if I am planning to go still faster. I write from Germany and at the moment I have no plans. I shall have to have a word with "Kim" (Cecil Kimber) about it when I get back. The engine is in perfect condition and could run again in the smaller class if a new block were fitted.

The M.G. MIDGET
DROP-HEAD COUPE

Externally, the latest TB-type M.G. drop-head coupe looks just like its forerunner, the T-model. The coachwork is equally successful when one is using it as a closed car (left) or an open car (above). The head can also be left in the mid-way position.

New TB-type Proves Delightfully Lively and Comfortable

THE fitting of a drop-head Tickford coupé body to the well-known T-type M.G. Midget chassis last year produced a car that was refreshingly different from the usual run of small cars—a model that appealed equally to the somewhat conflicting interests of the driver who likes and appreciates sports-car motoring and all that it stands for and who also has a weakness for refinement and comfort. It was, at one and the same time, a machine that could be used for long-distance high-speed touring, for exuberant cross-country journeys of the type to which sports car owners are partial, or for sedate town-carriage motoring, when boiled shirts and dance frocks are the appropriate wear.

All these things seemed equally fitting in this versatile little car. The word "little" is used advisedly because the Midget coupé is, frankly, a two-seater and no more. There is a nice big space behind the seats for luggage, and the seating accommodation itself (of which more in due course) is in every way ample for two people.

Beyond providing for these requirements, however, the designers cast a very stern eye on unnecessary inches, which attitude is responsible for one of the charms of the car.

The latest model of the Midget drop-head coupé, the "TB," possesses all these good points of its forerunner for the simple reason that it is, in fact, practically identical, so far as the coachwork and general chassis design are concerned. The only difference is in the engine-gearbox unit, which, as mentioned in the review of the current M.G. light-car range elsewhere in this issue, is of redesigned type with a different bore and stroke ratio and a counterbalanced crankshaft.

The alterations have produced considerably more power and have resulted in the peak output being delivered at 5,250 r.p.m. as opposed to 4,800 r.p.m. This, naturally, has made a revision of gear ratios desirable, and on the TB model the ratios are: 5.22, 6.92, 10.0 and 17.32 to 1 (compared with 4.875, 6.44, 9.95 and 16.84 to 1 on the T type). In other respects the chassis is substantially unaltered.

On the road the TB coupé handles very much like its predecessor, except that it is even more lively. Contrary to what one might expect, lowering the gear ratios has not made the car in any way more fussy—just the opposite, in fact, because the latest-type engine, with its counterbalanced crankshaft, is sweeter at high revs. and is mechanically quieter. The fact that the rev.-counter needle is just a little farther round the dial comes rather as a surprise than otherwise. Just how much farther that needle moves can be gathered from the fact that at 60 m.p.h. the new engine is turning over at 3,800 r.p.m. as opposed to 3,600 r.p.m.

Whilst on the subject of revs., incidentally, the speeds in gears at peak revs. may be noted. At 5,250 r.p.m. the car travels at 25 m.p.h. in bottom gear, 43 m.p.h. in second and 62 m.p.h. in third. These speeds compare with 24 m.p.h., 40 m.p.h. and 60 m.p.h. respectively at the peak engine speed of the T type, with its slightly higher gears; in other words, there is a small all-round increase in the speeds available.

Peak Revs. in Top

When the corresponding figures are plotted on a graph for top gear one finds that peak revolutions in the "TB" coincide with 83 m.p.h. compared with 80 m.p.h. in the case of the T type.

Turning from theoretical figures to actual performance on the road, one finds the "TB" a most satisfying car to handle. It shoots off the mark in most comforting fashion and, for all its coupé top and general comfort, easily upholds its makers' well-known slogan about being faster than most. The change from first to second gear is much quicker than before, and the changes from second to third and from third to top are just as quick as one likes to move the lever.

Second gear is particularly handy in traffic, as the clutch raises no objection to its use when starting from rest, and in this ratio one very rapidly reaches the legal built-up area limit, when the lever can be brought across the gate straight into top without the use of third gear.

That is not to say that third gear is not a useful ratio. Quite the contrary. In traffic it comes in for extensive use as representing a nice compromise between too many revs. for comfort and too few for acceleration, and on main roads it is a sheer delight. With the easy and quick change one naturally and easily resorts to third for overtaking, and when a main-road gradient begins to bring the speed down a little in "top," the original gait is instantly restored by a drop from "top" to third.

In top gear the maximum at the driver's disposal makes high-speed cruising possible with a nice margin of revs. in hand. A genuine 60 m.p.h. is a pace into which the car seems to fall happily and naturally, and there is then a very useful amount of throttle movement in hand for hills or overtaking. Also, that margin is always available if one wants to hurry—and the Midget can do that most effectively.

Road holding, brakes and steering in no way cramp full use of the lively performance of this versatile coupé. The car is steady both on the straight and on corners, the steering is pleasantly high-geared and accurate, and the brakes always seem adequate to the occasion. The combination of the Lockheed hydraulic system and a well-designed chassis which plays no tricks when they are used hard sees to that.

To some aspects of the coachwork reference has already been made, but more needs to be said about this very pleasing little body. It is in every sense of the term an all-weather type. With the hood erected it offers every comfort of a saloon; with the hood down one can enjoy real open-car motoring, with the added advantage of wind-up glass windows to give side protection at a moment's notice.

The only points upon which the car is inferior to a normal open body in this respect are those of every other drop-head coupé, namely, a slightly thicker windscreen frame and the fact that rearward vision is, to some extent, obstructed by the folded top.

The change from the open to closed position is very easily effected, more easily, in fact, than putting up the hood of some open cars, whilst in showery weather one has the advantage of being able to leave the hood in the coupé de ville position, in which one has only to roll forward the front part to close the car.

Good Driving Position

The body is nicely planned and the driving position has been carefully studied. Both seats (they are of the bucket type) are on sliding runners, and the steering column is both telescopic and adjustable for rake.

A stubby remote-control gear lever is just where one wants it when required, and the hand brake has a fly-off, or racing-type, ratchet, which makes it particularly handy in traffic. It is really powerful, too.

The instruments are nicely laid out on a polished-wood facia panel and include a large-diameter revolution counter on the driver's side and a corresponding speedometer on the near side. A tall driver finds the top of the speedometer a little obstructed by the windscreen-wiper knob on the passenger's side; this is a small fault, however, and could easily be overcome by reversing the instrument so that the hands started their travel near the top.

In all other respects the general arrangement of controls and switches is above reproach and one instantly feels at home in the car, especially in view of the excellent forward visibility. From the driving seat one has an uninterrupted view of the wing tips, whilst the screen pillars are pleasantly narrow for a car of this type.

Sports-car enthusiasts will certainly take to this latest M.G. model whether their tastes veer towards open or closed-car motoring.

(Left) The nicely planned facia panel with its large-diameter speedometer and rev. counter. (Below) Room for large suit-cases is provided behind the tipping seats.

(Left) The T.B.-type engine fitted to the latest M.G. Midgets. Note also the tool locker, fuse-box and under-bonnet screen wiper motor.

165

47,000 No-Trouble Miles

A LONG WAY. The mileage covered in thirty months is nearly equal to twice round the Equator.

Some Notes on a 2-litre M.G. with Tickford Body, Based on Daily Use for 2½ Years.

By LAURENCE POMEROY, Junr.

I BELIEVE it was Oscar Wilde who coined the aphorism that it is always a sorrow to part from a short-time acquaintance. There is, in any case, more than a grain of truth in the statement, in both human and material affairs. It is far more usual to have the first flush of rapture followed by a long term disillusionment than it is to have enduring and steadfast pleasure.

Certainly this is so in the case of motorcars. High performance, good springing, silence and a host of other desirable features may make a given model an extraordinarily attractive proposition during a test run. As, however, the miles pile up and pass from ten to twenty and well beyond the 30-thousand-mile stage, small deficiencies, a falling off in power, and, above all, a general deterioration of the vehicle as a whole, are apt to destroy all one's initial enthusiasm.

In the case of the 2-litre M.G. AMO 604, which I took for its first run at the end of July, 1937, I can honestly say that I have had nothing but faithful service. As I write this article on November 1, AMO is being stored for the duration, one of the war's sacrifices on the altar of economy.

A Best Car

Mr. Cecil Kimber would not, I imagine, claim that this model is the best car in the world. But it is certainly the best car I have ever owned out of a considerable number, built both in England and on the Continent. When I had it first I had spent a good many years in development and experimental work, in which the shortest run of, say, 100 miles, was always used for tuning, modifications or some adjustment. As a somewhat natural reaction I desired, having said good-bye to these activities, to have a car that would run for thousands of miles without anything other than routine attention. I had expected, of course, that above the 10,000-mile mark a decoke and the usual etceteras would be required. I was pleased indeed when this was not the case.

When the car had reached 20,000 miles without any trouble and without any adjustments, save brakes, and with no new parts, I wrote an article in *The Motor* about it, giving it due praise. At 23,000 miles the car was taken to Abingdon for certain atten-

tions. In particular, shackles had worn badly and were rattling and the clutch had suffered as a result of many restarts whilst obtaining photographs of a freak hill in Cornwall, later used for the London-Land's End trial. The engine, however, was not touched, nor did it show any need of it. The car returned running suavely and smoothly as ever, and shortly after it was a year old it piled up 30,000 miles.

Condition at 30,000 Miles

Then came a disaster. For various reasons not really connected with the car at all, a big end became slack. It was impossible to effect immediate repairs and before the necessary work could be done the crank and main bearings had developed a lot of wear. There was nothing for it but to renew the crank, main and big ends at 33,000 miles.

The rest of the engine, however, was in excellent condition. Some new

piston rings were fitted, also a valve guide here and there, and from then until a few days ago, when the speedometer clocked 47,000 miles, no further attention has been given to it. It still shows no signs of needing a rebore, the oil consumption, even when driving reasonably fast, being 800-900 m.p.g. In fact, if I exclude, as I think I am justified in doing, the big-end bother, the only renewals called for with a mileage equivalent to nearly twice the circumference of the globe, have been new brake linings, new clutch, a set of shock absorbers, a set of shackles, one speedometer and three sets of plugs.

It is worth mentioning that so far as shackles and shock absorbers are concerned, the later types of 2-litre have improved design but it has not been possible to incorporate them on my car.

Reliable Electricity

Such excellent service from the car itself has been matched by the results obtained with the components. The Lucas electrical equipment, for instance, has given absolutely no trouble whatever and it has only had the attention of new dynamo brushes. The Bishop steering gear, of the high efficiency type fitted at about 5,000

PROPORTION. The balanced aspect of the car is well shown in this head-on view. The Lucas wind horns and FT67 pass lamp are later additions which have given excellent service.

OPEN AIR. On fine days the Salmons body can be opened right out.

QUICK COVER. For normal open-air motoring the position shown right is best.

miles, has not been adjusted and still gives light and accurate control with extremely rapid castor action. This is, by the way, a special fitting as the standard steering is rather too heavy for my liking, although completely free from road shock. With the high efficiency gear one can definitely feel the road on the hand, but this is something I am willing to accept.

The brakes, of course, are Lockheed and this explains why the operating mechanism has needed no attention; as I have said before, only linings have been fitted, the drums still being the original.

So far as tyre wear is concerned the car again has some remarkable figures to show. The rears were renewed first at 22,000 miles, the front tyres running on to 33,000. Since that time the rear tyres have been renewed again, as have the front as a precaution, one tyre having suffered a percussion burst when I accidentally drove into a near-side kerb at about 70 m.p.h.

Tickford Merit

Finally, of course, there is the Salmon Tickford body. I have previously launched out in praise of this construction and it gives me pleasure to state again what a first-class piece of design and workmanship it is. The head can be converted from closed to open really quickly. As a matter of interest a doubting colleague timed the operation, with the following results:—

Closed to half open, 27 secs.
Closed to fully open, 32 secs.
Fully open to shut, 51 secs.
Half open to shut, 43.5 secs.
Half open to covered, 6 secs.

The time of real significance is, of course, the last named. I find little advantage in having the car fully open as only when one has a low sun behind the car does the driver or front passenger derive any benefit from having the back half open. Assuming then the half-open position to be normal, it will be seen that should a sudden rainstorm occur both driver and passenger are under the cover remarkably quickly, it being possible to perform the other evolutions of fixing the sides, raising the windows, etc., at one's leisure.

Both the Connolly hide upholstery and the general structure of the car have stood up to wear, tear and time in an exemplary fashion. The car was painted cream and black and could now, it is true, have a recellulose with advantage, the colour being faded somewhat. It is still, however, free from undue rattles or squeaks, and although the hood has developed a hole here and there, it does not let the wet through and could go some time yet before renewal was a necessity.

Pleasure in Driving

Some enthusiasts have expressed surprise when I tell them I like driving this motorcar as they feel it lacks some of the traditional M.G. sporting qualities. True enough, it is no faster than the old Magnette or N.A. type and I doubt if its standing quarter-mile time would be as good. Also when thrusting gentlemen with high power-to-weight ratio models come whizzing past on the Kingston by-pass the 2-litre driver must let them go on their hectic passage with good grace. It is not a car to flick through roundabouts at 50 m.p.h., to stand on its head or perform other carobatics.

Where it does score is in its amazing capacity to roll steadily along at 60-65 m.p.h. in supreme comfort so far as springing is concerned, with entire absence of effort from the engine, and in quietness and in peace. The latter seems to be derived in three ways: the double bulkhead between the engine and the passenger space isolates engine noise; the steel-cum-wood-cum-fabric top construction of the body is an effective sound damper and reduces road disturbances; and, finally, and perhaps most important, the square cut of the body seems to eliminate wind noise, to my way of thinking the most painful and misery-making phenomenon of all.

As a result one can quite easily drive 150 miles, conduct one's business and return home the same day, afterwards perhaps going out to a show and thence on to a road house and doing another 40 or 50 miles without any sense of having done heroic long-distance motoring.

When one tries to work it out in detail, the mileage I have done on this car is the equivalent of about 100 miles per day of use, or, say, $2\frac{1}{2}$ hours or 3 hours per day. If one employs a car in this fashion one demands, above all, comfort of mind and body. This is certainly supplied by Old Faithful.

Aid to Enjoyment

Assistance has been had particularly from two components fitted since the car was bought. One of these is the Lucas FT67 pass light. This now remains as a sort of war-time mockery but has previously been found to give so good a flow of light that on well-known roads head lamps are redundant and have, in fact, been removed to see if the appearance of the car was improved.

The second thing is the Philips radio set, which is remarkable for its reliability and brilliant realism of its tone, there being a freedom from excessive bass effect. Many foreign stations can be found, an advantage in these times.

For the ensuing period of war the car and all it has meant is but a memory. It is, however, more than that. So long as it can be viewed warm and safe in its garage it is something to associate with the days of peace which we all hope will not be too long deferred. When that time comes I shall, I hope, again be able to sit at the wheel and watch the milometer turn round to 50,000 miles and, I trust, well beyond.

DRIVING the big M.G.—the 2.6-litre, that is—leads to two main thoughts at the present moment; first, regret that in these times such a car cannot prosper as it should, and, secondly, a host of M.G. recollections going back to Mark Is and Mark IIs on which a great deal of capital motoring was done in other days.

The memories of smaller M.G. models tried in the meantime fade momentarily, the mind automatically reverting for comparison to the larger earlier models that were so well known, though not forgetting the 2-litre which remains current as companion car to the 2.6-litre.

In the latter, M.G.'s have produced a car that is very different indeed from the old bigger six-cylinder models, and different, too, from any of their existing cars. Each of these—the Midget, the 1½-litre, and the 2-litre—has its own particular appeal size for size, but in the " 2.6 " one senses the underlying aim to produce an M.G. of a kind not achieved previously.

To start with, it is definitely a big car. Although the wheelbase is the same as that of the 2-litre the track is wider, there is a distinctly long bonnet, and the effect as a whole is that of a car of impressive appearance, well proportioned, and spacious inside the body. Such a machine cannot be particularly light in weight, but M.G. ideals in the matter of performance are maintained by the power produced from the six-cylinder overhead-valve engine, with its two carburettors, rated at 19.82 h.p., and of 2,561 c.c. as an exact figure. Incidentally, the old Mark II engine was almost exactly the same size—2,468 c.c.

Especially to anyone who knew the earlier models, the 2.6-litre is a striking illustration of the changes that have come into the type of machine known broadly as a sports car. Chief among these is the use of a considerably softer suspension system in the interests of comfort. The outcome is a car that corners fast in the required style, but that is also really comfortable. There is little to choose between the back and the front seats from a passenger's point of view, and this is a notable achievement. So good is the suspension that a back-seat passenger can rest his head against the squab perfectly comfortably at high speeds.

Dual-character Performance

There is a fine surge of power from the engine, which is smooth and quiet also, and the characteristics of the power unit are such that in one and the same machine are given admirable top gear qualities and also the potentiality of fierce acceleration if it is elected to use the gear box. You can either trickle off from a standstill, using second gear to start, and put in top within a few yards, or by revving well up on the three indirect gears send the car shooting away up the road even in present conditions, on Pool petrol and with a retarded ignition setting to suit.

There is that element of the " road train " in the way in which it travels at 60 to 70 m.p.h. free of all effort and with fine power in reserve. The exact speed maintained is a matter of the road or the personal whim of the moment, not of the car, for the whole machine is still happy when the speedometer needle is put well past the 80 mark.

More strictly, of course, in present terms it is a matter linked up with petrol, for, obviously, no machine will give its best consumption if very high speeds are attained. Tests of consumption were made, using a special tank, and with a moderate driving style but at no crawling pace, not exceeding 45-50 m.p.h.. and coasting in neutral where any good opportunity of doing so arose, a figure of 24.4 m.p.g. was obtained and another in less favourable circumstances at 22.4 m.p.g.

Pool petrol is not ideal for high compression engines, but pinking was kept within reasonable bounds on this fuel by turning the hand-operated vernier setting of the ignition distributor well back towards the retarded position.

Through the years the practical people responsible for

The " Two Poin

Impressions of the Latest and La
and Many Special Fea

By H

the design of M.G.s have fully realised the importance of driving position. That of the " 2.6 " is admirable. The steering wheel is nearly vertical, and can be moved in and out on a telescopic adjustment so that an individual driver can suit himself exactly. The seat, besides being comfortable, is firm to the back. The result is a straight-up, confident position, which proves extremely comfortable for continuous motoring.

The gear lever is a fairly long, vertical remote-control type working in the familiar open gate used by M.G.'s, with a positive but easily operated stop against reverse. Second, third and top have synchromesh ; quick changing is allowed without any particular tendency to clashing, whilst a silky engagement of the gears is obtained by a

particular advantage on this car. Twin master cylinders are fitted, affording independent operation of front and rear brakes. There is no feeling of lost pedal motion before the brakes start to take effect. On the other hand, they do not "crowd on" too fiercely. A progressive decelerating sweep results from a quite moderate pressure on the pedal, and the braking effect as a whole is smooth, besides being really potent in emergency. The fly-off type of hand-brake lever is no more, the same applying to one or two other cars that used to have this fitting.

One of the best impressions, and something which embodies the justification of a car of this type and size, is the feeling of pleasurable anticipation with which a journey is begun in it. You know after a very little experience of the car that it can swoop over the hills, cruise at round about 70 without hurting itself, and make a hundred miles seem more like fifty owing to the ease with which it does all its work.

It is a car of a calibre that can achieve exceptional averages on any main road journey, and with the clearer driving conditions of to-day one frequently receives surprises when it is realised how far it has travelled in an hour without ever seeming really to have hurried. Very reasonable speeds were maintained at night with a Lucas mask of the approved type fitted on the off-side head lamp.

There are some special points, both mechanical and in the bodywork. An oil pre-heating and cooling system is fitted. Broadly, the engine oil supply circulates through a coiled pipe line which is in contact with the water cooling system. Upon starting from cold the normal thermostat short-circuits the main water radiator, and, the water in the cylinder jackets thus warming up rapidly, the effect is to bring the oil to the desirable state of fluidity quickly. Subsequently, however, the engine water temperature remaining moderate in comparison with that attainable by the oil, the effect is that of an oil cooler.

Unrestricted Luggage Locker

As a detail point one always admires the neat, flat, octagonal radiator filler cap, and the view along the bonnet from inside the car is particularly handsome and businesslike. The fact of the spare wheel being carried alongside the bonnet saves considerable luggage space, making the locker really big. In the thickness of the lid of the luggage compartment the small tools are nested in rubber. Four-wheel hydraulic jacks are part of the equipment, and a system of grouped lubricators placed conveniently under the bonnet, with pipe lines running to the bearings concerned, makes for ease of chassis lubrication. The two S.U. carburettors are supplied by two petrol pumps. The engine always started at once and needed little use of the mixture control, warming up quickly from cold.

A coachwork feature is the provision of hinged flaps in the rear as well as the forward door windows to act as extractor ventilators in bad weather. These are easily operated, and shut securely. Another special point is a shield forming part of the rear doors, preventing the mud that inevitably collects on what is normally the lower part of the rear wings from being transferred to passengers' clothes as they get in and out. When the car lights are switched on the roof lamp lights up if either rear door is opened.

A neat and practical instrument panel includes a rev counter as well as an engine thermometer, the shape of the dial surrounds conforming to the traditional "sign of the octagon." There is supplementary lighting for the switch panel, an impressive array set beneath the actual instrument panel, which is mounted high for easy reading. One would prefer that in this selection of similar-looking switches the starter knob should be distinctive. When a switch is pressed a check of engine oil level is given by an additional calibration on the petrol gauge.

In general, this M.G. is a well-balanced machine, partaking in full measure of the modern dual personality, that is, highly satisfactory in its flexibility and light handling for town driving, and an express flyer out on the open road.

odel from Abingdon : Fine Performance
Chassis and Coachwork

NFIELD

slightly more leisurely movement—not slow motion. Top to second and second to top, and such unorthodox changes can be made well. The latter is a useful movement with this car when pulling away from rest or after a severe check due to other traffic. Third might well be mistaken for top at times, being all but inaudible, and the other two gears are quiet. Top gear is 4.7 to 1, third 6.77, second 10.3, and first 17.4 to 1.

A little reaction is transmitted from the front wheels to the steering wheel, but this tendency never becomes pronounced, and it is the kind of steering that needs only fingers lightly resting on the wheel to hold the course at high speed, and there is strong caster action.

The Lockheed hydraulic braking system shows up to

RACING CAR DEVELOPMENT
The K3 MG Magnette

WHEN THE MG Car Co. was at the height of its racing activities in the nineteen-thirties they offered the 1,087 c.c. supercharged K3 Magnette as a ready-to-race model, in sports car trim with mudguards and lamps or stripped in pure racing trim. Many of them were turned into pure single-seater racing cars and one of them was constructed as such from scratch. This was number 23 in the production series and it was specially built in the Abingdon racing department for Capt. George Eyston, and consequently had the works number EX135 given to it.

Eyston's idea was to have a dual-purpose car that could be used for road-racing events as well as track events, using suitable body styles for each activity. In the normal K3 Magnette the engine and propshaft were mounted on the centre-line of the chassis, with the driver sitting alongside the propshaft. This placed the seat on top of the chassis side-rail, so it was not a particularly low, but it did mean that regulation two-seater bodies could be fitted for sports car events, or offset single-seater shells for racing events. In EX135 the engine was mounted at an angle of 6-degrees to the centre-line so that the propshaft ran diagonally towards the left rear corner of the chassis. A special rear axle was made with the differential/crownwheel and pinion housing offset to the left, and the left-hand chassis side rail was made with a bulge in it to accommodate the housing. This layout allowed the driving seat to be mounted *between* the propshaft and the right-hand chassis rail, giving the possibility of building a much lower car. A special semi-circular radiator core was made and a very simple aluminium bodyshell was made for road-racing, which followed the lines of this radiator. For record-breaking and track events a very sleek bodyshell was made, with a minimal opening in the front for radiator air, only the driver's head protuding form the cockpit surround, and a long pointed tail with head-fairing behind the cockpit. This special body was painted with longitudinal stripes of cream and brown, the MG racing colours, and the car was nicknamed "Humbug". When EX135 was being built at Abingdon in the spring of 1934 MOTOR SPORT went to see it and called it the "Magic Magna", following on the popular name given to Eyston's previous record-breaking car which was the 750 c.c. "Magic Midget". The Magna was a production 6 cylinder sports MG, and the Magnette was a more exciting competition version of it. By the time EX135 was completed it was being called the "Magic Magnette".

During 1934 Capt. Eyston raced EX135 in the International Trophy at Brooklands, where it retired with clutch trouble, in the Mannin Beg race in the Isle of Man, where it finished 3rd, and in the British Empire Trophy Race at Brooklands, on an artificially contrived road-course, which it won. At the end of the season the road-racing body was removed and the sleek track-racing body was fitted. In this form it ran in the 500-mile race on the banked Outer-circuit and was in the lead at one point, averaging 116 m.p.h. Then a ball-race seized in the rear axle and the car spun off the track. This was followed by a bout of record-breaking at Montlhéry in which Eyston took records in the 1,100 c.c. Class for the flying-start mile and kilometre, the 200 kilometres and for 1 hour.

In 1935 the car passed to Donald Letts, still in its record-breaking form as regards bodywork,

Capt. G. E. T. Eyston is seen finishing 3rd in the Mannin Beg in the Isle of Man in 1934 with the "Magi. Magnette", alias K3023, alias EX135, in its road-racing form.

The special K3 MG in its record-breaking form driven by Major A. T. G. Gardner, using the chassis fron EX135, the engine from K3007 and with totally revised body form by Reid Railton. Standing behind the ca are, from left to right, Cecil Kimber, Lord Nuffield, Major Gardner and Reid Railton.

and he raced it at Brooklands with the Bellevue Garage of Wandsworth, South London, doing the preparation. Meanwhile, in another part of the K3 MG world which was subsequently to affect the fate of EX135, Major A. T. G. Gardner had acquired K3 MG number 7 from R. T. Horton. This was a narrow single-seater which Horton had developed into a very fast track-racing car, with the assistance of R. R. Jackson and his Brooklands tuning shop.

In October 1937 Major Gardner took the ex-Horton car to a "Speed Week" held on the Frankfurt-Darmstadt autobahn, and he set Class G records at 148 m.p.h. which was a pretty impressive speed from 1,100 c.c. in those days. German engineers who were there with Auto Union suggested he should fit an all-enveloping bodywork, enclosing all the wheels. The following winter Gardner got the support of the MG Car Company to build a pure record-car, for K3007 was really no more than a highly-developed track-racing car. With the blessing of Lord Nuffield and Cecil Kimber a serious project was started by the MG

experimental department, with Reid A. Railto. assisting on the aerodynamics of the bodywork and Robin Jackson continuing the developme: work on the engine. The first step was to acquir K3023, or EX135 as they still knew it, fron Bellevue Garages, in order to utilise the speci. offset transmission line and low seating positio: As the car was only going to run in a straight li: the driving position was laid back at a shallo angle to reduce overall height, a rectangul: steering wheel being used, with high gearing s that it only had to turn a few degrees in eac direction. The Jackson-developed engine wa taken out of the ex-Horton car and put int EX135 and Railton designed a superb bodyshe which enclosed all the wheels. It had a ducte radiator system and each wheel was enclosed in i own box, with great attention paid to air-flo over, under and through the car. Railton was on of those natural geniuses with a flair for getting right first time, and without recourse to wind-tunnel he made all his calculations. Th result was that the first record-run by th rejuvenated EX135 saw a speed of 186.58 m.p.

SCRAPYARD CLASSIC

Ralph Clarke found the major components of his 1935 MG PB
mouldering in a scrapyard in 1966. By 1980 his
painstaking rebuild was ready for the road.
Herman Fourie tells the story...

MENTION the name "MG" to anyone born after 1960 and you will get a hazy response — these youngsters may recall seeing an MGB or Midget, but mostly their automotive memories will yield nothing more than images of boring BMC sedans of one kind or another. Occasionally the name TC or TD may crop up, but any attempt to suggest to our present generation of space age computer game freaks that those spindly-wheeled post-war two-seater MGs were the real sports cars of their time, will arouse some incredulity.

The history of MG cars goes back to long before World War Two, of course. To 1929, when a man called Cecil Kimber saw that the time was ripe for a small affordable sports car and produced his first M Type Midget. It used the mechanicals of Morris Minor sedans and was simple, inexpensive yet competitive on the race track. The M type had one failing — a fragile, two-bearing crankshaft — and if the little 847 cm³ engine was driven with too much verve the crankshaft would flex and snap.

Otherwise these little MGs had engines that were technically interesting, with an overhead cam and a vertical generator forming part of the gear drive to the camshaft. Driven carefully they could produce a fair turn of speed, probably

RALPH Clarke is director of product engineering for Leyland South Africa and has been with the company for more than 25 years. After school he started an apprenticeship at the City Tramways in Cape Town and progressed so well that he was awarded a bursary to attend UCT, where he did a degree in mechanical engineering. He is married and father of two children.
Apart from the P-Type MG, Ralph is presently involved in an even more exciting project — that of restoring one of the last remaining R-Type single-seater racing MGs, with supercharged o-h-c engine and fully independent suspension.
This car was first raced at Brooklands in 1935 and eventually became the property of Roy Hesketh in Pietermaritzburg. Watch this space for a full report on the R-Type when the restoration is complete...

as fast as one would wish to go on the roads of the time.

In 1932 the new J Types saw the light. The J2 was the more interesting of the two types with a sporty two-seater body, and it was the direct forebear of the P Types, which were first announced in 1934. These had delightful styling and more important, a robust new three-bearing crankshaft in a rugged engine that responded well to tuning. 2 000 PAs with the 847 cm³ engine were built, to be followed in 1933 by 526 PBs with the 939 cm³ engine.

The PB was announced to the motoring public just before the Olympia show in 1936 and stole the hearts of the motoring public. A journalist who tested a PB for the British journal *Autocar* had the following comments to make about the car:

"It does so much for so little. It is almost as fast as can be used reasonably. . . its acceleration is good and it runs happily at 50, 55 and even 60 miles an hour. . . its maximum would lie around 75 or 76 mph, given space in which to attain it. . . 50 mph seems a natural speed for open roads."

Scrapyard discovery

Ralph Clarke found the major components of his 1935 PB in a Cape Town

The dashboard (left below) is an exact copy of the original, with rebuilt instruments and satin-finish burr walnut. Four-spoke steering wheel does one and a half turns lock to lock. The PB MG uses an overhead cam

939 cm³ engine (right) with three-bearing crankshaft and crossflow cylinder head. Induction is via two SU carburettors. Note the row of spare spark plugs on the scuttle.

Brilliant red body and black mudguards suit the little MG, but in 1936 customers had a choice of many other colour combinations. The fuel tank is strapped to the body (below) and the spindly spoked wheels carry "Marie Biscuit" tyres. . .

scrapyard in 1966. R25 changed hands and he was committed to a course which was to end only 14 years later when the restoration was completed. Many important parts were missing and the body was in a sad shape.

A completely new wooden frame for the cockpit had to be made and new steel panels fitted and beaten by hand over the frame. Both doors had to be re-made in the same way.

All the upholstery, trim, seats and hood were missing and many hours were spent researching old material to find the correct styling and patterns to ensure authenticity. The door trim panels had the famous MG octagon embossed into the leather and a special die had to be made for this purpose.

The dashboard and instruments were missing and exchange units were collected from various sources, both locally and from the UK. The dashboard is now an exact copy of the original, with burr walnut veneer overlaid on a waterproof plywood base and satin finished.

The mechanical side of the restoration involved remanufacturing all existing components. Special attention was given to the engine, gearbox axles, brakes and steering. Vital new spares had been collected over the years and these — including new crown wheel and pinion, half-shafts, cluster gear, steering drop arm and sector shaft — were installed. Some vital parts had to be made up from old engineering drawings, or copied from existing models.

Painstaking work was required to restore trim and body parts to their original state. Door catches, headlamps, rubber trim strips and a multitude of

other bits and pieces were collected, bought or made to enhance the finish of the restored car. Finally the PB was given its present colour scheme of red and black, although catalogues of the time revealed that many two-colour schemes could be ordered by prospective customers.

On the road

We set off early one Saturday morning to sample the delights of open air driving and to experience at first hand the handiwork of a superb craftsman. The little PB was already waiting in the driveway to Ralph Clarke's house when we arrived and looked really tiny — Midget was the right word and two pre-war sized individuals formed a capacity load for this car.

Ralph coaxed the little beauty out onto the road and we set off in search of suitable pastures in which to photo-

graph it. We settled on the golf course, where the green grass and tree-lined backdrop formed a perfect setting for the brilliant red of the MG. Golfers preparing to tee-off stopped for an admiring glance at the dainty little carriage under the trees.

Driving the MG was like having to knead and bake your own bread after having seen nothing but pre-sliced cellophane wrapped supermarket loaves. There was a lot to do to get and keep the car in motion and above all, a constant awareness of things happening around and underneath you.

The designers of modern cars try to keep the users of their products as far away as possible from the mechanical workings. They know that the average driver prefers to remain uninformed about all those greasy bits that are necessary to make the car go — the modern

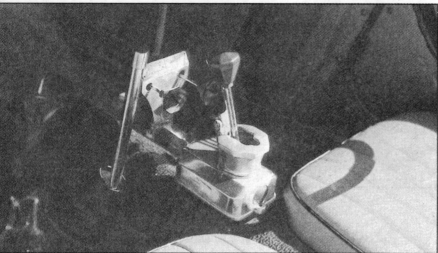

The famous MG octagon is embossed on the leather facing inside the door cubby hole (top). The remote-control gear lever protrudes from a neat aluminium turret with a latch to blank off reverse position (centre). Both hand throttle and choke are provided and the handbrake is of the fly-off type. Stripped-down chassis of the PB (above) shows the ash frame on which the metal bodywork is fitted.

car has become a household appliance and is made to do its job as unobtrusively as possible — kitchen cabinets on wheels, in fact.

The PB in motion is as far removed from the modern car as can be imagined — beam axles fore and aft, cart springs, rudimentary shock absorbers and narrow, high "Marie Biscuit" tyres make driving down the road a sensual experience. Every little bump or corrugation transfers itself to the seat of your pants,

and to your hands on the steering wheel.

The steering wheel has four spokes and fills about half the width of the car. It is bolt upright, close to vertical and takes one-and-a-half turns from full lock to full lock.

"Don't try to steer. . ."

"Don't try to steer it" says Ralph and I relax my grip on the wheel, which up to now had seemed to have a mind of its own. Sure enough, it settled down. We were going down the highway at 80 km/h and left to its own devices, the car went straight as an arrow.

The steering position felt odd — none of that classic straight-arm stuff. The wheel is about 200 mm away from your body at chest height, and holding it was rather like reading a newspaper in bad light.

Coming off the highway and around a fly-over necessitated some gear changes. No synchromesh here and a firm hand and superb sense of timing are required. From standstill you engage first, which is to the right and forward. Clutch travel is about two centimetres and the tiniest motion of the foot sets the show in motion. The change to second can be quite tricky because the ratios take quite a jump between first and second.

I try to keep the speed up in first, declutch, move the gear lever to neutral, out with clutch and quickly in again, and ease the lever into second. It is a bit of á gamble, because if the dog clutches inside the gearbox happen to be *precisely* lined up at the instant you change, you're in luck and a silent shift ensues. If not, "crunch" and you cringe.

Downshifting is, if anything, slightly easier, especially in the top three gears, where the ratios are quite close. Declutch, lever into neutral, clutch out, speed up the engine with a dab on the throttle, declutch and pick up the lower gear. Easy, if you know how. After a couple of tries, we had it taped.

Excursion into yesterday. . .

The car lopes along at 80 km/h in top gear and obviously feels at home in this speed range. We find no trouble in keeping up with normal traffic and a drop to a lower gear provides adequate acceleration for most eventualities. The brakes operate via steel cables but are quite up to the task of slowing down this tiny car.

Our excursion into yesterday is over far too soon and we head back home. Coasting down a longish hill, the MG produces a few rather unladylike pops from the exhaust pipe. "Running a bit lean" comments Ralph. Those modern-looking SU carbs are quite sensitive to changes in the atmosphere. "You set them up right for a sunny summer's day, but they run lean on a cooler day like today," explains Ralph. Anyway, when you're going on 50 years old, you should be allowed a few quirks like that. . . ●

TWIN MIDGETS

The M-type Midget was the model that made MG the leading British
sports car make, and Britain the leading sports car maker.
They were simple little cars that gave more than their money's
worth of performance and fun. Geoffrey Bewley reports on
two M-types that are more closely related than first meets the eye.

A nifty little thing.

*Centre right: The single
overhead cam 850 engine
was a willing performer,
but the two-bearing
crankshaft doesn't take
kindly to over-revving.*

THE FIRST MG M-type Midgets appeared on the MG stand at the Olympia Motor Show in London in 1928. Until then, MGs had been middle-sized, middle-priced, fast, well-fitted touring cars, based more and more loosely on current Morris models. But MG's manager, Cecil Kimber, was always inching toward the sports car field, and the M-type made the breakthrough.

The year before, Sir William Morris had introduced the Morris Minor to compete with the Austin Seven of the rival British automotive giant. Kimber had got hold of an experimental Minor chassis and engine, modified the controls and wrapped it in a simple two-seater body.

Kimber thought of it as a sporty car rather than a sports car, but the press called it a true ultra-light sports car, and a works team won the Team Prize in the Brooklands Double-Twelve-Hours Race in May, 1929. It was taken up by not-so-wealthy amateurs and enthusiasts for club races, hill-climbs and trials.

The M-type became the first of a range of light sports cars that proliferated in amazing variety until World War Two, and stretched on for 10 years after. It made MG the leading British sports car make, and Britain the leading sports-car-making country. With 3235 M-types built between 1929 and 1932, it was the biggest-selling MG until the post-war TC.

The two M-types in these pictures live in New South Wales. The red one belongs to Ian Heather, senior, and the blue one to his son, Ian Heather, junior. They've been in the Heather family now

Classic lines.

for the best part of two decades, running safe in good hands after long, hard lives.

Ian senior got his first. "We saw it advertised in the Sydney Morning Herald," he says, "and went over and had a look at it. A fellow over on the North Shore had it, and he wanted a little more than it was worth. It was in a very, very sorry state, and in those days the MG M-type was a forgotten cause.

"Anyway, after a week I rang up and he still had it, so I borrowed a trailer and went over with some money and came back with the car. Then we started the long road back, bringing it to what it is today.

"It didn't have a gravel guard or front mudguards. It didn't have the right dashboard or steering wheel, and it had twin carburettors. And the main thing was to bring everything back to stock standard, which we have done.

"The metal body was made at Parramatta in the mid-'50s, and we kept that. The front mudguards I made at Lithgow Technical College, with the assistance of two apprentices. The little side-lights we've got on it were given me in New Zealand during the International Rally there. Later, my son found out that his car was blue when it left the factory and mine was red, so we changed the colour to red.

"The motor is stock standard. The tank of course is not original, it holds twelve and a half gallons. Yesterday I said to my wife — well, I'd better go and put some petrol in The Pram (it's known as The Pram in vintage circles), because I haven't put any in since January.

"It didn't have the big tank originally. It had the same as Ian's got in his, a five-gallon tank. But of course when you're doing 45 to the gallon you can go a long way on five gallons.

"It was the only MG on the 1970 Cook Bi-Centenary rally. It's been on every International so far, successfully. It went on the Vintage Sports Car Club tour of Tasmania, and it's competed in historic race meetings.

"I drive it as often as possible. We stick to the limited *club plates* movement and I'm very particular about this. I fully appreciate the privilege the Department of Motor Transport has given clubs of this type, and I don't like to see any abuse of it."

Ian junior has had his M-type nearly as long. "It became available just after we bought Dad's, in August, 1962. Maxie Hamilton rang me up and said, do you want to collect two M-types? And I said, oh, fair enough. But we didn't finalise the details until October, 1964. He was moving and he had to sell the car. It was just a rolling chassis with a radiator underneath a tree in his back yard at Hurstville."

The Heathers collected it on a trailer, with a load of Morris Minor parts, and stored it with a friend who had a TA Midget.

"I started virtually from the ground up," Ian junior recalls. "I stripped it in August 1966 and sent the chassis away

to be straightened. It had a history down the South Coast of being used as a dune buggy, virtually, from what I could see, and it was bent to go around left-hand corners.

"Anyway, the late Ray Whitbread straightened it for us and we just started from there. Unfortunately in those days the MG Car Club had no interest in anything earlier than MGAs, so I joined the Vintage Sports Car Club in Great Britain. I sent over a list of what I wanted and I got quite a lot of stuff back.

"I built the body from scratch by myself. The bonnet came out from England by parcel post but I did the fabric finish myself. My local upholsterer told me I'd never get the material to do it, and I said, oh, come on, what do they use on the roofs of Holdens and Valiants?

"So I got the fabric, and one of the blokes in the club, Ray Powell, was doing a Riley special then. And if you look at his body and look at this they're very similar, because he was the bloke who showed me how to put the fabric on."

The blue car's fabric body is shaped like the original aft to a point behind the back axle. Where the sides ought to begin to curve inward to meet at a stubby boat-tail they're cut short, and the car is squared off across the back.

"When I built the body frame I built it as a pointed tail for the 1970 International Rally," Ian junior says. "But the Rally was coming up rather quickly, so I cut it off. It's under the house at home and that's another future modification. I've got enough blue material left to do a frame.

"The boat-tail and the V windscreen

was the standard factory car, but nobody can really say this is not original because nobody knows what the original body was in Australia. Very few vintage cars came out to Australia with bodies, because there was an excise on them. There were a whole host of body manufacturers in Sydney."

Neither of these M-types is, let's face it, a thing of beauty by today's standards. Even lovers of vintage lines must find them a bit wanting. Kimber's staff did their best 51 years ago, but the high little Morris chassis with its six-six (six feet, six inches) wheelbase didn't give them much leeway. All M-types look pretty much on the stumpy side.

Still, in 1929 they looked pretty good beside their first cousins with Morris badges. They outshone the sports Austin Sevens on the road, and matched the supercharged Seven Super Sports on the track. Their little four-cylinder 847 cm³ overhead camshaft engines were very susceptible to tuning.

The M-type engine was a Wolseley design, based on the Hispano-Suiza aero engines Wolseley built during World War One. Morris picked the engine for his projected light car when he took over Wolseley in 1927, and had it detuned so it wouldn't startle its undemanding prospective buyers. Kimber had the engine un-detuned for his sports two-seater.

The reference books say the three widely-spaced forward gears propelled it at 25 mph in first, 45 in second and 65 in top. It cruised at 50, which was as fast as contemporary tourers with three times as much power. It was reputed to be nippy

and handy. Light weight made for good acceleration and short stiff springs, with big shock absorbers done up tight, gave good road-holding.

Well, that was in 1929. We've come a good way since then, and often in the right direction. The familiar radiator and the spidery wheels suggest the M-type is like a pre-shrunk TC, but in reality it's as far from a TC as a TC is from a B.

Getting in you find the cockpit is pretty roomy considering the car's overall dimensions, but space in behind the wheel is lacking. If the wheel was a bit farther back you'd have a better chance of fitting your knees behind it.

There's not much space down around the pedals, either. The brake is the one on the right that feels like part of a brick and doesn't seem to do a great deal. The clutch is the soft one on the left, in the usual place. The accelerator is the small one in the middle that's hard to find.

This sounds as if it could give the unwary driver some trouble, but it doesn't work out like that. There's no chance of hitting the wrong pedal without thinking, because the tight fit down there means you have to think before you move a foot anway. Generally, you find you have to shift both feet so you can move one.

"If there's a major mechanical breakdown or there's something you've got to do to it," Ian junior says, "and it's off the road for three or four months, you've got to take it for a couple of runs to learn to drive it again, it's so different from the usual sort of car.

"I drive an MGA to hack round in. I suppose the hardest part is the central throttle on the M. But then I've done over 11,000 miles in it since the restoration and I suppose it's second nature now, jumping from one car into the other."

Both Heathers drive the M-types with more dash and confidence than we can show. It's best to start by finding a nice straight piece of road so you don't have to make too many heavy navigational decisions while you're shuffling your way up through the gears. Luckily the engine is flexible and forgiving.

The steering seems a little wavery, but it's not bad enough to scare you. The road-holding is quite good, about as good as you'd thought it could possibly be, and a lot better than you feared. The ride is okay, just okay, on a good surface, and jittery on a poor one. Acceleration is better than you'd expected, although fantasising that you were George Eyston would take a lot of imagination.

The brakes are mechanically actuated, with half cable, half rod system in front and all rod at the back. "You have to adjust them about every thousand miles," Ian Heather, junior, says. "What you do is, you put someone in the car and you jack up the wheel and then you adjust it so you can't move the wheel when the person's foot is on the brake. They can be adjusted up quite stiffly."

He says the M-type is fun to drive when you get used to it. "It's not a really fast car, so there's no problems there. I've got it up to about 60 mph, but it's capable of more than that. That was just cruising. But the one thing you've got to watch with these is, they're only a two-bearing engine. You've got to keep speeds down otherwise you'll break the crankshaft."

He doesn't drive his M-type very often, because the Vintage Sports Car Club doesn't run through suitable events. "When we do go out we generally try and do one longish rally a year, of about a thousand miles," he says. "We've just come back from the Vintage Vehicle Club's tour to Coffs Harbour, Dorrigo, Armidale and Tamworth.

"It's been across the Tasman with Dad's car to the International Rally in New Zealand in 1972, and round Tasmania with the VSCG. It's been to Adelaide and back and last year we took it up to Brisbane and back for the International rally. I like to use it, to get it out at least once or twice a month even if I don't do too many miles on it, just to keep it freed up."

Reader, by now you've been looking at these pictures long enough to decide the title of this piece is a slight exaggeration. The Heathers' cars are the same make and model, true, and still pretty readily identifiable as such, but the years have brought a few too many changes. It's a case of kinship, but not twinship.

But the best is saved for last. Twinship is proven in the cradle, remember. The scars of long life and the wrinkles and grey hairs of age can't sever the initial filial knot.

"My car is chassis number 580, made on August 27, 1929, and Dad's is chassis 582 which was made on August 28. They still have service records which show that 581 was a home car. So 580 and 582 were consecutive export cars. □

The M-type originally had a five-gallon tank; the non-standard version holds two and a half times that much and gives vast cruising range.

MG MIDGET J2

Just over 50 years ago, MG staggered Britain's sporting motorists by introducing a peppy open two-seater that sold for less than £200. Cyril Posthumus tells its story

FOUR YEARS is no time at all in the production life of a modern car, but go back half a century, and every summer was 'new model' time. Week after week, from July to the Motor Show in October, *The Motor* and its contemporaries would come out, almost panting with hot news on the multifarious new models, at a time when most major manufacturers produced four or five different basic models with many coachwork variations. It was 50 years ago, in the early August of economically bleak 1932, that the marque MG sprang a big and welcome surprise with their updated Midget, called the J2.

The genius behind this exceedingly pretty little sports car was Cecil Kimber, who was to MG what Sir William Lyons became to SS and Jaguar. Both were masters at "reading" the market, in adapting readily available components to their particular needs, and in practical styling. Kimber knew the appeal of sporting lines when he established the MG concern, using Morris parts back in the '20s, and his first big coup came in September 1928 when in one hectic fortnight he and his happy band of men transformed the new and boxy Morris Minor baby saloon, powered by a pro-mising Wolseley-designed 847cc four-cylinder overhead camshaft engine, into the cobby little MG Midget sports car.

With its fabric-covered boat-tail body of plywood seating two people in the open instead of four under a roof, a price £40 higher than that of the Minor saloon, and a modest maximum of just over 60mph, the Midget or M-type still sold as hot cakes are alleged to. With periodic improvements it was on the market for 3½ years, in which time 3,235 were produced, its looks and appeal outweighing the inherent shortcomings of a two-bearing crank-shaft, three speeds, fabric disc universal joints, a fuel tank under the scuttle, a ball-change gear lever, and 3-stud wheels. The J2, which was its lineal successor, was immeasurably better, thanks chiefly to the lessons of two hard seasons of racing. Seldom, indeed, could the benefits of motor racing be better argued than in the development of the MG Midget.

That there was good stuff latent in the M-type came as a surprise even, one suspects, to the MG works, newly moved to Abingdon-on-Thames. Its ohc Minor engine was deceptively robust and very receptive to tuning, and after a gentle initiation in the 1930 JCC High Speed Trials at Brooklands, the car emerged much modified, as the first "750" to exceed 100mph early in 1931. That same astonishing season it won three classic races in the British Isles – the Double 12 Hours at Brooklands, the Irish Grand Prix at Phoenix Park, and the RAC TT in Ulster. When Sir Henry (Tim) Birkin spoke of the "scuttling kindergarden" of small cars that foiled his efforts to win with big ones, he was primarily sniping at the MGs. Of course handicapping helped, but the little cars performed so outstandingly that they were almost always a jump ahead of the handicappers. Besides being reduced to 750cc to qualify for International Class H, the racing Midget acquired a revised camshaft and fresh valve timing which produced several invaluable extra bhp, eventual supercharging, a 4-speed gearbox, and a rear underslung chassis.

All these improvements, apart from the supercharger, went into the new J2 road model, but this car's most striking feature was its appearance. While the boat-tailed M-type had echoed French Amilcar and Salmson practice of the '20s

The J2 owed little to any other car, unless the main body "theme" was inspired by the vast Le Mans "Speed Six" Bentleys of 1929-30. An entrancingly pretty little two-seater, the J2 had the racing-type underslung frame, a long, low bonnet, cut-away door sides, fixed cycle wings, a 12-gallon "slab" rear tank to which a spare wheel was "strapped" by a triangulated metal clamp, and neat scuttle windscoops behind a fold-flat windscreen. Rudge Whitworth quick-release wire wheels, quick-action filler caps, and the new MG radiator with its distinctive tiebar completed as pretty a picture as £199 10s. could convert into reality. Rarely was a design so incisive, so simple, and so right in proportions and looks, and only the small 8 inch diameter brakes (with aluminium fins shrunk on) and Dunlop 4 × 19in. tyres imparted a certain skimpiness.

Beneath the prettiness was some skilful engineering, largely learned through racing at home and abroad. True, the 57 × 83mm, 847cc four-cylinder engine retained the M-type's 2-bearing crankshaft and the camshaft drive serving also as the armature shaft for the vertical dynamo. It acted as a useful damper, but received the dubious benefit of the cam gear lubricant, earning derision as time passed as "MG's oil-cooled dynamo". But the "J" engine had a new crossflow cylinder head with staggered inlet and exhaust valves, the result (in conjunction with twin semi-downdraught SU carburetters) being 36bhp at 5500rpm to the M's original 20 and best of 27bhp at 4500rpm.

The then-new smaller 14mm sparking plugs were employed, and the engine embodied a tubular front mounting to which the radiator was rigidly bolted, divorced from frame flexing. A new lightweight 4-speed gearbox was used, and another design refinement inherited from the track was the use of phosphor bronze guides instead of shackles for the aft ends of the semi-elliptic springs at front and rear, thereby achieving extra lateral rigidity. They were given oil via a convenient cluster of Tecalemit lubricators installed on the scuttle bulkhead for the welfare of the springs, brake cables, steering box and column, and brake cross-shaft, all getting their dose of gear oil every 500 miles.

Stoneguards for the headlights and radiator were among the optional extras, and the exhaust note was naughty but nice, though cries of "boy racer" in 1932 parlance could effectively be refuted since the J2 echoed MG's own racing experience. Not that the J2 raced; it was the big seller and breadwinner of the Abingdon family, and despite its launch during an acute economic depression and a production span of under two years, 2,083 (plus 380 four-seater J1 variants) were built, sold and enjoyed. Inevitably private owners competed with it in trials, club speed events, rallies and driving tests, a very low first gear and a road weight of just over 11cwt materially assisting in competitive performances.

But Cecil Kimber erred when he supplied the leading weekly magazines with "prepared" J2s able to attain 80mph. Thus the headline to The Motor's description shouted "80mph MG Midget for under £200", while The Autocar achieved 80.35mph in their road test. When eager customers received their production J2s they found they were lucky to get 72mph out of them – still not bad for 847cc in 1932 – but persistent complainers had to be mollified by free tuning at the works to find at least some of the missing mph.

Overall, however, a lot of athletic young people got a lot of pleasure from the J2 Midget, no matter that its standards of speed, comfort and weather protection would seem abysmally low today. In the light of its time it was nippy, exhilarating and inexpensive – a real fun car for the youth of Britain, and one that also gave aesthetic pleasure. Imitation may be the sincerest form of flattery, but Kimber and his men perhaps had mixed feelings over the way in which their open two-seater format, loosely known as the "Le Mans" style with its cutaway doors, wind-

Above: the prototype of MG's highly successful J2 Midget. Below: the 847cc engine with overhead camshaft and twin SU carburetters. Several of these engines blew up when owners attempted to emulate the 80mph top speed of the original, carefully-prepared road test car

scoops, slab rear tank and strapped-on spare wheel, was swiftly "whipped" by the opposition. Singer, Triumph, Aston Martin, Wolseley Hornet, SS Jaguar, Morgan, HRG, BSA and AC adopted the theme. MG themselves perpetuated it on subsequent P and T-series models right up to the TF in 1955, while Morgan retain it to this day.

But there was one change MG had reluctantly to make during the J2's production run. With no internal valances on those rakish fixed cycle wings, every turn of the steering wheel on wet roads (encountered almost any time in Britain) threw up a shower of spray and mud, most of which was blown back on to the screen, the driver, and the passenger. Tough and tolerant though sporting motorists of the '30s were, this was sometimes "a bit much".

With J2 manufacture keenly costed, Abingdon was well aware that long, sweeping wings with running boards would cost more to make, but at the 1933 Olympia Show the J2 appeared with them for the last four months of its production life, still undeniably pretty, if robbed a little of that saucy "racing" look.

The improved J2 also had an outrigger bearing at the front of its two-bearing crankshaft, foreshadowing the model's replacement early in 1934 by the P-type Midget with three-bearing crank – a car smoother and more powerful, better braked, a little sturdier, longer, heavier and more comfortable, and a little dearer. It had to happen; refinement was essential and inevitable, but the J2, seeming crude and spartan in contrast, had done a great job in creating so enduring a fashion.

MORE INFORMATION FOR THE MG ENTHUSIAST

Brooklands Books have been collecting motoring journals for nearly 40 years and have over 180,000 items listed in their files. Less than 10% of this material has found its way into books. As a company, our main objective has always been to make available to enthusiasts as much motoring literature as possible and therefore, we have decided to offer an added service for our readers - **Classic Car Files.**

Classic Car Files will be made up with articles etc. that could not be fitted into our regular books because of space limitations. They will in the main include road tests, new model announcements, and stories on tuning, racing, history, maintenance and period advertising. They will be individually photocopied to order and will be presented in a laminated folder for safe keeping.

All of our pre-war MG titles have been out-of-print for some years and to fill this void we have compiled this Gold Portfolio to cover the most interesting years of that period 1929-1939. To supplement this book we are making available the following **Classic Car Files.**

MG Classic Car File No. 1

Covering Sports 2 Seater, MK I 6 cyl. Salonette, Midget, Montlhery 750. 18-80, Magna and 1100cc Magnette (1925-1932 approx.)

60 Pages - £10.00 plus P&P.

MG Classic Car File No.2

With stories on P Type and Supercharged Midgets, the Magnette, KN and 2 Litre Saloons and the 750cc racer. (1933-1936 approx.)

60 Pages - £10.00 plus P&P.

MG Classic Car File No. 3

With stories on TA and TB Midgets, record breakers, 2.6 Coupés, 11/2 Litre Saloons and drophead and an article on overhauling the J2 Midget. (1936-1945 approx.)

60 Pages - £10.00 plus P&P.

One other out-of-print publication on MG can now be offered in photocopy form.

MG Cars the Early Years

Published about 1969. This book tells the story of MG from 1924 to 1931. Mike Allison reports on MG development during this period and uses contemporary advertisements to illustrate the text.

66 Pages - £10.00 plus P&P.

Payment: Sterling cheque or quote us your Visa, Access/Mastercard number. When ordering please quote credit card number, date of expiry, full name & address plus contact 'phone or fax number. Orders may be 'phoned, faxed or sent by post to:

Brooklands Books Ltd., PO Box 146, Cobham, Surrey KT11 1LG, UK.
Tel: 0932 865051   Fax: 0932 868803

All orders will be despatched within 14 days. Every effort will be made to make these photocopies as clear as possible, however, it must be remembered that some of the original material that we will be working from is over 70 years old!